Navajo
Blessingway
Singer

The Autobiography of Frank Mitchell
1881-1967

The University of Arizona Press
Tucson, Arizona

About the Editors . . .

CHARLOTTE J. FRISBIE has been involved with Navajo studies since 1962. She received her B.A. in music from Smith College, her M.A. in ethnomusicology from Wesleyan University, and her Ph.D. in anthropology from the University of New Mexico. An associate professor at Southern Illinois University, Edwardsville, she has also been chairperson of the Department of Anthropology there and editor of the Society for Ethnomusicology's newsletter. Among her publications is the book *Kinaaldá: A Study of the Navaho Girl's Puberty Ceremony.*

DAVID P. MCALLESTER is one of the founders of the Society for Ethnomusicology and is a past president and former editor of its journal. Holding an A.B. from Harvard and a Ph.D. from Columbia, he became professor of Anthropology and Music and director of Graduate Studies in Music at Wesleyan University. Since 1957 his principal research has been in the area of Navajo studies. Among his publications are the books *Peyote Music, Enemyway Music,* and *Readings in Ethnomusicology.*

THE UNIVERSITY OF ARIZONA PRESS

Second printing 1980
Copyright © 1978
The Arizona Board of Regents
All Rights Reserved
Manufactured in the U.S.A.

Library of Congress Cataloging in Publication Data

Mitchell, Frank, 1881-1967.
    Navajo Blessingway singer.

    Bibliography: p.
    Includes index.
    1. Mitchell, Frank, 1881-1967. 2. Navajo Indians —
Biography. 3. Navajo Indians — Religion and mythology.
4. Indians of North America — Southwest, New — Religion
and mythology. I. Title.
E99.N3M64   784.7'51'0924 [B]   77-75661
ISBN 0-8165-0611-6
ISBN 0-8165-0568-3 pbk.

*To the memory of Frank Mitchell and to
the many members of his family whose
unfailing hospitality, kindness and
interest made this book possible.*

Contents

ILLUSTRATIONS

Foreword

Two ethnomusicologist-anthropologists, Charlotte J. Frisbie and David P. McAllester, have truly accomplished a labor of love in editing the life story of Blessingway singer Frank Mitchell, a man known to his people as Ólta'í Tsoh, or Big Schoolboy. The labor involved many hours of interviews, both directed and nondirected, supplemented by countless hours of ethnohistorical research and many miles of travel, in order to clarify the chronology of Frank Mitchell's life and times. The love was centered on a grand old man who was a true patriarch of his tribe, on his people and their culture, and on their harsh but singularly beautiful homeland.

Most of the archival-library research was done by Frisbie, who searched through great masses of minutes of Navajo council meetings and numerous other files and records for confirmation of dates and the like. The results of her research are summarized in the chapter notes and four appendixes. Appendix B presents a particularly useful chronology of events from 1856 to 1972, embodying not only items pertaining to Frank Mitchell's ancestry and life history but much additional information concerning the Navajo tribe and country.

The editors continued to work rechecking data with members of the Mitchell family and with other Navajos for eight years following Frank's death. Then came the tremendous task of selecting and correlating data, arranging the materials chronologically, equalizing the English style of the several interpreters employed, and attempting to make the final version conform as closely as possible to Frank Mitchell's style of narration in his own language.

The Blessingway rites according to the Navajos themselves constitute the backbone of their religion, controlling all the other ceremonials. The Navajos also give the Blessingway historical precedence, placing its origin just after the Emergence. This set of rites is the only one in the vast complex of Navajo song ceremonials which is preventive or prophylactic in purpose rather than curative. In spite of their central position in Navajo life and ceremonialism, these relatively brief and simple rites have been shamefully neglected by scholars in favor of the more spectacular curing chantways, with their prayersticks, sandpaintings and body paintings.

We are therefore grateful that Frisbie and McAllester, led by their special interests in Navajo music and poetry, decided to embark upon an intensive investigation of the Blessingway based upon the life story of a prominent singer. But Frank Mitchell's narrative contains much more than his career as a singer, for there are many anecdotes and explanations dealing with his activities in public service, as a headman, as one of the first members of the Navajo Tribal Council, as a Chapter officer and as a judge in the Courts of Indian Offenses.

In Chapters 7 and 8 Frank Mitchell gives much material of great use to students of Navajo ceremonialism. He tells about the structure of the Blessingway rite and the details of procedure in performing it, the necessity of renewing it theoretically after every four performances, the rules for construction and ritual renewal of the indispensable mountain soil bundle and a wealth of information about the uses of Blessingway. Of particular interest are the passages in which he describes his trips with Father Berard Haile and other Blessingway singers to the sacred mountains of the Navajo country to gather mountain earth for the bundle.

Chapter 6 presents a myth of Blessingway which is essentially an abbreviation of the longer one that Frank Mitchell dictated to Father Berard Haile in 1930, with a few interesting differences (see L. C. Wyman, 1970, *Blessingway*, University of Arizona Press, Tucson, Arizona, pp. 341-492). Like the longer story, the abbreviated one is mainly concerned with Post-Emergence Events, with particular attention to the Origin of Clans. This chapter is a prime example of the style and devices which a knowledgeable singer employs when he finds it expedient to abbreviate a long myth.

In the editors' introduction to this book there is a feature of special significance — a frank and detailed account of their field methods and of their relationship to their informants, the Mitchell family. With complete openness, they recount the intimate and affectionate interplay that developed as they became "daughter" and "son" in what "became, for each of us, a second family of our own." In most accounts of fieldwork, these are matters which are altogether too skimpy to satisfy readers interested in fieldwork methodology. In this and many other ways Frisbie and McAllester have made *Navajo Blessingway Singer* a personal document of lasting worth.

LELAND C. WYMAN

Introduction

In his life and thought, Frank Mitchell embodied the qualities of Navajo religion. He was a man essentially practical, focused on this life and its problems, and deeply involved in moral and ethical values. The religion that sustained him, and through him a wide community of Navajo people, is similarly practical. The many deities and Holy People in its cosmology established the essential rules by which life should be lived. The hereafter receives little attention, for the emphasis is on the present world and its enrichment by a profoundly literary oral tradition of myths, prayers and song-poems. Myths provide the stories to which the prayers, some of them an hour or more in length, and the song cycles, totaling many hundreds of songs, refer. It is no exaggeration to equate any one of the longer Navajo chants with the Iliad or the Odyssey in sheer literary mass and in intellectual scope.

The people who practice this religion and who have produced these impressive arts live on a reservation in the American Southwest which is vast and spectacular in natural beauty, but also bleak and impoverished. In an area the size of Belgium live only about 140,000 Navajos, and yet the population is more than the land can sustain. Within this number are an estimated three or four hundred singers, any of whom may be expertly versed in the texts, sacred properties, procedures and philosophy of from one to as many as five or six great curing ceremonials. In addition, almost every adult man and numerous older women know and perform shorter rituals taken from a repertory of prayerstick cuttings, jewel and pollen offerings and "short sings," whose extent probably can never be fully assessed. Although much of the tradition is fixed, the possible combinations and recombinations are endless, each one being carefully planned to fill a particular personal need. Navajo ceremonials are personal and occasional rather than group-oriented and calendrical, and their purpose is to restore an individual to a harmonious relationship with the physical, social and psychological worlds. At the base of all the ceremonials is one that is preventative in purpose, prophylactic rather than curative; this ceremony is known as *Hózhǫ́ǫ́jí* or Blessingway.

To help other outsiders appreciate this extraordinarily rich world of ceremonial arts, we have presented the life story and thought of one man,

Ólta'í Tsoh, or Big Schoolboy, a noted singer of Blessingway who was widely
known by his English name, Frank Mitchell. He was first of all a family man,
greatly loved by his immediate relatives. He was among the first Navajos to
attend the government-established boarding school at Fort Defiance before
the turn of the century. He later worked as interpreter-handyman at two
missions and two trading posts. He was also one of the principal freighters,
hauling goods between Chinle, Arizona, and Gallup, New Mexico, in his
wagon before the advent of the automobile on the reservation.

When Frank began his career as a ceremonial practitioner, he was called
upon for public service. After serving as a headman, he was one of the first
members of the Tribal Council on the reservation. Later he also served as a
Chapter officer in Chinle and as a judge in the Courts of Indian Offenses,
traveling widely throughout the reservation in the latter capacity.

Frank's outstanding quality was his love of life and everything that it
has to offer. His earthy humor, his practical jokes, his love of language and his
reverence for the gifts of the Holy People, combined to produce an
exceptional man. Despite his achievements, he maintained a true humility and
recognized all good as coming from sources beyond human power. Although
he was one of the most traditional of Navajos, he never overlooked the
possible value of the new ways, ideas and material items that came to his
people from other cultures around them.

Frank took delight in the similarities between traditional Navajo beliefs
and Christianity, between supernatural power and modern technology and
between native and non-native medicine. Baptized a Catholic during his school
days and again in the last few weeks of his life, his funeral service took place
at the Franciscan mission in Chinle, where he had served in his youth. Yet,
after the Christian ritual was over in the cemetery, his saddle and bridle went
with him to the grave as did the spirit of his favorite horse, Weasel, who was
put to death in a nearby arroyo by his oldest son in fulfillment of one of his
father's last requests.

SPAN OF THE FIELDWORK

The materials for *Navajo Blessingway Singer* were gathered over a
period of eighteen years, beginning in 1957. With support from the John
Simon Guggenheim Foundation, McAllester began, that year, a long-term
study of Navajo ceremonialism, with particular emphasis on its music and
poetry. His interpreter was Albert G. Sandoval, Jr., who, when they were in
the Chinle area, suggested a visit to his "uncle" Frank Mitchell, a well-known
Blessingway singer. On September 23, 1957, they found Frank at home. A
tall, imposing man in his seventies, Frank was friendly and hospitable.
McAllester's project was explained at length, and Frank was keenly
interested, especially when he learned that the recorded materials would be
preserved in the Library of Congress and other archives. He remarked that the

essential spirit of the Navajos was contained in their ceremonies and especially in Blessingway. He predicted that when these were gone, the Navajos would also be gone. At the end of the visit, Frank invited McAllester to return.

A month after the first visit, McAllester returned to the Mitchells' and one of Frank's daughters, Augusta Sandoval, suggested that her father's Blessingway ceremony should be preserved on film and tape. Frank expressed his interest in such a project, and in December McAllester attended a family council at which, after much discussion, it was agreed that a film and tape record of the Blessingway would be made. The family stipulated that the film could not be shown commercially or to casual audiences unfamiliar with the deep religious significance of the ceremony. The filming took place a week later. Frank's youngest daughter, Isabelle, took the role of the one-sung-over since she was expecting a baby in about a month. Because she had also been having bad dreams, the Blessingway ceremony was preceded by a two-night Protection Rite, which was also put on film and simultaneously recorded on sound tape.

When the prints were returned, the whole family saw the unedited film, and McAllester spent three weeks checking the translations of song and prayer texts. In 1961 he returned to Chinle with the edited film and soundtrack, and Frank checked it carefully for possible errors in ceremonial sequence and the accuracy of the soundtrack. He then proposed that a number of additional sets of Blessingway songs be recorded, and McAllester spent a month in this work.

In 1963 Frisbie, who was then Charlotte I. Johnson and a graduate student at Wesleyan University, joined the project, which was now supported by a National Science Foundation grant. We spent three weeks in June assisting the American Indian Films, Inc., group in filming and recording the puberty ceremony, Kinaaldá, of Marie Shirley, one of Frank's granddaughters. Frisbie remained at the Mitchells' until August 20, studying the puberty ceremony, Corn Grinding songs and specific types of Blessingway songs with Frank. She also interviewed and recorded other singers and girls and women in the area in conjunction with the study of Kinaaldá, and collected some Enemyway music.

It was during this summer, on June 26, 1963, that Frisbie asked Frank if he would be willing to record his life history. He replied, *"Daats'i"* ("Maybe"). The request was repeated on June 29, and later that same morning, Frank announced that he was ready to begin. Thus began a series of sessions during which he spoke into the tape recorder's microphone without interruptions, directions by Frisbie or translations. By 9 p.m. on June 30, a total of twelve hours of narration had been recorded and Frank announced that he had finished telling his story. Later that summer, Albert G. (Chic) Sandoval, Sr., went over the tapes with Frisbie, providing line-for-line translations.

The 1963 tapes were transcribed and studied during the following fall and winter, and in the spring of 1964 Frisbie prepared a series of specific questions to augment several portions of the narration and to clarify certain events and references. McAllester spent a week in July interviewing Frank on Blessingway music and on portions of his life history. After completing work in the Fort Defiance area, Frisbie went to Chinle on August 5, and on the following day began directed interviewing with Frank on his life history. This work, which resulted in a total of 1,155 pages of typescript, was completed on September 6, and Frisbie left to begin doctoral work in anthropology at the University of New Mexico. Later that fall, she spent another week with the Mitchells, this time with her fiancé, Ted Frisbie.

In 1965, McAllester spent two weeks in July with the Mitchells, recording additional Blessingway songs that Frank had not included in the filmed session of the ceremony. He assisted at the Flintway ceremonial given for Frank at that time. In short visits from February through September, Frisbie spent a total of four weeks with Frank, checking details in the life story and Mitchell genealogy. She also interviewed Frank on House Blessing procedures and Navajo weddings and recorded additional song sets that Frank had not used in the film.

In 1966, Frisbie spent a weekend in February and five days in August at the Mitchells'. Frank was becoming increasingly ill with cancer of the prostate but was still very much interested in the recording project and spent two days checking previously recorded Blessingway prayers. He realized the seriousness of his illness and spoke about his hospitalizations and the little time remaining to him. He was noticeably weak and thin and was eating poorly.

In January, February and March 1967, Frisbie made three-day visits to Chinle. Frank's illness was progressing rapidly; he finally returned to the hospital in Ganado, where he died on April 15. At the funeral in Chinle on April 20, Frisbie was asked to keep the record book of attenders, and McAllester was appointed as one of the pallbearers. Frisbie continued to visit the family that spring and summer while studying the House Blessing ceremony, a project supported by a fellowship from the American Association for University Women. In August, she began directed interviewing with Augusta to clarify some remaining family details in Frank's life history.

In 1968 and 1969 McAllester made several two-day visits to Chinle and the Mitchells, and the following year one of Frank's grandsons, Douglas Mitchell, came to Wesleyan University as a Visiting Artist in American Indian Music. In 1971, Frisbie received support from the American Philosophical Society and her institution, Southern Illinois University, Edwardsville, which made possible two months of archival research in Window Rock, Saint Michaels, Fort Defiance, Ganado, Gallup, Canyon de Chelly and Chinle. The study of the ethnohistorical and chronological aspects of Frank's life history was begun at this time, and pertinent documents and photographs were also located and copied. We both visited Chinle in July and worked with Augusta on details of the life history. We also spent two weeks at the Verde Valley School in Sedona, Arizona, indexing the accumulated mass of typescripts and outlining the shape of the narrative. Augusta visited us there and participated in the discussions.

On August 2 we went back to Chinle for a conference with the Mitchell family on the question of publishing the narration as a book. Our original agreement with Frank was reconfirmed, and we were given permission to begin editing the materials, with two stipulations: that the work convey the pervasiveness of Frank's religious beliefs and that the family have the right to review the manuscript and illustrations before a publisher was sought. An agreement was also reached at this time on the allocation of any income that might result in the event of publication.

After completing the manuscript, we returned to Chinle in June 1975, and the contents of each chapter were reviewed with Frank's daughters in a family conference on June 16. Deletions requested by the family were made at this time. The illustrations were discussed, the financial agreement reaffirmed and the process of locating a publisher was considered. The mood of the meeting was one of satisfaction that we were this far along in the realization of Frank's wish that a book on his life would live after him, and a sense of "family" unity arising from our long years of cooperation.

HUMAN RELATIONS IN THE FIELDWORK

Within the past fifteen years many anthropologists have become increasingly concerned with the particulars of fieldwork and the complexities of human interactions involved therein. Much thought continues to be given to reexamining and redefining the relationship between anthropologists and their co-workers or collaborators from other cultures. The assumptions implicit in the dyad, "scientist and subject," are no longer tenable in an era of ever increasing sensitivity to human rights and self determination; increasingly, the implications of legality, ethics and common courtesy are becoming very much a part of the anthropological consciousness.

Among the topics needing more adequate treatment in many anthropological works is the description of one's relationships with collaborators. As Langness (1967) and others have indicated, all too often the reader is told only that the researcher was considered to be a friend or was treated as a kinsman. Human relations are not easily described, especially as they change over a long period of time from the initial development of rapport to their continuation through various projects and on into the realm of lifelong friendships with mutual obligations and responsibilities. We would, however, like at least to attempt a description of our relationships with Frank Mitchell.

McAllester came to the Mitchells as an anthropologist and ethnomusicologist interested in studying with Navajo practitioners the general area of ceremonialism, with specific emphasis on its music and poetry. Frank was immediately interested in assisting with the project. Some of his reasons coincided with McAllester's intention to preserve ceremonial arts, as fully documented as possible, for the future purposes, whatever they might be, of the Navajo people themselves. He invited a continuation of the relationship, and within a few months McAllester was considered "one of the family." Frank pointed out to his children that McAllester was so much like his own son, David, who had died in 1938, that he seemed to be a replacement for him. McAllester was called "son," by Frank and his wife and "brother" by Frank's sons and daughters. This relationship continues into the present, with mutual correspondence, phone calls, financial obligations and visitations between Arizona and Connecticut.

McAllester's role in the family was something like that of a well-to-do relative who visited occasionally and sometimes hoed in the garden or lent a hand chopping wood. He was made welcome at family ceremonials and accompanied the Mitchells to ceremonial events outside the family. One difficulty arose when Frank insisted, over the protests of the sponsors of an Enemyway, that McAllester was his son and should be allowed to witness certain secret rituals. McAllester had to disobey Frank in order to leave and take his place with other outsiders. On another occasion, when McAllester praised a tasty Navajo meal, Frank said, "Why don't you divorce that woman in Connecticut and settle down here? There are plenty of women here who cook like this all the time."

Frisbie came to the Mitchells as one of McAllester's students, assisting in the Blessingway study and especially in that aspect of it concerned with the Girl's Puberty ceremony. Her initial purpose was to document this ceremony with specific emphasis on music, prayers and myths in a study that would lead to a master's degree in ethnomusicology at Wesleyan University. She also came as a student of Navajo culture and expressed her hopes of learning to cook in Navajo style, grind corn, herd sheep, butcher, spin, card, and, possibly, weave. Frank asked her "nationality" the first day and equated the Pennsylvania Dutch part of her background with Germans, stating with a laugh that this meant that she was an "enemy." She was given the name "Yellow Woman," and was told by Frank to call his children "brother" and "sister," and him, "grandfather."

From her initial days as observer, Frisbie became, functionally, one of Frank's daughters. In addition to participating in the Navajo aspects of the daily household life, she also provided the only means of automobile transport, wrote letters and loaned money. The days of that first summer, and subsequent visits, were divided between studying with Frank, household tasks and driving people to trading posts, the post office and clinics, missions, the welfare office and the homes of relatives. Trips were also made to locate diagnosticians and singers when members of the family needed them and in several cases, to take Frank to perform his Blessingway ceremony for someone outside the Chinle community. Frisbie was, and still is, the brunt of good-humored jokes about her attempts to learn Navajo language and behavior.

In daily life, Frank acted as a benevolent, protective grandfather toward Frisbie and introduced her as his "adopted daughter" at ceremonials and other gatherings. He was a true research collaborator as well as a source of information in the Blessingway project; he was interested in the numerous ways in which ideas affect behavior. He questioned Frisbie about many of her beliefs, opinions and habits and came to know her not only as a person but also as a bearer of her own New England culture. The rare awkward moments which did occur arose from Frank's regrets when he felt he should refuse to record certain materials and from a certain ambivalence about Frisbie's work with other singers.

Frisbie's relationships with the rest of the Mitchells vary with the individuals concerned, her closest ties being with Frank's wife, Tall Woman, and his daughters. She remains a "school girl chum" to several of Frank's grandchildren and is now introduced as a "friend of the family from years ago" to family friends and the newer great-grandchildren. The friendships continue into the present, as do the implied obligations and responsibilities.

METHODS OF FIELDWORK

During the times that we were studying the Blessingway and other areas of Navajo culture with Frank, we lived with the Mitchell family, participating in and observing the daily routine in Chinle. McAllester worked with Frank in various ways. There were recording sessions during which song series were sung through without interruption. After such efforts, several days would be spent in playing back the material, transcribing texts in Navajo and interlinear translation and discussing the material. These discussions led in many fruitful directions, including material on Frank's life history. There were directed interviews specifically on the life history with the assistance of interpreters Albert G. (Chic) Sandoval, Sr., his son Albert Jr. and Frank's daughter Augusta. These sessions were taped, with the narration alternating with the interpreters' translations. McAllester accompanied Frank on one of his Protection Rites and acted as his ceremonial helper. He attended various performances of Frank's Blessingway and a Girl's Puberty ceremony, and was present at the Flintway done for Frank in 1965. McAllester also accompanied various family members on visits to ceremonials held for Navajos outside the family; these included Shootingway, Red Antway and Enemyway. Some of the material in the life history comes from the notes on these ceremonial experiences and the conversations that occurred at these times.

Frisbie put in the larger amount of field research time directly on the life history project, using directed and nondirected interview procedures, as mentioned above. Translations were provided by Augusta Sandoval and

Albert G. Sandoval, Sr., and were usually recorded on the same tape as the narration. In some instances, tapes made with one interpreter were retranslated with the other in order to benefit both from the father-daughter relationship of Frank and Augusta and from the extensive ceremonial knowledge and anthropological expertise of Chic Sandoval. In the case of the nondirected life story tapes made by Frank in 1963, the translations were made several weeks after the recordings.

Frank and the interpreters were paid in cash on an hourly basis for the time they spent recording, translating and discussing all of the materials. We paid a daily rate for room and board and helped the always slender family resources with occasional gifts of food, clothing and money and also with personal services and assistance of various kinds.

EDITING PROCEDURES

Frank, of course, is the author of *Navajo Blessingway Singer*. Our job has been to collect the data, edit the narration and, with the assistance of able interpreters, put it into English. By utilizing both nondirected and directed interviews, over the years much duplicate material was collected in Navajo, which was then translated into English by one or more of several interpreters. Part of our job as editors has been to render the widely different English styles of the various interpreters into a translation that seemed consistent with Frank's Navajo in flavor, style and implication. In some cases, this has meant rephrasing a particular interpreter's various idiosyncratic usages, such as the sometimes elaborate social science terminology developed by Chic during his work with Edward Sapir and his years as Tribal interpreter.

In several specified instances, verbatim materials given by Frank to other scholars and researchers, including Mary Shepardson, Clifford Barnett and Irene Stewart, have been incorporated, with permission, into the life story. Here, too, we have tried to maintain the unity of narrative style.

Several changes have been made for the sake of readers. Where possible, we have translated into English all place names and personal names, though Frank and the interpreters gave these, almost invariably, in Navajo. The few Navajo words in the text and notes are those for which no translation could be secured. We have also eliminated repetitions. Although there are many repetitions of stories and events in the fieldnotes and tapes, for this book we followed the principle of selecting the fullest account for presentation. Points at which conflicting information was gathered, from Frank himself at different times, from other family members or from ethnohistorical and library sources, are indicated in chapter notes, which show the source and nature of the differences.

We have also attempted to arrange the narrative in chronological order. In the 1963, nondirected version of his life story, Frank followed his own scheme — an undated progression of events from his youth to the present, with many side anecdotes and cross-cultural comparisons. He commented at length on the younger generation, the future of Navajo ceremonialism and what seemed to lie ahead for the Navajo people and the world at large. The later interviews were directed at expanding portions of this first document, and there are, of course, other materials resulting from Blessingway studies with Frank which also contain life history information. The relationship between many of the events in Frank's life and events which can be documented through ethnohistorical and library research is illustrated in chapter notes and in Appendix B, Chronology.

ANALYSIS

The narrative offers useful data on the process of enculturation; the transmission of ceremonial material in the oral tradition; relationships in myth, prayer, song and ritual; cultural values; the role and status of a Navajo singer and politician; cultural change; and native philosophical speculations. All these are in addition to the wealth of detail about the Blessingway ceremony itself, the ceremony which has been and still remains the cornerstone of traditional Navajo religious thought and practice.

Though, to our knowledge, there is no other "complete" life history of a ceremonial practitioner, a number of other personal documents have been published and offer fruitful comparison with *Navajo Blessingway Singer*. For the Navajos alone, there are Dyk (1938, 1947), Kluckhohn (1940, 1956, 1960), Kluckhohn and Rosenzweig (1947), Leighton and Leighton (1949), Roberts (1951), Jewell (1952) and Vogt (n.d.). Life histories are also among the materials collected by the Navajo Tribe itself in recent years: Johnson et. al. (1969) and Hoffman and Johnson (1970). We hope to consider some of these resources as well as others, such as Kluckhohn (1945), Langness (1967) and Mandelbaum (1973), which deal specifically with the anthropological value of life histories, in future analytic discussions. The length of the narration and the amount of historical and ethnohistorical data in the present volume seemed to us to preclude such excursions here.

Navajo Blessingway Singer and most of the other published life histories of Navajos are of men. Frisbie's recording of the personal narrative of Tall Woman, Frank's wife, and Shepardson's similar studies with several other Navajo women are initial steps toward redressing this imbalance. We hope that these and other personal narratives of women will become available to add an essential dimension to this genre of material in Navajo and other cultural studies.

Copies of the ceremonial materials recorded by Frank and of the tapes of his life story are deposited in the Fine Arts Library at the University of New Mexico, the Archive of World Music at Wesleyan University and in the Library of Congress, where their use has been restricted by the family. Frisbie and the Mitchells also have personal copies of these materials. Typescripts of

Frank's narrative as well as the unedited interviews are in our possession. Early drafts of the edited narrative are keyed to the taped interview typescripts. These and our field journals contain material for close analysis of emphasis, repetition, the Navajo sense of sequence, humor and its context, effect of situational variables and the different results from directed and nondirected techniques. The fact that the entire narrative exists in Navajo encourages the hope that there may sometime be a Navajo language edition.

Navajo Blessingway Singer then, is Frank's life story, and it is our hope that in the process of editing his materials, some of the spontaneity, fullness of detail, high humor and serious intent and commitment that went into its telling have been preserved.

CHARLOTTE J. FRISBIE
DAVID P. MCALLESTER

1. The Early Days

*Frank learns about early times from Chee Dodge and his own
parents... what the soldiers were like and what they were
called... early life of the People and their clan divisions...
conditions at Fort Sumner... provisions for the release of the
People... back in the Navajo country... his parents meet.*

I got all of my stories about the early days from Chee Dodge;[1] the first time I
heard about these things was when we went over to Chee Dodge's place to
check on a rumor we had heard about him. Chee had a whole house for
himself; he invited us all to sleep there with him. That night while we stayed
at his place I heard Chee Dodge talking about all the old time days; he told us
what he knew about when the People[2] went to Fort Sumner. He told us
about that right from the beginning; you see, he was one of the ones who
went there. I think he was just a little boy when he went there; he
remembered it all so clearly that he told us everything about those days. That
is how I learned about how the People went over there and how they were
treated, and how they came back from that Long Walk.[3]

A lot of the old men, the ones who had been on that trip to Fort
Sumner and back used to come together at Chee Dodge's place and discuss
these things, what had happened in the past and how the People lived in the
old days. They talked about the hard times that they had had to endure, and
about the fighting. Chee would ask them how they lived way back, and he got
that all in his head. After I started serving on the Council, Chee told me those
things, and that is how I learned most of what I know about that. The People
must have gone through some very hard times. They even used to eat dog meat.

My father and my mother told me that they went to Fort Sumner on
that long, long walk. But they did not tell me much about the times before
Fort Sumner or what happened during the time they were gone over there.
My mother barely remembered the Long Walk, and the same was true with
my father. They had no way of knowing how old they were when they left.
After they returned from Fort Sumner they started living together. Much
later on, they told me how they used to live after they returned from there.

My parents said that before they went to Fort Sumner, they had a
much harder time of it. The Navajos were warlike; they would put up a fight.

[11]

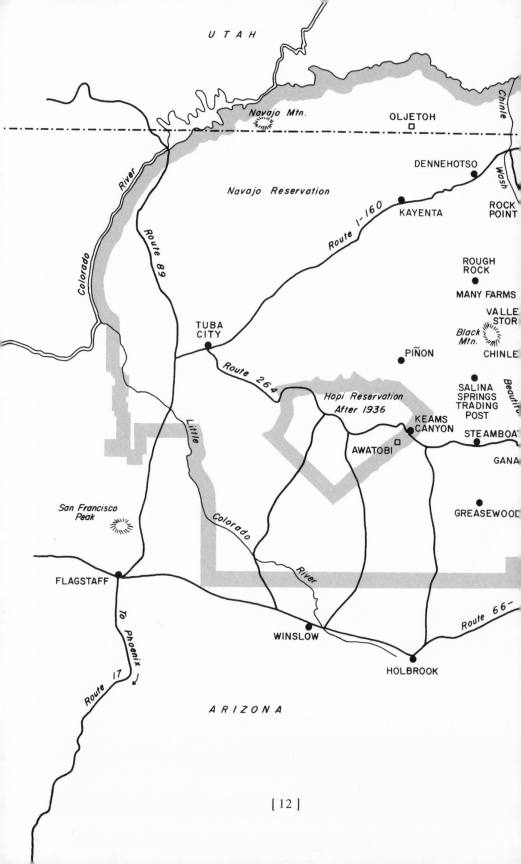

U T A H

Navajo Mtn.

OLJETOH

DENNEHOTSO

Chinle

Wash

ROCK POINT

Colorado

River

Route 89

Navajo Reservation

Route I-160

KAYENTA

ROUGH ROCK

MANY FARMS

VALLE STOR

Black Mtn.

CHINLE

TUBA CITY

PIÑON

Route 264

Hopi Reservation After 1936

SALINA SPRINGS TRADING POST

Beautif

KEAMS CANYON

STEAMBOA

AWATOBI

GANA

Little

San Francisco Peak

Colorado

River

GREASEWOOD

FLAGSTAFF

To Phoenix

Route 17

WINSLOW

Route 66-

HOLBROOK

A R I Z O N A

[12]

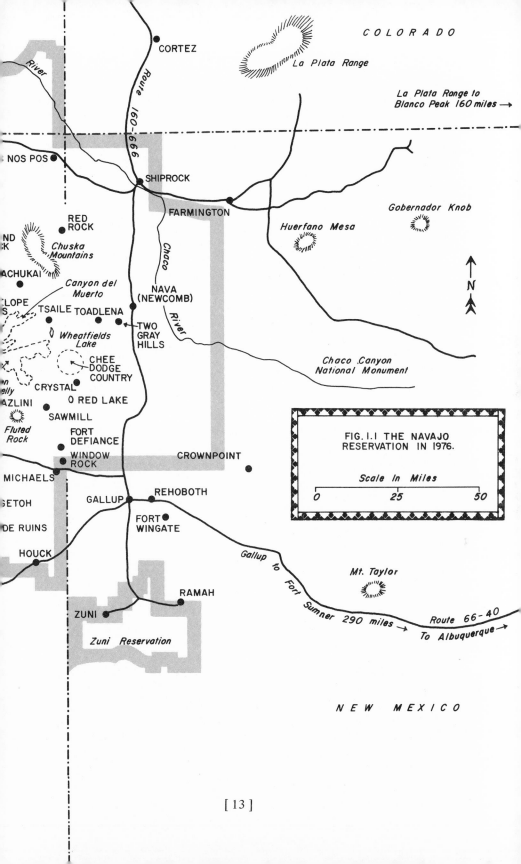

FIG. 1.1 THE NAVAJO RESERVATION IN 1976.

Scale In Miles

0   25   50

COLORADO

CORTEZ

La Plata Range

La Plata Range to
Blanco Peak 160 miles →

River

Route 160-666

NOS POS

SHIPROCK

FARMINGTON

Gobernador Knob

Huerfano Mesa

RED
ROCK

ND
CK

Chuska
Mountains

Chaco

ACHUKAI

Canyon del
Muerto

NAVA
(NEWCOMB)

N

LOPE
S

TSAILE TOADLENA

TWO
GRAY
HILLS

River

Wheatfields
Lake

Chaco Canyon
National Monument

CHEE
DODGE
COUNTRY

elly

CRYSTAL

AZLINI

O RED LAKE

Fluted
Rock

SAWMILL

FORT
DEFIANCE

WINDOW
ROCK

CROWNPOINT

MICHAELS

GETOH

GALLUP

REHOBOTH

DE RUINS

FORT
WINGATE

HOUCK

Gallup to Fort Sumner 290 miles →

Mt. Taylor

Route 66-40
To Albuquerque →

RAMAH

ZUNI

Zuni Reservation

NEW MEXICO

[13]

There was nobody down in this Chinle valley then; everyone was hiding out in the mountains somewhere, and they were really suffering.

Before the People went to Fort Sumner, they were encircled by their enemies. They could not go out into the open without getting killed or something happening to them. They were having trouble with the Utes, the Santa Claras, the Apaches, Comanches and the Mexicans. They were also having trouble with the Hopis; so they were having trouble all around.

The Navajos started all of this themselves by stealing things from the other tribes. They used to go raiding through the country here; they raided the Mexicans from one direction, Apaches from another and the Chiricahua Apaches; besides those, the Pueblo people were attacking them from other places. The Navajos stole things from the Hopis just like they did from the Mexican people who moved across the country here. That was the main thing that started all of that trouble, and that is why the People were rounded up and taken to Fort Sumner.

The People were open to enemies from all directions. They did not have anything to eat, and they could not go out and get anything. Most of the time during the day all they did was hide. As soon as a Ute or an Apache spotted them, they would just go after the Navajos until they had killed them. There was no safe place anywhere; there was really no protection from anyone.

You might think that the Canyon[4] here would be a safe place where the People could hide out, but even there it was not safe because there were times when people were killed in the Canyon, especially near Mummy Cave, where a whole group of Navajos were killed near the cave there. The Navajos were in there unseen by their enemies going down the Canyon; the Utes were going down the Canyon,[5] and the Navajos were way up near the top, inside a big cave. I do not know how many families had come together for safety up there. When the Utes were moving along the base in the riverbed, some crazy man yelled at them. He thought they were safe, that they could not be attacked. That is what drew their attention to those Navajos.

The Utes came back and camped right down at the base of the bluff. The Navajos could not see them because there was a rock formation near the cave, and the Utes were back of it. They could not touch the Navajos that way by shooting, because the People were behind a bank for protection. So some of the Utes stayed there to watch the People and another group went around on top of the Canyon and found a place where they could see into the cave. There was no protection there. The canyon wall went around in a circle. That is where they started shooting into the cave and killed the People. Of course when they started shooting into the cave, subduing them that way, the ones down in the Canyon came up the bank and rushed in there and just killed them all off. That is a place name now, "Where the people were shoved off the bluff." It is a little above Mummy Cave, where the ruins are. You go around another point of the mesa and it is right there inside Canyon del Muerto. It was because of the massacre of those Navajos in the cave that they call that the Canyon of the Dead.[6]

Over on the other side there, right by a peach orchard, at a place called Peach Orchard in Canyon de Chelly, there is a small cave. It is the place where a small band of Navajos were murdered. They were killed by rocks which were rolled into the cave to force them out. I have seen fresh blood marks on the walls of those rocks, and also bullet scratches on those walls. You can see the blue streak marks made by the bullets and the human blood smeared on the rocks; I guess they were wounded and were wiping blood off and wiping their hands on the rock.

Some time ago, I walked down there with a man who knew about that spot where the Navajos were killed. We took a trail leading down into the Canyon right by that cave and we saw all these things. It all shows that we were classed as coyotes at that time; you know, when you see a coyote running, the first thing you want to do is kill it. I guess that's the way we were looked upon, as being just no good for anything. They were trying to kill us all off; the object was to eradicate the Navajos from the country.

It was awful in those days; the Navajos starved to death and it was so bad they even had to eat dogs and lizards and every living creature they could find, like rats and mice. Some of the stories from before Fort Sumner are so bad, I can hardly believe those things really happened to our people in those days. My parents said it was much worse before they were taken to Fort Sumner. One time my grandfather's family had a dog. They were out in the woods, hiding in the mountains, and their enemies were here on the plains. The minute they knew the enemies were coming, they ran for cover and stayed there until they were gone. One time they figured that if this dog saw those enemies coming up from the plains he would bark and attract their attention, and those people would come and raid their place. So they decided that they would kill that dog and use it for food for a few more days.

The People really suffered then because only the men who were able to ride were sent out in the open to gather what little food they could get. If they were lucky, they brought back a handful of something to feed their families out there in the mountains. They really suffered during those times. But when they went to Fort Sumner things were altogether changed. I mean that while the People suffered there, it was not as bad as before they went there. That is what my parents said.

There were small troops of soldiers here and there which would go across the country every now and then. The People were hiding out in the mountains in various places, and they would see these white men who were soldiers out in the plains. They would watch them from there, doing their cooking outdoors wherever they camped. This was the first time the People heard of white men.

These Navajos were curious, and they would watch the white men from a distance; they would see them build big fires, put on big pots and cook supper. They would see the steam coming out of the kettle, and then many times after the soldiers moved from the camping ground, the Navajos would go over there and see these big chunks of bones lying around on the ground. They would also see broth or coffee that the soldiers had not drunk; they would see it thrown on the ground, and they would notice that they had just eaten little pieces of meat off the bones and thrown those away with meat still on them. And they would wonder just what these people ate because all of those bones still had some meat on them. So they would think that it was just the steam that had been eaten. That's where one word for white men comes from; it's really the word for steam, "One who eats steam."

The Navajos would see all that steam coming out of the coffee kettle, and then later the soldiers would throw the grounds right there and also the coffee that they had not finished; the Navajos would see the remains of it there on the ground. Because they did not know what coffee was, they wondered if the soldiers just ate the steam and threw the rest away.

The soldiers wore those caps, and another name the Navajos called them was "Ones with the pointed heads." Another word they used before the word *bilagáana* came into use was "Ones who cover up their ears."[7] One of those caps they used in the wintertime covered their ears and all down their heads. The People used to see the soldiers wear those as they traveled through this territory here. The Navajos used to think that the white men could go to sleep just like that, with those caps on and their ears covered up.

Those soldiers used to have long winter coats, big ones. The People saw them wearing those and they gave them a name for that too — "Those who had two coats." These coats had a great big collar that came down and then met a second coat. The People had all kinds of funny names for those white men. They used to say if a white man picked up a stick he could light it; I guess they saw them with matches, but they never remembered seeing the soldiers take the matches from their pockets. I guess the People just thought it was a stick they had picked up and struck on their pants to light a fire.

I used to think when I heard all those different names the People had for the white men that every one of them was a different kind, like a sheep is a different animal from a dog, a dog is another different animal from a cat. So I thought there were all kinds like that among the white men, some with pointed heads, some who slept with their ears covered.

The word *bilagáana* originally came from other things the People saw. Before they went to Fort Sumner they saw these white soldiers. Every time there was a dispute between some Indians in different territories, a whole troop would go out there, and then half of that troop would never come back; they would be killed when they were in battle with those Indians. Then some more troops would be sent out, and even this second group would lose half of their men, and then still more troops would come. That's where the word *belaga* comes in; it means, "They are being killed." They just started calling white men *bilagáanas*.[8] It comes from the word *bi'dagáni*.

In the days before Fort Sumner, we were increasing rapidly, and the People were not farmers. Naturally they had to have food, so they started looking around to see who had something to eat. Then they went out raiding those people. Things kept getting worse; finally it got very bad. All of that time we did not know that we were under the Mexican government; there was a governor at Santa Fe whom the Navajos called "Chopped Up Scalp."

The time came when gold was discovered in California, and people from the East started coming through this country. Of course the Navajos did not know any better, and they kept shooting at anybody, any strange people they saw in order to get something to eat. Those conditions kept getting worse, and finally, in 1846, there was the war with Mexico. That is when the United States took over and this "Chopped Up Scalp" surrendered to the United States government. He made peace with them and told them just what kind of people the Navajos were; he told them that we were warriors and that we could not be trusted.

Sure enough, the United States government found out what kind of people we were and they rounded us up, got us together and started to do something about all of these things. That is when they took us away to Fort Sumner. There were other people coming into our tribe, joining certain clans. They were getting their names by their property, and by the places where they lived. That is the reason there are so many kinds of people among the Navajos now. There are many clans among the People now, but there are only six original ones. There are so many in the Navajo clans because of all the pueblos there in New Mexico; those are the ones that joined the Navajos. They had their clans just like us, and they went by certain clan names too.

Long before Fort Sumner, the missionaries moved into their territory. When the first missionary came out, the Spanish people went out from Santa Fe and built their towns everywhere. I guess the Pueblo people did not like the missionaries so they got rid of them; they killed them. After that, the other missionaries found out about that, and the Pueblo people were informed that there would be soldiers coming out to punish those who killed the missionaries. So they got scared and a lot of the Pueblo people came across into the Navajo country from there.

That was where some of our clans originated. There were really only six original Navajo clans. These were Standing House Clan, Bitter Water Clan, Near the Water Clan, Mud Clan, Water Edge Clan and Two Streams Meet Clan. Those were the six clans according to my story of the Navajos coming forth on the earth. Our clans originated from Changing Woman.[9] Besides those six, the others, such as the Hogan on the Rock Clan which came from the Pueblos, were just picked up along the way.

After we were taken to Fort Sumner, of course, the government rounded up the Chiricahuas, the Mescaleros, and put them together with the Navajos. And when we were released to come back to our country, some of the Apaches came along with us. Naturally they became Navajos and joined various clans; some of them kept their original names, like Chiricahua, but some of them just joined ours. We have a Chiricahua Clan and we have some Mescaleros, but we do not have a Mescalero Clan. They just joined the Red

Streak Clan. I do not know what those Apaches were called among their own
people, or whether they had any clans or not. There is a clan called the
Meadow Clan. They really originated in San Mateo as Mexicans, and when
they drifted among the Navajos in the mountains there, they joined the Edge
of Water Clan. That is how they became related to the Edge of Water Clan.

My parents were not married at the time they went to Fort Sumner and
they were not old enough to understand what was going on over there. They
never really told us how things were there, just a few things about going and
coming back. Most of what I learned about that Long Walk was from Chee
Dodge after I started being on the Council. You see, when I was learning
Blessingway from my father, he told me to just forget about those things; he
said, "They do not go with what you are learning." On the other hand, my
wife's father, Man Who Shouts, had a little taste of war in him. His uncles and
other relatives participated in these raids, and when I was learning
Blessingway from him, he used to have a lot of interest in talking about these
things. He encouraged it.

The People were not tortured or separated as much as some people say
they were during that time. When they were going to Fort Sumner, they were
all gathered at Fort Defiance and from there, they were in the hands of those
soldiers, the cavalry. They protected the People all the way to Fort Sumner,
and they were well protected over there too. The Utes were the main ones
who were still trying to attack the Navajos; that was because the Navajos had
been taking horses and things like that from their country, and they had
become our enemies. The soldiers were always there to protect the People.

I guess the ones who suffered were those who got away from the
soldiers. They just ran into the other Indians who were out there waiting for
them. Those were Utes, and there were some Mexicans who were at war, too,
with the Indians. The Navajos never knew where they would be attacked
from. My parents never really suffered because they were well taken care of
as soon as they were turned over to the soldiers at Fort Defiance. They took
them all down to Fort Sumner; I guess they had to walk all the way.

I do not think that my mother and father met during the time they
were going over there because they were put in different groups and were not
all together. There were many, many groups; there was this family and then
another one, and then this one; the soldiers I guess could not handle all of
them at once, so they put them in groups and took them along that way.

At Fort Sumner, they suffered in one way or another, I guess. You see,
the People were held prisoners up there for some time, and I guess they were
really lonesome for the Navajo country. That is how they really suffered;
they were lonesome for their land over here. They were not used to the type
of country over there and that was real torture to them. In a way, it was their
own fault; they stole from all of those different people; if our people had not
done that, they would not have suffered so much. The Navajos may talk
about how much they suffered at Fort Sumner and during that Long Walk,

but that is nothing compared to the things my grandfather and father told about; it was so much worse before they were taken to Fort Sumner.

The People were held at Fort Sumner a long time; they were told at that time that as a whole they still were not ready to be on their own because they were still like little children; they needed to be trained and brought up, just like children. The people from Washington said they were not going to tell the Navajos in a harsh way what they were supposed to do, or try to force them; they were going to go along very easily with them until the day when they would be able to carry on their own tribal affairs. They knew if you said harsh words to the People, they might get mad right away and scalp people.

A lot of the older people back during the time of this Long Walk were like that. They used to say that they would not take any rough talk from a white man; any white man who talked like that would be shot right then and there with a bow and arrow. A lot of those older people said things like that, that white people should not be allowed to live. Some of them did not know any better and did not think about what they were saying. The people who had parents and relatives who had been to Fort Sumner and back also talked like that even later. I guess they had just been hurt by all that happened to their ancestors over there. They did not forget that deep in their hearts, and they had hard feelings toward white people.

When the People went to Fort Sumner, they were told that the only way they would be released was if they promised not to use guns or bows and arrows or other weapons. They were ordered to stop shooting each other; the government told the People that there had better not be any shooting just because some white men happened to be in the neighborhood.

The Navajos signed a treaty there at Fort Sumner, and that is why the government finally released them. When the People returned from there, from captivity, they were told just what the program would be for them in the future. They were told not to start any more trouble and to quit stealing.

Manuelito, the man whose statue you see standing out there in Gallup at the crossing, was one of the main warriors in those days. Before the People went to Fort Sumner, Manuelito was an outstanding warrior; he was in lots of battles and was experienced. Of course all he wanted was to fight and fight. When the People were subdued by the government and taken as prisoners over to Fort Sumner, they were ordered to stop fighting. It was then that Manuelito laid aside his weapons and swore not to fight again. He laid aside his gun, his arrows and bow and his shield that he protected himself with, and he said, "I have no use for these; I don't want to use these further because I see there is no hope in the future for us as long as we keep this up. As long as we're fighting and raising trouble, we're just doing harm to our people. I have found this out, so we might as well just forget about it and lead a peaceful life for the welfare of the People. We'd just better make up our minds to take the advice of the white people." Manuelito went before the People and told them they would have to quit fighting and live in peace, as the white people wanted. They agreed, and so they were released after they signed the treaty. With that understanding they moved back to Navajo country.

Manuelito was recognized as the spokesman for the whole tribe. He was made the head chief and from there on, of course, he was a leader, a spokesman for the rest of the leaders.[10] I learned about what Manuelito said from Chee Dodge.

At that time the People promised to live peacefully and get educated. Before they left Fort Sumner they made an agreement that they would get their children educated in school. Not until the People returned did the government start having schools out here, like the ones at Fort Apache, Albuquerque and other places. The government agreed to help us with food for at least ten years if we would send our children to school. The Navajos were to provide the transportation to Fort Defiance, where the school was, and in return we were to receive help with our food and also receive tools. So the People agreed to send their children to school.

The People were also told at the same time that they would have to get out and form a Council themselves and find a man they could look up to to settle any difficulties that came up. They were told that they would have to get their own police force later on, and their own judges too — everything that we are doing right now. I guess they realized right then that only if they were educated could they go on like that themselves. They were asked if they were willing to take that step; they all agreed that they were going to do it. So they let the People come back from Fort Sumner to Navajo country.

After that time a headquarters was established at Fort Defiance. Some of the people who came back wanted their children to go to school, but many of them still had the same opinion about white people; they thought that anything having to do with white people would have bad results. So for this reason, many of them did not want their children to be in school. It also was stated in that treaty that the People could get 160 acres assigned to them for their use to take care of their families.[11]

After the People got back from Fort Sumner, they all lived in the Fort Defiance area for some years. I guess the government did not want to turn them loose to come back out here because they thought the Navajos would start trouble all over again. The government wanted the People to realize that they were doing the wrong thing themselves. And they wanted to get the Navajos to start living right, not going out and stealing from people. So they taught them to do something for themselves, instead of just stealing.

When the Navajos returned to Fort Defiance, a detachment of soldiers camped right at Cow's Head, on the present state line. That used to be called Haystack. Another group camped at Saint Michaels, another, west near Sawmill and another, northeast near Red Lake. The camps were for protection and control of the People. The Mexicans to the east, the Chiricahua Apaches to the south, the Hopis to the west and the Utes to the north were old Navajo enemies. The government kept the People there for some years again at Fort Defiance, and at the same time helped them with their food and all those things.

So that is how we got started. We were issued buckets and tea kettles, pots and pans, cooking utensils and things like that for our home use there at Fort Defiance. Of course, before that time, there was no such thing as a cooking utensil for families. It is not like the present. Every home now has any number of utensils. Before those things were issued to us, we had maybe one clay bowl where the food was set for the whole family. We did not even have any spoons to eat with; we just had to use our fingers.

We were also issued tools, such as axes, shovels, picks, saws, hoes and other things which we would use around our homes. These things were bought by the government for our use; we were issued these tools so we could build ourselves a home or whatever we wanted to build to live in. In that way we were to improve our living conditions. Later on, leaders from each area went out, got the People together and taught them how to use these tools.

We were also given food. The rations we got at that time depended on how many there were in the family. You were questioned to see how many members you had in the family, and then they gave you a paper to that effect and you presented that at the counter where you got your rations. The government spent a certain amount of money for that, depending on how many were on those ration lists; in that way, they took care of the People and issued rations to all those entitled to get some. That was what they agreed on at the time they signed the treaty; the government promised to take care of the People with rations for a ten-year period. That was all in the written treaty, how they were going to be cared for by the government for ten years. After that time the People were to support themselves; they would probably be on their feet again and able to care for themselves without rations.

It's just like what they do today, like the surplus commodities they give out at the Chapter House. We are given a little card which we have to show for those things. In the summertime now, when most of the children go back to school, if they go off the reservation it has to be reported that they have gone back and left fewer people at home. Of course, those who go to public school are home all winter. They went by rules like those at Fort Defiance right after Fort Sumner. It was government items that were given to the People.

We were asked to pay back the government for the expense of those ten-year rations. And we got in a dispute with the government over the 160 acres of land that were to be assigned to the People for use in caring for their families. Old Man Dodge got stubborn about that and told the government people, "You promised this to us and never did live up to it and therefore I don't think you have a right to these lands. We are the original inhabitants here, and so by rights, the land is ours."

No one has ever gone back begging for anything after that period when the People got those first rations. At the time they received rations, each head of the family told how many dependents he had. Figuring that into money, of course, amounted to quite a lump sum. The government wanted us to reimburse them for that expense, but that never did come about. They stopped issuing rations to us after that.

When the People came back from Fort Sumner, some of them still went ahead and did what they had been told not to do; they started raiding white people and stealing their flocks and everything else. Some of the People could not resist the temptation of going out and raiding again, and so it soon went from bad to worse again. So Old Man Manuelito went and asked for help, and got the government to station some troops nearby to keep peace. That was how the first army station, Fort Wingate, was established. It was probably about then that MacArthur was there as a little boy. He told how he saw all those Navajos herding sheep and doing other things.

So the government got those soldiers and stationed them there at Fort Wingate. The soldiers chose some young Navajos to help them; that was when so many of our Navajos were taken care of by the soldiers. They helped guard us when we were still having trouble with the Apaches and the Comanches on one side, and also with the Hopis and the Utes. The Navajo soldiers and white men went around and tried to keep peace. The soldiers used to pass through here to see that the People were not starting more raids with the other tribes. They traveled through here and camped every now and then just to keep the peace. This was when Jeff King was a soldier; he was one of the old soldiers from way back who worked to keep peace between the People when they were having all these disputes. I knew him well; I guess he deserves the honor of being taken to Arlington Cemetery because he has been with all those well-known generals and others who fought for their country.[12]

I do not know how far apart my mother's people and my father's family were living while they were at Fort Sumner. I don't know much about the living conditions in those days. From what I heard, my grandfather on my father's side, Man Who Speaks Often,[13] was always a well-to-do man. My mother said he had a large herd of sheep and horses as his own property and that he took all of them to Fort Sumner and came back with them; so he never was without stock at that time. Man Who Speaks Often was respected by the others because he was an outstanding man; he had a brother by the name of Big Man. They were all pretty well-to-do.

After the people returned to Fort Defiance, they were confined in that area for a certain length of time because they were being issued rations. Man Who Speaks Often settled down a little this side of Fort Defiance for the time being, and then I guess my mother's people moved into that same area. That is when my mother and my father got to know each other; they were living near each other near Fort Defiance. My mother said that about a year after they returned from Fort Sumner, during the time they were at Fort Defiance, she and my father started living together as a married couple. They did not get married in the Navajo way because everything at that time was unsettled. No one was untroubled enough to conduct ceremonies in a peaceful way; the People were not settled then.

The common practice was to marry girls when they came of age to older men, such as those with property and those who were singers. Now when we marry them, we match them according to age. In most cases the girls did not want to have anything to do with old men, but they were forced to because their parents said maybe that man was a witch or something. Many people now will not tell you these things; they try to pretend the Navajos were perfect, even though they know how it used to be.

My father was from Pointed Red Rocks; his name was Water Edge Man. He belonged to the Water Edge Clan and got his name as he started living around this part of the country. Before he and my mother were married, I do not know what name he went by; probably just Son of Man Who Speaks Often. My father spent most of his time around the Steamboat area. He was not a singer but he did know Blessingway.

My mother went by the name of Tall Woman; men and women were slim and tall then rather than chubby like today. My mother was from the Two Streams Meet Clan, and she lived with her mother, Two Streams Meet Woman, and her father, who belonged to the Mescalero Clan. Two Streams Meet Woman moved around all the time with the sheep, near Whiskey Creek, Lukachukai, Tsaile, the Chinle Valley, Black Mountain and Keams Canyon. My mother's father, Big Moustache, was half-witted; he was not normal. He came from the Wheatfields area. He was not a singer and spent most of his time looking after the horses of his brother, Big Man, who was a roamer. Big Man used to trade with the Utes for almost anything — horses, cattle, buffalo robes. Big Moustache would take care of Big Man's horses; he spent his time carving wooden frames for saddles and making hobbles and halters from cowhide and horsehide.

My father's father, Man Who Speaks Often, was a Blessingway singer and a recognized leader and headman for the people in the Wheatfields area. He taught my father the Blessingway and how to make the sacred bundle. The father of Man Who Speaks Often also knew that ceremony and passed it down; he went by two names, Thin Man and Yellow Bouncing Man. He was also from the Wheatfields area. My grandfather, Man Who Speaks Often, belonged to the Bitter Water Clan. I do not know what his wife was called; she passed away when I was almost two and I never really knew what her Navajo name was; she was probably called Wife of Man Who Speaks Often. She belonged to the Water Edge Clan, and she roamed around the Chinle Valley; her people came from the Canyon del Muerto area of Canyon de Chelly. I never really got to know her and her husband very well, but I heard that they were well-to-do.

She was also known as Disappeared Beard's wife. Her husband brought that name on himself by plucking his beard; all white men should have this name. Disappeared Beard belonged to the Salt Clan, and he and his people roamed the country near Steamboat and White Cone. They congregated around the areas with water; there were no tribal wells then, just natural springs. Water was only available in the rainy season. I did not know him; we did not live as close neighbors, and I never heard what he did. My mother's relatives were "my people." Disappeared Beard probably did not farm because that was not done very often then; the People were mostly raising stock.

EDITORS' NOTES

1. Henry Chee Dodge, known as Chee or Chee Dodge, was a well-known Navajo leader who lived from 1860 to January 7, 1947. He served as tribal chairman in 1923-1928 and 1942-1946, and had been elected to a term as vice-chairman under Sam Ahkeah (1946-1950) at the time of his death. Frank relates the circumstances of his night at Chee's house in detail in Chapter 9.

2. The Navajos refer to themselves as *Diné* — the People, and this practice has been retained herein.

3. The Long Walk refers to the forced removal of the Navajos to Fort Sumner in 1864 after they were rounded up by Kit Carson. The People were released in 1868 after years of hardship which included starvation, disease, crop failures because of drought, grasshoppers and other plagues, and failure to receive promised supplies. The Navajo population at Fort Sumner during the incarceration varied between 7000 and 9000 people. For details, see Bailey (1964) and Thompson (1976). Walker and Shepherd (1964) and McNitt (1964) describe conditions prior to the Long Walk, and the United States-Navajo Treaty presents the 1868 Treaty which concluded the event. Jett (1974) evaluates the destruction of Navajo orchards in Canyon de Chelly.

4. Canyon de Chelly has been established as one of the National Monuments in Arizona. Located in the northeastern part of the state east of the community of Chinle, the area is well known for its spectacular reddish sandstone canyon walls formed more than 200 million years ago. It is also the site of impressive rock formations, rock art and prehistoric ruins built mainly between A.D. 350-1300. By about 1700, Navajos from northern New Mexico began to occupy the Canyon; today, there are scattered families, gardens and peach trees along the canyon floor. For detailed histories of Canyon de Chelly, see Jett (n.d.), Brugge and Wilson (1976) and Grant (n.d.).

5. Throughout this section, Chic Sandoval disagreed with Frank, insisting that the latter's references to Utes should be to Spanish. "It was the Spanish who did that in 1805; that's in Spanish history." Chic of course was correct. (See Narbona 1805.)

6. This is a widely promulgated misconception. Canyon del Muerto was actually named by Colonel James S. Stevenson after his 1882 visit there (Brugge and Wilson 1976:2).

7. For other names, see the Franciscan Fathers (1910:129), where other translations are also provided for these two names, specifically "Whose Forehead Protrudes," and "Who Sleep on Their Ears."

8. According to Wall and Morgan (1958:20), *Bilagáana* derived from the Spanish "Americano."

9. Changing Woman is a benevolent Navajo deity; see Reichard (1963:770). For an account of the origin of the clans, see Chapter 6.

10. At this point, Chic Sandoval said:

> I want to add something to that myself. The main one who signed the treaty as the head of the Navajos was Barboncito. Manuelito was in the subordinate rank there. Barboncito lived for three years with his people after coming back to Fort Defiance. This is pretty reliable because I got this from old man Charlie Mitchell; he was eighteen when he came back from Fort Sumner, and Chee Dodge was only eight. Charlie used to tell me about this. Barboncito was the man who was really looked upon as the main chief of the tribe. He was originally from the Canyon country.
>
> After he died, three years after the return, they appointed another man, Slim Yellow Man, who lived on the south of Fort Defiance, somewhere in the neighborhood of Houck, Arizona. Old Charlie used to say that Slim Yellow Man was kind of a quiet, level-headed fellow who hardly ever said anything. All he did was roll one cigarette after another, and smoke all the time. When he wanted to talk, he'd have his cigarette in his mouth, and you could hardly understand what he was trying to say.
>
> After he passed away there were two leaders: Manuelito for the New Mexico side, and Mr. Totsoni for Arizona. These two were appointed instead of one main leader. They would meet at Fort Defiance to discuss the People's problems. That's the information I got from Charlie Mitchell.
>
> When these two leaders were appointed, they got together in Fort Defiance every so often to discuss the Indian problems in their areas. The People were gradually spreading out and coming into community settlements like Lukachukai, Chinle, Canyon de Chelly, Black Mountain, Shiprock, Ganado, and all of those places. The Indian Agent suggested that they appoint spokesmen for each of these communities through these two leaders, from whichever area they were in. Manuelito looked after that portion of the reservation, and Mr. Totsoni did it over here on the West side. They were the ones who recommended somebody for Chinle, the Canyon, Ganado, Black Mountain, Keam's Canyon and for each community. So Manuelito recommended for his side of the reservation. They recommended promising leaders; they never recommended the young ones, but suggested mature men the People would respect and listen to.
>
> That is the way these communities got started. Each time they would get together, they would bring in these men; one man from each community was brought in, presented to the agent, and given credential papers recognizing him as spokesman for that community. They got his name and gave him a slip of paper with the agent's name signed to it. That was their authority when they were talking; if they had that paper from the agency signed by the agent, they were recognized.
>
> That is the way it went up to about 1927 or 1928, when the Chapters were organized. That originated with Mr. John J. Hunter from Leupp. That was where he first started the Chapter organization, and

that gradually did away with the old community leaders. In their places they established three officers of the Chapters: President, Vice President, and Secretary. That's the way it is now.

Before the Chapters were organized, the Council was organized in 1922 or 1923, by election. The People never did anything about electing before that time; they didn't know that the government was operating that way, so the Council was patterned after the United States government.

When Manuelito asked for a military post to be established near the reservation to keep peace, law and order, the People were still not settled. Things were still in turmoil; they had not really quieted down yet. They were still in commotion with the Chiricahua Apaches, Geronimo's band. They were also fighting the government. Of course, too, once in a while there would be an outbreak among the different Apaches and the Utes. On Manuelito's advice, the War Department asked for volunteers, for Indian scouts. They came into the picture then. They came in and volunteered at Fort Wingate, the army post. They were the ones who went after Geronimo and subdued him.

After that, things turned for the better. There were quite a number of old Indian scouts who drew pensions for a number of years. Jeff King was about the oldest one and served about the longest. He has been recognized as a hero.

11. At this point, Chic Sandoval elaborated as follows:

I've read through that treaty a number of times and translated it to the Council a number of times. It states if an individual, a single young man, wants to pick up land for farming purposes, he is entitled to 80 acres, if he's single, unmarried. Now if a married man wanted farmland for his family, regardless of what size family he had, then he is entitled to 160 acres. Farmland, not ranchland; that's where a lot of the People misunderstood it. They thought it meant they could just pick a big chunk of land and claim it as their own. But it was not that way. The treaty meant that as long as the People were going to use the land to cultivate and raise crops on it, they could use that much land. A single person, 80 acres and a married person, 160.

You see, the understanding the People got by this assignment of land for their use and for the use of their families was that the individual would fence in a piece of land for his own use and cultivate it. On top of that, he was to be equipped with some implements to operate his farm. That never did materialize. The government promised that, but I guess through some fault of the People themselves, they did not get those implements.

12. Jeff King died during the summer of 1964, and the obituary in the *Navajo Times* was widely discussed.

13. None of our Navajo consultants could translate this name, *Dich'aali;* the translation given here is from Franciscan Fathers (1910:123). See Appendix A for kinship charts, comparative census record material, and a compilation of genealogical information.

2. Boyhood

Frank and his siblings... early memories: sheep, cere-
monials, travel and kinds of hogans... containers, implements
and foods... saddle- and moccasin-making... life with his
mother's family: trading with the Hopis, following the sheep and
his grandmother's temper... farming with his parents... the
teachings of his paternal grandfather... training for hard-
ships... his father's wanderings and his mother's second
marriage.

I do not know too much about when I was little; there is nothing good in
that, nothing to tell. Those things are foolish and ugly. I was too small and I
did not think at that time.

My mother told me that I was born thirteen years after the People came
back from Fort Sumner. When I figure it out according to what she said, I
figure that would be 1881. You see, they have taken census figures so many
times since Fort Sumner days that all of my records have different dates on
them. But my mother said that about a year after they came back from Fort
Sumner, she and my father were married. Then two years later, their first
child, my oldest brother, was born. The People called him Tall Two Streams
Meet Man. I was the first one that got the name of Mitchell. Then after
awhile, when white people came around for something, they asked me what
the names of my brothers were. So I gave them their English names; I called
Tall Two Streams Meet Man, Jim, and the others, John, Jimmy, Sam and
Tom.

After Jim was born, there was just the space of one year before my
next brother, John Mitchell, came along. I remember my mother telling us
that he was born three years after she and my father were married and that
Jim and John were the only two of us that were a year apart. From then on
down the line, all of their children were two years apart. I guess John Mitchell
got his name from Charlie Mitchell,[1] too, like I did, because he worked with
them in later years on those irrigation projects. John and Jim grew up with
me, and we spent our early years taking care of our father's horses and our
grandmother's sheep. We had no liberty of our own in those days, even

though we were always on the move; we were confined to our daily tasks and never went off on our own.

The third one in the family was born two years after John; his name was Slim Two Streams Meet Man; in English, people called him Jimmy Mitchell. This brother was not raised with us because he was over with our grandfather most of the time. His occupation later in life was breaking horses; he castrated them and worked with them for our grandfather, Man Who Speaks Often.

After Jimmy there was a girl we called Woman at War; she was born two years after Jimmy, and she was later the mother of George and Billy Mitchell. Two years after her birth, another sister was born whom we called Warrior Woman; she became the wife of Curly Hair and then died early in life from what I guess was tuberculosis. Two years later a baby boy was born; he died in childhood and never was given a name. I came in right after that, two years later. My folks were living at Wheatfields when I was born.[2]

After me, my younger sister was born. She was called Little Woman, and she was the one who later lived with my mother's second husband, Star Gazer's Son, after he had left my mother who was sick. This sister also became sick early in life, I suppose with tuberculosis, and died a little more than a year after our mother passed away. After this sister was born, my mother had two more children with my father. My younger brother was born two years after my younger sister; his name was Generous Warrior, and in English he was called Sam Mitchell. Two years after he was born, the last child my mother had by my father was born. He was known in English as Thomas Mitchell, and he had more schooling than all the rest of us.

When my mother started living with her second husband, Star Gazer's Son, she had two more children. The first one was a boy who went by the name of Little Man; he lived over by Black Mountain for fifteen years; later he passed away at the sawmill. The other child was a boy who died in childhood before he got an established name.

Before I went to school and got the names of Frank Mitchell and School Boy, I know I had another name, a pet name. But I have forgotten what I was called when I was small, it's been so long ago. Since my school days the People started calling me "School Boy," even the family. That became the name most people used. Then, later, it was changed to "Big School Boy."

I was just a small boy when I began to remember things. We happened to be living at a place called Tsaile; that is where I first began to remember things. I remember that I had a grandmother, and my mother had some sisters besides herself. In those days a family like that used to stay close together. We moved around together; when we moved from one place to another, we always went in groups.

My grandmother had a band of sheep. She was the only one who had some livestock. Of course I remember that at the start my mother and her sisters all lived together with us. The older people would go off places; I do not know where they went or for what reason. We children would just stay home; we did not go anywhere.

In those days, the men who were singers and performed ceremonies were the only ones who went around and treated the sick. That is what they were occupied with. I had an uncle on my father's side who was very harsh. He would scold us all of the time. One time there was someone sick in the family and they were performing a ceremony. While that was going on, we were told not to go to sleep. Whenever we fell asleep, they would wake us and make us stay awake. Finally I got so sleepy that I could not stay awake any more. I was sitting next to this uncle of mine who was pretty harsh, and I guess that I fell asleep and just rolled over right beside him. My uncle jumped up, grabbed me by the hair on the side of my head, and yanked me up, putting me back down in sitting position. I could see that he was pretty angry. Of course, I did not look straight at him; I just glanced sideways over there every now and then to watch him. After that, I did not go to sleep again; I just stayed awake for the rest of the ceremony until it was over. Then we were told, "Now you can go to sleep." That was something I remember very plainly because of course I was old enough to remember things then.

The People moved around most of the time, herding their sheep from place to place. After they were released from Fort Sumner, they all came back to their own land. Of course we did not have things such as barbed wire or grocery stores, or food that could be bought from the store. When I was little, we had no trading posts or white men around; we were really poor. There was no trading post in Chinle at that time; the only post we heard of was over at Ganado, and that was too far away.

There were no roads whatsoever, and there were no wagons or anything of that sort in those days. The People had to travel on horseback or just climb all over those mesas on foot. That was really hard. The trader at Hubbell's in Ganado used to get his merchandise from Gallup, because one or two Mexicans would help haul those things out from there in mule trains or a wagon. They had to make many trips because the wagons did not haul too much. So they brought a little bit out, and in no time it would be gone again. There were no Navajos around here in this area that I know of who had wagons at that time.

The People traveled mostly on horseback; when we moved with the sheep, we used horses to carry our belongings. We, being children, of course had to go along. Whenever the family started moving like that, we children would sit in back of the rider. We were small and fell asleep sometimes, so they used to take anything they could find and tie us around the waist to the rider so we would not fall off. That is the way we moved around, tied to the riders so we could sleep sitting on those horses. The main reason for moving around like that was to look for new grazing ground and water for the sheep and horses.

The first hogan I lived in was something like my present one but it was all round.[3] It did not have notches in the corner where the logs came together. The logs were set on top of each other without any notches. We put mud and dirt in there all the way from the bottom to the top. Then we covered the whole thing with dirt just like those Eskimo houses that you see all covered with snow.

When the People came out to farm or went up in the mountains, they would build temporary hogans, with one pole sticking up in the middle. They would just lay the wood up against the pole standing there in the center and then just stack the rest of the wood all around to hold it together. That kind of hogan was for temporary use; if we were going to spend a winter somewhere, we usually just made a round one.

In the summertime we just used any trees we could find; we would move to where there were trees or some kind of bushes, and we would just cover them with something and use that for a shade.

There were some other kinds of hogans we used too. There was a kind that we put up when we planned to have a ceremonial, like a five-night doing. We would put up one that has four or six legs and do the chanting there. If the ceremony was just going to be a blessing one, a small ceremony, we used the hogans with four legs. For the big ceremonials, we usually made those with either four or six legs, and then made them a little bigger by adding eight or ten posts all around. We used to call those "the hogans with the big nose" because of how the entry was made. The hogans each had two posts for the doorway, and then there were two rafters that ran from there through the center to join the others as supports for the roof. This entryway stuck out like a porch. Then the hogan was covered with dirt and mud, all over, from the ground up to the top.

That was the kind that I was raised in and saw all the ceremonials performed in when I was a small boy. My folks lived in that kind too. It's only been recently that there have been such things as wagons and good lumber. When I was a boy, we just used anything we could find for wood. And we went out on horses or with one or two teams and just dragged those posts in, two or three at a time. Another way we got posts was to ask a group of men who were known for carrying posts or hauling heavy things to bring them. There would be about ten or more men altogether. They set a day to bring the posts in; then they got together at one place and had the women fix food for them. Then they went out and brought in the wood on their shoulders. They would make two or three trips like that, and then you would have enough posts there to make yourself a hogan.

It was about 1900 when we started using wagons and some farm tools, like plows, harness sets and other things that they were giving out from Fort

Defiance to the People. About then the Navajos started to settle down. At first they just used to go from one place to another with their sheep and horses and cattle. They wandered all across the country and did not have permanent homes on the reservation. But after that, they started settling down, farming with things such as wagons and equipment. It was about 1900 when they started using log posts for hogans. It was only about fifteen years ago that we started making hogans with tarpaper, not dirt roofs. We never did that before. The ones that you see now with concrete walls are really modern; they still build those with wood, but then you stucco over that.

We also used stone hogans during the time that the People were having so much trouble with other tribes. You can see ruins of those in canyons and different places. The People built those like hogans, but just used stone, I guess for protection. Those hogans were not used for living purposes or for any ceremonial reasons. During the time when the People were scared and were fighting, they just built anything to protect themselves. They would build it right up in front of a cave as a defense.

In the days when I was a small boy, the People had water jugs that were woven by the women and smeared over with pitch to make them waterproof.[4] They used the horse's tail, or the mane and the tail, to make a braid which was woven around those water jugs, just like a sack to hold them in. Those braids had loops on them, and with those, the People hung them on the saddle or tied them there and used them to carry water. We also used goat hide for water bags. When a young goat was killed, instead of butchering it as we do now, we would just cut it across the legs at the rear end and peel off the skin. That was used to carry water in, after you fixed it so the neck opening was closed. You did that with a string, and also closed the leg openings that way. Then you filled it with water and put it across your horse, carrying water that way in front of you while you were riding.

We moved around all of the time, mostly by horseback. Since we had no wagons to carry our belongings, we carried them on horses. Moving around like that, nobody bothered about farming a piece of ground. We just moved around with the sheep and also our few head of horses. We never stayed at one place very long; we would spend a few days here and then move on to some other location. That is the way we lived, even in the wintertime; in spite of the cold and the deep snow, we moved even then.

At that time we had no shovels to use or any other kind of tools, except that we did have an axe for cutting wood. There were no blankets for us to use as bedding; the People used sheep wool and wove blankets to use from that wool. There were no store blankets available in those days; the homemade blankets were all we had. Later on people began to bring in some of those black blankets; they claimed that they came from Mexico. Some were black and some red. They brought just a few of them in, here and there; just some people had them. Of course we did not have those; we used sheep pelts to sleep on.

The only food we lived on was milk. When the sheep and goats were brought in from grazing, people milked them and fed us the milk. That is about all the food we ever ate in those early days; we lived on milk. The people used to make cheese from that milk, too. We used to pick those purple weeds that are right out there in my fields now, the ones with the round leaves, purple flowers and yellow berries that are about the size of marbles. The People, especially those who had lots of sheep and goats, would go and gather those berries, putting them in a big sack. Then we would put them out in the sun to dry, and then keep them through the winter. Any time during the year we could put those dried berries right into the milk; their juice makes cheese form on that milk.

We used to eat a lot of that cheese. The People made pots, large ones shaped like the little cooking pots used in ceremonies today. We would use those to boil the milk in; then we would put some of the juice from those berries in there. You pick the yellow berries and crush them up; the juice comes from those seeds. You soak them in water and it turns brownish. Then you strain it, put it into the hot milk, and let it set. When it forms cheese, like cottage cheese, the water comes to the top, and the cheese forms underneath when it cools. You remove that by hand and squeeze all the water out. Then you roll it into balls and set them on tree branches. We used to expose our food to the weather outside to keep it; we would leave those cheeses out there and use them when we needed them.

We also put those cheeses on big thin rocks that were clean; we would shape them with our hands and set them on top of those flat rocks and let them dry. Sometimes the People would make a big ball like that. My mother told me that we used a lot of that; she would just slice off that cheese, reheat it, and we would eat it like that. The other thing we used in making that cheese was the insides of a baby lamb or goat. We would take out the milk bags from their insides when we butchered them, and we would dry those bags out. Then we would grind these up, just like we did with those seeds; we would grind them up very fine and put them in the hot milk. That makes the cheese form in that milk, too.

We stored that cheese on rocks anywhere, in the shade or the sun. We just had to set those rocks so they were off the ground and the dogs and other animals would not bother them. There are some places around this area where you can still find those rocks, flat rocks like that, set in the tops of trees; that is what they were used for. You need plenty of milk to make that cheese, even to get a little cheese. You have to go around asking for milk these days, or milk the goats and save it until there is enough, at least five gallons.

There was no coffee in the early days. My grandparents used to talk about using the spike of the yucca plant to make a drink because they had nothing like coffee. There are two kinds of yucca, the wide-leafed one and the thin, narrow-leafed plant. My parents used that drink a lot too, and once I tried it. After I was a grown man, I was hunting one day for my uncle's horses somewhere around the Tsaile area. We had already been out a day without anything to eat and we were really hungry. So we came across one of those yuccas, and we picked that spike. In the summer you can pick them; they have fruit which is long and looks something like a banana. It tastes really sweet if you pick it at the right time. We picked that and took it with us.

On the second day we got really hungry; we still had not located the horses yet, so we went to a campground some people had left and found some coffee grounds there. They looked clean so we took all the grounds and put them in a can and went to the nearest water hole. We set this can of coffee grounds there and added some water to it. When it started boiling, we added some other grounds and made coffee. Then we roasted this yucca blossom in those grounds and had a meal. That blossom was really good; I was half starved because we had been out there a day and a half already. When I think of that now, it seems as if I had biscuits and coffee at that time; that yucca blossom took the place of biscuits.

Coffee beans did not come into the area until after the People were back from Fort Sumner. The People received rations after they returned from there, and it was during that time that they got coffee. My folks and I would go over to Fort Defiance on certain dates each month when we were told we could get those things at the headquarters there. It was like the government surplus commodities we have today. People come out here every month and the People go to the Chapter House and pick up shares of food, like powdered milk, canned foods, flour, lard, peanut butter and things like that. The school gets part of that too; it helps a lot on food prices because we get those things, like beans, pintos and things like that from the government at no cost. During the days when we used to go to Fort Defiance for those things, the coffee that was issued by the government was not roasted. We each got half a hundred pound sack of green coffee. When we got those beans home, we would roast them ourselves and then grind them.

We also got a kind of yellow soap from Fort Defiance, and flour and sugar too. It was brown-colored sugar, not beet sugar. I guess it was maple sugar.

When I was a boy, we also had wild carrots and wild onions that we picked almost anywhere and used as food. During certain seasons, we gathered pinyons and yucca fruits, and harvested weed seeds from wild weeds. Some of these things could be put away and stored; other things, such as apricots had to be put to use or dried. We also gathered a plant which tastes like celery. We would squash it and put it in hot ashes to scorch its seeds. Then we would take those plants out of the ashes, dry them a bit and then make a powder out of them. That plant grew everywhere and we used it in making stew. We even put it in cornmeal. We put the water on, put some of that dried powder in it and boiled it. Then we would add a little cornmeal so it thickened, and add some salt and maybe some sheep fat. And that is what we used for our food. We ate mush a lot when I was young, and I got sick of it. One day I tried to make a mush out of sugar and water when everyone was out of the hogan. No matter how much I stirred, I just could not make it thicken.

There were no saddles like the factory-made ones of today. In those days we used homemade saddles, made from wood of local trees. Some men knew how to make them; not everyone, but only some. I never made one of those, but I watched people doing that. They used rawhide or tanned leather, and that leather came from the government too; we got that at Fort Defiance at the same time they gave out food. It depended on how many you had in your family; the more there were, the more leather and food you were given. Some people who had big families got two rolls of leather for their use. We used that for saddles and for the soles of moccasins and for those long-strapped shoulder pouches that are decorated with silver buttons and used to keep small belongings in.

There were several different ways of making those saddles. The foundation was made from wood; the People used to take a handaxe or hatchet and go out into the woods. They would look for naturally formed roots of trees or maybe the upper parts of trees where they form curves. The main part that supported the whole saddle had to be formed in the round; the People could not make it round or shape it because they did not have any other tools except a small hatchet and a round file that were given to them at Fort Defiance.

After you found the wood, you had to fix it up. There were no screws or drills to use in putting it together, so all we used were two or three pieces that fit together naturally. The very first saddle was just a narrow piece of wood with sides on it to fit the horse's back. It did not have a horn — just two sides padded with deer hair, with a cinch and wooden stirrups. Those were called "parallel pairs"; — they would lie on either side of the horse's backbone.

Later on, the People got the idea of pack saddles with horns on them from the kind of saddles that the Mexicans were using. They also got tanned leather from the Mexicans and used that to make cinches and straps for their saddles. Some of the saddle horns were just crosspieces, like a pack-saddle frame. The back piece was rounded, made from curved wood. The sides were just pieces of flat wood. The People used wood files to smooth the wood for those saddles. We did not have any braces or bits to drill holes through those pieces, so we just used pieces of fine wire we found here and there; we put those in the fire until they turned red hot, and then we used them to burn holes through the wood. It took a long time to drill a hole in the wood that way. After all the holes had been made, we tied the pieces together with whatever wire we could find.

After the wooden skeleton of the saddle was put together, then we would get either horsehide or cowhide and cut it up into little, fine strips. We would get those strips really wet so they would stretch and then use them for sewing the saddle together. When they dried, all of the pieces would be tight together. Then we would thoroughly soak cowhide or horsehide and cover the whole frame over with that, putting it out to dry in the sun. When it dried against that wood, it was just as hard as steel. Then on top of that layer, we would put more layers. We would find bigger wires to burn more holes when we needed them; we put two straps in the back and two in the front for carrying things. You could not do anything to break those saddles when they were finished.

It took a long time to make those saddles. There were some men who did it really well; their saddles were just like the ones we have today, except they were plain. Some of them were even better than those that are being made now. Those saddles brought good prices; the People would give sheep, or sheep and horses and other things just for one saddle. Some of the men who were experts in making saddles used to get a girl for that. Families in those days would just go out and ask certain men to marry their children. They did not have to get acquainted or anything like that. The People would always look for a man who was good at making saddles. When they found one, they would be willing to give their daughter away for that, so they would have someone in the family who knew how to make saddles.

These are the things that I remember now about how it was when I was a small boy. As far back as I can remember the People had moccasins. The machine-made shoes came only recently, after the traders started moving onto the reservation. For a long time all those traders had were groceries. After they got settled down, we noticed that they started getting shoes, clothing and things like that.

The People were suspicious of those things at first; whenever they came across a white man in shoes, they were too shy even to touch those shoes. They said those were made by white men and they were not supposed to wear them or even touch them. There were times when they would find clothing, like pants, shirts, coats and even hats, and they were scared to wear those things. The old people said you were not supposed to wear anything made by a white man or belonging to a white man. So they did not use those things, even if they found them. They just let them go. All they did was make their own moccasins, even for the little children.

The main reason for that was that during the time when the People went to Fort Sumner, they were mistreated. And for that reason, they would not touch anything that belonged to a white man; they said that all of those things were not good. We were told not to wear white men's clothes because those people were our enemies and we would get sick from the effects of using their clothing. If the People were given some clothes, they would just throw them out. I was raised during the time when the People were afraid of those things, but I am not like them.

When I was a boy, the women wore high moccasins, the ones that wrapped around the calf; those were made out of undyed buckskin. They are disappearing now, except over in the western part of the Navajo country. Those high moccasins were wrapped around the legs; at the end the buckskin narrowed down to a narrow string, and they tied them with that. Now they are using silver buttons or coin buttons in some places instead of that tie. The men wore low-cut moccasins; they were like those of the women, only shorter.

There are several things used in tanning the buckskin for moccasins. You can burn juniper and use the ashes. Then there is a bush that grows high up in the mountains; you take its bark, dry it, then chop it up and grind it into powder. Then you boil it and add some other roots of bushes that grow in the valleys. You peel those roots, pound up the thin layer that covers them and boil that for a long time. You lay out your buckskin and apply the ashes of the burned cedar bark, in ground powder form. Then you rub in the liquid from those boiled plants, getting the buckskin soaked in that and going over it many times so it is even. You have to do that right so that the tan is even. Then you just roll up that buckskin and put it somewhere where the liquid will soak in. After it dries a bit, you put it in the damp ground until it softens up. Then you remove it, shake everything off and hang it up to dry. When it dries thoroughly, you have to rub and stretch it many different ways by hand to soften it up again and get it back to its original shape.

The People also used to dye some buckskin black. They used the leaves of the sumac bush for that. You can also use the yellow clay from under the surface of the ground; you dig out that clay and burn it in the fire until it is black. You can also use pinyon pitch, burning that and mixing it with the clay to get that color. You mix those together, stirring them while they burn so they do not cake up too much. When you have the right consistency of paint for your use, you cook it over an open fire until you know it is time to mix it with the liquid from the sumac leaves. After awhile, when you are sure it is right, you put your buckskin into that. That color never fades. We used that for dyeing when I was a boy and also for making the wool black for the rugs. When the traders moved in, we started getting those commercial dyes. They do not stay black; when you wash them, that color comes right out.

In my boyhood days, buckskin was scarce. I wore moccasins, but mine were made just any old way; all that mattered was that they covered my feet. Mine were made from moccasins that had been used before and had worn out; the materials were just handed down from my mother or others in the family.

I learned to tan buckskin from my mother's second husband, Star Gazer's Son. Buckskin was still scarce when I got married and had my own family, and it was not until I got into Tribal affairs that I realized I could get buckskin with the little money I was making. I started making moccasins then, and I was really surprised that I still remembered how. Star Gazer's Son used to be a moccasin-maker; I had watched him when I was a boy, and later I just copied him. He was married to my mother at the time, and we lived on the rim of the Canyon. My mother and he used to make moccasins, and I watched him. He had three different ways of sewing: one that went around like wrapping, another that went through and another way where you could not see the stitches. We sewed those moccasins with sharp pointed implements – awls made out of deer bone. They were just as hard and sharp as any steel, and we used those to punch through the leather and the buckskin. Then we put our sinew through those holes to sew them.

When they enrolled me in the Indian school, I started wearing American-made shoes. I never wore moccasins any more after that, and because of those machine-made shoes, my feet got all out of shape; I had bunions and other things on them, and they were all out of form. I was ashamed to let people see my feet in moccasins, so I used to wear those factory-made shoes even when performing ceremonies.

I probably would not wear moccasins today if it were not for a woman telling me what a singer should look like when he is performing a ceremony. One time I went over to Black Mountain country to perform a Blessingway. I always put on good-looking, clean clothes for that, and shoes. Although my hair was cut short, I dressed decently.

When I finished the morning bathing ritual over there, I went out and then came back into the hogan. I saw an old lady sitting there, looking at me when I sat back down in my place. For awhile she was quiet; then she began talking to me, telling me that in the early days, men who performed ceremonies wore moccasins and homemade knitted stockings. They also wore their hair long, fixed in the back, and they looked nice. She said now the People no longer do that. "When you hire someone to perform some ceremony, he comes in all dressed clean and decently. He has his hair clipped off in the back and looks ugly. All of those men now wear those American-made shoes, which make them look like big draft horses with iron shoes on."

I never forgot what that woman told me; she was the one we used to call "The Woman You Plead With." She gave me some ideas on changing my clothing, and from that time on I have worn my moccasins whenever I am going to do a ceremony. I cannot make my hair grow; it bothers me every time it grows even a little. I think it looks better doing ceremonies in moccasins in the traditional way. I believed what she said, and from that time on I began wearing moccasins again.

I started making moccasins only recently. I have made them for my wife, my daughter Isabelle and my grandchildren when they were small. I have also made a few for some of my white friends. I never made them for pay, and now I do not make them any more; my eyesight is getting too poor for that. I sewed mine with sinew from along the backbone of a sheep or goat; the goat sinew is tougher than that of the sheep. You get it out from where it lies in the meat with a knife, and then you dry it. Then you strip off the size you want and twist it real tight and hang it up to dry again. When it dries, it is stiff. I used a needle that looked like a quilting needle; you just use that for making holes. You have to have good eyesight, because you just use the thread alone to go through the holes.

When I was a small boy, just starting to notice things, the family used to move around. My people used to roam around with us from Black Mountain, back and forth across the Chinle Valley here, from Tsaile clear across to the west of Black Mountain, and then over to Hopi country. There was no permanent home for us then. We just went from one place to another, all the way from there across and back.

When my father was living with us, we used to live mostly over at Black Mountain. My father and two of his sisters had a lot of sheep, as did my mother's mother. Neither family did much planting or farming. They just moved around the country with the sheep, going to different places where there was grass and water. Most of the time we moved around with my grandparents on my mother's side. This grandfather had a younger brother who was called Big Man. He had a lot of horses, and my grandfather used to tend them.

Late in the spring or during the summer, after there were a few people down in the Chinle Valley who had started farming, we would come down to them when the corn was ripe. We would go to the people we knew at harvest time and give them sheep or something and get corn from them. We ourselves did not start raising corn or anything like that until later. We had horses at this time, but we never worried about feeding them corn because there was plenty of grass for them all around. One of those big sacks of corn would last a long time for our family, but two or three hundred sacks of corn would only last about a week for the horses.

Our winter home was there in the Black Mountain area. One of the reasons we went there was to trade with the Hopi Indians. They had no sheep or other animals, and they were always looking for meat. So we did our trading with them. The only thing those Hopis had was food made from various kinds of cornmeal; we would trade with them, getting bread in exchange for meat.

Many Navajos traded mutton and beef with the Hopis. During those days none of the Hopis had sheep or cattle. So the People took mostly meat from here. The Hopis also did not have much wood; their homes are up on the mesas where it's hard to get wood for the fire; I guess they had wood around that place some time ago, but they had just used it all up. And they had to go many miles away to get it; usually they took donkeys with them;

they would pack them with wood and bring them back in a day or two. So the Navajos took wood over there from here. What they traded for was mostly corn food, like corn bread and a thin bread the Hopis called *piki*. The Navajos would trade for these things, and corn itself — dried corn, ground cornmeal, corn on the cob and corn in the many different ways the Hopis fixed it.

I remember that my family did that. They went over to Hopi country mostly in the wintertime, because that was the time the Hopis really needed wood and all that meat. It was also cold then and a good time to carry things between here and Hopi land. My people never did too much trading in the summertime on account of the heat, but in the wintertime, it was easier. I myself was too young then, and I never went there, but my folks did that. That was how they got most of their corn; I guess most of the corn that we grow now came from there.

Another thing the People used to take to the Hopis over there was rabbits. In the wintertime, a whole group of men would join together and go out; they would just sift through an entire area where they knew there were rabbits. There were times when there were jack rabbits in flocks, and the men would form a circle around them, close in on them and then just gather them up. They never used a net or anything like that, just clubs to kill them. They would kill as many as they could, but some would escape. Those men always came out with a lot of rabbits. Then they would pick them up; they would not clean them or anything; they would have the horses and everything ready to go, and they would take those rabbits over to Hopi country. The Hopis really liked those rabbits, and our people would trade them for other things.

The Hopis would clean the rabbits and save the skins and everything else. Then they would have a big ceremony over them. They would get cornmeal and give their blessings over all those rabbits that the People had killed. My folks used to tell me about that ceremony the Hopis had for the rabbits when they took them over there. They watched the Hopis do it but never took part in it. I think some of the Hopi old-timers still do that; whenever they get a lot of food or something, they bless it with ground cornmeal, like a blessing before they eat or use up the meat.

This way of catching rabbits, by circling them, came from the Hopis, too. We never knew much about that until we started trading with them. The rabbits in that area had become scarce. So the Hopis told our people that they knew a good way to catch rabbits, and the Navajos learned it.

That way of catching rabbits usually takes more than ten men; these form a circle, and they do not stand too close together. They leave a big space in between, and the circle is usually about two or three acres around. They stand there and sometimes they have dogs with them. Then they start coming together. They usually do this in the wintertime; the snow in those days used to get so deep that you could catch a rabbit easily because they could not run fast in the snow.

The Hopis cut those rabbits in half and dried them like that. Then they would take a little piece every now and then and use it for their meal. They did not have any sheep or cattle, and that is mainly what they used for meat. They are up on the mesas and nothing grows too well over there.

My mother's mother usually moved her camp across the valley to the Black Mountain area; there was better grazing over there in the winter for the sheep, and she could also trade with the Hopi Indians. Her main reason for moving over there was because it was easy to trade with the Hopis. But my grandfather did not like to go along. He never did care to go across with her when she moved her camp. So he stayed back here, tending those horses.

There were a number of us boys who were just young fellows; we asked our grandmother, "Grandma, why is it that you move across the mountains to the Black Mountain area and our grandfather never wants to go along? Why is that? Why don't you persuade our grandfather to go along when you move camp? What's the reason he doesn't care to go?" We knew why he did not want to go, and so we were just merely asking her for fun.

So she said, "I think he must be a bear. A bear isn't supposed to go to the Black Mountain country. That's the reason I guess he doesn't want to go; he must be a bear." She gave us that answer.

Then we said to her, "Why don't you try to persuade him and try to get him to go along with you in a nice way?"

When we asked her that, she said, "I don't care to plead with him. Even if I should put a rope around his neck and try to pull him across, he's liable to die before I drag him over there." That's what she used to say.

While she was scolding him like that, he never said anything. He never quarreled with her. He would just sit there and keep his mouth shut and never give her an answer; she would do all the scolding. Then at times, too, she would be in a rush to have him do something around home. He would always take his own time; he never got excited about anything; he just moved slowly to take action. Of course, he would do what she wanted, but he would take his time about it. Sometimes she would just lose patience with him and get angry at him. Then she would say, "I wish I could shoot him with an arrow and see if he'd notice it!" Those are the things that I remember in my boyhood days about my grandmother and grandfather, and how we used to live with them.

Of course, when she moved with her sheep to Black Mountain country, he would stay back here to take care of his brother's horses. He had one horse that he used all the time, and it was really over-used. There used to be a place where the family moved to now and then, and there was a corral built there for the horses. One day my grandfather drove those horses into that corral. He was going to saddle his horse, the one he was riding over and over and using too much. It was getting a sore back.

It so happened that some family near there had lost a baby; probably that baby miscarried. In those days the People never bothered about burying a baby in the ground; they just wrapped it up in something and put it up in the tree branches. So this particular time, my grandfather drove those horses into that corral and got his horse to use, and found that it was getting a sore back. He started looking around to see what he could use to cover that sore spot before he put the saddle on. As he was looking around, he saw some kind of a rag up in a tree. So he walked over there and pulled it out. Maybe he thought it was some rag that was used on horses that had sore backs. When he shook it, there were some human bones that dropped out of there. So, of course, he did not use that cloth after those baby bones fell out of it.

I guess my grandfather told my grandmother about it and she got angry about that. She said, "That devil,[5] that devil, do you know what he did while we were across the valley in the Black Mountain country? He went and robbed a grave and never even purified himself. And when the children came back, well, there he was lying around and they've been playing with him. He is a devil. So don't get too close to him; don't be rubbing against him," she said, as if she were telling us that he was poison and not to touch him.

After spending the winter in the Black Mountain area, when the spring came, we would start moving back to our summer place, away from Hopi country, over here on the east mountain range. That is the way we kept moving around until finally we came here to this location, Chinle. My family began to do a little farming then, and so it happened that we stayed here. My mother and some of my brothers stayed here around Chinle; only my grandmother and often my brother John kept going back over to Hopi country. We stayed here even in the wintertime; that is how it happened that I settled here. This is where we started farming, and even after we grew up we stayed right here. We did not go out anywhere for anything. We children were always busy looking after the sheep and the few head of horses that we kept with them. We settled down right near Chinle, at the mouth of the Canyon; that is where we started to live permanently and where we built a hogan.

In those days when we started farming, we did not have fences to divide the farm lands; we just had markers so we knew from which point the land was ours. We would plant corn and other things early in the spring and then leave as soon as the planting was finished. We would go to the mountains so the sheep, cattle and horses could get some grass; out here on the farmland, they would get into the corn patch. So we moved with the sheep and all the stock; we used to drive the horses in great big herds just like the cattle in those days, and we would move up into the mountains with them and stay there until later.

In those days we did not know of any kinds of animals that would harm the crops as they do now. We never heard of grasshoppers or corn worms, and we never saw chipmunks or small squirrels. Now we have so many of them that they just go into the fields and chew up the crops, destroying them. In those days we never knew there were such things that would come along and damage the crops. We never heard of a crow, and we did not have to worry about putting up a scarecrow. As soon as we planted, everybody would leave for the mountains.

For several weeks we would be up there in the mountains tending our sheep and cattle and horses; we would come back when the corn was about a foot high. The men would come back here on horseback with their sheepskins and whatever lunch had been prepared for them. We brought mostly boiled mutton and ground corn bread fixed in many different ways, like blue corn bread, when we came out to hoe the weeds. We would bring hoes, sheepskins, blankets and a little food and come out and spend a couple of days hoeing the weeds. In those days, we did not have as many weeds in the field as there are now, so it only took a couple of days to do all that.

When we finished hoeing, we would go back. We never had to worry about how the crops were going to be; we just forgot about them and went into the mountains and came back when the corn was about ripe. Every now and then someone would come out and check to see how things were in the fields. But we never had to put up a scarecrow.

There is another thing — it was not just one or two people who came out to hoe. One thing that kept the People in the whole area together was that if any of them decided to move away and start on their own, they knew that sooner or later they would go hungry. If they stayed together, they knew that if they ran out of food other people from the families nearby would always have something to help out with. That was one thing that kept us close together. If one of us needed help there was always somebody there to offer it.

When the hoeing season came, there would be groups of men who would always get together and come out on horseback and hoe. It used to get hot in those days too, just like today, and when it did, what those men did was take off their clothes and cover themselves with white clay, which protected them from the sun. They would stand out there like that and hoe all day. When they finished an area, which would usually be in a day because so many of them helped, they would go to another. All of the people in the area did the same thing. They would go to one place and help, and when they were all finished, they would move to the mountain again, all at the same time. When it was time to hoe, they would move altogether and start hoeing together; when they finished in one field, they would go to another. They were just about through with everything that way in a few days.

Today the People do not do that. The Ten Days Projects[6] have ruined us. Now it has gotten into the minds of some people that if they do a little work they should get paid for it. Back in those days when I was a boy, people used to help each other all the time. All it took was for the People at each particular place to prepare the food. The rest would come and help, and would be willing to help as long as there was food for them. That is the way they did things in those days.

When we settled down and started to live permanently at the mouth of the Canyon, axes were scarce, and at times we had to borrow them from one another. Families would borrow an axe to chop wood and to cut the poles to use in building their hogans. The hogans were roughly made then; they were not really good ones. Of course there were still no stores in the area; the nearest store we had was at Ganado. Some of the People used to go over there and bring home things from that store. They had things like cloth there.

After some time, a store was started at Tsaile, and then the people who lived around there began to go to it. But the store did not have things such as tools to use around home as they do now. The main things that that store had were flour, coffee, sugar and some cloth. That is about all they had there for trade. The cloth was not a good kind of calico; all they had there was cheap cloth. Then later they began getting some of those wool carders, and that is how the People began using those carding combs to card their wool. They also started getting different colored commercial dyes, like black, red and other colors. The People started dyeing their wool with those, and that is how they began to decorate their blankets with designs of different colors. I do not remember how long the store at Tsaile operated in that way, but we finally heard that place had burned down; I never learned what happened there.

When we were living near the mouth of the Canyon, and even before then, my parents used to make me get up really early in the morning and run. I dreaded that, getting up so early and running I do not know how many miles, and for that reason I was glad to go to school when we heard about it. I also had an uncle on my father's side who was called Blacksmith. The folks would make me get up and work the bellows for him; I would have to stand there and do that for him while he worked. I dreaded that too. My uncle was mean to me; he scolded me all of the time. I was glad to get away from him, too, when I went to school.

There were certain people in those days who were appointed to be headmen[7] in each area. We did not have any policemen, and there was no such thing as going to court or jail. The People were just scattered all over; they were so far apart that they did not have time to gossip about one another or to get each other in trouble. They were too far away. In those days, the People really listened to each other; they did whatever they were told to do or not to do by these headmen. If there was help needed, they went out and helped one another. Now the People do not do that. We live too close together, and someone is always gossiping about someone else; when the story gets big enough, soon they start throwing one another in jail for that.

When the Council was formed there at Window Rock, we began having councilmen, chapter officers and Navajo police to work for the tribe. Ever since that was started, the People outside of Window Rock just looked at those officials and saw they were getting paid to work; since then people do not come out and help if you ask them, like they did when I was a boy. All you had to do then was prepare a big meal for them and they would be there to help with whatever there was to be done. Now whether you feed them or not, they still want to get paid. Now I hate to ask anyone to help me because I know they will expect me to pay them. Things like the Ten Days Projects have really ruined the Navajos; even the People who work just one day now want to get paid.

My grandfather on my father's side was one of the headmen who used to talk to the People. He used to talk to boys who were my age and tell us that young boys who are growing up are very active in every way. There are some that are not polite; they think they know everything and soon start misbehaving and getting into mischief. If a boy starts that kind of life, sooner or later he is going to end up doing something wrong. My grandfather tried to tell us that young boys should not carry on like that at any time during their lives because the earlier experiences the People had showed that it does not pay in the long run.

My grandfather would tell us about the times when the Navajos thought they were doing something great by stealing and taking property from others. They were men and should have known not to steal, but they went out on raids, and many went right along with them. They all really suffered from starvation. Often the families of those men who were out stealing suffered starvation high up in the mountains somewhere. My grandfather would tell the People that he himself was one of those men who had suffered like that. He was one of those who ate dogs for food and also the white spikes of those great big yuccas. The People used to roast them in the ground and eat them because there was nothing else to eat. He would tell all of us young boys not to misbehave in any way; he said the real trouble starts when you think that you can do things your own way and you end up stealing; that really brings trouble to you.

My grandfather would tell those things at every gathering the People had. He told all the young boys what stealing had done to their ancestors and how they suffered from it. I guess to make it funny, he told us that those cactus they roasted in the ground had now turned into these big homemade flour tortillas, and the big yucca leaves that they roasted in the ground had turned into young calf ribs. These leaves look like calf ribs after they cook. Then, too, he said that the dogs they ate had become those funny looking sheep that white men raise; I guess he was talking about angora sheep, those great big old sheep with skin that is all wrinkled. I guess he said those things to show that he knew then that in the future the People would have calves for meat and flour for bread and they would even have sheep here on the reservation. Sure enough, those are the three main things the Navajos eat: mutton or any kind of meat, store-bought flour bread, and ribs from cattle, not dogs.

He also told us that when the People were starving they were nothing but skin and bones; you could see through those people, especially around the collarbone. You could see their big veins and how the bones were structured, and everything. The People looked horrible then. Now instead of the People looking that way, where we once had necks full of bones and veins, turquoise in many strands has taken the place of the great big old veins.

The People just laughed about those times when my grandfather talked to them this way. He used to talk at big gatherings, like Squaw Dances,[8] and try to make us young ones see what our forefathers had gone through. I guess he wanted us to realize that the People had really suffered in the past and that things were much easier now. He wanted us young people to realize that and to make use of everything that came along in life to make things easier than the way they had been in the past.

In the days when I was a small boy, there was no such thing as welfare or relief workers. No one ever said that an old couple, or an old person, was unable to support himself and should be given help. People in that condition just had to suffer that way and do the best they could to get by. One of the things we were told during my childhood was to prepare ourselves to make a living. We also learned about farming and sheep-raising, but we were told these things do not last forever. In your young days you are not handicapped, and you are able to endure a lot of hard work and hardship. But when you get old or disabled in some way, that is the end of your work. You are not able to continue to operate your farm as you did in your younger days, or tend your sheep as you did before. No matter what kind of occupation you have, as long as you are physically able to carry it on, you can enjoy the benefits of it. But once you get handicapped in some way, or old and feeble, well, that is the end of that. All of those things, like farm work and raising sheep, end. The only occupation you can make use of until the end of your days is that of a ceremonial singer.

When I was able to remember things and to think about them, those were the teachings of the People. Of course, before that time things were unsettled. The People were fighting then, and I suppose their instructions to the younger people were different from those that we were given.

When I was a boy, the folks would get me out of bed when I was asleep; they would jerk me out, and if it had happened to snow the night before, they would make me go and roll in it. They would tell me to go and jump in the water and take a cold bath, and they would tell me to go and run a race in the morning and not to be sleeping. They used to tell me when I was a boy, "If you don't harden yourself for these things, you're going to be taken advantage of by your enemy. You're liable to be found sometime lying on your belly with one arrow in your back, showing that you were not hard enough for these things. But if you are strong and brave, then you'll be found with plenty of arrows sticking into your chest. If you get killed that way, it shows that you have fought bravely."

Some of the People who told me about those things were the ones who earlier had gone out raiding and stealing from their neighbors. These people were thieves and, of course, their enemies came and attacked them and took advantage of them, and they had to take the consequences.

While I was growing up and learning all these things, my father was starting to run around wild. Sometimes he would not come home for a long time. He had many wives, I do not even know how many, but any young man with clothes and wealth had lots of women attracted to him at that time. My father was that way; he had children by other women in other places; he had some in Round Rock and Wheatfields that I know of, and he had plenty of horses. I had no occasion to listen to him in my early years because he was never home. On his mother's side there was a lot of livestock to provide for him, so he was pretty well dressed. In those days, men were just out for a good time. They never thought about providing anything like a permanent home for their family. My father made no plans for the future of his children. He always had a horse ready to take off on. Early in the morning he would leave for one, two or three days. Then he would come back.

My mother was somewhat half-witted. She was ordered to look after the sheep. She never had a chance to go around, and she did not have a mind of her own. Her mother told her to go herd the sheep. My father never told her anything because he was too busy running around. Her duties were to feed the family and herd the sheep.

Because my father was living this way, I had some half brothers and sisters. One of these is Slim Man; we had the same father, but his mother was Red Woman. Her mother, Mexican Woman, was one who was captured and taken away by the Mexicans. Thus, his mother was part Mexican.[9]

When I got older, my father took up with a woman from Wheatfields and moved back around here. That woman was a close relative of Big Man, and she had plenty of sheep. My mother's mother had moved back to Keams Canyon, but my mother was staying here with our family. We had become quite poor because my older brothers had gambled and given away almost all of our property, including many of the livestock my grandmother had given us.

While my father was gone up around Wheatfields, Star Gazer's Son, of the Those Who Walk About Clan, came to live with my mother, since she was no longer living with my father. Their marriage was arranged by the family; they asked her to accept him. We all went in Canyon del Muerto with him and settled down there.

EDITORS' NOTES

1. Charlie Mitchell, one of the early leaders in the Chinle area, was one of Frank's clan uncles. The circumstances under which Frank was given his name are related in Chapter 3 of this book.

2. In an interview Irene Stewart conducted with Frank on July 17, 1965, in conjunction with the Doris Duke American Indian History Project, Frank elaborated on his birth as follows: "My mother told me that I was born just south of Tsaile. She said, 'It was fall and your father and I were down in the Canyon getting some peaches because they were ripe. We didn't go on horses then because we didn't have any. We just walked. We were getting peaches when you started giving me labor pains. So we hurried home and that's where I gave birth to you.' My mother never told me which month I was born in, but it was fall, the month of the big harvest. That's when the peaches ripen. In English that would probably be October. I don't know what day it was. In those days, the People didn't count days. They just kept track of the months." (Typescript #965, Oral History of Canyon de Chelly Series, Doris Duke American Indian History Project: 25-26.)

3. For further information on hogan architecture, see Mindeleff (1898), Kluckhohn, Hill and Kluckhohn (1971:143-162), Spencer and Jett (1971), Jett and Harris (n.d.) and others. For ceremonies associated with hogan construction, see Haile (1937b, 1942) and Frisbie (1968, 1970).

4. For comparative details on all aspects of material culture, see the encyclopedic work of Kluckhohn, Hill and Kluckhohn (1971).

5. Although "devil" is one possible translation of *ch'įįdii*, the Christian theological connotation is not to be inferred. See Haile (1950:310-311).

6. The Ten Days Projects are short-term work projects planned by the local community and funded by the tribe. These provide self-improvement opportunities, on-the-job training skills and wages, as well as potential group assistance with specific tasks such as construction of homes and school bus shelters, wool carding and spinning, weaving, etc.

7. At least by the beginning of the twentieth century, when the need for the earlier war chief vs. peace chief distinctions had declined, the Navajos were represented by numerous headmen who served as local leaders. Chosen by popular consent, these *naat'áani* (headmen) or *nant'á* (speakers or spokesmen) directed some local community activities, arbitrated disputes, and represented specific areas at larger gatherings, communicating opinions and news to political figures, other headmen and those they represented (see Franciscan Fathers 1910:422-424, Hill 1940, 1956, and Shepardson 1963).

8. See Chapter 4, n. 5.

9. According to Frank, Slim Man's people were originally from Jemez Pueblo. Thus, a Coyote Pass Clan or Jemez Clan affiliation seems implied. For a life story of Slim Man, see Johnson et al. (1969).

3. School

News of a school at Fort Defiance ... trouble at Round Rock and subsequent agreements ... how enrollment went at first ... Frank is enrolled in school ... the trip to school ... arrival in Fort Defiance ... school routines and various incidents ... Frank goes home for several years and gets name Ólta'í Tsoh ... returns to school with brother Tom ... Frank gets restless and runs away with a classmate to find work.

We had built a hogan when we heard that at Fort Defiance they had put up buildings in order to get the children of the People into school. My uncles were the ones who used to go over there, but of course we children never did go. And we heard that from these people who went over there; they brought back these words about the school.

Then some more years passed, and of course I was a little older. I had grown up. Maybe I was fourteen or fifteen years old. These old people who used to go to Fort Defiance brought back word that their children were to be placed in school to get educated. That's what they were saying. The buildings were ready for the children. They told us that the children were going to be fed over there and they would sleep over there and be taken care of, and learn to read and write and know how to work the papers. That's what they were starting to tell us. So these headmen, the leaders of the People, went around trying to persuade the People to agree to it, but the Navajos in general were opposed to it. They said, "Well, who wants to give his children away to somebody else, especially to a white man? Nobody wants to do that." But these spokesmen would try to persuade the People to consent to do that.

When one of those men would come to see us, coming to our hogan, the folks would tell us, "Go on, hide; get away from here, get out of sight!" And they just chased us off and told us to hide in the caves or in the creek or in whatever we could hide in. And then we would just be peeping up now and then to see; we would do that until the man would go away. When he left, then we would go back to the hogan.

Finally, after awhile, they said, "Well, there's a new agent at Fort Defiance, and he's getting pretty strict. He wants to get the children in school." And we heard that around the Fort Defiance area, he was taking his police force out and picking up children for school. When that was told to the People, of course that made them more opposed to it than ever because they were being forced to give up their children.

During that time the People were pretty much against enrolling their children in school, and they were determined not to give their children up. A new store was started at Round Rock; it was put there by one of our own men, Chee Dodge. He and a white man had put the money together to start that store.[1]

I think that it was about two years after that store was in operation that trouble broke out. I suppose that the agent would get together and discuss these things with the headmen, the spokesmen there. Of course we were unaware of it out here, and that was the whole difficulty. I suppose that when they got together with this new agent[2] there, he talked to them and persuaded them to go out and recruit children for the school. And I guess they and others who favored the school agreed to it. Old Man Dodge favored the school; of course he was the only one who spoke English at that time. There was another fellow by the name of Old Man Silversmith, and there was Charlie Mitchell, my clan uncle. Over here we had our spokesmen, fellows by the name of Weela, Man Who Shouts and others.

Some of the People were strongly opposed to sending their children to school. These were people who lived over on the other side of the mountain, over towards Shiprock and then also along the San Juan River there; that is what we heard. People were saying that the agent and his group of Navajos who favored the school were on one side, and on the other side were the ones who were opposed, especially these people from the north side there. We heard that they were very much opposed to it and had said that they were not going to give one child to the school.

So for that reason, a date was set to meet at the store at Round Rock at a certain time; there all these questions would be cleared up. The agent would come out there and explain everything about why this was being done. And when those people over on the north side, the Shiprock side, heard this, they said, "Well, we're not going to give one child to him; if that agent does try to force us to put the children in school, we're not going to do it. That's final. When he comes and starts to talk like that to us, we'll tell him that we don't want to do it, we don't favor school at all, and if he insists on it, when the time comes, when he just insists on it and wants us to do it, well, we'll grab him and throw him out of the store."

They had arranged that among themselves and made this agreement, and they were pretty well united on that when the day came that the agent was to be at Round Rock. A man by the name of Black Horse was appointed as the spokesman for this outfit from the north side that was opposing the school.

"When the agent comes there and starts to talk to us, let him talk and explain just what his plans are regarding placing those children in school. When he gets through, you tell him, 'No, we're not going to do it; we don't agree to it.' " They instructed Black Horse in this way. "Now, if the agent says for the second time 'You have to do it,' you tell him 'No, we're not going to do it.' If he says it three times, you tell him, "No, we're not going to do it." If he still insists, then give us the order to throw him out." That was the way old Black Horse was instructed by his people to face that agent and tell him that they were not going to let their children be enrolled in school.

So that was the plan. When the time came for them to discuss this with the agent,[3] they went inside the store where this meeting took place. Of course, the agent started to tell them all about school and that they would have to put their children there, that that agreement was in the treaty. Black Horse said, "No, we're not going to do it." And then the second time the agent said, "No, you have to do it," and for the second time Black Horse said, "No, I told you no." And for the third time and the fourth time the agent said, "No, you have to do it, you have to place your children in school." And for the third and fourth times Black Horse said, "No, I told you no." Then he said, "Go ahead, grab him, throw him out."

The People were all waiting for this; they just ran in there, grabbed hold of that man and rushed outside with him. They were throwing rocks and sticks and everything at him.

There were some men there who lived around Round Rock; Weela was one of them, Long Moustache was another and Bead Clan Gambler was still another one. They had a hogan there where they stayed all the time, just spending their time playing cards and gambling. When this happened, of course they noticed what was going on. They saw the agent being tossed up and down by this mob of people.

Bead Clan Gambler, a big husky man, was the leader of these card players. He ran in there where these people were tossing the agent up and down and throwing rocks at him from a distance. The mob wanted to take the agent out, away from the store and stone him; that's what they were going to do. So Bead Clan Gambler began to elbow his way into that crowd; finally he got to where the agent was and grabbed him. Of course, he had a lot of friends who were with him in his gang. And when Bead Clan Gambler pulled that agent from out of that crowd and rushed him back toward the store, of course those fellows encircled him, protecting him and the agent. And so he ran back to the store with this agent and took him right inside, while the others were keeping the attackers back. For that reason, Bead Clan Gambler was made an Indian policeman and was a policeman for years.

By the time they got the agent back into the store, he was out of his mind, very frightened, I guess. You see he didn't know what was going on. When that happened, of course those who were attacking the agent were surprised and angry that they had lost their captive, and they started to attack the store, set fire to it, tear down the stone wall and chop at the door. They were yelling and threatening, and these fellows who were between them and the store kept them back. And that's what prevented any more trouble there. And of course things quieted down after a while and finally, one group was on one side, and the group that was with the agent was inside, and there was a group between them which prevented any more trouble. And so that's what happened there on account of the agent getting too rough with the People; he almost got murdered on that account.

Just at that time, there was a detachment of soldiers from Fort Wingate over near Tsaile hunting bear.[4] Inside, the agent talked about writing a note to those soldiers; he discussed it beforehand with that group inside. He said he did not know whether those soldiers would come to help them out or not; because, you see, the soldiers were from the War Department and he was from the Interior Department; they were two different departments under the government. But he finally said, "I guess I'll try and see what happens," and he wrote a note.

Chee Dodge's horse was there; it was a big horse with white stockings, and it was a pretty fast horse. The horse was saddled and prepared for the rider; it was led up to the store, out of view of the attackers; they were on the north side of the store, and the horse was brought in from the opposite side, so they did not see it. Of course we do not know what Black Horse's group was discussing over there, what they were planning to do next. Over here on the agent's side, you see, that is what they were planning; they wanted to send a note out by somebody with a fast horse. And there was this third group, interfering in between and preventing any further trouble. These people just pleaded with Black Horse's group not to do any more than they had already done. They said, "You are just going to bring hardship not only on yourselves but on everybody else, on all of us." And they pleaded with them and said, "Please, please don't start anything else." That is how they prevented further trouble.

So the note was given to a man, and he got on the horse and started off behind the house; he did not want these attackers to see him, so he stayed in line with the house as a blind until he got away some distance. And then he went across a low place there, sort of a hollow place, and then he went up on the ridge in the direction of the paved road. That's the way he started off toward Lukachukai. The flat was quite a distance to cover before he could get to another hill to get out of view. Of course, when he came out into the open there on the flats, that is when he was noticed by these attackers.

The opposing side thought he was carrying a message, a paper or something. So a group of young men started chasing him. "Either catch him or shoot the horse from under him if you get close enough to do that"; that's what the spokesman said to these fellows who started chasing that rider. But the horse the man was riding was pretty speedy, so the group had no chance to overtake him. The horse was too fast for them; it was gradually increasing the distance between them and him, and they couldn't even start to catch up with him on their horses. So finally they just had to give up because his horse was going too fast; at last, they just turned around.

I guess he delivered his message to the camp over there and the hunters were all back at the camp when the message came. The note was delivered to the officier in charge there, and he read it over and said, "All right." He told the messenger that they'd start off as soon as they could get ready. And I suppose they went to work to pack up and saddle their horses. They started moving at night, and went along all that night until daylight, and when they had just a short distance to go, they prepared themselves for trouble. Then the officer in charge went on ahead. The soldiers all arrived at the store together.[5] Of course I did not see these doings: this is just a story that was told to me by somebody else.

Those attackers, a crowd of them, were still there, and a messenger was sent to them on horseback. The officer inquired about Black Horse, and they said, "Well, he's in the crowd over there." And so then, he got off his horse and started to walk over there. Of course he was asking about Black Horse as he was walking along; he wanted to know where Black Horse was and to have him come over.

Then Black Horse came up. They met there and shook hands. Then he was questioned, asked why he had done this, and he told his story about why he did those things. I guess he said, "Well, the reason we did that was because of the way the agent was treating us. He was treating us roughly; that's the reason we did that."

The officer began to talk about this question of a school and to explain it. He talked with Black Horse for some time, and he calmed down the feelings of the group. After some time they quieted down, and then the officer said to Black Horse, "Let's go over to the store; you and the agent can talk this over there and come to some understanding." The army officer brought those fellows over with Black Horse; the agent was shaking as they brought him out of the store. And then he shook hands with Black Horse.

After quite a discussion, Black Horse was informed that this school business was not going to be put aside and that it was here to stay. "You have to comply with it whether you like it or not. That's your agreement with your government; in the treaty you agreed to do that and you have to comply with it. They're not going to quit; they'll just continue to go on. This was decided by your government in Washington, and it doesn't only apply to you Navajos, it applies to other Indians also. So there's no use trying to get away from it, because you have to agree." It was also explained that the plans were for everybody; that nobody would be excused from school; that the children all had to go to school and get educated.

After awhile, everything was agreed to and friendship was restored. Food was taken out of the store, flour and things like that, and the women from both sides were told to get together and start cooking for the crowd, which they did. I do not know how long they all were there, whether they stayed there another night or not, but I imagine they just stayed there until everything was settled and friendship restored; then they dispersed. At that time, of course I was a boy, and this is just a story handed on to me. After that, they said, "Well, we'll meet together at Fort Defiance and we'll discuss this question again there and we'll definitely agree on some kind of policy."

Of course Black Horse was worried about himself; he said, "What's going to happen to me when we meet at Fort Defiance; what's to happen to me then?" Well, he was told he would have to wait until things were discussed over there. So that was the end of their discussion on that at Round Rock; then they dispersed.

After they returned to their homes, a certain day was set to meet at Fort Defiance. They got together; they had some officials come from Washington to meet with the Indians there, and an investigation was held into how this agent, Shipley, had been conducting his work and handling the Indians. That was all investigated. They found out that he was getting rough with the People, that he was to some extent at fault for doing that. And he did not stay very long after that; he was transferred. These officials from Washington did the investigating, and the People told everything that Shipley had been doing. Then the officials said that it was not all the fault of the Navajos, that it was the fault of the white officials, too. They said, "Well, the agent started to pick up children by force; he has overstepped himself in some places and that's what caused this uprising." So he was discharged from his duties and asked to leave. Black Horse was never punished for what he did; he was just made a headman, one of the leaders of the tribe.

After that was settled, another agent was appointed; Shipley was replaced by another man, who was told that he had to handle this problem gently. He was told not to get too harsh or too rough with the People, because they did not understand. "You have to be patient with the Navajos and persuade them in a friendly way. You have to explain these things and make them understand, not just go in there and get rough with them that way. Naturally people don't like to be handled in that way."

And the spokesmen and those who were supporting the agent were cautioned; they were told not to go around making threats: "You scare the People that way and that isn't the policy at all. You're to go around and try to persuade them to agree to these policies, because they don't understand and you have to explain it to them. If they understand it correctly, of course you have no trouble, but if you go around and threaten them with force it brings trouble. Now this education is something that is going to be beneficial to your people; you have to be careful about how you go about it. If you handle it the way this Shipley was handling it, you're bound to bring trouble on yourselves and on the government officials. You have to handle these things carefully and easily and not with threats."

The headmen from various areas were told to go back home and tell the People about education, and why the government officials wanted it for the children. "It's going to be a benefit to them, and it's going to be a benefit to the tribe; it's a good thing to have your children educated." They were also told, "Fort Defiance is the headquarters for all your people, for all the Navajos; that's where you should come and discuss these things with people in general. You must understand that these headquarters were established for your use and to help you discuss your problems." That was the policy in the beginning, right after Fort Sumner; after their captivity the Navajos were told what the programs were for them in the future.

The government promised to finance education without any expense to us. What we promised in the treaty was to enroll all children of school age; of course, at that time, nobody had any objection to that; all the People wanted to go back home, so they just promised anything.

It required a lot of patience, a lot of work to persuade the Navajos to put their children in school. These men would start working early in the summertime to get children enrolled by fall. It took a lot of coaxing and persuasion to get the people to agree to it.

At that time things were issued to us for our use in preparing food, such as skillets and pans to mix the dough in and other cooking utensils. These cooking utensils were issued to the Navajos at Fort Defiance, and they brought them home and began using them. Of course, not everybody got these issued to them. Just here and there we began to get these things brought in from the agents.

That, of course, created some rumors and gossip. Some Navajos said, "Those things you're getting from the government, from the agency, are payments for your child whom you've enrolled in school." The People began telling each other that. On that account, people were confused; they did not know which was which, which way they should go. But most of them objected to school.

Another of the drawbacks was that these men who went to recruit the children for school were receiving wagons and farm implements, harnesses and things like that. And of course, the People got suspicious. They said, "Well, just because he's recruiting the children, he gets so much for each child that he gets. He's selling a lot of children and getting things like that for it."

One of the main objections to enrolling the children was that white people are not Navajos. They are foreign people, people of another race. The People were suspicious; they thought that if they put their children in school, the white people would take the children away from them and either kill them or do something so they would never be seen again. Even if they remained alive, the children would just go further and further from their homes and before the People knew it, they would never come back. That's what they used to say.

In the beginning, they only enrolled the children of the servants of the well-to-do families. And these servants were usually new to the Navajo Tribe. Many of them were Pueblo Indians who had come and joined the Navajos; some of them married Navajos and had children, and they were the ones who put their children in school first. They were not classed as Navajos. And then there were others who were just used as servants to do chores for the well-to-do people. Children of those families were also enrolled, and some of them were pretty well advanced in age, closer to twenty when they were in school. The People did not want to risk placing their own children in school.

Old Man Dodge used to bring that up in his talks with the People. He said, "If we had any sense at all, if we were wise, we would have enrolled the best Navajo children in school. We might now be in a better position to make a living. Instead of that, we just put these servant children in school. Now they are ahead of us in education, and they turn around now and are more or less our enemies."

The leaders who were appointed after they returned from Fort Sumner were the ones who went out and did the recruiting. They were the ones who urged the People in their areas to enroll their children in school.

The children were supposed to be voluntarily placed in school and not forced at all. But sometimes they were really forced by their parents. The parents were the ones who were willing to let their children go to school. You had to get your children to Fort Defiance yourself. People would take them over there on horseback or in a wagon; that was the only way they had then.

I guess the reason some of them were willing to take their children to school was that for doing that they would be given, free of charge, some farm implements like shovels, picks, hoes and axes. That's how they started out; the tools were in exchange for the trouble of getting the children into school. The People would get together at Fort Defiance for these different tools and utensils. They were told there what they could be used for and how. Then of course, they would go home and use them. This was part of the agreement they made at Fort Sumner. The government agreed that if the Navajos brought their children into school, the government would help with the food that was given them for at least ten years, and with all the tools and utensils.

The People who enrolled their children at that time probably gave them bad advice. The boys especially in their teens or past that age, were told, "If any of those white people try to punish you, beat you or mistreat you, you just get a knife and stab them; cut their bellies open." That is how wild we were.

The school accepted just any children, regardless of what conditions they were in. Some of those children were brought to school very badly clothed; there was just nothing clean or whole on them. They were brought into school in the condition they were in at home. Everything they had on was what their parents had provided; they did not have any stores then where they could buy clothing to dress them up in. They had no shoes or overcoats or real protection.

The incident I told you about at Round Rock happened in the fall. The winter after that, sometime after Christmas, about that time they started going around recruiting children again. That's when I was enrolled to go to school. I do not know how old I was then; maybe fourteen, fifteen, or even seventeen.[6] I was the first child in our family to be placed in school; that's because I was sort of the black sheep. They said the most ugly ones were put in school first; I guess I was the ugliest one in the family.

Now when they started placing children in school, they didn't take the prime; they took those who were not so intelligent, those the People thought could be spared because of their physical conditions, and those who were not well taken care of; those were the kinds of children they enrolled first. Some of them were actually half-witted. Of course there were any number of such children among the Navajos. Some of them were children of Navajos who were a little better off than the rest and had servants.

The leaders who went around recruiting children for school talked to the People about what the advantages would be in the future, if they would put their children in school. The People would get angry and say, "No, sir! Absolutely not! I'm not going to give up my child; while I'm still alive, I'm not going to turn my child over to those foreigners. Outsiders are not going to take my child away while I'm still living." That's what they used to say. They would sometimes get out a butcher knife and toss it in front of those doing the recruiting, and say, "Well, go ahead, cut my throat first; you'll have to do that before you can take my child." It was mainly the women who would stand in front of their children, not wanting them to go to school. The men were willing to put them in school, but it was always the women who acted like that when the recruiter came.

My mother was the worst one. She really objected to my going to school; she did not want to release any of her children for school. My uncle, Charlie Mitchell, and other relatives tried to persuade her to put one or more of her children in school, but she said, "Absolutely not!" She would not talk of such a thing.

Finally, the day that the recruiting police came to Round Rock, she gave in and let me go. When the People heard they were coming, all of them had to go over to the trading post and gather there with their children. My parents came down from the Black Mountain area at that time and went over there. I was the only one who came with them; I was the ugliest one in the family, so they put me in school and kept the others back. My brothers and sisters did not come down from Black Mountain at that time; I was the only one. There were several others from around this area who went to school then and are now still living; one of them is Hair String Man, who lives around

Valley Store; he's an old man now, but he still remembers me and our school days.

When I was being enrolled in school, Charlie Mitchell said that my name would be Frank Mitchell. That's how I got that name. Word came around that there would be several wagons that would come to pick the children up and haul us to Fort Defiance. When I was enrolled to go there, there were no wagons to take me down to where they were gathering the children together, and so I went with somebody else, sitting in back of the rider. That's how I came down to the place at Round Rock where they were gathering the children.

And sure enough, big wagons were waiting there to take us in. There were three or four wagons, big covered wagons with about four or six horse teams on them. That was the type of wagon the traders used to haul groceries and other things from Gallup at that time.[7]

When we got to Round Rock, the recruiters prepared us for the trip. They brought clothes along for us; our old ones were pulled off, and we were given some new clothing to put on. That was the first time I came into contact with clothes like those. I had never seen trousers or shirts like that. That was the first time I saw a white man and white man's clothing. Before that, we had knitted stocking and moccasins, but not even dyed ones, just of a whitish color.

Each child who was going to be taken away to school was given clothes; these were distributed just as they now distribute commodities through government service. The material was all the same, like corduroy. It was a yellow-brown color, and the coat, pants and vest were all made out of that. We had a cap, something like golf players wear, out of that brown material, and we were also given heavy socks and Army-type shoes, with real wide toes and soles. They were wide and they were not beautiful; they were made with a wide toe, and there was no shape to them. At that time there was no rubber, as there is today. The soles and uppers were all of leather; it was striped with blue. They also gave us shirts to put on, and even some underwear, in one long piece, like a Union suit. We didn't know how to unbutton those, so that's why we dirtied ourselves.

The shirt was one piece with no collar or anything on it; just an opening on the top; that was all it had. Of course these clothes I am talking about were made differently from the way they are today. The People before this time did not have these long legged pants with buttons on them to open them up. So when they brought all those clothes there, all those pants and shirts, it was the first time some of us had ever seen buttons on pants. Some of them did not have a belt; you just had to hold them up and if you let go, you would lose your pants. We did not know how to wear those pants. When I think about it now, I think about how ignorant we all were and how little we knew then about white people's ways of living and how their clothes were made. This was the first time we had experienced this.

The trader there at Round Rock put out food, and the women cooked it and fed the children. After that, we were given the clothes, and all of us young men got dressed up in them. We did not know how to wear those clothes. There's a certain way that you button those pants and tie ropes there, and we did not know anything about it. A lot of us did not know how to work the buttons in front, and many just wet themselves. We had to learn how to undo those pants. Those people were trying to show us how we should put them on and take them off, and it took a lot of explaining and a lot of work to get used to how to do those things. When we had to go to the toilet, we did not know how to unfasten the pants so that we could sit; they had to teach us how to do those things. After they would do that, they had to dress us up again, pull up our pants and button them and fasten them together. That's why we had to learn to wear those kinds of clothing. It's embarassing to talk about these things, but you ought to know them. I guess that's one of the reasons no one will ever come out and tell anyone these stories, the whole truth about how the People used to be ignorant about working buttons and those things.

While we were being prepared for the trip, this was also the first time that we had our hair cut. We all had long hair. You see, those boys with their long hair had lice. Some of them even had open sores on the back of the neck from them. So our hair was all clipped, cut short to get rid of the lice and nits. In this way, some of the children who were enrolled in that condition, dirty and with bugs, got cleaned up. When they returned home for visits, the older people used to ridicule them, just because they were cleaned up. The children would also talk about themselves, and what condition they were in when they entered school. Some of them tried to say that they were already clean.

We did not cover much distance in those days when we traveled. We left Round Rock, went just a little ways, and then camped out fifteen miles from there. That's about as far as we went in one day. Of course they had bedding for us to use at night and also food to eat on the road.

We left for Fort Defiance and went along the base of the mountain all the way. I think we spent four nights on the road from Round Rock into Fort Defiance. The second night we camped over near Tsaile, on the other side of Greasewood and the third over near Whiskey Creek, on this side of Crystal. From there we traveled from morning until late that night, when we finally got to Fort Defiance. After about four days of traveling we finally arrived. Now it takes just a matter of hours to get there from those places.

I did not feel lonesome or anything during the trip; I was just glad to be going along. I guess everybody kept looking forward to the next town, because most of them were half starved out here since they were not settled down yet. The People had just come back from Fort Sumner and they were not too well settled yet. My family was always on the move.

At night, they had everything for us. They had an extra wagon for the food they fed the children with, and also the men who were along. A lot of men, like the headmen from each area went with us. We were accompanied by these leaders who had recruited us. They traveled by horseback along with the wagons. Of course, they talked with the People along the road and told stories to one another, too. Sometimes Old Man Dodge would be present. He would talk with the People; that was the way with the men who were accompanying us, but we boys were not thinking of telling any stories or talking about anything. The main thing on our minds was food.

At night, we would stop to sleep. There were plenty of blankets, really heavy ones of different colors – red and some other colors. They were even better than what we had to sleep on at home. Each of us got a blanket and just lay out any place on the ground. We had to fix up our bedding the best way we could. Most of the boys would go to sleep at night; some would just tell jokes and funny stories. The older men who went along with us would sit around the campfire and talk about how they were going to get the People in a better condition and all of that; mostly I guess they talked about trying to get the people to understand that their children should be more educated.

We ate meat, tortillas and coffee on our trip, beef and mutton and other things that we ate at home. But the food was prepared for us in different ways, which we really enjoyed because it was not the same thing over and over like what we had at home. As we went along, they bought sheep from the Navajos living along the way. The majority of the People on the reservation at that time had sheep; they did not have many traders and the traders would not buy sheep from them, so sheep were very cheap, anywhere from $1.50 to $2.50 for white sheep. The men who came for us from Fort Defiance were given money from there so they could buy fresh mutton and whatever they needed on the way back. Every time we stopped, they butchered a fresh lamb.

There were no girls in our group to help with the cooking. But the road we were traveling on was the only one used by people in that area and many lived near it where they could get to the store and other places. There was always somebody along the road. Past Lukachukai and Greasewood were hogans of families living along the road. It was the same way at Wheatfields and at Whiskey Creek. From there on, there was hardly anyone living along the road until we reached Red Lake. That's where we had another meal and then we left in the afternoon. It was sunset before we got to Fort Defiance.

Those men who rode with us always went a couple miles ahead when it was nearly time to eat to where they knew there was a good place to stop. They would go around on horseback and tell the People who lived near that place that the children were coming through and they needed help and someone to cook for them. The women who lived along the way would come out and help. If their hogans were close enough to the road, then we ate at the hogan. If they lived too far away, then they came out and met us on the road and did the cooking there for us. The men who were leading us would build a fire close to the road and have it ready by the time we got there. They would buy a sheep, butcher it and have everything ready for us. All we had to do was get out and pick up some wood here and there; then we would be ready to eat. We did not have to do any of the work that was required for our meals; we just had to get out of the wagons and eat. Then we would get back in and start moving again.

As we traveled, we just sat in the wagon. We did not play cards or anything during the trip. Some of the boys who went with me had never been in that part of the country, and they were so surprised to see the differences in the country they were going through that they just sat there and stared. We did not do too much talking. Some of the boys happened to know the location of different landmarks. We would see them and they would tell us what the name of that place was, what it was like and all of that; we would just watch. Sometimes we got restless just sitting in those wagons, and we would ask to get out and walk along the side of the road to pass the time. When the wagons would go up a steep hill, they used to get us out and make us walk. When we got to the top, then we would get back into the wagon again. We would sit on the crosspieces which they put across the wagon box; two or three of us would sit on one crosspiece. Sometimes it was so crowded on those benches that some of us sat on the floor of the wagon.

With wagons, the traveling was very slow; the men on horseback could cover the country much faster. And so they were already waiting for us by the time we reached a stopping place. Some of them would be lying down in the shade sleeping; others would be busy keeping the fire burning. The horses would be out grazing around. As soon as we got there and got out of the wagon, they would tell us to get some wood for the fire. We did that, because in those days, when a command was given, it had to be followed, it had to be done. It is not like today when you tell children to do something and they do not pay any attention. In those days, an order was an order. You had to do it. After we finished our lunch or whatever we had, then the women who had done the cooking would take those things home with them.

We got to Fort Defiance after dark. It was the first time that I had been there. I did not know what to think about that because it was the first time I had seen artificial lights. It just made me wonder what that was.

I remember seeing those brown-colored cabins along the side. One of the first council houses was there; the old hospital was still the general hospital when I was going to school. They were just then digging the foundation for the stone hospital. I had trouble with my eyes, and I had to go there and get treatment at that general hospital, and be in school at the same time.

They told me when I was in school that that old stone house on the hill used to be the hospital a long time ago. At that time they were using it for the sanitorium. I think they have torn down all those old buildings now except for the hospital. Most of the patients then were tuberculosis patients; in those days there were many of them; some were treated there in the general hospital, if they were not too far gone; those who were really bad were sent off to Albuquerque.

As far as I remember, those brown-colored cabins were standing there, and they told me that those were there already, long before I came to school. One of those was a council house or something like that, like the one they have over at Window Rock now.

When we got there we saw that there were a lot of houses and there were a lot of children already in school. So they just dumped us among the children who were already there. I was not afraid of anything; I did not know what fear was at that time. When I entered school there was plenty to eat there, more food than I used to get at home. We had different foods at Fort Defiance, like rice and beans. And we had some dried fruit that we ate, like apples. Besides that we had meat, beef, which was bought for us at school. So I was happy about that; I was willing to go to school if they were going to feed me like that. The clothing that I got there too gave me joy. I was proud to look at the clothes and the shoes, and to walk around in them.

When we entered school they cut our hair short and they kept us clean all the time. Sometimes they would use a louse medicine, a poison or whatever it is; I think they used to call it "blue ointment." It's a kind of salve they buy to kill the bugs. They checked our heads every now and then and would give us treatments. They kept us clean by bathing us every so often. And of course, finally, they got rid of all of those scabs and sores. When we were in school, once a week, usually on Saturdays, we used to change our clothes. We took them off and sent them to the laundry, where they were boiled so there was no chance for lice to be on them. Eventually we cleared ourselves of lice.

I learned a lot from that experience. I have taught my family all about it, so you will not find any bugs around here. That's one good thing I learned from that. When I go off to do some singing for different families, sometimes they are careless, and they are covered with bugs. They are dirty and do not keep themselves clean. Naturally they have those bugs. So if I visit a place like that, as soon as I get home I notice that I have brought bugs with me. You should not sleep on sheep pelts just anywhere; they may be full of bugs. You are liable to collect a lot of them and bring them home.

I remember when I started school we used to go all day. But later on, I do not know just how much later, we went for only a half a day. Half of us went in the morning, and half in the afternoon. The other half of the day we would do chores around the school, whatever there was to be done around there.

By the time I entered school, the big stone buildings were already there for the boys' building and the girls' building. They also had a stone building where we had our meals and a kitchen. They rang a big bell to tell us the time of day. We learned what the bell meant.

Now at that time, a little before I entered school, Nelson Gorman, John Gorman, Stanley Norcross and White Singer's brother were already there. These men were already somewhat advanced in their schooling, and they transferred to other schools, like Fort Lewis, Colorado, and also Phoenix, Arizona, and Riverside, California. Those older students, of course, have all passed away now; some of them died of old age. They were all older than most when they entered school, and that was before my time. Those who went off to non-reservation schools returned sometime later. They were in school before my time, and I do not know how the grades were operated in those days.

We had desks and chairs, and writing materials were provided for us. We had a blackboard and a big, wide book which had pictures of various animals in it, like cat and mouse and things like that with the names under them. They told us what those were and what their names were, and how you spelled them. Then they taught us the ABCs and 1, 2, 3 and all that. As soon as you get up to 10 you knew you were qualified as educated. That was the beginning of our schooling. We never had tests or grades; we never knew who was on top of anyone else.

At school we just went by the bell. It was a big bell like the one they have there by the cattleguard at the Franciscan church here in Chinle. At a certain hour we would go to bed. Every time that bell rang, it meant that we had to get in line, or go to bed, or get up and get ready for breakfast, or dinner or supper.

Whenever it was time to go to bed, we all went in. There was always someone there to see that we were all in bed securely, and not making too much noise. When it was time to get up, they usually rang the bell which told us that it was rising time. Then after we got up, we were put in the charge of the caretakers outside. We used to do morning exercises, drill around and exercise for about one hour and then we were taken in to eat breakfast. After that, one section would get ready for school and the other would go off to do chores.[8]

One of the problems we faced there was that we did not know how to eat at a table. We had to be told how to use the knife, fork and spoons. And when we started eating, we were so used to eating with our fingers that we wanted to do it that way at the school, and we had to be taught. Although we had things there to eat with, like a fork, we had never used them at home, so we did not know what they were or how to use them; so we always wanted to stick our fingers into the food. Of course, it took some time before we got used to how we were to conduct ourselves with those different things.

One winter that I was there at school, I was detailed to feed the hogs all winter, to haul the slop to the pig pen. The slop barrels were on a sled in front of the kitchen, and all the excess garbage from the dining room and the

Cosmos Mindeleff, photographer; from Link 1968:34

FIG. 2. Group in front of the Fort Defiance Boarding School, 1893. The bearded man on the right is Agent Dana Shipley.

kitchen was dumped into those barrels. My duty was to hook a team of horses to that sled and drag it over to the pig pen and feed the pigs that way. For doing that I used to get twenty-five cents a week.

I also had a job in the horse barn. They only had one team of horses which I looked after; I had to feed them, water them, brush them and clean out the stalls. That did not take much time to do, so after I got through with that, then I was free to go anywhere around the school grounds.

Some of the other boys were detailed to work around the buildings, like in the classrooms. They would sweep out the classrooms, mop them up and clean up all around. They would work the same way in the dormitory buildings. Of course in those days we only used the coal stove for heating. Some boys were detailed to clean out the stoves, bring in fresh coal, build the fires and keep the places warm. Others were told to work in the dining room, wash dishes, clean the tables and sweep the place. It was the same thing with the kitchen; boys were told to help around in there. Others went to the laundry to help wash and hang up the clothes. In those days, they did not have these coin-operated machines; they had those old hand-operated ones, with hand-operated wringers. These washing machines had a handle which you pushed back and forth to turn the clothes in hot water; that's the way they would wash the clothes.

They also had about twenty or thirty head of milk goats there at the school; I do not remember the exact number. Some of the boys were detailed to herd them on the range from morning to noon; then others tended them in the afternoons. And there were still some others who were detailed to milk these goats every morning early, and in the evening again.

Navajos always want to slip something away, to steal it. Naturally when the boys milked the goats, they would pour part of the milk in an old tin can and hide it away for themselves. When they got a pan full or a bucket full, after they had eaten their dinner or their lunch, they would go out and go behind a hill, and boil their milk, having a good time drinking it sitting around the fire.

These jobs were changed and passed around after awhile; they set a time on each detail, and when it was up, usually after about a month, they would switch the boys to something else. Of course each of those places had a foreman, an overseer to see that the work was done.

The girls had jobs too; they had to do what women learned to do, like sewing, mending, cooking, washing and ironing, helping in the kitchen and baking bread for the school. And of course they had someone over there at those places to direct them on how they should go about those things. The bread-making was a little heavier job than the other chores. There were some boys that worked in the bakery too; I think that was the highest paid job in the school. They were getting about thirty dollars a month, a lot more than any of the others did. When the girls baked bread, they delivered it to the kitchen. In the kitchen, they got the waiters there to put that food on the tables for the students.[9]

That was the routine there at the school. On Saturdays we used to take our showers and put on clean clothes. There was nothing else to do. We just loafed. We would go off for walks, and if some of the boys' homes were close enough they would go home for a visit. If they lived too far from home, they would just go out walking, visiting other places. The officials would not let us go to the Navajo sings unless they were close by in Fort Defiance. We could not go home for those things.

On Sundays, the next day, we all went to church.[10] At about nine we went to the assembly hall, where we would be preached to by church people and priests and others from other denominations. The preacher or whoever was there of course did not have any interpreter in those days, and of course we did not know much English, and we did not understand what they were talking about half of the time. They talked about God, and most of us did not understand it. So I guess they were just talking to themselves.

At that time they did not have any Protestant missionaries. Everybody that went to school there was eventually baptized a Catholic, and they just had those Franciscan fathers from Saint Michaels, those long-robed priests who were already there at Saint Michaels. They used to come around and talk to the children. Father Weber was head at Saint Michaels then, but I never got acquainted with the priests who came out on Sundays. We never heard of Protestant missionaries at that time.

Then, sometime later, we noticed there was a white man living on the hillside there where the road comes down off the hill. That's the first time we heard of another missionary. He used to talk about the Great Spirit, the Great Holy Spirit. He used to talk about that so we nicknamed him the Great Holy Spirit. We did not know those missionaries by name; we did not know the difference. The only one I remember is Father Weber, a Catholic priest. He was the Superior at Saint Michaels mission, and he used to send some of his men to talk to the children. They came up in an old-time, little buggy with one horse. Of course in those days there were no cars.

They had church in the classroom because they did not have a church building there at school. I think the priests came out twice a week, on a Sunday in the morning, and then on Wednesday in the evening, too; in the winter, it was Thursday. When they came we were all sent to listen; all the students were made to listen to the preaching of those missionaries. They came to talk to the students there about religion. I do not know what they talked about; we never could understand it. I remember a priest who used to come out to Fort Defiance, and every time he got there he always talked to the children. He would begin his talk by saying, "My dear children," (átchíní) but instead of saying it that way, he used to say "diichiłi" (abalone shell). There was a missionary there too, kind of an elderly man. He used to come out and talk to the children at night. And we did not like him. So we nicknamed him "that devil," and called him Billy Jones.

None of the officials, teachers or other employees of the school knew any Navajo either; not even enough to translate the talks there to the children. If one of the children understood a little English, they would use him to translate. We did not talk much English; most of the time we talked Navajo, our own language, to one another. They did not understand us and we did not understand them. We could not even memorize the names of the teachers. So we would give them names in our language. I had a teacher, a woman teacher, who was very slim and skinny; at times she got mean. So we named her "Miss Chipmunk." There was a lady we worked for in the laundry; she was a tall woman and really light in complexion; that's why we called her "Red Corn." Then there was another one who worked in the kitchen; she was an awful-looking thing, and we called her "The Woman Who Makes You Scream." We had all kinds of names for them. The times they looked the worst was after they got all cleaned up. You see, we did not have any men teachers. I remember that when I first came to that school, there were no men teachers there, just women.

I know that I did a lot of things that I should not have, even while I was in school. For instance, while I was there, if somebody died, we did not bother about observing the rules that we were supposed to when we were at home. We ignored all those things when we had to help bury somebody at school.

A lot of boys ran away from school. The only place anybody could find a job was on the railroad. A lot of them just took off and worked somewhere on the railroad. Whenever a child was missing from school, they went out and hunted for him; they did not just let him go. It was like that for me; even though it was not during the school year, but after school let out when two of us ran away from there, just the same they had a search party out for us.

When they located children missing from school, they brought them back but they did not whip them. They just punished them by having them do some chores, or stand in the corner for a certain length of time. It was mostly the girls who had to stand in the corner for the whole day or something like that. When I was there, if a boy ran away and was caught before he was very far away, when he was brought back, why of course he used to get a whipping. If you were stealing something, like I did one time when I was stealing apples with some other boys, you were caught. They locked us up in the disciplinarian's office. When he came in he got a great, big, long strap. After the spanking, he locked us up all day. That's the way we used to be punished. If you were disobedient in the classroom, they used to hit you on the palm or the back of your hand, and then make you stand in the corner.

If it happened to be big boys who deserted the school, then when they were caught, they would get punished in a different way. They would make them carry a big log, a piece of fence post, over their shoulder walking back and forth. Just like those unknown soldiers' guards, they go back and forth, back and forth. I was never naughty like that or punished that way. I was always obedient because I was a little scared of them and so I always did what I was told.

On the school grounds and in the school buildings, whatever happened there, there was always someone in charge, like the teacher. If someone was disobedient she gave out various kinds of punishment, depending on whether it was a boy or girl. They always had someone out on the grounds also to oversee your play and all that. If they caught you doing something that you were not supposed to do, of course you got punished.

When I started school at Fort Defiance, I did not get there until after Christmas. I stayed there that winter until vacation time; I finished out a whole half year there. Then it was summertime, time to go home. My folks brought a horse down there for me to ride home, so I came home that way. When I arrived home, my folks were crying. They said, "My goodness, look what they did to you; they surely must have been abusing you. Look at your hair. They even cut your hair!" And they said, "We won't let you go back; when it's time to go back, we won't let you go back. Stay home."

When I came back, the family called me *Ólta'í Tsoh* – "School Boy." They slapped that "School Boy" name on me, and when they called me, they always said, "School Boy." So I did not lose that name, and even now they call me the "School Boy." A few years later I was going around with my close relative, Charlie Mitchell, who was one of the headmen in this area. Another man, Curly Hair, my clan uncle, told me that I was the same height as Charlie, that I was stout and husky like him, and that I had the same voice. So he said, "Why don't we call you 'Big School Boy,' after Big Charlie?" So that is how I got the name "Big Schoolboy." Now I am well known by that name in Navajo, you know. People outside of Chinle know me by that name and also by another, Two Streams Meet Schoolboy. They call me that because I belong to the Two Streams Meet Clan.

So I just spent one winter there in school, and when it was time to go back, I did not go. I do not remember exactly how long I stayed home; I think maybe it was three years without going back to school again. My mother did not want me to go back; they kept telling me that if you live among the white people, you are going to get sick later on from that, and you cannot be cured from that. I guess I did not go back for many years because my folks were scaring me saying that I should not mingle with the foreigners because it would make me sick and have a bad effect on me. The People scared me away from going back because they talked to me that way. So I did not want to go back to school again.

I had been wearing the clothing that was given to me at school when I came home. I wore that clothing out, and I dropped back to the same way I was before I entered school. So I was running around with white calico pants again, and even my shoes were worn out. When I realized what condition I was in again, I got to thinking about going back to school.

When my family finally gave in again, this time they decided they would send my younger brother, Tom Mitchell, along with me to school. So that's what we did; I wanted to go back, and I went back; he and I went, the two of us went back together. That's how come I went back, because my brother was going with me.[11] When I returned to Fort Defiance the second time with my brother, I informed Old John Brown, the ex-policeman, that we were going to school. He said, "Wearing a badge beats going to school."

When I went back the second time, my brother and I stayed there about another three years. We came home for vacation and then went back again, after vacation was over. So altogether the schooling that I had was about four years.[12] Of course, one was not a full year at the beginning; half the school year was over when I enrolled. So that was just only half a year at that time in the beginning. When I went back the second time with my brother, I stayed about three more years, then left and never did go back to school again. When John Brown and I used to get together and talk about our old school days, we used to talk about the red boots that he used to wear.

After awhile I thought I had had enough of school life so I took the first chance I got when I heard of some work that was available down on the railroad. The reason that I did not stay at school was because another boy, a schoolmate of mine, and I planned together to work on the railroad in the west somewhere. We planned this secretly, skipped out from school and went down on the railroad. The Navajos were already working on the railroad then, the railroad that was coming out of California, around Needles, and all down this way. So without telling my folks or his where we were going, we sneaked off.

EDITORS' NOTES

1. Letter Book 20 of the Fort Defiance Agency states (p. 224) that a license was issued by Navajo Agent Lieutenant Edwin H. Plummer to Dodge and Aldrich to trade at Round Rock on 12/25/1893. Dodge requested severance with Aldrich the following year and permission to establish a trading post at Fort Defiance. However, Dodge and Aldrich were still operating the Round Rock store in 1903 (Letter Book of the Fort Defiance Agency 28). For further information on trading posts and the history of their establishment on the Navajo reservation, see McNitt (1963), Underhill (1953) and Hegemann (1963).

2. Dana L. Shipley was the Navajo Agent from 1892 to 1893, being replaced after the Round Rock Trouble by Lieutenant Edwin H. Plummer, who served as Navajo Agent from 1893-1896 for the Fort Defiance Agency. It was Lieutenant Plummer who took a group of Navajos (including eleven men, one school girl and two school boys) to Chicago, October 13-24, 1893, for the World's Columbian Exposition.

The Trouble at Round Rock occurred during October 1892. Discussions of living conditions of the Navajos before and during these times, the compulsory law of 1887 requiring all Indian children to attend school, the building of the Fort Defiance school in 1879 and its opening in 1881, and detailed accounts of the Trouble at Round Rock occur in the following sources: Van Valkenburgh (1938), Lipps (1909) and Letter Books of the Fort Defiance Agency, especially Volume 17 (3/28/92-1/19/93). The best and most accessible source is Left-Handed Mexican Clansman, et al. (1952). The latter includes a forward and detailed summary of the events (based on the above sources) by Robert Young, an account of the incident by Left-Handed Mexican Clansman and shorter versions by Howard Gorman and the Nephew of Former Big Man. There are also brief references to the event in the biography of Henry Chee Dodge (Hoffman and Johnson 1970:186-212) and in the life history of Albert G. (Chic) Sandoval (Barnett n.d.). A longer version by Sandoval, obtained in 1963, appears as note 4 below.

3. At this point, Frank stated that Agent Shipley was the first white man he ever saw. However, this seems unlikely, since he was not there. His account on p. 58 seems more likely.

4. At this point in the translation work, Chic Sandoval added his own version of the story, saying that Frank's did not take both sides of the story into account. His narrative follows:

What Frank is talking about, this uprising happened in November, 1892. The reason that I happen to remember is because that is the year I was born. My father told me that that happened the year that I was born, the following month; I was born around Christmas and this had happened in November, and that's how come I happen to know my birthday. According to the reports of the Indian Office, that's the way it's recorded there; it happened in November; I think they give the date too, but I don't know.

Well, I got this story from both sides. A fellow that was on the agent's side, a fellow by the name of Charlie Mitchell, was one of the men who was recruiting children. Frank mentioned him; Charlie was his clan uncle. They had split the party at Tsaile and Charlie Mitchell, Frank Walker (he was an interpreter also), and a fellow by the name of Navajo Dick (he was just a sort of a servant for these two men), came down to Chinle here, and stayed here that night. They left here the next morning and before they got to Round Rock, they stopped at somebody's place for a little lunch. While they were there, that's when it happened over there. They were there, you see, before the soldiers arrived.

Charlie Mitchell said, "We left there and were going on our way and a man met us. That man was one of the enemies of these agents. He knew about what was happening; that was the reason he was coming, but he never said anything to us. He just passed us. And we were going, three of us," he said, "and we met another man who happened to be friendly; he was a clan relation of ours. He stopped us.

He said, 'There is trouble over there; you better not go over there.' He said, 'They threw the agent out and they brought him back, and they're threatening to tear down the house, the store, so you better not go.'

"No," said Charlie; he was kind of stubborn, you know; he was hard to advise. Charlie said, "No, we're going over there; it's our business to be over there."

"Well," this man said, "I think there are too many on the other side; if they see you and recognize you, they're liable to attack you." So he said, "You just hold still here and I'll go back and get a group of men for your protection."

And so he went back and notified some of those young men who were not on either side, I guess; they came up with him in a group. Charlie said, "Well, we got in the middle of them and we were surrounded by them; one going ahead of us, and some on the side, and some in the back. And we rode down like that, and Black Horse's outfit didn't recognize us until we were right by the door there. These men, my partners, Frank Walker and Navajo Dick, they just ran in. Navajo Dick didn't go in; he stayed out. Black Horse was riding back and forth and shouting and talking. He recognized us and he said, 'Charlie, Charlie, come closer, come closer.' "

Charlie never let anybody talk to him like that. He said, "I turned around and said, 'You come closer. What are you doing over there? If you want trouble, come and start trouble over here.' " And just then, he said, "The storekeeper grabbed me and said, 'Oh, hush up'; he pulled me into the store and closed the door."

And, of course, they slipped out a note by the agent, and they sent off a horseman on horseback; they were using Chee Dodge's horse;

it was a fast horse too. They asked Chee how fast his horse could go; he said, "Well, he's pretty well-winded; he can run a long distance." So they had the agent write out a note to these soldiers at Tsaile and they slipped the paper out to this man and they had the horse ready over there. Chee's horse was in the corral, all saddled up; that man went over there and jumped on it and dashed off.

When he was about half a mile away, Black Horse's group noticed him. Black Horse said, "There goes somebody. Go and catch him. Don't let him get away. Go and catch him." So a whole group of his men started after that man, but the horse was too fast, you see; he had a good start on them. They chased him all the way.

I'll tell you where they gave up. There was a rock canyon he had to go across, and the horse was pretty well out of wind at that time; there were a lot of juniper trees around there, so near there, that man kept looking back to see how far Black Horse's men were behind him. When he went over the ridge and saw these trees, he rode behind one of them and faced his horse back, let his horse get some wind. Then he noticed them coming up on the ridge there. They stopped and looked across there. They thought there was no hope; they said, "he's gone across; that rocky canyon is pretty steep. He's already gone across there." They didn't know he was waiting there in the bush. They stood around for a while, and then they returned. And it was one of these fellows who chased the man on the horse that told me this story. His side of the story, of course, is against the agent's side, but they pretty well agree on what happened.

What Frank said is correct. Black Horse wasn't really the agitator; it was only because he was outspoken that they appointed him as the spokesman for the group that was opposing the agent. And so Frank is right on that. And Charlie Mitchell was with the agent, you see, and he told his side of the story and this other fellow that was one of the pursuers of his horseman, he told his story to me, and they pretty well agree on that.

The fellow just kept hidden in the tree there and then, after a while, those fellows finally gave up. They stood around there for a while and rested their horses up, I guess, and then they disappeared over the ridge. Then he turned his horse around and started off. He went across that canyon, and got to the soldiers' camp that night, I guess, sometime after dark, and delivered that note. And right away he got these boys together and put packs on their pack mules; the soldiers were on horses, and they left right away. They were on their way when daylight came. It was very shortly after sunup when they arrived there at Round Rock. When Black Horse's group saw the soldiers coming, they knew right away that those were the soldiers coming. Well, Black Horse began to lose his group; they started drifting away from him and by the time the soldiers arrived, why his group had trickled down to just a handful.

The Army officer brought the soldiers all in here right at the door. They unpacked their things and threw them in the store. Charlie was in there, and he said that they unrolled the cartridge belts out on the floor and started loading their guns. Well, I guess they had them loaded, all set to take action. And he said that if those men caused any more trouble, if they started any more trouble, the soldiers were going to open fire on them. But Charlie said, "I was delegated to sit with an old soldier, gray haired fellow; he was chewing on hardtack," he said, "and as he sat there, he wasn't even shaking, he wasn't even nervous; he just sat there chewing on those crackers."

Charlie said, "Here we had spent all night long in the store, and when I heard that the soldiers were coming, I said, 'Well, come on, let's go out and attack them.' Here I was all excited; I wanted to jump out there and just fight hand-to-hand. I grabbed my shirt and split it open and threw it aside; I wanted to run out there naked and fight it out with them. But the soldiers said, 'No. No, don't do that; keep quiet now, the officer will fix it.' "

The officer stepped off his horse outside there and started walking over there to those men. He knew that that was the outfit over there. Black Horse was on horseback talking, and the officer recognized him right away. The soldier said, "Come on, come on, Black Horse, you come out." And somebody from here said something to the officer over there. He reached down, and he had his cartridges there and his pistol. So he unbuckled them and threw them back over his shoulder. One of the soldiers ran over and picked those up and brought them in; so the officer went over and met Black Horse unarmed.

Black Horse hesitated for a while; he didn't know whether to come or not. When he saw those soldiers in the store there, prepared to shoot, of course that changed his mind. It was no use trying to fight that way. Finally, I guess, the men in his group said, "Well, you'd better go up there." The soldier held up his hand to Black Horse. Black Horse hesitated. "Come on, come on, my friend and shake hands." Finally, he decided it was the best thing to do.

Then the officer said, "Call the agent out here. Tell the agent to come out here and shake hands with Black Horse." And the agent was inside the store there just shaking like a dry leaf. He didn't want to come out. Finally, they said, "Go on out and meet him; it's all right, the soldiers are out there; the soldiers are here to protect you; go ahead, get out there."

So they forced the agent to go out there. "Come up; now shake hands here," they said, and the agent shook hands with Black Horse. The soldier said, "Now come on, let's get together and discuss this thing over."

And Black Horse was kind of hesitating; of course he wasn't the agitator, you see; he was only appointed the spokesman for the group, and he kind of depended on the rest of them. They finally said, "Well, let's talk then." The soldier said, "Well, go on, bring some flour out here, and coffee, and things, whatever you have in the store there, and feed these people. We'll take care of the expenses of it."

So he started talking with Black Horse and he said, "What you did is wrong." Black Horse wanted to know how much punishment he would have to take for doing that. And the soldier said, "No, none at all. You didn't do any damage; you abused the agent, that's all. But I don't think we'll do anything to you. As long as we make peace here, well, that will be over."

So Black Horse didn't believe him; he said, "No, I think I did a pretty serious thing. I am not going to be forgiven that easily."

The officer told him again; he said, "No, no; well, I'll put in a good word for you so that you won't be punished."

So that was the end of it, that uprising, and that's what Frank told here. You can see the difference between my story and his story; of course, Frank got his story from somebody else; I got this story from both sides, and both of those men agreed in their stories.

5. At this point, Frank said that the soldiers were the second time he saw white men.

6. Frank's mother was living with her second husband in Canyon del Muerto, close to Frank's father who had moved back from Wheatfields around the time that Frank was enrolled in school. As notes 7 and 11 below indicate, Frank probably was initially enrolled in 1894 when he was thirteen years old. His estimates here seem to reflect the Navajo sense of time and the fact that he returned to school in 1903.

7. The Letter Books from the Fort Defiance Agency contain a wealth of information about the Fort Defiance school, and the attitudes about enrolling children. For example, in Volume 20 (dating 10/11/93 to 2/2/94), there is a letter (p. 194) from Lieutenant Plummer to Henry Dodge, Round Rock (carrying only the 1893 date) in which Plummer urged Dodge to send the area children in, promising to give some axes in return, "but if they want me to do what is right by them they must do what I know and tell them is best." In another letter (dated 1/8/94) to Mrs. Whyte of the San Juan area, Plummer urges speed in bringing in the neighborhood children in return for shovels, coffee pots, axes, pails and coffee mills. The Navajos were to show that they were "worthy of them [the utensils] by bringing their children into school and they must hurry as a large party is coming in from Round Rock with a large party of children. . . ."

Two letters refer to children brought in from Round Rock. One, dated 1/19/94 (Letter Book 20:403) from Lieutenant Plummer, Acting U.S. Indian Agent to Mr. Frank Walker of Gallup, reports "fourteen children came in tonight from Round Rock. This makes sixteen from that neighborhood. We have now one hundred and twenty four pupils." Another, dated 2/1/94 (Letter Book 20:488-489), was sent by Lieutenant Plummer to the Honorable Commissioner of Indian Affairs, Washington, D.C.; it reads:

Sir:
I have the honor to submit herewith voucher for expenses incurred in sending for and bringing in school children.
The children were gathered near Round Rock, about seventy five miles from the Agency and were to have been brought in by their parents on ponies but a severe cold spell of weather came on accompanied by a very heavy fall of snow, making it impossible for them to get the children in in that way. Word was sent to me and I sent a wagon out for them. I provided forage and what rations I supposed would be sufficient to bring the party in but owing to the condition of the roads it took four days to make the trip, each way, and it became necessary to procure additional supplies. The meals charged for were furnished the Interpreter and teamster.

There were sixteen children gathered in the vicinity. The place where Agent Shipley had a fight with the Indians about a year ago, while attempting to procure children for the school by force.

Very respectfully
Your obedient servant
E. H. Plummer
1st Lieut. 10th Infantry
Acting Indian Agent

It seems quite certain that Frank came in with this group of students from Round Rock.

8. An idea of the typical day at the school is conveyed by a copy of the Bell Schedule contained in Letter Book 30 (dating 1/2/1903-6/1/1908). The schedule (pp. 51-52) is dated 9/1/1903 and is given as follows:

Navajo Boarding School Bell Schedule by
E. R. Ferguson, Actg. Supt.

6 a.m.	Rising Bell
6:55	Breakfast bell (first)
7:00	Second Breakfast bell
7:30	Bed making bell
8:00	Work Bell
8:55	First Bell for School
9:00	School Bell
10:15	Recess
10:30	Recess Closes
11:30	Work Closes
11:55	First Bell for Dinner
12:00	Dinner
1:00	Work Bell
1:25	First Bell for School
1:30	School
2:45	Recess
3:00	Recess closes
4:00	School Closes
5:00	Work Closes
5:25	First Supper Bell
5:30	Supper
7:15	Dark Bell
8:00	Retiring Bell

9. Some of the other information available in the Letter Books about the Fort Defiance school is shown below:

Letter Book Volume and Date	Date of Entry	Data
F.D. Agency #11	11/2/1888	80 students enrolled
F.D. Agency #17 (3/28/92–1/19/93)	1/2/1893	105 students enrolled. Supt. Wadleigh was at school during Round Rock Trouble.

F.D. Agency #21 (2/2–5/4/1894)		174 students in attendance, "nearly 100% more than last year. The children are still being brought in. All have been brought in voluntarily instead of being arrested, kidnapped, etc. by Indian Policemen as formerly." Clothes at school were cashmere but gray kersey uniforms preferred.
F.D. Agency #22 (5/5/94–7/21/94)	5/30/94	183 enrolled
F.D. Agency #25	10/15/98	64 students enrolled
F.D. Agency #25	8/26/99	134 students enrolled
F.D. Agency #27 (9/6/1899–8/23/1900)	10/25/99	112 enrolled
	11/1	128 enrolled
	11/11	164 enrolled. Frank Walker is the interpreter at this time.
	11/27	170 enrolled; chicken pox epidemic
	1/25/1900	Boy dies from measles on 1/23
	1/27	170 enrolled; room for 6 more girls. Government now giving wagons to Navajos in return for hauling 20-35 loads of wood. Boys outnumber girls at school 3:1 Fire protection at school poor; phonetics and note singing are being neglected; fence requested to keep out horses and old Indians.

Underhill (1953:227) provides other interesting information; for example, in 1891, a Civil Service Commission Certification became required for all teachers appointed to Indian schools, and by 1896, pupils were coming to the Fort Defiance school without urging and were staying there the whole year.

10. Missionaries were permitted to hold services at the school at least by 10/20/1903; Letter Book 29 (dating 5/8/03-1/5/04) states (on 10/20/1903) that Catholics held services Wed. p.m. and every other Sunday; others held services Thursday nights and every other Sunday.

11. Letter Book 30 (dating 1/2/1903-6/1/1908) contains a series of letters describing conditions at the Fort Defiance school in 1903, which would have been around the time when Frank returned with his brother Tom. Among the major concerns at that time were the following: students were speaking Navajo while at the school and boys were not using the walks, being courteous, removing their hats, responding to bells promptly or being orderly in their conversations. These problems are specified in letters from Mr. P. H. Sayles, disciplinarian at that time; reference is also made to Miss Mary Keough, who was matron at that time.

Amidst these letters is another by J. C. Linengood, Superintendent of the Navajo Boarding School (Vol. 30:13), dated 2/20/03 and directed to the topic of Fire Signals; in part it reads: "The fire brigade will always report immediately to me at the building on fire. Fire Brigade — Isaac James, Francis Lope, Hoska Nata, and Frank Mitchell."

Other information is shown in chart form below:

Letter Book Volume and Date	Date of Entry	Data
F.D. Agency #28 (7/1/1902– 4/11/1903)	7/21	Buggy price: $110; spring wagon: $125; 2 horses: $200; double harness: $40.
	7/25	Indians required to cut hair by 1/8/1902; to be rewarded with light colored hats. Efforts to stamp out Indian religion documented in letters.
	8/4/1902	Oscar Waddell is disciplinarian.
	8/19/1902	171 enrolled. New dorm was occupied in 10/1900. Slightly later, 300 had hair cuts; one boy punished with jail for refusing.
	10/22/1902	Police rounded up 26 run-aways from the school. 175 enrolled.
	1/23/1903	Round Rock store still in process with Aldrich and Dodge.
	2/2/1903	Supt. Linengood's time; documentation of squads of little boys carrying out wood and coal, getting timber, and working in shoe and carpenter shops (Blacksmith and carpenter shops added in 1902 according to Underhill 1953:227).
	3/6/1903	201 enrolled.

12. When discussing this in 1964, Frank counted it as "two full years in school plus a half, with altogether three years of schooling." Appendix B, a Chronology of Events from 1856-1972, suggests that the second time Frank went to school he stayed only a year.

4. Going Out Into the World

Working on the railroad ... adventures on the work crew ... his uncle brings him home ... conditions around Tsaile at that time ... wrestling with Tall Water Edge Man ... Frank's subsequent illness and treatment ... his natal family ... Frank works at the government warehouse in Chinle and at the Fort Defiance Trading Post ... his job at Saint Michaels and the woman there ... return to Chinle and work at the mission there ... an attempted rape and the attack on Reuben Perry ... learning from Son of the Late Little Blacksmith.

The reason we decided to leave school and go out and work was that we had seen men go off to work like that and come back with good clothing. They also had money which they would then use to buy things like jewelry and dry goods for their families. Of course, we wanted to have some of those things. Lots of boys went off like that because there were not very many jobs around here. There were no jobs for anybody, and the only place you could find any work was on the railroad.[1] So lots of boys and men went to work somewhere on the railroad.

Another reason was that in those days it seemed as if all that you had was just the clothes you had on; nothing else was yours. Now children say, "My shoes are wearing out; I need another pair," when their shoes are getting a little bit worn. Then their parents go and buy some new ones. When I was that age, you could not say that. You just had to patch up what you had on. That was yours and nothing else outside of that could be yours. It is like all of the stock that I have. I've given one or two of them to each one of the grandchildren, and now those belong to them. In my boyhood days the People did not have anything like that, and so they just went off and worked somewhere else, trying to make a little money for themselves. Because of these things, this boy and I ran away, even though the salary was very, very little. We only earned $1.10 for a whole day's work!

When my friend and I left school, my older brother John was already working at the store in Fort Defiance. We went to his place the first night and stayed there overnight. The next morning, of course, he had to leave in time to go to work. He told us to stay there and stay put, but instead, we ran off again. We were walking along the road when somebody came along in a wagon. We jumped into that wagon, and the man took us all the way into Gallup.

When we drifted into Gallup, we heard that a fellow by the name of Gold Tooth[2] was recruiting workers for the railroad. So we went there and found two other men who were going down to work on the railroad. That made four of us who wanted to go. We all got on a train, and this man gave us some food and blankets. We were told to go to sleep until about midnight. Then there would be a train coming through; that was the train people took when they wanted to work on the railroad. So when it was time for the train to arrive, we were awakened by this white man. I did not know that those things were being done by clock time. I guess that is how he knew that the train would be coming pretty soon. He told us to get up and be ready because the train would be there in a little while. So we got up and washed and prepared ourselves to go. By then the train had come. We just walked out and climbed on.

We traveled on the railroad from Gallup past Flagstaff and beyond. We went to Needles, where there is a big wide river flowing through there. We passed over that and continued going. Somewhere beyond there a lot of Navajos were working, and when we arrived we were let out to join the crew.

The next day, of course, we were registered to go to work; papers were made out for us, and then we started working right away. What we did was to get those railroad ties out; we were replacing the worn, old ones with new ones. Our crew went ahead; after we took out the old ties, the next crew came and replaced them with new ones. Then another crew followed that; they filled in with dirt and tamped the dirt down in. That is the way we worked in separate crews, one crew for this and one for that. We moved westward, working like that.

At night, after working during the day, we would pass the time playing cards. We did not sing songs or anything like that for passing the time. You see, most of the men who were working were pretty well advanced in age. Of course, there were some young boys like myself, but in those days boys my age were backward about speaking out in public. So we just joined in with the older men, the fellows who were playing cards. One of the games we played was called Coon Can. Several men would sit in a circle to play that; that's a Mexican game. Others played what was called Monte.[3] That's where you put a pair of cards on one side and you bet on one of them. But there is a lot of crookedness connected with that Monte game. That game is the one where we'd lose all our money. Of course, we did not know that there were a lot of crooked tricks that those older men used.

There are lots of stories I could tell about my days working on the railroad. One happened in a place just beyond Needles where the railroad track has a lot of bends in it and goes up a steep grade. Passenger cars were sometimes used to transport the men from their camp to the place where they worked during the day. These cars were hooked up to a main freight train, which then pulled them over to the place of work. One time it happened that there was a long freight train coming through loaded with sheep. One of these passenger cars was attached to it about halfway back in the train.

Some men, including one from the Black Streak of Wood Clan and one named Winslow, got into this passenger car. These men and the rest of us were hungry for meat; at that time meat was very scarce. These men intended to take advantage of this train when it stopped at a certain spot. So when the freight train stopped, they jumped off and broke the seals on the freight car. It was just a thin strip of tin that they had to break. These four or five men went inside where the sheep were and started tying up the sheep. When the train got to the point where it had to go up this steep grade it had to slow down. And when it did that, these fellows started throwing out those sheep they had tied up in the boxcar. They threw them out beside the tracks, and then they jumped out and started picking up those sheep. It happened that one of them got loose and ran off.

That night I had been over to where the men were gambling and playing cards, and these fellows who threw the sheep out were in our camp. When I returned home that night to my camp, I noticed that Those Who Walk About Man, Winslow and several others were bringing in some butchered meat. Of course, I took part in eating the sheep which had been stolen. In our camp there was a woman too, a relative of one of the men who was there.

The next morning a white man came by who was a patrolman traveling up and down the railroad. He had spotted the loose sheep running wild. The men from our camp had gone out and chased it and caught it. The white man caught them as they were ready to kill it and said, "Don't harm the sheep. Don't do anything to it. Chances are they'll be inquiring about it."

So he called on ahead of this train that was carrying the sheep and told people about it. And then we got the news that there were a lot of sheep missing. So they rounded us up and began questioning us about this. We got worried about it; the whole crew was afraid that they would get these men. It was reported that there were some guilty ones among us. Those men were afraid that they would be put in jail. So we agreed to deduct about fifty cents from all of our wages to pay for the sheep. Then we got word that this was agreeable to the owner. So we all had to pay in order to prevent these fellows from being put in jail. I imagine that some of the crew did not even have a taste of that mutton.

Another time we were working about ten miles from our camp. One evening the train came to pick us up after we quit work. We started back to camp on a platform car; it was open, with no sides, and we used to go back and forth to work on it. We were on that car and we were ready to go back when two of the men got into a fight. I think maybe at first they were just joking and kidding around with each other, but it got serious. They fought and wrestled around, and they finally fell off the car. They were still wrestling, fighting there on the ground when we passed out of sight. Later in camp, everyone started worrying about the younger one, The Son of One Who Has Cows. They were afraid that the older man, White Man, was kind of mean, and they thought that he might have killed the younger boy or harmed him. But nobody went back to investigate.

Sometime later that night, the younger boy came home. His shirt was all torn and almost gone. The men asked him what had happened to the man he was fighting with. He said, "He's still over there. I fought with him and I hit him and knocked him out. He was still lying on the ground when I left."

Towards morning the older man came home. He was pretty badly beaten up; his face was all bruised and cut up and swollen. The railroad people got after those fellows; they were told they should not have done that. "We are working here in harmony and you should not fight like that." That was the only fight I remember.

Now back at home, of course, my folks did not know where I was. I never even let them know that I was going to do that, and so they missed me. They did not know what had happened to me, and they got worried and started inquiring around about it. They were using hand-tremblers and star-gazers[4] to look for me. I guess when this friend and I went to Gallup on that wagon, some people noticed us. When my brother inquired around, he learned that we had gone to Gallup and were probably headed west to work somewhere on the railroad.

Everybody at home started to get suspicious about where we were, and my late uncle, my mother's brother whom we called Old Man Short Hair, inquired around and learned that it was likely that we were with the railroad crew somewhere to the west. So he went into Gallup and asked to work on the railroad. Of course, he really did not want a job; he just wanted to look for us. He went all the way to Needles, California. We were working on the other side, beyond there. After we had been there for about three months, all of a sudden he appeared over there. He was looking for me and another boy from our area who was working as a water boy with our crew.

I was so ashamed of the condition I was in, I did not want to see my uncle. After Old Man Short Hair arrived, he went to work with our crew, and so the three of us were working there together for about another month and a half.

All of the workers kept gambling over there. Every time we were off, we played cards. I got a fever to play cards with them, and I did not know that there were a lot of crooked tricksters who knew how to cheat. So when I played cards with them, of course I was bound to lose every time. The wages that were paid me, I lost as soon as I was paid.

When I first arrived in that camp, I had some decent clothing and some decent blankets. But I lost even those in gambling. Then I bought an old quilt covered with rags and waste, and I used that for my blanket to sleep on. I kept playing cards and losing my money that way. Every time I got paid, the money just went to card games, and I had no chance to buy anything decent. My clothes were all in rags, and that is all I possessed. That quilt and an old blanket that I had with me, even those were half burned up. One night when I was out gambling somehow they caught on fire and got all burned and full of holes. They were all I had, so I just had to keep them. That is the way I was carrying on at that camp in California.

After my uncle overtook us and worked with us for a while, the railroad moved our crew back towards Flagstaff to a place called Seligman, Arizona, at the other side of Ash Fork. They had a railroad camp there where we all worked for a while. Then we were told, "You'll have to move now, go back to your country. There is no more work here."

When the time came for us to go back to Gallup, the boxcars we had been living in were hooked to each other. That is how we came back to Gallup. Before we left for there, I thought of getting off and getting stranded over there. But there was nobody whom I could go to. I was in a strange country with nothing in my hand to live on. My uncle did not want to leave me behind, of course, so he persuaded me to come along. So I came back with all of them on that train.

I was ashamed when I watched so many of the men get on the train with big loads of nice things they had bought while working on the railroad. When I got to Gallup, I was so ashamed of the things that I had, that burned blanket and quilt, that I left that bundle of burned things on the train and walked out empty-handed. I guess my old rags stayed on that train and went on. When I tell that to others, they always say, "Well, why don't you sue the railroad for taking your property along?"

So I did not go back for any more railroad work after I had learned all of those lessons. At Gallup, we got out of those boxcars, and from there we just walked on foot. We finally reached home, this side of Tsaile.

When I came back from working on the railroad, my folks were living on this side of Tsaile. Right after I returned, my mother, Star Gazer's Son and the rest of us moved across the Canyon to the west side on top of the mesa. I cut some timber to build an old-style hogan. We accidentally moved next to my father up in the foothills toward Lukachukai. This was the first time that we had been close to him since the year I started school.

My father had moved back from Wheatfields because he could not get help with herding and taking care of his horses. He also moved back here because many other men were interested in his wife, Big Man's niece, the one they called Woman With Goats. These men had begun picking on my father and her; he moved back here to escape from the young fellows up there in Wheatfields. My father returned to his original home and found his maternal nephew, Tall Water Edge Man; he brought him back over here to work for him. Then he also remembered that he had children of his own who were the right age to work. He began to think of me as his boy again. He would take me over to his place to herd that woman's sheep and to look after her horses. While I was over there, my father used me as a servant; he did not teach me anything.

When I got back home, of course, I did not go back to school again. I did not even go back to work. I just stayed around at home. I do not know how long I lived like that. I just did not go around very much. Once in a while I might go to a Squaw Dance,[5] but in those days they were kind of rare. We never heard about many Squaw Dances. The People had them, but they were very scarce. It was probably that way because the People were not living too close together like we are doing now. In those days the People were just scattered all over. They were so far apart that only once in a great while would you see somebody from the other side of the hill coming across. And another thing, the People at that time were always on the go, moving from place to place with their flocks to wherever they could find grass. Very few people lived down in this area or on either side. In the summertime people would go up in the mountains and spend their time there. When they went up there, quite a lot of them got together in the same close area. Then they sometimes had Squaw Dances. I just heard about those; I never went to many until I was older.

It was the same with the Yeibichai[6] Dance too. There was not much water out here on the flats, but there was always water up in the mountains; it rains up there in the summertime. The People could not very well have any ceremonies like the Squaw Dance or Yeibichai Dance in places where there was no water. A lot of people, when they wanted to have a ceremony like that, would move up into the mountains. The mountaintops had lakes and springs; in other places, like in the Canyon and on Black Mountain Mesa, there were dams to collect and store water. In these places the People had all the water they wanted for these ceremonials. They could also get all the wood they wanted; wood was needed for the shade, the shelters and for the hogan poles and also for the fire. In those days there were no wagons to use in hauling that wood. But in the mountains, the People would have wood within walking distance. They could walk over and cut it down and make things. Everything would be right there.

The People did not even have many Blessingway[7] ceremonies at that time because there were not many people in one place. There were only one or two families so many miles apart. When they had a Blessingway, there would be about three or four families all in one group at the same time. This would be about the only time they would come together, and even that was hard because few people had wagons. Most of the time they traveled on horseback or walked. At the same time, there was not much sickness or illness around then when people were scattered so far apart. Nowadays people are so close together that when they get together at one place, all these sicknesses spread.

While I was staying around home, I got to chumming around with this young cousin of mine, my father's nephew. This cousin, Tall Water Edge Man, was a strange, bluish-looking boy; my father brought him over to live with Woman With Goats and the one daughter that she had had by another man before my father started living with her. So the four of them lived right near us. My father's stepdaughter's name was Woman at War. He and Woman With Goats had no children together.

This cousin, Tall Water Edge Man, and I would always go around together; he was a month older than me. He and I would play around with his rifle, just for the fun of it. My own father had built a hogan just a short distance away from us, and so this cousin lived right here. Every time we got together we wrestled and played around, doing this and that.

We would always get to wrestling when we would be out somewhere. We would do that just for the fun of it; it was not a real fight. One time in doing that, he injured me somehow, and that injury almost killed me. It was during the winter when that happened, and I was pretty sick for quite a while because of that injury. We were wrestling, and he twisted my body so that I got internal injuries; I almost died from the effect. Ever since that happened, I remember things; everything from then on is clear up to this morning and what I had for breakfast. Before that time, I could remember where I had been but I just never thought it was too important to remember much of anything else.

This time, after I had come back from the railroad, I met my cousin again and I said, "Why don't we go and have a sweat bath together?" We set the date for the next day. So the next day, I went out into the woods and chopped down some wood for the fire, for the sweat bath. I chopped down this great big old cedar and trimmed off all the branches. Then I started carrying the wood on my shoulder to the sweathouse. It was quite heavy; I just barely made it.

In those days we did not have a permanent sweathouse. We would just get four or five poles together, lean them upright against each other and then cover the whole thing on the sides with blankets. There would be no air going in there, and it would get hot very quickly. Nowadays we make sweathouses and keep them in the same spot. The foundation is the same as it was before, but the outside is covered with dirt; the only place we have a blanket is at the entrance. When I was a young man at permanent homes where we would spend more time, we usually made a sweathouse like that. But if we were out somewhere, camping with the sheep or something like that and we wanted to take a sweat bath, all we did was just get some logs or poles together and cover them up with a blanket. The Navajos took a lot of sweat baths in those days when we were not as busy as we are now. We do not do this too often nowadays.

The People used to say, "If some older man or one of the headmen, a man considered a little higher than you, happened to come and visit, he will want to take a sweat bath. He will ask you about your sweat bath, and if you say that you do not have one, then right away that man will consider you a lazy type. You will be considered too lazy to set up a sweathouse, and he will think that you have no sense and don't amount to much." We were taught that as long as we have a sweat bath near our home, we would be considered men. Having a sweathouse shows that you are planning ahead.

In those days we used to sing a lot in the sweathouse; we would sing all the time we were in there. There are special songs for that purpose, songs about the sweathouse itself, the Sweathouse songs. You can also sing other songs, like Blessingway, Monsterway,[8] Self-Protection and Horse songs. Songs like the Hogan songs and Dawn songs are never used, but others, like Mountain songs and other Blessingway songs, can be sung in there.

According to the legend, the first sweathouse was built by the Holy People. Since it was built by the Holy People, it had its own songs. The Holy People used to go to the sweathouse to discuss things – how the future should be and what the Earth People should do. We still sing those songs when we take sweat baths. You cannot sing those songs in just any place. You have to be in a sweathouse where there is no light of any kind. You just cover yourself up in there. That is the only time, in the pitch dark sweathouse, when those songs can be sung.

Anyway, the sweathouse that my cousin and I were going to use was closer to my home than to his, so I brought that wood over there. When I got there with that cedar, my cousin was waiting for me, lying against the sweathouse watching me carry that heavy wood. As I dropped those logs, he got up and rushed for me to wrestle.

I think that I must have already been out of wind and that I had injured myself carrying that wood quite a distance. I was tired, too, from carrying it. When I started that wrestling, right away I knew something was wrong because I usually ended up on the top, and that time I was always on the bottom. I could not seem to get my strength back to get him down. I tried to get him down, but three or four times he pinned me down. Then he would get off; I would say that I still thought I could pin him down, so we would go after each other again, starting to wrestle. The third time we wrestled, we rolled down a little slope. My cousin gripped me with all of his force, and as we rolled over, I landed on the bottom and he came up right on top of me. After that I just gave up.

Tall Water Edge Man got off and started chopping wood. I got up; I felt kind of strange, sort of dizzy. I went into the sweathouse and fixed the rocks there, setting up the outside so we could build a fire and heat the stones on it. My cousin chopped wood, and I went home and got blankets to cover the doorway. When I came back, we went in there; I went in two times, and the second time I went in, I remember I got a bad headache all of a sudden. I felt it coming on more and more, so I told Tall Water Edge Man that twice was enough for me.

I went home, and when I got there, I found that both of my parents were over at my cousin's place; they were having some kind of little ceremony over there. It was late in the afternoon when I got home, so I just lay down; one of my younger sisters was there. I just lay down, and I felt the pain growing stronger in my head. Later, sometime that evening after sundown, I got so sick that everything just went black; I stayed unconscious for about nine days. After I went unconscious, my sister went over to the other house and told them that I was sick. When they got back, they started asking my cousin right away what had happened to me. He told them that I was all right when I left the sweathouse; I was not complaining of anything then.

So my parents went and got a man who lived a little way from there; they asked this singer to do hand-trembling over me. When he did that, he told them that it appeared that I had been injured by carrying a log or something; it seemed that I had been injured by lifting something heavy. That same night my older brother went over and got a man who performed the blackening ceremony from Lifeway,[9] and brought him back over to our place that night. This man got his sacred bundle and started singing over me right away. I did not know it, because I was unconscious for nine days. This is what they told me. This singer, Man With a Hair Bundle,[10] just sat in the hogan with me and sang over me for nine days straight. Day and night, night and day, he sang, until on the ninth day in the morning, all of a sudden I woke up.

I felt hungry and wanted something to eat. So they gave me something to eat, and that made me sicker. I just threw up everything they gave me and got sicker than before. So that man just kept singing and giving me medicine for another two or three days. About two or three days after I regained my consciousness, I felt very sharp pains across my chest. That is when I really suffered. Before that, I was unconscious and I did not have any feelings or know too much about my suffering. When the pain started in, it was so bad I could not keep still. I just kept rolling around and around with pain. Man With a Hair Bundle just stayed there with me. He must have spent about two weeks singing over me day and night and just giving me herb medicine he mixed with water for me to drink.

In those days singers would stay with you until they knew you were getting well. They would not quit until they knew that you were recovered enough to walk out. They used to say, "I'm not going to leave you before you get up and walk out." They used to do that in those days.

After I regained consciousness, that man knew he was bringing me back, so he just kept singing until I noticed the pain. For about two or three days after I awoke the pain was really bad, but he did not give up. Singers in those times were really active in their singing. They were not lazy like the ones we have now. Man With a Hair Bundle just sang on and on until finally, about the third day after I had felt that pain, it began to go away. The pain was going away gradually and finally it was completely gone. But that man still kept singing over me. He did not want to leave me until I was able to get up and walk around by myself. So he stayed with me another three or four days after that and sang until I was able to get up, go out and do some things myself.

Every time I smelled food, it made me sick to my stomach. All the food had a bitter odor to me, and I could not eat anything. I tried eating other things, and those just made me sick too. So my family went down into the Canyon to where people dry peaches in the summertime. There are big cactus down there, and the People dry the wild fruit from those cactus, those big red fruit, in the same way. The People in the Canyon had some of that fruit left, so they brought some of it, dried, to me. They boiled it well until all of the juice was coming out, and then they strained it really fine. Then they put cornmeal in that juice and made a mush out of it for me. That was the one thing that did not make me sick. So I started eating again. Then I was able to go out and walk around.

Man With a Hair Bundle said, "Well, you're getting over your sickness now so I think that I'll just go home. There's no danger of your getting a relapse." After that I improved. My injury was healing up, I guess. I was able to go out and walk around. So that is what happened to me from that wrestling with that cousin; I almost died.

Man With a Hair Bundle was an old man; he had lots of hair, and it was very thick. Every time he would tie it up behind his head, he had a big hair bundle. Imagine how different he was from those old men now who have scanty ones. Now these old men are baldheaded on top, with just a little bit of hair here and there around the crown. There is an old man in the Canyon like that now; he sits around at Valley Store a lot, and he's so jealous of my hair, he always teases me.

While we were living in the Canyon, my brother Jimmy was staying over with my grandfather, Man Who Speaks Often, near Wheatfields. After Jimmy came of age, he began to get into a lot of mischief. He used to go after other men's wives, and Tall Man, White Hair and Son of Mr. Mule were three of the men who beat him up. These men lived in the Canyon, and all had young wives. Jimmy was young, and he used to saddle his horse in the afternoon and go over in the Canyon to run around with these women. It was not far for him between Wheatfields and the Canyon. Sometimes he was caught right then, and if the men did not see him, they sometimes tracked him. Other times they would wait for him the next time with a club and use it on him.

After Man Who Speaks Often died, Jimmy came back to our family. He soon married his first wife, a woman by the name of Sticky Mouth's Daughter; her father always clicked his mouth when he talked. There was no ceremony when these two were married. This girl had already been running wild and had many children. My brother and she had two boys together. One of them went to school and played in the band. By blowing on the instruments, he got an infected throat and died while at that school in Santa Fe. The other one, who was older, was killed while catching a ride with a man hauling a water drum from Sawmill. That tank turned over and crushed him. Both of the boys died, however, after their father did.

When Jimmy started living with this girl, he bought livestock and started a farm in the Chinle Wash, this side of Valley Store. He started a nice home. They also grazed sheep at Black Mountain. But his wife died after a short while, from smallpox or measles. Then he had to take care of his two boys and two nephews named Billy Mitchell and George Mitchell as well as himself.

Those two nephews were the children of my oldest sister, Woman at War, who was married during the time while my people were living in the Canyon. It had been arranged for her to marry Tall Big Bitter Water Man, who came from the Nazlini and Sawmill area. They had a regular marriage ceremony. She only had two boys with this man, Billy and George Mitchell. Then my sister died. Her husband married again, and his next wife had two children and then died. He married for the third time, and that woman also died. I guess he must have been some kind of a witch or something.[11]

While my sister was living with Tall Big Bitter Water Man, he had no real job; he just broke horses for riding. His maternal relatives were well-to-do people, though, with lots of livestock; they used young boys to look after their horses. These relatives had a sense of their importance; they said that wealthy people were the most valuable and that the Canyon people were of little worth.

Tall Big Bitter Water Man only knew how to break horses. He did not participate in Squaw Dances or in the Yeibichai. His mother had lots of sheep, and when my sister and he had George Mitchell, Tall Big Bitter Water Man's mother butchered meat and sent it over by his younger brother, Slim Bitter Water Man. Well-to-do families like that always have a feeling for their new grandchildren, if they are the man's parents. They send food to help them out and in return they hope that the child will be brought to them so they can pet and hug it. When Tall Big Bitter Water Man died, he was living up toward Black Mountain near the gas station close to Cottonwood.

Another of my sisters, Warrior Woman, was also married while my people were living in the Canyon. My family agreed on her marriage, but there was no ceremony. Her husband was Curly Hair, and his parents were well-to-do people. My sister carded wool and spun it for blanket-weaving while her husband ran around. He broke horses for a living and gambled a lot. He liked to play tricks on women. There is a game they called "Don't Laugh." You don't laugh when the clown is coming in; if you do, you have to forfeit to the clown. Curly Hair was the clown; if the clown laughs, he forfeits.

My sister and he had no children. They lived as married people for about two years or a little less. Curly Hair would take off for months, just like a lot of other men did during those days. Men did not feel responsible for their wives, children and their homes. Later some of them would return to all of those things, while others would just take off for good. Curly Hair left my sister when she began to get sick. She moved back with her family. In those days, the mother-in-law and son-in-law could not see each other; that is, the girl had to move into a separate hogan near her mother's home.

Curly Hair went back to Wheatfields to his parents and then we heard he began living with one woman after another, leaving children scattered all around. The last place I know he went to was across the wash to live with a Standing House Clan woman. She is not related to any of us. That Standing House Clan came from Changing Woman in the West. They passed through here picking up members as they went through the villages that were inhabited at that time. These people were Pueblos and Canyon people, not Navajos.

My sister grew weaker and weaker. From all indications she had tuberculosis. It is thought to be transferred from one member of the family to another if you are living together. I was away a lot, and I guess that is why I am the only one left. Almost all of the rest died of tuberculosis. My sister finally passed away when my family had moved back around Tsaile.

One of my younger brothers, Sam, was still staying around home when I was there at this time. He never had an occupation until later, when I took him over to Sawmill. My youngest brother, Thomas, was gone during these years. He was the last child my mother had with my own father. Thomas went to schools in Fort Defiance,[12] Sherman and the Carlisle Institute[13] and had the best schooling of all of us. At Fort Defiance they had no definite time for schooling; in Albuquerque they had a five-year period; you took longer if you wanted to go through the grades. Thomas had the best command of English of any of us; he was in school a total of five or seven years. While he was over at Carlisle, he began to feel sick. He came back around here and got a job as an interpreter at the Protestant mission there in Fort Defiance. Gradually he got worse and had to leave that job.

When my mother was living with her second husband, she had two more boys. One of them died in infancy, and the other, Little Man, just recently died. During this time, my mother became sick with a chronic ailment. Thus, she did not want to have anything more to do with men. Therefore, she gave her daughter, my youngest sister, to her second husband, Star Gazer's Son, to live with him before she left him.

When my mother was living with Star Gazer's Son he had no occupation. After she left him, he began to perform Monsterway; he also found the causes of illness by star-gazing. This man was elderly, and my youngest sister was a teenager. When my mother gave her to him, my sister did not care for him. After two or three years, he finally left her. They had no children. After that, they got another girl for him from the family of his mother's sister, so he would teach the boys in that family about star-gazing. Red Canyon Man was one of those. Many others claimed to have learned star-gazing from Star Gazer's Son, but they changed it so much that Red Canyon Man just gave up practicing it. Star Gazer's Son's Monsterway consisted of repeating prayers all night long and only a few songs. Now that is just reversed.

After my mother left Star Gazer's Son, my own father came back to us. He and Woman With Goats split up because she started going around with White Singer. In those days, the elders in the family talked about such things and said, "If your wife does this, do not abuse her or get jealous of her. She has this privilege; she is a human being. You have the choice of leaving her or staying with her regardless of what she does." So my father took his choice and left her. She stayed on their farm at the end of the land between the two washes and grazed her sheep northeast of the wash. She died down there.

Before my father left Woman With Goats, her daughter married this cousin of mine, Tall Water Edge Man. This girl started making herself the boss of that family. She did not recognize her own mother or father as the head of the family, and she did not obey her mother. After she married Tall Water Edge Man, they became the recognized owners of all of the sheep, horses and cattle. For a while, my father got another nephew, Little Water Edge Man, to do chores for him, but finally my father convinced him to leave and marry into another family. Thus, by the time my father and Woman With Goats split up, Tall Water Edge Man and his wife had taken most of the property. When Woman With Goats died, all the rest of her property went to her male children. My father was left without any property.

When my own father, Water Edge Man, came back, he recognized me and his other children. He brought us clothes and gradually gave us some stock. His mother also gave us gifts. It was because of this that my mother did not get jealous; now my father was taking care of his own children in the proper way.

In the spring, after the wrestling with my cousin, my family moved back to Chinle. I guess I must have been about twenty or a little older then; I was starting to become a young man when I came back from the railroad and suffered that injury. I was still weak and was not much help around the home; I did not do much work. Everyone else was planting corn and tending the fields and the farm, but I did not do anything because I was still getting over my sickness.

My father, who was quite old when he came back to us, soon started thinking about Those Who Walk About Woman.[14] At that time she was living in Black Mountain, and my father started going over there courting her.

When I got over my sickness, I stayed around near Chinle. I still was not married or anything like that. I was still staying around here when all of a sudden the People found that there was a store, a warehouse being built. It happened that the government was buying a lot of tools and other things for use on the farm and at home, and they were issuing these things to the leaders of the community. They brought quite a few of these items out here to Chinle, and they appointed a white man to take care of these things and issue them to the People. That government store was over the hill from the Thunderbird. They were bringing those things out here from Fort Defiance.

When my own father and mother moved back to Chinle, of course, I did not have anything much to do but just stay around home. I understood and talked a little English by that time, just from experience. Of course, I had picked up what little English I knew by going to school for those three years, but I did not pick up much then. Besides that experience, though, I worked on the railroad and picked up a little more English there. And so, I could understand a little bit.

In Chinle at that time there was only one trading post,[15] the old one over past where the Thunderbird Trading Post is now. Charlie Day was the trader there at that time; they were operating that trading post, and they spoke Navajo quite well. I went over there, and those Day boys said, "I think that man, that government man, could use you." That's what they told me. They told me to go over there to see if I could be of any use to him. When that government man came to the store the next time, the Day family told him about me, because they knew I spoke a little English and he needed an interpreter.

The next time I went over there, the Day boys told me that that man at the government warehouse wanted to meet me. I have forgotten his English name, but among the People he was known as Tight Pants. So I went over and saw him; I talked with him a little bit. And sure enough, he said that he needed a helper and that he could use me. He had a light wagon and a team of horses that he used to go back and forth to Fort Defiance. I stayed there with him, and we used to go into Fort Defiance occasionally to pick up some tools and other implements and bring them out. Those things were from the government and were to be issued to the People.

I did a little interpreting for Tight Pants. Of course, lots of times people would come around asking for something that I did not understand. I guess I spent about a year and a half working for him. About that time, there were others who had picked up a little more English than I had, and so eventually he got somebody else in my place and I dropped out.

About this time, my father and our maternal uncles began discussing the marriage of my oldest brother Jim. Since he was the oldest, he had lots of clothes and other goods. There was a ceremony in the Navajo way when he married this first wife, who was from the Salt Clan. They had one child who died in infancy. After that, my oldest brother started going wild with women. He acted like a billy goat and never produced offspring properly. Since he was well provided for, he roamed this area. His only occupation was taking care of stock and breaking horses for several families. Maybe he had other children; I do not know.

At the same time, my next oldest brother, John, was roaming around. He took up with some of the wild girls who were running around on the bluff of the Canyon. They were Bitter Water Clan people, and no marriage ceremony was ever performed for him. He was not settled at this time, and I do not know what he was doing for a living. After a while, though, John started working on the government project which had crews building irrigation ditches around Wheatfields. During that time, he became acquainted with a white man, C. C. Manning. This man was originally a government employee who was an engineer for that irrigation system. He surveyed ditches around Wheatfields, Tsaile and Lukachukai and also over the mountain and along the San Juan River. When the crew was working at Wheatfields, both John and C. C. Manning were working on the same project. They moved up around Shiprock after finishing the work in Wheatfields and spent about three years up there together. When they finished over there, the crews moved back over around Red Lake and spent another two years. From there they went over around Fort Defiance.

When the irrigation crews moved to Fort Defiance, this C. C. Manning became interested in the trading post business and quit his government job. Since John was already well acquainted with him at that time and they got along well, my brother started to work at the store Manning bought in Fort Defiance.[16] John's first job was to freight goods from Gallup; he used the storekeeper's team and wagon. In Gallup, C. N. Cotton, who was the wholesaler over there at that time, would give him things to take back to C. C. Manning's post at Fort Defiance. That was John's main occupation, freighting back and forth. He would stay one night in Fort Defiance, one night between Fort Defiance and Gallup, and then one night in Gallup, before coming back again. So I guess he just kept freighting like that, in circles.

When John started working for Manning, he was living with a woman from Deer Springs who was from the Big Water Clan. They had lots of children, but most of them passed away very young except for one girl. I did not know her name because I was still over here in Chinle at that time with my mother. John and this woman moved to Fort Defiance with their three children when he began working at that store.

Her mother started to complain soon after that; she would ask why John was only feeding his wife and children. She quarreled and nagged and then began to argue with her own daughter. The daughter said, "Well, if you don't like it, I can break up and go wild with other men." So that is what she did. She left John, took the children and started running around.

John stayed in Fort Defiance and began to chum around with the Shirley boys; they all started drinking, and those boys persuaded John to marry one of the Shirley girls at Deer Springs. He had three girls by that woman; only two of them are living now. One is Alfred Hardy Jr.'s wife and I do not know about the other one.

John was working for this C. C. Manning at Fort Defiance when the government man in Chinle put someone else in my place at the warehouse. When I lost my job, I did not know what to do. I just stayed around home again. I do not remember how long I did that; maybe it was about a year. I just was not doing anything during that time.

My brother John finally gave me word that this white man, C. C. Manning wanted somebody to work at the Fort Defiance trading post in the kitchen. My brother told this man that he had a brother who might be willing to work for him like that, doing little chores around the house, washing dishes and helping around there.

When my brother had started working for Manning, of course, he had done those kinds of chores at first. He helped tie up the pelts, sack the wool and other things like that. At that time, John did not understand a word of English; he never went to school. But after a while, he gained more experience, and so Manning moved him from piling the merchandise to waiting on the customers. Gradually he worked his way up like that, and as he got more experience, they moved him right along. After a while he was well experienced in trading with the Indians. He knew the prices of things, how to handle money, work that scale and cash register and many other things.

When my brother came over here and asked me if I would be interested in going over to Fort Defiance, right away I decided to do that. So he and I went back together, and I decided to start working for this C. C. Manning. He was a tall, slim man who had a really red moustache, and so he was known among the People as Red Moustache. This man was nice and friendly; he was harmless, and so right away I started doing the dishes there for him. The pay down there at that trading post was better than at the warehouse in Chinle. Over at Fort Defiance I earned about fifteen dollars, while over in Chinle, when I was working for Tight Pants, I earned about ten dollars a month.

I stayed over there at Fort Defiance and worked for quite a while. My duties there were mostly those of helping Red Moustache's wife in the kitchen, doing the heavy lifting and dishwashing for her. The trader was always having people come for dinner, and he always gave them a big meal. They really had a lot of kitchen work over there. White people would come and visit, and the missionaries would come around and eat at the place too. My main job was to take care of all those dishes. I also did some chores around the place, including some work in the store. So I had a little experience doing kitchen work, including a little cooking.

I was still working there as a dishwasher when Manning sold out. He told me that he and his family were going back to Gallup, and he asked me to go along with them. But I did not care to go, so I just stayed behind. My brother, who had been with Manning for about twenty years since the start of those irrigation projects, was kept on by the new owner of that trading post, but my own job was over. So I was left stranded after that.

During this time, John was still living with that Shirley woman. My youngest brother, Thomas, was getting weaker and weaker, and when he finally quit his interpreter's job, he took all of his belongings over to John's place with that Shirley woman and put them in a trunk there. Shortly after this, Dr. Wigglesworth[17] came out to work among the People, and he began to try to treat Thomas.

About that time, John began to have problems with the Shirley woman. She said that he was stingy with what he earned at the store and her parents also began complaining. They said that John had a farm and did not help them with anything. Finally his in-laws said, "If you are not going to help us, go back to where you came from." So John built himself a separate hogan and he left that woman. He was peculiar in that way; he was not very sociable.

The Shirley boys began to pick on him and argue with him. So John started chumming around with another close friend at Sawmill; that man was He Who Seeks War, and he was a Blessingway singer. Part of the trouble with John was that he never contributed or helped the family or his close relations. He had two sources of income, from the store and later from the Blessingway he learned to do at Sawmill from He Who Seeks War. But he saved his income for future use. He used to trade things from the Fort Defiance store to Black Mountain. He would get livestock and give those to Jim Mitchell, our older brother, without his own wife or children knowing about it. When they started complaining about that, he put those things in his brother's name so he would not have to give them to his wife and children. He was very stingy like that, and he kept all of his property secret so that when he finally passed away, it was lost.[18] No one knew exactly where it was or what it was.

When he split up with the Shirley woman and left Fort Defiance, he was given another woman from a family near Sawmill. At that time, he had cattle, horses, a farm and a house. They thought that he would help them, but they found out after about a year that he would not, so they took that girl away from him. John had one child by this woman, Little Left Handed's Daughter-in-law; she is still living.

Like I said, for a while after my job ended there at the Fort Defiance Trading Post I did not know what to do. But I guess that my former employer had put in a word for me, and had told others in the area that I had a little experience in doing chores and odd jobs. At that time, the Franciscan Fathers at Saint Michaels Mission[19] were looking for a man to help inside the house over there with the cooking and other things like washing the dishes. I guess the trader who sold that store told the Fathers that I was a pretty good worker, pretty dependable, and that I was available for a job of that sort. The Fathers told Manning to tell me that they would like me to come over to the mission. So I went over there.

When I got there, a priest by the name of Curly Haired Priest [Father Anselm Weber] was there; I do not know how many others were there, but he was the Superior. Frank Walker was also there at that time; he was a young man then and was the interpreter at that mission. The Fathers told me what my duties would be if I accepted the job. I would be given quarters in a house where I could live with them.

A lot of the leaders of the People at that time, like Chee Dodge, Silversmith and Charlie Mitchell used to come and meet with the Franciscan Fathers. I guess they talked about plans of how they could work among the People. Men from other areas, like Chambers also came; they would all come together at Saint Michaels; they would meet at the Fathers' house, eat there and stay there.

The Fathers gave me a place to stay; I had my own room with a bed and everything in there. I had only one horse with me at that time. It belonged to my older brother, John, and I did not want to get rid of it, so I took it over to the mission and told the Fathers that I would like to keep it there, so taking care of it would not interfere with my work for them. The Fathers said, "Well, we have a pasture here that you can let it loose in, and anytime, maybe on Sundays, when you want to go visiting, you can take it out and ride around on it."

After I had been at the mission for about a year, the next summer I got acquainted with a woman. She used to come to me and I used to sneak over to her place. She did not live very far from the mission. I think she was kind of running wild. She trapped me; that is how we got together. I do not know what her name was or what her clan was. Maybe she was one of my cousins or somebody. I would go over and see her at night when time permitted.

Of course, there at the mission most of my work was cleaning up the kitchen and washing the dishes. When the priests had visitors from the outside, it took longer to clean up and do that work. Sometimes it would be late at night before I got through. Sometimes I just did not get over there at all. Of course, I had a place to sleep there at the mission, but when I got to running around, whenever I got through with my work, I would pretend that I went to bed, and then I would sneak out and go down and visit this woman. I would stay overnight there with her, and the next morning I would get back early so I was not noticed.

I did not realize that this woman was jealous. Of course, I never thought of any such thing at all. I did not suspect anybody, and I was under the impression that she trusted me and had faith in me. Sometimes she would start questioning me when I came in late. She would say, "Where have you been? You are so late in coming back here." One particular time there were other priests visiting there at the mission and so it took me quite a while to get through with my work in the kitchen. It was pretty late at night when I finished, and I started to go back to that woman's house. I was on my way down there but before I got there, I came to some hogans where there was a light. So I went in to see what the people were doing; in there a whole group of men were gathered, and they were gambling. They were playing cards. I watched them, and it was tempting to me to see so much money passing around from hand to hand. So I stayed there watching that game, and I stayed longer than I meant to. I did not join them because I did not want to take a chance on gambling again after what I had been through in California while working on the railroad.

It was after midnight when I started off. When I got to this woman's place, she was still up, sitting there all alone, spinning wool. She was still up waiting for me. So I just entered the hogan and threw myself down on the ground. She did not seem to pay any attention to me; she just kept sitting there spinning wool. Finally I got up and went over to sit right next to her. She still did not say anything; she just kept on spinning. She would not look at me or say anything.

So after a little bit, I just reached over and tickled her belly. When I did that I did not know that she was in a bad humor, that she was suspicious of me going after some other woman. I guess that is what was on her mind at that time. When I tickled her, she grabbed a wooden poker that she had lying next to the fire and hit me across my shin just as hard as she knew how. She was very angry. Of course, that was painful; that hurt.

I did not say anything for a long time. I just sat there until the pain began to go away. She never paid any attention to me even after that; she went ahead spinning wool again. After some time, when the pain eased a bit, I got really angry. I jumped up and doubled my fist and gave her one big blow on the side of her head. She fell over; when she did that, I just dashed out of the hogan and rushed back to the mission. Of course, I had a bed over there and a room where all of my belongings were. So I just went back there and went to bed. I do not know when she got up. Maybe she passed out from that one blow.

I did not go back there to see how she was. I just did not bother about her. I stayed there at the mission until my swollen shin was better. I used to watch for her; I expected her to come around sometime. Sure enough, once in a while I would see her coming. Then I would just sneak into the house and go up to the second story and stay there until she went away. I guess she came to the house and waited for me down there on the ground or some place. But I never did bother about going back to her. When I saw that she was going away, I would go back down and work around there.[20]

This woman kept after me, and I stayed out of her way all through the winter and the early part of the spring. By then, I was getting uneasy about that. I just did not think that it was safe for me to be around there, so after a while, I decided that I had better go back to my home in Chinle. This woman just kept after me like that without any rest. She was after me whenever I went anywhere; she always seemed to follow me around. Towards spring, I had had enough of that. Like I said before, I had my horse there at the mission; I kept it inside the fence, and I used to ride it. So I finally went to the Superior and told him that I was getting homesick and lonesome and that I wanted to go home.

After I talked to the Superior about my intentions, he said, "All right, if you want to go, you can go. But you are a pretty dependable worker and I think you have a chance to continue with the mission. We have a mission at Chinle[21] where there is a big, stout priest. He is alone there and needs somebody to do chores for him around the mission. So when you go back over there, maybe you can go to him and help around his place just like you have been doing around here."

So he told me I could go home and visit for a while and after a few days I should go over and see this other priest. He said, "I'm pretty sure that he will accept you because I will give you a letter to take to him which you can hand to him on your way home. Then go home and stay a while and then go back. When you give him this letter you can set a date with him when to go back to him. Be sure and do that; go back to Father Leopold[22] and cook meals for him, just as you have been doing here."

So after he talked to me like that, he wrote a letter to Father Leopold for me. I saddled my horse and took off. I delivered that letter to the priest here in Chinle, and he read it over. Then he said, "All right; I guess it's all right. You come back here anytime but don't wait too long. I would like to get you here as soon as you can come." So I agreed with him that I would come back some time. From there, I went on home and I visited at home for a while.

When I got home I found that my mother had moved out near the valley, over at Tsaile. So I went back over there. In the spring, they moved over towards the rim of the Canyon, towards Chinle. By that time my oldest brother Jim was married. He was living on the next hill back in there across the wash. He was married to the sister of the woman who is now my wife. So our family was all over there with him.

After I had been home for a while, I went back to Saint Michaels. When I went there, I told the priests, "I think that I'll just go back to Chinle for good. I found that my mother is helpless. She does not have anyone to care for her. She has no one to chop and haul wood for her, so I had better go on home." That was agreeable to the priests at Saint Michaels, but again they told me about Father Leopold. He was alone at the Chinle mission and I could be of some use to him. They said, "From the mission it is not too far to your mother's home, so you could help him out, too."

After that was decided, I left Saint Michaels in the early summer and came back to Chinle. On the way back I stopped at the mission and talked with Father Leopold and told him that I wanted to do some chores around home for my mother before I came back and worked for him. Then I went on home.

I spent some more time with my family. During that time, I used to go over and visit at my oldest brother's place. That is when I finally noticed a certain young girl. Jim moved over toward where we live now after a while, and by that time people were beginning to settle more closely around here. Two of those who were here were Scouting Man and Slim Many Goats, while over on this side of the Nazlini Wash, over by the cottonwood grove, there were Old Man Many Goats and his children, a man named Mescalero, another called Singer's Son and others. When they started living closer together like that, they started having more Squaw Dances. Of course, I attended a number of them after I came back from Saint Michaels to stay. I stayed around and quite often I stayed with my older brother Jim, who was living near Chinle here. I would help my mother and would also help down around Many Farms, planting and farming and doing things like that.

At the same time, I was working around the mission for Father Leopold. There was not too much work to do there; he was alone and it was not much work to fix meals for him and then wash the dishes and do little chores around the house. The rest of the time I would just sit around the mission and do nothing. Then I would come back over here and stay with my family. Father Leopold only had one brown horse that he rode around on. He did not have a car or wagon or anything like that. I also rode that horse. If there was a dance going on around here, then my older brother would let me use one of his horses to go to that dance.

I stayed around the mission just one summer. I guess it was around 1906 that I was working for Father Leopold. It was around 1904 that I was at Saint Michaels. The only building near Chinle at that time was the Franciscan Father's house. There was also a trading post near where the Thunderbird Lodge is now and where that old warehouse was where I had first worked. That building and an adobe house there burned down some years later. That place used to be called Place Where the Mule Burned or Burnt Mule because a mule burned to death there. It was not until 1910 that they started building the schools and all those other places here in Chinle.[23]

In the fall, after I had worked at the Chinle mission for Father Leopold for one summer, a man called Son of the Late Little Blacksmith[24] was sent to Chinle to keep peace and order. This man was a kind of headman and was sent here from another area because of the uprising when several men attacked the Superintendent.[25]

Before Son of the Late Little Blacksmith arrived, we heard that there was some trouble brewing up around the Canyon.[26] The thing that really triggered that trouble was the activities of five or six men who were just gambling and roaming around. Two or three of them were the same ones who gambled while working with me on the railroad. I guess after they came back they did not settle down to make a living; instead they just kept running around and gambling. The People did not like them because they used to roam the country in a group, arm themselves and cause trouble. The leaders of that band were Thankful One, White Man and Lichen. The Winslow boys were also in with them.[27]

I guess things would not have been too bad if it had not been for the Yeibichai Dance. A man held a Yeibichai Dance around the summit near Saint Michaels, and these men went to it. They were there just playing cards and gambling. After they had lost everything they possessed, they left. Coming back, Winslow came across a woman who was out herding sheep. He tried to rape her, but that woman really put up a good fight. Later she reported him to the headman in the area, and it was reported in Fort Defiance.

The Superintendent, Reuben Perry, wanted to talk with these men, and he asked them to come into Fort Defiance. But instead of doing that, they armed themselves and went across the valley here to the Black Mountain country. After that, the agent got into his wagon and started out for Chinle. Of course, there were no such things as automobiles in those days,[28] and so he came in his wagon. When he arrived here in Chinle, he started inquiring about those men, trying to learn where they were located. He was told that they were somewhere over around Black Mountain and that some people over there with them were urging them to continue making trouble.

Someone around the Steamboat area told one of these men that whenever the agent at Keams Canyon wanted to see them or had anything against the Navajos in that area, they usually took him aside and made him do as they wanted. This man told these troublemakers that when they did things this way, the agent just gave them everything and let them loose and never punished them. It was on the basis of that that these gamblers got the idea to seize the agent over here in Chinle. They thought that they could force him to drop the charges against Winslow.

John Brown from this area and several others from Lukachukai and the surrounding areas had been appointed policemen.[29] They started hunting for Winslow and his friends; that whole group was considered dangerous after that incident. I guess the word got around over there in Black Mountain that the police were looking for these troublemakers. There were several men over there that let this group stay at their places during the night. I guess the men in this group told the People in the Black Mountain area that they were going to fight with rifles and guns against the policemen who were looking for them.

So these men decided to come in from the Black Mountain area and meet with the Superintendent. They seized him, just as was planned. But the policeman who was with the Superintendent told these men not to do that. They released him and then one of them said something in a joking way to the policeman, but the policeman took it seriously. I do not think that when these remarks passed between the policeman and Big Tom either one of them really meant action. But they should not have made those accusations in public that way because this incident was a serious matter. So the Superintendent agreed and said, "All right." I guess he had only one policeman with him and that was not enough to subdue these men who had arms. Of course, when he said that, he did not mean that he was just going to forget the whole thing.

In those days, you see, the feeling was pretty bitter against the government and those agents. The majority of the People had a grievance against the government, and they were always looking for a chance to take revenge in some way. When the Superintendent realized that he could not control these men, he just agreed to everything that they said and so they released him. Then he and that policeman went back to Fort Defiance.

It was then, I guess, that the Superintendent called for the troops. He wrote to the Army officer. Of course, the soldiers at Fort Wingate could not take action on their own accord after that message came in from the agency, and so they passed the word along to Washington. I do not know why the Indian police could not bring in those men. Maybe they were afraid of them and did not want to bother touching them. Therefore, it was decided that troops should be sent out there to find them. That was a hard job because those men were sneaking around in the badlands and were hard to find. We heard that the troublemakers had moved across the valley to the Black Mountain country again and that they were hiding out somewhere and that people were sneaking food in for them. The Superintendent was also hearing these things from various places. The government kept sending policemen over there, but they could never bring those troublemakers in. Because of that, the agent asked for assistance from the War Department, to subdue those fellows over there before things got worse.

A detachment of troops came to Fort Defiance and then just a few of them were sent off to Chinle. When these soldiers arrived here in Chinle, they called in some of the leaders, those who were recognized as headmen of the community here. They told these men that they wanted to take them to Fort Defiance. There was no such thing as tribal policemen or courts at that time.

The Superintendent and the other government people down at Fort Defiance wanted to talk with these headmen to find out which side they were on, whether they favored the outlaws or the Superintendent. They told these leaders that the troops were ready to take action, but that they did not want to start anything until they knew where the leaders of the community stood. They also told these leaders that if they did not want any trouble to be started, they should step in and help subdue these troublemakers.

So the Superintendent called them in and talked with them to see what intentions they had and how they stood on this matter. He told them that if they did not want to help get these outlaws, then, of course, the soldiers would go ahead and take action. He told these leaders that if the soldiers did that, it would be bad for everyone, not only for the troublemakers but also for everyone else. It would be very harmful. He also told these headmen what the results would be if nothing were done to subdue these fellows. They were told that things would go from bad to worse, and that the hard times would happen all over again, just like before the People went to Fort Sumner. People would start shooting at just anything they saw coming towards them, and everyone would be harmed. He also told these headmen that those troublemakers were liable to turn against other peaceful Navajos, like the headmen themselves.

The headmen were asked to go ahead of the troops and get all the information they could about the strength of those men and how many new ones had joined them to resist the government. When they knew those things, they were told to come back and report so the authorities would know just what the situation was. So the date was set, and as they returned from Fort Defiance, these headmen spread the word around that on a certain day everyone would get together and talk about what they should do.

I do not know why those other men were going around with Winslow trying to defend him for his wrongdoing. He committed that crime and had never done anything like that before, so there really was nothing much against him.

The headmen came back ahead of the troops and passed the word around and told the People what was being planned about that. Of course these troublemakers heard about it at the same time. When they learned this, they got kind of scared. They knew that the result would be bloodshed. So they sneaked back across the valley from Black Mountain and went up into the caves in the Canyon at night, somewhere around the junction of Canyon de Chelly and Canyon del Muerto. Of course, when they went into hiding up there in the Canyon, they all had rifles, pistols and ammunition. The other people living in the Canyon learned that they were in the area, and they did not want to have any trouble started there. So they got together and talked with these troublemakers. They told them that there was no use sneaking around at night, trying to avoid the soldiers and the law. These people talked to those men and said, "You'll only make yourselves suffer more; you will never win in the end. If you are determined to do something, if you want to be harmed or killed, then why do you sneak around after dark? Who are you after? Who are you mad at? Who do you want to harm? Why do you sneak around after dark like that?"

Someone also told them that if they were angry at certain people, they should go out there and do what they wanted to do in the plain daylight. The people said to these troublemakers, "Our advice to you is to go and surrender; just give yourselves up. We don't think you have done anything serious, and we think it is foolish for you to be acting this way. To avoid all of these troubles and hardships, you should go in and give yourselves up and just see how you come out."

"The only thing you've done wrong is that you refused to go in with the police the way the government wanted you to. We don't think that it will be very difficult to remedy that. Outside of refusing to obey the police you have not committed any crime, so there is no reason for you to be acting the way you are. You have come back here amongst us, and you are just bringing hardship on yourselves and on the people in this community here. If anything more drastic should take place, then innocent people will be harmed and it will be your fault. So we think you should willingly give yourselves up and go into Fort Defiance."

When those men heard this they decided that there was no sense in resisting. So they stripped themselves of their arms and ammunition and they left the Canyon with some of these men who had been talking to them. They went up to Crystal, where one of the headmen, a man by the name of Silversmith, was living. It so happened that Silversmith and these trouble-makers were from the same clan, and so they went there to talk this matter over with him. Silversmith, who was an old man then, said, "All right, I don't see that you committed any serious crime. You simply disobeyed the order and I don't think that that should amount to much. So I will take you in myself. No doubt you will be punished some for disobeying the order but that will not be much. I think it's a good thing that you came to me to discuss this thing, so I will go along with you to Fort Defiance."

Silversmith went into Fort Defiance with these men. It seemed as if most of the People sided with these troublemakers; that is the way the stories were spreading around, especially from the Black Mountain area where the People were really bitter against the government. When they heard that these men were going in, they kept urging them to go ahead and build up trouble so it would become serious and the People would be at war with the government.

After these men gave themselves up at Fort Defiance, they were kept there for a while. Some of the People remember seeing them while they were waiting for their trial. They had chains around their feet and their hands, great big balls and chains. They were chained together in a row, and they had to wear them even when they wanted to go to the bathroom. The policemen watched them all the time, even when they wanted to walk outside and stretch.

After about three weeks in Fort Defiance as prisoners, they were put on a train and taken to San Francisco and beyond there to an island in the ocean. I guess they went to visit their mother, White Shell Woman; she is supposed to be on an island out there.[30] They were taken over there to that penitentiary called Alcatraz. They were all sentenced according to their crimes, and they were sent to that penitentiary mainly to let them see for themselves with their own eyes what it was like when you were a criminal and what you had to go through for causing all of that trouble. They saw what conditions were like in those penitentiaries and what kind of people were in there. The main purpose of that was to educate them so that when they came back home, they would tell other people about what it was like. Each of them was given a different time according to how much he deserved to be punished. Sometimes I wonder about that, though; that did not look right because Winslow, the one who tried to rape that woman and another one were the first to come back from Alcatraz, and they were the ones who had caused all that trouble. They were sentenced to about three years;[31] the other troublemakers stayed over there for about four years.[32]

The first night after these men got out of jail, there was a Yeibichai Dance over near Chinle. These men traveled all the way back from that prison, and they arrived in Chinle on the first night of that dance. You know that when there is a Yeibichai Dance, different groups come in to dance and they will announce them as they appear. They always say, "These dancers are from so and so, and they are coming out to dance next." Those three or four who got out first just ran in there and joined that dance. The People were probably kind of short on dancers, as they are sometimes. When that happens, anybody can help fill in the places, and that is what those three did who were the first to come back from prison. They danced in that Yeibichai the same night they got back.

The next morning, the first thing, Silversmith made an announcement to the People. He was the one who had escorted these men to Fort Defiance years before, and he knew that they had been prisoners. He announced to the People that all of these men here were foreigners, that it was bad for them to have come out to see this Yeibichai Dance because now the People had even seen and heard some dancers from way out on an island. This man kidded with the People and joked with those men about that. I guess those men had learned their lesson by then; everybody around there just started laughing about it. Those men did not think it was a joke. I guess that all of those experiences made those men learn a lesson.[33]

I guess that the government did not trust the Navajos out here around Chinle very much after that happened,[34] so they wanted to get someone to come out here and stay with the People to talk to us and serve as a guide and a peacemaker. As soon as these men had been taken away, the leaders of the People got together and discussed these things. The headmen of the various communities[35] talked about the way the government was handling the People. They decided that the blame was on different agents, the different individuals who were sent among the People. They thought it was the individuals, not the government as a whole that were to be blamed for these problems. These officials and agents came in with different ways of handling the People, and their policies did not seem to be uniform. In some cases things worked smoothly, and in others it seemed as if the agents and other officials just came in to stir up trouble instead of preventing it.

The headmen decided that the Indians should be handled differently so that no more things like this trouble with Winslow and the others would happen. They decided that this trouble was the fault of government people who came out to run the affairs of the Indians according to their own ideas without proper instructions. With that in mind, the headmen suggested a policy of sending a well-informed man from one area into different areas where he had no close relations. This man was to give advice to the People without favoring any side; he was to be honest with them and to try to teach them.

On the strength of that, Man Who Shouts, Little Man, White Goat and others who were community leaders got together and went to Fort Defiance. There they talked to the government people. They were told about the treaty again that the Navajos had made with the government. Leaders of the People had signed that, and part of the treaty stated that from that time on, any individual who committed a crime on the reservation would be sentenced to punishment by a court. These leaders were told to keep that treaty in mind and to teach others not to side with men who violated the rules. They were told that cases like that should be an individual's business. If a person commits a crime or misdemeanor, let him take the consequences. No one should join in his defense. They were told that even the guilty ones would not be handled too roughly. They would be brought in peacefully and given a fair trial before they were sent to jail for their punishment.

The headmen talked with the government people in Fort Defiance about their ideas for handling the future affairs of the Indians. They reached a decision together over there to send Son of the Late Little Blacksmith out here to Chinle to be a guide for the People. Although he was a police officer, still he was not sent here to enforce the law but more to teach the People what the government policy was toward the Indians. He was to inform the People in Chinle about these things and to serve as peacemaker and sort of a judge. If anyone got into trouble he could advise them as to what they should do about it.

Son of the Late Little Blacksmith was not an educated man. He was from the Crownpoint area and had been an Indian scout and a soldier at Fort Wingate. That is where he became more experienced about these things than the others we knew about. He had been with the army on several occasions in the Apache wars and also in other Navajo battles, including some with the Pueblo Indians. Whenever any uprising happened and a troop had to be sent out, Son of the Late Little Blacksmith would be one of the scouts to go. Because of that he was experienced, and the headmen recommended that he be the one to be stationed here in Chinle. He was to be a guide and a peace officer and to teach the People what he had learned from these experiences.

He was like Jeff King, Charlie Mitchell and Old Man Short Hair, too; they were Indian scouts, and that is where they picked up a lot of their ideas about the rules and things the People should follow. These men got a lot of their ideas as I did, by attending those meetings with these men who were talking to the People. That is where I started to learn to talk to the People and how I learned what the rules and regulations were. That is how I myself learned about white man's laws.

When Son of the Late Little Blacksmith came here to instruct the People, he did not have any place to keep his horse. The mission was the only place where Indians could stay in those days. Their only way of traveling was on horseback. So the government asked the mission to set aside a quarter section, 160 acres of land, on which the Indians could graze their horses inside a fence when headmen and others from outlying areas came here to get together for a meeting. The mission agreed to do that; the Fathers put up an enclosure where the People could keep their horses, and the mission planted some hay for them to use. There was also a plan to establish a school at Chinle and to be able to take care of the parents of the children who would be coming from far away. So that was agreed to and there was an understanding among the People that they were welcome any time at the mission and that there would be a place for them to sleep overnight and to graze their horses there.

Son of the Late Little Blacksmith was told to remain in Chinle and, with the help of the mission, to try to give the People some help with the things they did not understand. He was told to use his own judgment about violations; if he thought a problem needed to be taken to the Fort Defiance agency, then he should do that; if he thought that it could be settled back here, then he should do that. He was also told that when cases needed to go to court, he would be called upon to relate what he knew about the individuals and the case, and in that way he could help the agency help the People. In those days the courts were not patterned after white man's courts as they are now. A lot of the authority was in the hands of the headmen. Of course, the agent had full authority to impose sentences. The agent would serve as judge in those cases, because the headmen, the spokesmen for the People, were not educated to pass sentences on the different crimes. So while the headman was sometimes asked to make decisions, the full power rested with the agent. If the headmen made decisions, the agent had to approve them before they could be enforced.

The agent at this time was Tall Chief [Reuben Perry], and Son of the Late Little Blacksmith acted in the capacity of a bridge between the People and the agent. Although his title was policeman, at the same time he acted as a peacemaker. From time to time, he took certain cases into Fort Defiance. There he would explain the troubles to the agent, and on the strength of that the agent would advise what should be done. Some of those complaints would be dropped; when they were investigated, Son of the Late Little Blacksmith would find that there was no foundation to them, that they were just made up.

He told the People about the government policy toward the Navajos according to the treaty at Fort Sumner in 1868. He said that from here on, no Navajos would be allowed to go off the reservation and raid others as they had been doing in the past. If they did they would be punished for it. This was agreed to by the People and the government over there at Fort Sumner. At that time, the People were headed by Maneulito and many others who were also spokesmen. They all agreed with the government that they would do that, that they would not create any more disturbances. Son of the Late Little Blacksmith told the People that their leaders had agreed with the government on that and that now all of the People would have to comply with it.

Any question that arose needed to be investigated to see what was at the bottom of it and how it started. That was the only way the whole situation could be fully understood. That is the system that Son of the Late Little Blacksmith started using out here. When any complaints came to him or any trouble arose, he would go over there and investigate it thoroughly before he decided whether to take the matter into Fort Defiance or to use his own judgment about it. He said that with that policy, gradually, one by one, people would find the right road. He said the leaders needed to be patient and to talk with the People. Some of them started acting badly or talking without thinking ahead, and that is what brought on trouble and ill feelings among the People. He said that in many cases when matters were investigated, you discovered that it really was not a court case after all.

Man Who Shouts, who later became my father-in-law, and others, such as Bead Clan Gambler, Weela, and Long Moustache used to meet with Son of the Late Little Blacksmith to discuss the best ways to encourage the People to be more law-abiding. They would meet with him over at the mission, and while they discussed these things, Son of the Late Little Blacksmith would often tell them about similar situations that existed elsewhere on the reservation. He often talked about the hill country over near the Continental Divide, where some of the land is off the reservation and some is on.[36] He told these men that the way things got straightened out over there was that police were brought in and the People were encouraged to start coming together in communities. That is the reason we now have a community here in Chinle and another one up in the Canyon and others in other places.

When Son of the Late Little Blacksmith gave this advice and talked about ways of remedying situations, these headmen said, "Well, we'll work out a program like that. We'll send out police to meet with each community like Valley Store, Tsaile and other places where people have settled." So they agreed to that program according to the way that Son of the Late Little Blacksmith had advised them. In Chinle we had John Brown as policeman, and up toward Sawmill there was Old Policeman. And we also had Big Policeman, White Haired Policeman, Mexican Man, and Late Red House Singer; around the Wheatfields area they had Old Man's Nephew; they called him "The Policeman Who Undressed" because he discarded his uniform.

These were Son of the Late Little Blacksmith's policies when he was stationed here. He would travel around along the Canyon and between the canyons, down in the valleys and up on the mesas and over into the Black Mountain area. He would go around wherever it was necessary. If he knew of any people who were not going straight or needed to be corrected, then he would go right to their homes and talk to them directly.

When there was a group of people he needed to talk to, he would set a date on which they should get together and ask them to have a meeting. The policemen who were elected to work in the area with him were subject to his orders. When he wanted to hold a community meeting, he would send for them and tell them what date he had set. Then the policemen would notify the People that on that day there would be a meeting at a certain place. That way the headmen could come together and talk with the People. The People would spread the word about the meeting and its purpose. Son of the Late Little Blacksmith would get some of the headmen to go with him, and they would go over and meet with the People and discuss the problems together.

Sometimes if it was bad weather, they would have to meet in a large hogan. In those big hogans, when all of the People gathered together from somewhere, they would have a full house. A lot of the hogans at that time were quite large; those that were built in the four-legged style could be expanded. If it was warm weather, of course, they just met out in the open.

Son of the Late Little Blacksmith would arrange the meeting in a circular position, just as if it were a hogan, with the opening toward the east. He would seat people in a row as they came, starting from the east and moving around through the south. Then the speakers would come in. Of course, some of the People at that time were quite mean; they always wanted to make trouble for others and to disturb the peace. Some of those People did not want to obey any orders or anything that was told them from Fort Defiance and all the way from Washington. So it was Son of the Late Little Blacksmith's job to tell them just what the policies of the government were toward the People.

Son of the Late Little Blacksmith and the other leaders would call on each individual in the hogan and ask him to express himself. Starting with the last man or the first man and moving around south, they would call on the spokesmen for different family and community groups and ask them questions about what their personal opinions were on these matters. The individual would be asked to come and take a seat over here in front of the spokesmen so he could be questioned about his opinions. In that way, these men would discuss what they thought the best thing to do would be.

In these meetings, when Son of the Late Little Blacksmith would go around in a circle, there were two things in general that he would bring out each time. He would ask someone, "What is your personal opinion about these things?" Then he would go on and say that there were only two opinions; either it was good or it was bad. He said, "I would like to hear from you which is the best for you as an individual or as a community or what your opinion is on what is best for all the People. If you behave and obey laws and live peacefully and be friendly and sociable, then you will have nothing to interfere with your progress. Things like that are all for the good of you and your neighbors and everyone. On the other hand, if you lie or steal or cheat and lead a bad life, of course it will be bad for you and your people. If you are against something that is good, then you are on the bad side, which will not benefit anyone. So I would like to ask you which side you stand on."

That was the way that Son of the Late Little Blacksmith talked to the People. He more or less put them on the spot to express their personal opinions on these different things. Son of the Late Little Blacksmith would go around in a circle and question the main ones in the group. Of course a lot of them would not understand what he was saying, and they would just get confused. They did not know what to say or what to answer, and they would just get stage fright. Some of them said things without really thinking about what they were saying. Others, of course, knew right away what he was talking about and gave quick answers. Doing things that way, sometimes they might spend a whole day discussing these things.

One man by the name of Johnny Bida told a story about himself during one of these meetings. "When they were having a meeting, I was sitting in the audience watching each person go up there to be questioned on his personal opinion. I had my mind all set about what I was going to say about the good things and the bad things. I was going to get up and draw one line and say, 'Here is my opinion on that.' So when my turn came, I crawled over there to sit down and express myself. I went over there and sat down, and then everything just went blank. As I took my seat, I drew a long line and another one on the ground. What I wanted to say was that, 'this is the good line and that is the bad line.' I had that all planned out. But after I drew the lines, everything just went blank on me, and there I sat with two lines in front of me.

"I forgot all about how I was going to start. I just sat there dumb, not saying anything. Everyone was quiet, and one of the leaders said, 'What does that line represent? What do you have those lines there for?' I don't even remember what I said then; all I did was mumble something and then I went back to my place." A lot of the People were that way; they never learned to get over being scared of talking.

When Son of the Late Little Blacksmith held these meetings, he would help the People with different and difficult questions. Sometimes trouble would start somewhere in the mountain ranges over on the other side. The troubles in those days were mostly about land use; the People would usually quarrel about that. Other times, disputes would arise over livestock and the use of water. When these troubles arose, the People would usually take them to the headmen, like Charlie Mitchell, Silversmith, Old Man Dodge and others who were spokesmen for the People. They would bring their grievances to them, and if the headmen did not want to handle the case, they would refer those people to Son of the Late Little Blacksmith, who was stationed at Chinle. Of course he understood more than anyone else what the troubles were about. He was familiar with those things. They would ask him to investigate and find out just what was at the bottom of the dispute. After that was done, it could be discussed more thoroughly. Sometimes Son of the Late Little Blacksmith would decide that it was just a small matter which really could be straightened out by the headman.

It was good the way he taught the People. One of his teachings was that "the men who cheat and know the tricks are pretty shrewd; they can always manage to figure things out. On the other hand, the man who has his mind on making a living does not want to make a mistake. He does not know anything, and he is silent compared to those others." I started to notice that a lot of the things Son of the Late Little Blacksmith said were true. When the People were talking like that in a meeting, it was always the sneaky ones who would come out with the answer right away, while the others, no matter how much time they gave them to think about things, would just come up with a blank. That really was the way those things went, and I started to learn that from Son of the Late Little Blacksmith. That was part of his job, to get the People to learn to express themselves about what they thought was best for each individual and for the community.

Since he was stationed at the mission there in Chinle where I was working, I stayed with him; that is how I happen to know all about what he was doing. I stayed there with him for a whole year and a summer and another winter. When he held these meetings, I followed him around and got a lot of ideas from him. I would just go around with him as his partner. I would watch and listen to what he said and how he spoke each word. I learned how he talked. I guess Son of the Late Little Blacksmith noticed that I was getting better at talking, too, because after a while he asked me to come along to the meetings with him. That is the way that I learned what was being discussed by the People and what was being planned for them. Before that time, of course, I was unaware of those things. I suppose the People had discussions like that for various purposes before this time, but I never paid any attention to them. Finally, with all of those experiences, talking to the People started coming naturally to me.

After I had worked at the mission and stayed there with Son of the Late Little Blacksmith for almost two years, I left and did not return. The reason I did that was that I had started living with this woman I am now married to, and we had started raising a family. I had to support them and look after them; that is why I stopped staying at the mission.

EDITORS' NOTES

1. Around 1876, the Navajos received word that a railroad was going through the southern boundary of the reservation. Surveyors came through in

1876, laying track between Albuquerque and Fort Wingate for the Atlantic-Pacific Railroad (Underhill 1953:205). By 1879, Navajos in that area had started using the railroad ties discarded by railroad labor gangs for hogans in areas near the tracks (*Ibid*.:206). By the winter of 1881-82, the first train went to Wingate and on to Manuelito. From there, ox cart trails facilitated travel to Fort Defiance.

The railroad continued to move westward from Albuquerque between 1880 and 1887. By at least 1885, the line had been renamed the Santa Fe. Letter Book No. 26 from the Fort Defiance Agency shows that by 1899, Navajos were working on the railroad. An entry dated 10/18/1899 (Letter Book 26:474) states that the 320 Indians working on the railroad were earning a total of $7,000 per month. By 1900, the Santa Fe Railroad was operating all the way to the Pacific Coast (Underhill 1953:221), and mercantile depots had been established at Gallup, Defiance Station (Manuelito), Winslow and Flagstaff (Link 1968:41). Many Navajos continued to work for the railroad and also to explore other employment opportunities off the reservation, such as work in more distant beet fields. For further information, see Underhill (1953) and McNitt (1963).

2. Gold Tooth was the Navajo name for C. N. Cotton, a trader who was in Ganado c. 1899 and who was the first to sell merchandise in Gallup, both through the Gallup Mercantile and the El Rancho stores. Cotton had at least one gold tooth, and he recruited Navajos for the Atlantic-Pacific (later, the Santa Fe) Railroad.

3. Information about these two games is apparently extremely limited. As Culin (1907:32) indicates, games using playing cards are among those the Indians borrowed from the Anglos. Card games, played with cards purchased from the traders or with native copies thereof, are easily recognizable as common Spanish and American games (*Ibid*.:791).

The Franciscan Fathers (1910:478-479) refer to Monte and Coon Can, calling them the only modern card games with which present Navajos are familiar. Vocabulary lists on these pages of the Franciscan *Ethnologic Dictionary* suggest that the eight- and ten-spot cards are not used in either game, that the cards are turned up in Monte in a manner the Franciscans equate with *qa'i'nłłi*, or drawing out, and that *(neznd) dałhijł*, means "the (ten) cards are held, the game of Coon Can" (Franciscan Fathers 1910:478).

In Culin's study of "Chess and Playing Cards" (1898:665-942) the author refers to Apache playing cards which are modeled on playing cards from nineteenth century Cadiz, Spain, in which the eights, nines and tens are omitted. Captain John G. Bourke reported that the Apaches had borrowed many words as well as the cards themselves from the Mexicans. The Apache game was called *Con-quien*, "with whom?" and was also known by the native name, *DaKa-cunitsnun*, "Cards ten" (*Ibid*.:936). That this is similar to the Navajo Coon Can seems highly probable.

4. Hand-trembling and star-gazing are among the forms of divination used by Navajo diagnosticians. For further information, see Morgan (1931:390-402).

5. The Squaw Dance is the public part of the Enemyway, a three- or five-night ceremonial which cures dizziness, weakness and many other maladies attributable to ghosts of enemies of the Navajos. Mythologically based on the slaying of the monsters by the Navajo culture hero Twins, and on the war on Taos, the ceremonial was frequently used during the days of Navajo raiding and warfare to protect the People from the ghosts of the slain. Interspersed among the sacred rituals are some public ones, including the Squaw Dance, a rare, indigenous occasion where Navajo girls capture male partners and boys and girls dance together. According to his granddaughter Geneva Mae Kee (7/6/63), Frank described his first Squaw Dance to his grandchildren as follows: "I did not know how to dance when I went over there, so I tried to hide in my blanket. This girl came up and grabbed it. I tried to get away at first, and then I just started to cry. At that time, the People just wore breech cloths. As I ran, my blanket ripped. So I just cried again." Frank did not include a reference to this incident during the undirected taping of his life history, nor was it pursued through directed interviewing at a later date.

For further information on Enemyway, see Haile (1938), McAllester (1954) and Witherspoon (1975b:56-64).

6. The Yeibichai Dance refers to the Navajo Nightway ceremonial, which is held to cure eye, ear and other head ailments, rheumatism, arthritis and other body paralyses. The Nightway, which can be held in five- or nine-night versions, is restricted to performances after the first frost. While most of the ceremonial takes place inside the hogan in private, the last night may include a public exhibition by masked male dancers in an outdoor brush enclosure. The dancers, who personify selected mute male and female deities, perform in teams, singing and dancing according to the rules established by the Holy People. Yeibichai dancers may also perform during the Mountain Chant, Feather Chant and Coyote Dance. For further information on the Nightway, see Matthews (1901, 1902) and Wyman and Kluckhohn (1938).

7. The Blessingway is the only prophylactic ceremony among Navajo rituals. Its emphasis is on good hope, future well being, health, happiness and positive blessings rather than on curing. Among the ceremonies which are part of Blessingway are House Blessing, *Kinaaldá* or Girl's Puberty Ceremony, Seed Blessing, and the earlier known Chief Blessingway, Mountain Peak Blessingway, Enemy Monster Blessingway and Game Way Blessingway. For further information, see Wyman and Kluckhohn (1938), Frisbie (1967, 1968, 1970) and Wyman (1970).

8. For Monsterway, the deities and other ceremonial concepts, see later chapters in Frank's story, Reichard (1963) and Wyman and Kluckhohn (1938).

9. Lifeway is a Navajo ceremonial which functions to cure injuries from accidents, such as sprains, swellings, strains, burns and cuts. Unlike other Navajo curing ceremonials, the Lifeway is continued until relief occurs or the

form of treatment has been deemed useless. For further information, see Wyman and Kluckhohn (1938).

10. This name refers to the fact that Navajo men as well as women used to wear their long hair tied up in an hour-glass shaped bundle behind their heads. Some Navajos continue this practice at present. After the hair is brushed, it is folded into the bundle which is then tied around the middle with a white yarn hair string. The hairdo is known as a *tsiighéét*.

11. This joke is one of the few references to witchcraft Frank made while working on his life story. All of the others are related to his own role as a political and ceremonial leader and his own illness. For an excellent source, see Kluckhohn (1944).

12. There is no mention of Thomas Mitchell in the Fort Defiance school records from c.1903, when it seems likely that he was there with Frank. However, the Fort Defiance School Enrollment Record Book, Vol. 1 (1907), does record a Thomas Mitchell who was 5'7", 116 lb., and whose home was in "Chinlee."

13. Underhill (1953:227) gives the following dates for the establishment of the off-reservation schools which accepted Navajo students: 1881, Albuquerque; 1886, Grand Junction, Colorado; 1891, Santa Fe; 1891, Phoenix; 1892, Fort Lewis, Colorado; 1893, Fort Apache, Arizona; and 1902, Sherman Institute, California.

14. Frank said here, in an aside, that this woman was the grandmother of Wilson Yazzie, the second husband of his own daughter Ruth.

15. Information on early traders among the Navajos can best be obtained from McNitt (1963). However, Underhill (1953), Left-Handed Mexican Clansman (1952), Kennedy (1965) and the Letter Books of the Fort Defiance Agency also contain useful information.
   Between 1868 and 1878 the Navajos traded with Anglos, exchanging wool and blankets for the traders' staples. Stover and Coddington's store in Fort Wingate had Lorenzo Hubbell as a clerk in 1869, and Neale's store in Fort Defiance was bought by Damon the same year. Lorenzo Hubbell moved to Ganado in 1874 and by 1876 (Link 1968:39) or 1878 (McNitt 1963), established Hubbell's trading post in its present location. Shortly thereafter, Anglos began to come on the reservation in noticeable numbers. Many of them explored the possibilities of trading, and by 1900 there were about two dozen traders among the Navajos (Underhill 1953:208). Post offices had started at Ganado at Hubbell's in 1883, at Keams Canyon and Navajo Springs, also in 1883, at Houck and Tuba City in 1884 and at Tohatchi in 1898. Traders were assisted by the railroad, the mail and undependable wagon caravans which came from Santa Fe or Albuquerque (Link 1968:40, 41).
   According to Van Valkenburgh (1941:39) the first trading post in Chinle was established in a tent by Little Mexican in 1882. Closed by the

Navajo agent after a year, it was followed by a small trading camp, operated from tents between 1885-1886 by Ansom Damon and Sam Day, Sr., during their brief partnership. The first license to trade in Chinle was issued in 1886 to Lorenzo Hubbell and C. N. Cotton, who worked for one year as co-owners of the store later known as Garcia's (McNitt 1963:214). Successors included Michael Donovan 4/3/86, P. Washington and Thomas J. Lingle 1/23/88, Bernard J. Mooney and James F. Boyle 2/21/1889, and John Boehm 7/6/89 (*Ibid.*:214, n.2).

Letter Book No. 27 of the Fort Defiance Agency shows that on 2/19/1900, Charles L. Day requested a license to trade at Chinle, where he intended to buy out William Meadows, who had built another post below Canyon de Chelly about twenty miles southeast of Chinle in 1896. This was granted. About the same time, Hubbell built a second post in Chinle, and in December 1902, Franciscan Father Anselm Weber, Frank Walker, Miss Josephine Drexel and Sister Agatha visited there, evidently while contemplating the feasibility of a Franciscan Mission in Chinle. Among those who worked for Lorenzo Hubbell were Sam Day, Jr., Mike Kirk and Leon H. (Cozy) McSparron.

Sam Day, Sr., sold the large log trading post built in Chinle in 1902 to Charlie Weidemeyer of Fort Defiance in 1905, and Charlie Cousins went to Chinle to operate it, becoming involved very shortly thereafter in assisting Agent Reuben Perry when he was attacked near the Chinle Field Matron's house. This post later became Cozy McSparron's Thunderbird Ranch, and has continued in operation through modern times.

When his father Sam sold the Chinle post in 1905, Charles Day returned to Ciénaga Amarilla, where he remained in the trading business, operating the Two Story Trading Post. He opened a new store in Round Rock in 1916, but was killed shortly thereafter, in 1918.

Around 1917, Lorenzo Hubbell's Chinle post was sold to C. N. Cotton, who was trading in Ganado and shipping in Gallup by 1899 (Letter Book No. 26, 10/18/1899). Camille García went to work for Cotton in 1920, and by 1923, Cozy McSparron, Camille García and Hartley T. Seymour bought out all three stores in Chinle (McNitt 1963:215).

16. Fort Defiance, which was the site for the first post office in Arizona on 4/9/1856, and later in 1871, the first mission (Link 1968:19, 40), historically has been the center for much Navajo activity, including trading. In Fort Defiance, C. C. Manning purchased the trading post from Billy Weidemeyer in 1896, and it was owned and operated by Manning from then until 1906. The post he owned in Naschiti in 1902 was managed by Charlie Newcomb, and Manning's post in Crystal was bought by Newcomb in 1922. Manning, who reportedly was a fair trader (Letter Book 27:11/29/1899 entry) went to Gallup in 1912.

In the early 1900s many other traders were also in Fort Defiance, Chinle and elsewhere on the reservation as a perusal of McNitt (1963) and other sources indicates. The trading post owned by Aldrich and Dodge in Red Rock was still in operation (Letter Book 28:1/23/1903 entry), and the drama of trading continued to include fires, such as that at the Sampson Trading

Post on 12/6/1902 and at Weidmeyer's store (Letter Book 27:11/29/1899 entry), thefts and violence.

Despite the fact that agents decided which and how many traders should be licensed on the reservation, the quality was variable. By 1902, the Fort Defiance Agency Letter Books begin to contain references to unfair trading practices. Letter Book No. 28 contains a letter dated 9/5/1902 which reports that traders are forcing Navajos to freight and transport supplies and paying them only in trade at the low equivalence of 40¢ per 100 pounds. A letter dated 3/26/1903 states that, in general, Indian horses are so poor that little freighting can be done with them. Letter Book No. 29 gives some indication of C. N. Cotton's prices. On 11/24/1903 he is reported to be paying Navajos 50¢ per 100 pounds of shingles hauled as freight.

As Underhill (1953) so aptly indicates, the coming of the railroad and the traders deeply affected many aspects of Navajo culture, including household items, dress, farm utensils, housing style, dyes and warp and weft materials for weaving, and silver work, among others. For further information, see *Ibid*.: 191-230.

17. A doctor by the name of Dr. Albert M. Wigglesworth (see Father Emanuel Trockur 1964), is well remembered among the Navajos for his years of patient, humane service. Shortly after coming to the reservation, he became involved in combating the major health problem of the People at that time, tuberculosis. As Frank (1964) described him, "Dr. Wigglesworth was the first good doctor the People ever had. He taught the People about tuberculosis and the contagious diseases. He told Thomas to isolate himself at the first tuberculosis sanitorium that was built at Fort Defiance, and he did." Fort Defiance became the location of one of the first tuberculosis sanitoriums on the reservation. Dates for the establishment of this and other hospitals on the reservation (according to Underhill 1953:278 and Frink 1968:2, 95, 96) are given below:

1889 - closed 1947	Fort Wingate
1897 - closed 1929	First hospital in Fort Defiance; a small one constructed by the Episcopalians who, in 1894, established the Good Shepherd Mission there (Frink 1968:95 and Link 1968:19).
1901	Ganado — Presbyterian hospital, later known as Sage Memorial. Underhill (1953:299) gives 1904 as the date, while Link (1968:58) says the first hospital was completed in 1911. It was enlarged from twelve to seventy-five beds in 1930 (Salsbury with Hughes 1969:134).
1908 - closed 1942	Leupp (replaced in 1926)
1908	Shiprock (replaced in 1915)
1911	Tuba City (replaced in 1928)

1912	Fort Defiance government hospital (enlarged in 1929 and 1939)
1914	Crownpoint (replaced in 1939)
1926 - closed 1942	Toadlena
1927 - closed 1944	Kayenta
1927	Tohatchi — operating as health center
1932	Chinle — operating as health center
1933	Winslow — operating as health center

18. As the reader will see in the narrative, John is frequently criticized for his stinginess and lack of cooperation towards his family. Navajos expect a great deal of reciprocal social and economic support among all those defined as relatives.

19. According to Letter Book No. 26 (p. 477) of the Fort Defiance Agency and other sources, the Franciscan Fathers mission at Saint Michaels was established in October 1898. The mission boarding school run by the Sisters of the Blessed Sacrament opened shortly thereafter, and by 1/23/1900, Frank Walker was serving as the mission interpreter. About a month later, on 2/21/1900, Charlie Mitchell, one of the Navajo headmen, visited the mission for the first time.

The Fathers held their first baptism at Saint Michaels on 4/4/1900. Two years later, on 4/3/1902, with Father Leopold as missionary, their religious instruction at the Fort Defiance school was begun. That year also saw the start of construction of the mission's elementary school on 3/1/1902. The Saint Michaels' post office was established on September 1, 1902, and by 12/3/1902, the elementary school had opened, with forty-six children enrolled.

Although records at Saint Michaels did not always include names of Navajo employees, judging from Frank's contact with Father Anselm Weber it is most likely that Frank worked there between 1904 and 1906. Mission records from 4/12 to 5/12/1906 indicate a Navajo, Francis Mitchell, was paid for work at the mission during that time. Franciscan Father Emanuel and Frank himself doubt that these records refer to Frank, since they both remember a slightly younger Francis Mitchell who was also in the area at that time and whose name was often jokingly interchanged with Frank's in school and at the Saint Michaels Mission. For an excellent account of the Franciscans' work among the Navajos, the establishment of various missions, Anselm Weber and much early history see Wilken (1955). Rademaker (1976a and b), *Padres' Trail* (October-November 1973) and *The Navajo Times* (11/29/73) also contain useful information.

20. Both Frank's children and his grandchildren were well acquainted with this particular incident in his life story, and encouraged him to tell it repeatedly.

21. Although information about the establishment of the Franciscan mission in Chinle is available in Wilken (1955) and *Padres' Trail* (June-July 1973), the best source is a six-page typed manuscript by Father Leopold filed in the Historical Folder at the mission. When Father Leopold began going to Chinle for two to three weeks at a time, the only white people there were the Days (trader and family) and Father Leopold. The Days housed Father Leopold and occasionally others who came to Chinle to consider a mission site, on the strength of the rumors that a government school would soon be built there. 1903 brought a post office (Link 1968:40) and a mission site to Chinle. The mission site was selected on 4/16/1903, and on 6/24/03 a letter was sent to Washington, D. C., requesting a land grant for this purpose. On 9/27/1903, Father Leopold held his first public service in Chinle, and on 10/10/1903, the requested land was granted.

In the summer of 1904, Father Leopold and Brother Placidus came to Chinle and lived in a small "dugout" room in an old stone building near what later became García's store. On 10/15/1905, the site for the mission house was selected by Fathers Weber, Leopold and Ketchum, with the latter being from Washington, D.C. By January 1906, the Franciscan residence was habitable rather than completely finished.

It appears that Frank Mitchell worked at the Chinle mission after the middle of February 1906 until August of that year. On 2/19/1906, Brother Placidus died at the Chinle Mission. Father Leopold was left alone, and this corresponds to the time when Frank left Saint Michaels and was encouraged by Father Weber to go to Chinle to help Father Leopold. Frank remembered that Father Leopold had been in Chinle for more than a year and that the Father's house was already set up when he went there to work. In August of 1906, Brother Placidus was replaced by Brother Gervase, and Father Leopold was no longer alone. Thus, Frank's employment was probably terminated at this time.

In the summer of 1906, the mission house was finished. About this time, Son of the Late Little Blacksmith also came to Chinle to serve as law officer and peacemaker. Mission records show that he used the land at the mission for pasturing his horse.

In January of 1907, Father Marcellus went to Chinle, where he remained through 1915, when he went to Saint Michaels. Later, on 7/24/1907, a ceremony was held, raising the Franciscan Father's home in Chinle to a residence. The Annunciation Mission Church was built between 1910-1911, during the time when the government boarding school at Chinle was also under construction.

22. The Franciscan Fathers are commonly referred to by their first names, following the title of "Father." The complete names for the Franciscans involved in Frank Mitchell's story include: Father Cormac Antram, Father Berard Haile, Father Leopold Ostermann, Father Emanuel Trockur and Father Marcellus Troester.

23. The Chinle school construction dates vary according to source. Seya Mitchell (8/3/71) stated that construction began in 1910, but the school did not open until 1913. Records at the Franciscan mission in Chinle show two dates, one where construction began in the fall of 1910 and school opened on 4/1/1910 and another, where construction began in the fall of 1909 and school opened 4/1/1910.

Frank, having already suggested 1908, 1909 and 1905 as dates for his return to Chinle, refused to contribute to the attempt to date the Chinle school. Instead, he explained that he never cared to remember what happened or keep track of what happened at certain times before he learned the Blessingway. Only after that was he able to remember things clearly.

Other sources use the dates shown below for the establishment of boarding and other schools on the reservation:

School	Events	Date	Source
Fort Defiance	Boarding school building constructed	1881	Left-Handed Mexican Clansman 1952:1
	First day school	1869	Link 1968:19
		1869	Frink 1968:2,88
		1870	McNitt 1963
	Construction of Boarding school	1879-81	Frink 1968:2,88
	Boarding school opens (with 20 pupils)	1881	Left-Handed Mexican Clansman 1952:8
	Boarding school opens	1882	Frink 1968:2
	Boarding school established	1881	Underhill 1953:227
	Boarding school opens (with 84 pupils who did not stay)	1882	Underhill 1953:226
	Boarding school opens	1883	McNitt 1963
		1883	Link 1968:19
Grand Junction, Colorado	Boarding school established	1886	Underhill 1953:227
[1887 — Law making education for Indian children compulsory]			
Moqui-Keams Canyon	Boarding school	1887	Underhill 1953:227
Fort Lewis	Boarding school established	1892	Underhill 1953:227
Saint Michaels	Sisters of the Blessed Sacrament Mission Boarding school established	1898	Frink 1968:95 Underhill 1953:227
Tohatchi	Boarding school established	1900	Underhill 1953:227
Tuba City	Boarding school established	1901	Underhill 1953:227
Rehoboth	Christian Reformed Mission Boarding school established	1901	Underhill 1953:227
Saint Michaels	Mission Elementary school established	1902	Link 1968:59
Shiprock	Boarding school established	1907	Underhill 1953:227
Leupp	Boarding school established	1909	Underhill 1953:227
Chinle	Boarding school established	1910	Underhill 1953:227
Crownpoint	Boarding school established	1912	Underhill 1953:227
Ganado	Presbyterian Mission Boarding school established	1912	Underhill 1953:227
	Presbyterian Mission Boarding school established	1901	Frink 1968:95
Toadlena	Boarding school established	1913	Underhill 1953:227
Chinle	School plant still used in 1976 opens	1919	Van Valkenburgh 1941:39
Fort Wingate	School plant still used in 1976 opens	1925	Van Valkenburgh 1941:39
Saint Michaels	Mission High School opens	1946	Link 1968:59
First public school on the reservation at Fort Defiance for the Navajos		1954	Link 1968:19; Frink 1968

24. According to Frank, Chic, Augusta and others, Son of the Late Little Blacksmith was known both in Navajo and English by his Navajo name, *Atsidi yazhini'biye'*. Seya Mitchell (8/2/71) referred to him as "the first headman in the Chinle area," and stated that Nelson Gorman helped, too, but other records refer to *Atsidi yazhini'biye'* as a policeman and peacemaker and distinguish between him and the community leaders or headmen.

25. The Superintendent was Reuben Perry. According to Letter Book No. 29 (5/8/1903-1/5/1904) from the Fort Defiance Agency, on 9/26/1903, the reservation was divided and Reuben Perry was put in charge of the southern half, effective 10/1/1903. Perry served in this capacity until 10/16/06.

26. For what is probably the most complete account of this incident, which occurred late in October or early in November 1905, see McNitt (1963:284-290). This account is based on National Archives Records, Navajo File No. 121, and conversations with Lucie Cousins, wife of Charlie Cousins, one of the traders in Chinle at that time. Another account may be found in Wilken (1955:173-178). Two other accounts appear as footnotes 31 and 32 below.

27. As McNitt (1963:287) suggests, different sources provide different names for the troublemakers. Frank's story compares to the others as shown below:

McNitt (1963:286,287,290)	Perry's Letter (McNitt *Ibid.*, n. 11)	Wilken (1955:173-178)	Frank Mitchell
Dlad	Gladhy	Dlad	Dlad
Ush-tilly	Ush Tilly	—	—
Tsosi-begay	tsosa-Begay	Tsossi ni'Biye	—
Dinet-lakai	Denet Lakai	Dinelgai	Diné'łgai
Winslow	Winslow	Winslow	Winslow
Tol Zhin	Tol Zhin	—	—
Do-yal-ke	Do-Yal-Ke	Doyaltqihi	—
—	—	Linni	—
—	—	—	Ahyeehi

28. Among the earliest automobiles on the reservation was that of Lorenzo Hubbell, a high-wheeled, open car which Sam Day II often drove for him in the early 1900s. Roads were few and very rough, and tourists were kept away from much of the reservation by these road conditions and lack of cars. By 1915, the era of the automobile had arrived. In 1913, C. N. Cotton actively supported the routing of the transcontinental automobile highway through Gallup, and other traders, including Charles L. Day, participated in a Gallup-to-Albuquerque motorcade to increase publicity for the issue (McNitt 1963:215, 223-224). According to Link (1968:25), in 1915 five Navajos owned cars: Chee Dodge, Tom Damon, Willie Damon, Hosteen Yazza and Clitsoi Dedman.

29. In the early days before the formal establishment of the Navajo Tribe and its Council, officers and policemen, agents were assisted in their law

enforcement duties mainly by former war chiefs and Indian scouts, especially those who had earned prestige during the Fort Sumner incarceration and various Indian wars. For example, in 1872 Agent Thomas Keam organized a force of scouts to stop cattle-stealing. Ninety-five Navajos joined and earned five dollars a month, while their leader, Manuelito, earned eight during the few months the force operated. Ten of these men were kept on at five dollars per month when Congress ordered the original force disbanded (Underhill 1953:203-204). These men served in much the same way as did the policemen who later assisted Son of the Late Little Blacksmith, namely as trouble scouts and message carriers among the agents, other government officials, headmen and the People.

The Navajo Mounted Police were officially established in 1934 and reorganized in 1936 as the Navajo Patrol. Later this Branch of Law and Order was reorganized as the Navajo Police Department and in 1959 was placed under tribal jurisdiction (Link 1968:105).

30. See Reichard (1963) and Wyman (1970) for further Origin and Creation Story details about White Shell Woman, who is often equated with Changing Woman.

31. According to McNitt (1963:290), the seven prisoners were taken to Alcatraz on 1/10/1906 but were transferred to Fort Huachuca in south-eastern Arizona in August 1906, after the Indian Rights Association intervened for shorter sentences and imprisonment in a drier climate. Frank's ideas about the length of the prison terms do not match McNitt's information, which states that Winslow, Tsosi-begay and Ush-Tilly were released on 10/20/1906 after about eight months, and Tol Zhin, Dlad, Dinet-lakai and Do-yal-Ke in June 1907, after an imprisonment of about seventeen months.

32. Father Leopold's six-page typed manuscript on Chinle (housed at Our Lady of Fatima Mission, Chinle) contains the following version of this same incident: "Shortly after Father Leopold arrived [in Chinle], a group kidnapped the Superintendent near Chinle in anger over his arrest of a Navajo from Chinle for having more than one wife. The Superintendent was released after saying he needed to change the arrest at Fort Defiance. He went back there and returned with soldiers who arrested all the kidnappers. The ringleaders were sent to the Penitentiary and others were jailed for participating."

33. Van Valkenburgh (1941:39) gives another variant of the Perry incident: "In 1906 Navajo Agent Ruben Perry, while attempting to force Navajo children into school at Fort Defiance, was overpowered and held captive by DoyaL thi'ih, Silent One, and his followers for two days. Soldiers later captured the rebels and they were sent for a year to Alcatraz Prison in San Francisco Bay and later to Fort Huachuca, Arizona."

34. McNitt (1963:285-288) states that several days after the attack on Agent Perry, trouble erupted in the form of a theft of silver and turquoise at

Cousin's Trading Post in Chinle. This was resolved by the well-timed arrival of part of Captain H. O. Williard's K Troop, Fifth Cavalry from Fort Defiance, the Fort Defiance headman, Welo, and several other headmen. Further trouble expected by Agent Perry from whiskey consumption during a Yeibichai near Sam Day's post did not materialize.

35. According to McNitt (1963:289), the headmen involved in helping round up those involved in the Perry incident included: Silversmith, Atsitty yazzie-begay, Bish-klan, Bechi, Welo, Hosteen Tsosi, Hosteen Dilawishe and Nosh-gully. "Hosteen Dilawishe," or Man Who Shouts, was Frank's father-in-law.

36. This refers to "The Checkerboard Area," created by the Allotment Act of 1887, where Indian land allotments in the New Mexico area were interspersed among non-Indian holdings.

5. Family Man

Frank meets Tall Woman... Man Who Shouts advises them... they start raising a family... Frank works at the sawmill... the fight between two white men at Tohatchi Sheep Dip... conditions at home and Windway ceremonial for Tall Woman... sicknesses and deaths in Frank's natal family... getting a wagon... working on the bridge and the Chinle school... freighting... the story of Black Mountain Man... more children are born... a mule gets into Frank's corn to its sorrow... ceremonial treatment for Frank's back pains and his other ailments: Beautyway, Ghostway, Shootingway, Chiricahua Windway... Frank assists at an archaeological excavation... his thoughts on the ancient people... humorous use of sacred songs.

While I was still working for the Franciscan Fathers at Saint Michaels, my family moved out to the rim of the Canyon towards Chinle and stayed there in the summer. When I came back from working at Saint Michaels and began working at the Chinle mission, I spent most of my time with my parents as I have already mentioned. My older brother Jim was married to my future wife's sister, and was living there with her family on the next hill across the Chinle Wash. I would come out here in the early spring and bring the horses out from the Canyon to help my brother get the fields ready for farming and planting. I used to go over there and visit him. That is when I finally noticed this woman; she was just a young girl then.

Well, when I started to go out visiting my brother, I really went there to see that girl. I would see her when I came to help Jim with the farming, and there were a couple of nights that I came to see her when nobody knew about it. We gradually were getting close together. We spent a whole summer like that, and then in the fall we just got together, and we did not tell anybody what our plans were or anything. Well, we thought that nobody knew about it, but someone was already spying on us, and later, when I came over during the day again to see her, her father told me that her family knew all about what was going on between the two of us. He said that we might as well come out in the clear and start making a living for ourselves, because if we were

[120]

going to live together it was time to start getting the things that we were going to need to live with and to use in our future life. No one else was going to get them for us, so we might as well come out in the open and start making a living the right way, settling down there at her place.[1]

For a couple of times I went back and forth from her people's house to my folks; I was not really sure where or how to start out, and I just went between the two houses. One time, after I had returned to her place after spending a few days with my parents, her father, Man Who Shouts, came there and started asking me some questions about my life. He talked well because he was a headman and a Blessingway singer. He asked whether I had any horses or any kind of property. I said, "No, I don't have any kind of property. I don't even have a horse. The horses I use usually belong to somebody else; I borrow them to go to these different places that I want to go to. All I can call my own are the garments I'm wearing. Outside of those, I don't own any property at all. As for sheep, I do not even have one. Of course, my mother has a good flock, but since she has been sick, we have had to use them to hire singers. Now she has run the flock down almost to nothing. So I do not own anything there either."

After I told him about my full background, he told me this woman was the same way. He said, "This woman has a mother and father who own property. We have a large band of sheep,[2] cattle, horses and a wagon and some jewelry. She owns about three head of sheep out of that whole flock." He gave us a good talking to. He said, "You probably have sisters and brothers who own their own private property, but you have nothing to do with that. It is not yours; it belongs to them. The same thing is true with my daughter. She has brothers and sisters who have personal property, but she has nothing to do with that; it is not hers and she has no share in it. So you will never get ahead that way. Just get together and live like man and wife and start putting something away for the future, for your use."

Man Who Shouts told me if I wanted to live with her it would be best if we started out the right way instead of me just going back and forth between the two houses, spending a couple of days over there and coming back over here for a few more days. He said if I were just going to do that, later on after we started having children, I would end up in a mess, without anything to feed the children and with nobody to look after them. He told me if I was going to live with his daughter that I was to settle down there at her house and help with the work that was to be done around there, like herding the sheep, and plowing and working in the fields. He said later on we could start out on our own; we could divide up the little we got there and start living on it ourselves.

Man Who Shouts also told me what it was like to be married and to be living together making a living for yourself and your children. He said that that was a very hard thing if you were not prepared for it and if no one told you about it. He talked to me almost all night there, telling me about what it was like to make your own living and how hard it was. He told me that things were not going to be as easy as I thought.

It wasn't too long after I had started seeing this girl who went by the name Tall Woman[3] that they found out and her father had that long talk with me. Her father came over to see my father and talked it over, and then both of them came down and talked to us about it. They got us together and both of them said that if we were going to be getting together, we might as well start making a living for ourselves, because it was not going to do us any good if we were just going to run after one another.

When they got us together they talked with us and told us that things were not always going to be just the way we figured they would be. It was a hard life that we were going to live together, and it would be better if they gave us a little talk about what it would be like to make a living for ourselves. So they talked with us; her father was a very well-spoken man; he told me in a very clear way that I might as well make up my mind and start. Her father asked me what kind of a man I was, where I was from, and what I was doing around here and everything like that. I told him those things and that I was working for the Fathers here. He asked me if I had ever been married before or if I had ever been with a woman before, and I told him about the woman at Saint Michaels. I did not hide anything; I told him about knocking that woman out cold and running off. Man Who Shouts just laughed about that, but at the same time, he told me if I were going to marry his daughter, I had better not do that to her or treat her like that, because that was not what we were getting together for. He really talked to me, and his talk was worth listening to. I was really glad many years later that he had told me all of those things and that he had come right out and told me what it would be like.

Man Who Shouts told us we must plan for the future. We would have a home and responsibilities as husband and mother. My father and Man Who Shouts discussed these things in our presence. They told us to make up our minds about how we were going to do things in the future. My father said that Man Who Shouts was well respected and well-to-do and that I had better try to imitate him as much as possible. Man Who Shouts told me that I was not coming to their place just to be a servant to them. I should have a home and start acquiring property that would be for me and my children. He said that in our early married life we could depend on his daughter's family for subsistence but that we could not do that for very long.

After they talked to us, we were given to each other. They did not perform any ceremony for us when that happened, so we started living together publicly right after that; I started living there like that with this woman in the fall.

So from that time I just started living there helping out all I could. This woman and her people lived on the other side of the wash, not in this area where we are now. They lived over there where there are piles and piles of sand now. At that time, that was the best farmland in the area; over there against the hill is where the irrigation system was. Other people lived over there too, and over here where we are today was just one big unused space.

In those days there was no sand and no tumbleweed over there. The wind did not even blow very hard. In the early spring the wind blew, but not half as much as today. It blew for a short time, and we would know when it was going to stop. As soon as those winds calmed down, we would go out and work on their farm, plowing and planting, and because the wind did not blow right after we planted, the ground did not dry out so quickly. That is how we could raise such good crops.

But later the winds started blowing as they do today. They blow so hard that you cannot even see, and they dry up the ground in no time. Even if you plant when the ground is still damp, the wind dries the top of it so fast that by the time the corn has a chance to start growing, the top of the dirt is so dry that it does not get as big and as good as it did when I was living with Tall Woman's family. Now the winds also blow all the tumbleweeds; these come out and form great big bushes. The winds blow them off in a certain direction and then later blow piles and piles of sand on top of them, making sand dunes.

As I have said, Man Who Shouts was a headman. When I got to know him, I learned what his teachings to the People were. I learned that Man Who Shouts' talks were different somewhat from those that Son of the Late Little Blacksmith used to give when I was working at the Chinle Mission. I could see that they differed in a lot of ways. And the reason for that, I think, was that Man Who Shouts was using the old Navajo way of talking. As I observed it, it kind of confused me; the two talked so differently that I couldn't get the run of the language. I used to wonder why those talks were so different, but I guess that they both meant the same thing, although I did not understand that.

When I started living with my wife at her home, I was in daily contact with my father-in-law, Man Who Shouts. On my side, my mother was sickly and so were my brothers; they started dying off. In those days there were no hospitals anywhere.[4] They had just a small one at Fort Defiance, but it mostly issued medicine. For serious cases there was not any good hospital to go to. The People did not use the hospital very much; they depended mainly on the local singers for every sickness they had.

For several years I stayed around home here in Chinle living that way without working anywhere. A while after we were married, the firstborn was a girl[5]; we nicknamed her "Being a Woman" and "Billy Mahi" as she was growing up, but now she is known to white people as Mary Davis. Then another girl was born; we nicknamed her Aheejabah, but she was known in school as Mary Mitchell. She died later while she was in school at Albuquerque. Then a boy, Seya, was born. He never had a pet name around here. When they started building the school here in Chinle, Seya was a little boy and another child was about due; as nearly as I can figure, Tall Woman

and I started living together as man and wife about 1904.[6] I guess it was
about six years after I got married that they began building the school. That
was 1910.

After several years of staying home not working anywhere and just
taking care of my children, I got word that there was some work available at
the sawmill[7] in Fort Defiance. At that time the sawmill was new; it was just
beginning to operate. I moved over there and started working. I gradually was
able to start putting things aside for my family. Of course, I remembered the
advice of my father-in-law, and I kept that in mind.

When I worked at the sawmill, this other man by the name of John
Smith and I were in charge of a logging crew. We used a great big two-wheeled
cart to haul the logs to the mill. Those wheels were about as high as the
ceiling of my hogan here. That cart had a big log chain attached to the rear of
it, and you had to tip it a special way to load the logs on.

It usually took two men to handle that cart. The back part did not stick
out too far; there was another joint in the center and then a tongue, just like
on a wagon, way up at the other end. John and I would drive that around and
then set it at a certain place where we could pull those logs together with
horses to load them. The way we'd load them was to have a pole leaning up
against the wagon so that we could roll them up on there that way. If the logs
were not too thick, we could put five on one cart; if they were pretty thick,
then only three logs would be a load for us.

We'd fasten the logs with a chain and then hook the team onto the
tongue end of the cart. The ends of the logs would drag on the ground. While
one man drove the team, the other would sit on the ends of the logs. There
were no brakes on those wagons. The man who was sitting on the logs had to
put rocks on them and use his own weight to help slow that cart down when
we came to hills. As you went down the road, the cart would zigzag back and
forth because it was only two-wheeled. You were liable to fall off; it was like
tying a barrel to a tree limb and trying to ride that. That was the way you had
to ride those logs. John Smith drove the team most of the time, and I stayed
behind as brakeman. Sometimes I walked alongside of that cart; when we
came to steep hills, I used to jump on those logs to add weight to slow the
motion. I really liked that work, although it was very hard, especially when it
rained and when it was winter. It was not too bad when it was dry.

When we were not hauling, we were out in the woods. I supervised men
who were chopping trees down. There was always a group doing that. Then
there was another group down at the mill to run those logs through.

When we brought the logs in from the mountain, we would haul them
right to the door of the big building where the sawing took place. We would
take the horses off the wagon and turn the whole thing around. The logs were
already on the ground, so all we had to do was take the chains off and pull
them out of the way. Another man stood there, and he knew how to go

about things, so there was not much heavy lifting, even though they were big logs. That man would follow the logs on into the inside of the mill. They had special tools they used to roll the logs into the mill.

Inside there, they had special equipment to handle all of those logs and put them into position so they would go to where the machines were running. The logs went down a belt operated by a steam engine. First the outside bark was sawn off. The man standing there would turn the logs over while the steam cleaned the outside first. Then they would saw into the bark; they made the pieces very large. They cut off so much first and then turned it over and cut some more. By the end of that part they had a big square piece of lumber. Then the wood went to where they cut it to whatever thickness they wanted. There was a man out there who gathered up the wood and stacked it. Another one stood over on the side where the sawdust came down on the ground and shoveled that out of the way so it did not pile up. Now they have electric machines to do those things which we did there by hand.

During the week, we lived in six or seven log cabins right there near the sawmill. The cabins that are around that old sawmill now are not the ones we lived in. I think those first ones are all gone now. The only big house there was where the white man who supervised the whole thing lived.

After the sawmill started growing, people moved in there with their families and started putting up dwellings. Traders moved in, and a school was built there among the new cabins. That was after my time. The people living there on the north side of the mill, on the hillside, are the old-timers. They have lived there all their lives. They did not come from other places.

We worked mostly with Fisk pine; that's all there is high up in those mountains. We never had any accidents there because we watched things carefully. We got to know where the steep hills were and when we needed to put on the brakes. We knew it so well that we could even haul those logs through those roads at night.

When the snow came, we did not use that big two-wheeled cart; instead we used a sled. Those sleds were built high from the ground and were made to hold the logs. They had a platform box on them, made from lumber about twelve by twelve in thickness and fixed up with holes and pegs. The pegs were set in there to hold the logs in place.

You had to be careful how you loaded that, too. Sometimes we used a horse to pull the logs onto it; we would put the chain over the log and then the horse would pull it over. Sometimes we used mules, but they would get so stubborn you could not do anything with them. They would just pull and pull, and before you knew it they would just turn the whole thing over. I would get angry when that happened. But nothing else ever happened because we all knew we had to be very careful of how we did our work there.

In the early fall, we would start hauling logs to stack up in camp. Even when it became winter, we kept working if logs were available. We piled those logs up near the mill so in case of a heavy snow they would be there. Of course we could not do any logging in the heavy snow, but inside the mill where they were sawing logs, they would continue to work as long as there were logs to saw. In those days we used to get really deep snows. We used the scraps from the mill for firewood in our cabins. When the weather was bad, they would close the mill, and then we workers would haul that scrap lumber to where it was needed. I got quite a bit from that for myself. Always in the early fall when we knew that the snow was going to come, we would haul a lot of that wood in and stack it up so high that in the wintertime we never had to worry about hauling any more way down into our camp.

When the weather got a little better in the spring, the snow melted and the ground thawed out and got boggy. Then you could get into mud holes with that logging wagon. Even though it had wide tires on the wheels, still it used to get stuck. When that happened, of course, the only thing that you could do was to unload your logs right there and pull the wagon out of the mud.

There was always something to be done around there, and even when we were not logging, I always had other hauling to do with my team and wagon for people in that area. There never was a time when I was without a job or not doing something while I worked at the mill.

Sometimes in the summer we would be excused from work at the sawmill so we could help with hauling wood to where they were dipping sheep.[8] At the Fort Defiance agency they did not have enough horses or teams to take care of the dipping operations on the reservation. In cases like that, sometimes they would detail our team to do that work, to help with that dipping operation. They used quite a bit of wood then to heat up the water at those dips before they added the chemicals to it. I would always be on the go in the summer, hauling wood to those sheep-dipping areas.

One time we were told to haul some wood to the Tohatchi dipping vat with our sawmill equipment. There was a school over there already and a sheep dip there, and all of the people in the area were to help. That time we almost had a fight with a white man who was in charge. In my early days I sometimes lost my temper pretty easily. I was known for that nature of mine.

A man who was an animal doctor from Fort Defiance would go over the mountain with us to Tohatchi in the wagon. I guess he was in charge of the dipping. They used wood there for fuel too. This white man who took us over there told us to go ahead and haul wood to the dipping place from the school there.

On the trip, we settled down for the night at the foot of the mountain because it was getting late. We started cooking there; the food was provided from Fort Defiance; I guess we were on a government job. This man got out a whole slab of salt pork and cut some of it up; we used the drippings from it for frying other things. Instead of putting the whole thing back in the wagon, we just left the salt pork on the ground at the head of our bedrolls that night. After we ate, we put it in a sack and we all went to bed. That night a coyote came and took the whole slab; we did not even know when that happened, but in the morning we found the tracks; it took the whole slab of salt pork out into the woods somewhere.

So we went on to Tohatchi. The sheep dip was a little ways from the school, and people were gathering there. We went over to the school in the wagon and started hauling some of the school wood. The principal of that school found out that we were hauling that wood to the sheep dip. He got angry and came over and told our boss, this white man, that he wasn't supposed to take that wood from the school. He said, "You've got big men, you've got a team, you've got a wagon; go and get your own wood from the mountain."

The doctor got angry at him for what he had said; the man from Tohatchi was leaning on a stick there after he had told our boss to go tell his men to bring in their own wood. The animal doctor kicked the stick out from under the school principal. That made him angry, too, but he just went back across the creek to the school.

We put up our tent there because we were camping. We put everything in the tent. The school principal came out several minutes later with a gun in his hand. He came running toward us. Our boss from Fort Defiance went into the tent and took out his gun too. They almost had a battle there.

I did not want any trouble like that where I was, so I ran up to this white man I had come with and grabbed that gun. I told him I did not want any trouble and to just let the man alone, let him cool off. He was mad; he wanted to shoot that white man. But I told him not to. Then I took the gun away and took it back into the tent, and I sat in there holding that gun for a long time.

That other white man never took any action. I guess he was trying to bluff us. Finally somebody else came out and took the school principal back to his house. Then we packed all of our things into our wagon, took down our tent and started back for the sawmill after dark. We got back to Fort Defiance early in the morning, towards dawn.

I don't know the names of either of those men. The one we went with was a doctor from Fort Defiance, and he was the one who knew how much medicine to put in the water for sheep dipping. When we got back, he went right to the main headquarters and reported what had happened. All the details were taken down on paper. Later that afternoon, we were called in and questioned. Of course, our story was not different from what the doctor had told. Four days later the doctor was called in again to tell some more men who were there what had happened, so he told them the same thing again. That other man was called in to Fort Defiance later. I heard that he was told to leave. I guess right there they got rid of a white man off the reservation.

We were asked to go back over there and finish our work, but the doctor said he did not care to go back over there and face that man again. Now those doctors had certain areas they tended to in those days. They were under the Department of Agriculture, and during dipping season they were detailed to help with the dipping operations in certain places.

There is one thing that I occasionally think of about that trip. Our people used to say that anything like what happened with the coyote was a bad sign. If a coyote came around or you saw one or it passed over your path, it was not good. When you think about that coyote coming over to us at night and taking that meat, there must be some truth in that. Anything that involves a coyote never comes out well. The following day those men probably would have killed each other if it had not been for me.

A year or so later, this doctor left Fort Defiance and sent me a letter from Albuquerque. That's where those doctors usually came from. He mentioned the time when I grabbed the gun as he came out of the tent, and he thanked me for interfering so that nothing serious had happened. He told me that he was not sure what he would have done to that man at Tohatchi if it had not been for me. He said, "If you hadn't grabbed the gun from me, well, no doubt I would have done something I shouldn't have. I might have killed that man, and who knows if I would now be in the penitentiary or have even lost my own life for that. I want to express my thanks to you for doing that."

That's the way we were working there. Sometimes we used those vehicles to go into Fort Defiance. There were just a few of us working there at the sawmill, and every so often they would take us to Fort Defiance to buy groceries and bring us back in that same wagon. I think I spent about five years in all doing that kind of work over there.

While I worked over there, Tall Woman was here at home taking care of the children. After work on Saturdays, I would saddle up my horse and come home. Sometimes I would get off at noon on Saturdays, and sometimes I would leave right after working hours on Friday. I kept one horse over there to travel back and forth on. I would come over to my wife and the children and check on them and see that they had enough supplies. Then I would leave home sometime Sunday night in time to get back on the job early in the morning at the mill.[9]

When I was home, Man Who Shouts used to talk to me about saving and preparing for the future. I was making about twenty-five dollars a month at the sawmill, compared to the fifteen dollars that I used to make when I worked with my brother John at C. C. Manning's store in Fort Defiance. Sometimes when you are married, you are more or less the servant of the girl's family. Some of those people have no feeling for their daughters' husbands. But Man Who Shouts was not like that. He did not order me around like a servant. He talked with me and helped prepare me for the future. He said, "Every time we butcher, you eat part of it. But don't be depending on us for that forever. Save some things of your own." He did not order me to help with the work around there because of my job at the sawmill at that time.

While I was working away from home like that, the Shirley family offered Chee Dodge's old mother-in-law to me. I refused her because that group wanted to use me like a servant to take care of their property. I told them I already had a woman. And when they asked how well off she was I said, "Her people have some cattle."

In those days, while my wife was a young woman, she began to get sick. It started after she had had the first three children; before we started living together I do not know whether she had good health or not. But after she had borne about three children, she began to complain about indigestion. You know that that is very common with women. Sometimes she would get it quite badly. When she started these complaints, her father was still living. Of course Man Who Shouts was a singer himself, and although he and his wife were able to finance major ceremonies, he was kind of stingy with his possessions. So he himself did some minor ceremonies for her; he had some small ceremonies like cutting prayersticks and making small sandpaintings for her. He also was a hand-trembler, and he performed that for her to learn the causes of her condition. Then he would do one of his own minor ceremonies for that. When he did not know the proper ceremony, he would hire someone else to do it. We carried on that way for some time.

The first large ceremony we had for her was the five-night Navajo Windway.[10] We did that because her face was all paralyzed and crooked. The first one was performed for her by Ugly Base of the Mountain Man, who lived down at Many Farms. He did just the first four days of that; he only completed the four fire ceremonies because he was not qualified to give the whole ceremony yet; he had not been trained to complete it, so he did not want to do the final night. He said, "I'll complete the fire ceremonies because I know them. But for the final night, I'll let my brother, Slim Base of the Mountain Man do that." After he went home, Tall Woman felt a lot better. And since she had some results from that, we did not see any reason to have that man's brother come. As far as I was concerned, I did not have the financial means to stand the expense of anything like that. We depended mainly on her father for those things.

While I was working at the sawmill, my brother Jimmy Mitchell's wife died, and he moved back from Black Mountain, where they had been grazing sheep. John Mitchell was back from Fort Defiance then, and he talked with him about getting married in the regular way. They went over to Tsaile and got a girl who is still alive today. Her name is Genevieve, and she is a clan relative of Slim Man. This was the only time that Jimmy Mitchell was married in the regular way. They stayed together three or four years. Their daughter is now married to Nadi Davis of Lukachukai Boarding School. One of Jimmy's nephews, George Mitchell, was left to head the family of four boys. Every now and then Jimmy Mitchell would come out from Tsaile to Black Mountain to check on this first family of his – his own two boys by his first wife and also Billy Mitchell and Billy's older brother George Mitchell.

When Jimmy Mitchell got sick, he did not last very long. They sent an old man down here as a messenger. He took his time visiting down the Canyon, and he turned around at the store, leaving word there for us. Jimmy Mitchell's boy and I got the news secondhand, and we rode over there on horseback and found the hogan burning.[11] He had died the night before and was buried then. He had been sick and had died within two days.

My mother was sick then too, and was getting worse, and so was my sister Little Woman, who had been living with Star Gazer's Son for five years. They had no children, and then he left her. Later she had two children by Late Man's Son; the first was a boy who died in infancy and the second a girl who died at three months. My sister started to get sick before the second child was born. Late Man's Son left her after that.

During those times while my mother and sister were sick, my younger brother Sam was working with me at the sawmill. I had taken him over there with me during my second or third year there. He had no occupation, he just did odd jobs around there. During that time there were not many people from this area working at that place, just people from there. Others started working there from many different places after I left there. Then they started the stores and schools.

Sam was living with Willie Shirley's mother, Yellow Haired Woman, at this time. He had the name "Generous Warrior"; he was given that name during a Squaw Dance. It belonged to someone in the past who was a warrior and went stealing; this man brought enemy property home and gave it to his relatives. They beat the drum all night long and in the morning serenaded him, and then he gave away his property.

Sam got sick after about three years of living with Yellow Haired Woman. This was the first woman he took up with. She was much older than he, and they had no children. When he got sick he left her and came back to Chinle and began living here with his brothers. He had tuberculosis and died before our mother did.

My mother started getting much worse about this time, and I started taking care of her. By then, Star Gazer's Son had already left her; I am not sure why he did that because I was home only two or three days at a time, but it probably was because she was getting sick. My mother had been sick for a long time, and when she got worse I started helping out. By then Little Man, one of the boys she had had with Star Gazer's Son, had grown up to about nineteen years; he and George and Billy Mitchell had been growing up together and taking care of my mother while she was sick. The sheep were being neglected because of that. Some nights the boys did not have time to sleep, and then the next day they would sleep until night time and then come home. Once when that happened, those boys traced the sheep which had wandered off and found that two coyotes had killed almost all of them.

My sister Little Woman was very sick by then too; she and my mother were too sick to care for each other. Because they were poor, I got them next to me so I could look after them. I built a hogan for my mother, and we had a ceremony in it. Then she died, and we vacated that place and moved our winter home up nearer to Lukachukai. I tore down that hogan I had just built and put it up across the road, where our cornfield is now. My brothers, Sam and Jim Mitchell, came here with me to help take care of our sister Little Woman. Her second baby died in that new hogan, so we moved up the road from Jabah's place. That was where my sister died; she had been sick for about two years, and she died a little more than a year after my mother. They both died from tuberculosis. After that, we moved again.

After my mother died, George and Billy Mitchell and Little Man stayed at the place where John later died. John was at Fort Defiance, and he took George over to Deer Springs, where he wanted to use him as a laborer without pay.[12] John's in-laws were against that, and they quarreled with him on that account. George just left to herd sheep for Little Jesus Man. After a while he left there, and Little Jesus Man gave him some sheep. Then George went with Little Man to live with Jim Mitchell who was operating a farm. They stayed there helping him, and George combined those sheep with Jim Mitchell's. Billy Mitchell was not there because he was in school. Eventually Little Man acquired some land near my alfalfa crop, and Jim Mitchell arranged for him to be married into his wife's family, to a daughter of his sister-in-law, over at his place. Little Man spent the spring over here irrigating and planting, but after that he never cared for that land, and everyone came around and used it. Little Man had inherited that land from my mother; all of her cooking things and her grinding stone were stored at Jim Mitchell's place. Little Man used them when he came down here to irrigate. He had some children with that woman Jim Mitchell got for him, but they are scattered all around now, and I do not know them personally.

During this time, my wife and I had a separate dwelling next to her father's and mother's place. We lived there with our children, so we were not imposing. I was also trying to help her family out.

My youngest brother by my father had come back from the Carlisle Institute at this time because he was beginning to feel sick. Dr. Wigglesworth, who was the first good doctor the People ever had, taught the People about tuberculosis and other contagious diseases. He told my brother Thomas to isolate himself at the first tuberculosis sanitorium that was built at Fort Defiance. Thomas went there, but he did not get any better. He gave up hope, and we came and took him out.

Then Thomas went back to the sawmill to where Herbert Mitchell's mother was living with his father, Little Leader. They got a singer who was considered to be one of the best ones in the area for the Flintway to come and do that ceremony. He came and treated Thomas for a month. He had him take all kinds of herbs internally; he used prayers and songs. After a month, the singer gave up all hope. He said, "My children, he is not getting any better. I have used everything that I know – herbs, songs, prayers. So I am giving up hope; I have never had to do this before. I don't know what is killing him. So I am leaving."

Thomas kept getting worse; a few days after the singer left, he died. A woman from Fort Defiance complained that she had had a child by him and wanted some property. Thomas had left everything at John's place. John gave me the use of Thomas' saddle because I had done more than anyone else to help. That woman never got any of that property because she had no proof of it and because Thomas had very little. While he was sick, I had to come to Chinle on horseback to get groceries and take them up there to him.

When he died, I spoke some harsh words to John. I found out that Thomas had been baptized by the mission. I went over to see John as soon as Thomas died. He came out, partly dressed, to meet me as I sat on my horse. "Go to the mission and ask their help in burying the body," I said to him.

"I've got other things to do; go yourself," he said to me.

Then I said, "When are you going to help us and lift a hand? You always have an excuse to get out of these obligations." After saying that, I came back to Chinle.

My father-in-law always gave me a consoling talk whenever I returned after a death had occurred in the family. He would say, "Those things are to be expected in this world. Take the natural course in this world. Be courageous and don't take it too seriously. These things are bound to happen. You will still be faced with it in the future with your offspring. You'll feel it more then than with your brothers and sisters; you'll feel the same for your mother and your children."

I admired that father-in-law of mine for his talks. He never shed a tear over a death in his family. He just gave instructions for preparing the body. He would go to the dead person and talk as though the body were alive. "So and so, you have gone away from us now. Your soul is out of your body, which will be laid away properly. We still recognize you as a relative, but don't ever bring harm to us in the future."

We went through many expenses having ceremonies for those with tuberculosis. At the beginning there were no doctors, so we depended on the singers to cure these sicknesses. The government had first-aid stations out here with emergency medicine. There was no transportation, no x-rays, hospitals, doctors or medicine. We just had one-, two- or five-night ceremonies, one- or two-hour sandpaintings. The singers would go according to the hand-trembler's advice. If the sickness lasted a long time, of course, we had to have long ceremonials. These were expensive. But you have to do something with your mother and relatives dying right there in front of you. You lose sleep worrying about it. If you have anything to pay the singer with, you do not consider the value of that; you just do it. That is why I cannot understand John never helping us. It was all of these bad experiences that taught me what to expect in life.

I stayed over there at the sawmill about five years, coming back and forth to visit my family. While I was working there, I heard that at Fort Defiance they had some wagons for anyone who wanted to work for them. I also heard you could get other people to help you if you wanted to acquire a wagon. I did not know how many times the government shipped wagons there to be issued that way for work. One time I heard that there were a lot of wagons being brought into Fort Defiance for that purpose. So I thought to myself, "Well, I think I'll take a chance; I think I'll go over there and ask for one of them and see what kind of an answer I get."

When I went over there and asked about a wagon and said I wanted to work for one, they questioned me on various things. They asked me if I had any children, if I had a farm and a home. And I said, "I do, I have a family and I have a farm." I told them that at Chinle I had these things. That helped me to get my application approved. Then I was asked where I wanted to do the work to earn this wagon. I said, "Well, at the sawmill; maybe I can get some men to help me to work for this." So I came back and reported that my application for a wagon was approved and that I was going to work for it at the sawmill. Then I got some relatives who were willing to pitch in and work it out with me. At the sawmill we were told they needed some log-cutters and that we could do that to earn the wagon. I was asked to find some men to do the chopping, and I did. Then I was asked to be the foreman on the crew, and I agreed. The wagon came after all the work was done. It did not take very long for me to earn this wagon with the help of others, and I went over to Fort Defiance to get it.[13]

In those days, the wagons were really substantial. Those wagons were equipped with a double board side, side boards and end gates and with wagon bows and canvas cover and with a seat and with a set of leather harness. When I got to Fort Defiance, the wagon was given to me. Then I hooked up the team to it and came sporting home with it, with the white canvas cover on.[14]

I worked at the sawmill a bit longer, but the pay was not enough. In those days they paid about twenty-five dollars. Things like clothes and food did not cost as much as they do now; in those times, if you spent about three dollars you had quite a lot to take home with you. But it was still hard for me to make ends meet and to take care of my children. They were still over here in Chinle.

I had two horses that I broke into driving that wagon; that is what I was using for getting around. I had an uncle who was very much pleased with the way I got that wagon, and he talked to me about it. "That is worthwhile," he said; "Now you must take good care of it and use it to take care of yourself and your children." This uncle of mine, Blind Blacksmith, used to go trading for mules among the Utes of Utah, and he would bring back mules and horses. Every time he went there, it took him quite a while to come back. He did not own a wagon, but he had two mules that were broken to driving the wagon, and he told me to go ahead and use them. So I was able to use those two mules and my own two horses from then on, at the sawmill and then later, hauling freight back and forth from Gallup. I took care of those mules for my uncle and broke them in so he would be able to hitch them to a wagon if he ever got one later.

When this uncle went to Utah, he used to tan buckskin. The place was full of wildlife, like deer and other animals. I guess the Mormons who lived there went out and killed a deer when they wanted one. So they always had plenty of deer hides there, but they did not know how to tan them. So he would just go over there for about a year or even two years at a time and settle down there and tan buckskins. He tanned many of them and would always know which ones were the best. They always told him to take some of them as a payment. So he always brought the best ones, the big ones, back over here. They were fixed up really nicely, and he would take them to the trading post here. At that time, buckskins were really high priced. My uncle would sell them for about thirty dollars and in return would get some Navajo rugs that were being traded at the store by the Navajos. Then he would take these rugs back to Utah and trade them for more mules from the Mormons. By the time this uncle stopped trading, he had about twelve mules that followed him around like dogs, and one big American horse that he rode. He must have been the first one out here to have a twenty-mule team train.

This is how this Blind Blacksmith made a living for himself and his family too. He was my mother's brother and was a Two Streams Meet Man like I am. At the same time as this, another of my mother's brothers, Short Hair and my clan uncles Chee Dodge and old man Charlie Mitchell were all over at Fort Wingate, where they were Indian scouts.

When Blind Blacksmith came back from Utah for good, I gave him back his mules and then I got myself another pair of horses. While I was still using his mules and my team of horses over at the sawmill, I heard that they were going to build a bridge over here on the mountain, this side of the sawmill, between the sawmill and Chinle. They were building a road straight through from Fort Defiance and the sawmill to Chinle. They had some work on that road and bridge that needed to be done. So I just resigned from my job at the sawmill and came home. By then I was pretty well fixed up. I had my wagon, a team of horses, a team of mules, some extra horses, and my children had plenty of clothes and food. It seemed as though I was the only one here in Chinle who had a wagon to travel around in at that time.

When I started working on that bridge, I did the same jobs that I had done over at the sawmill. I hauled logs for that bridge down from the top of the mountain with horses. Of course, those people working on the bridge did not have carts like the ones we used at the sawmill. I just used my two teams and a log chain to pull those logs down to where they were building the bridge. There was a deep arroyo on the mountainside, and they wanted to bridge that. The poles were cut about forty or fifty feet long for the stringers. They cut those down on the mountaintops, and I used my horses to drag the logs down. The workmen piled the poles on top of one another and built the bridge with supports on both sides and then strung it across there. I also was sent back and forth to the sawmill to bring in really thick, heavy logs from the top of the mountain over there.

I must have worked on the bridge for about a month. On the weekends I would come back over here and visit my wife and my family; they were still living here with her family. We had only two or three children then; I remember that Mary Davis and Mary had been born and another child was on the way. We had some little ones who died too, so I guess there may have been others by then.[15]

I earned quite a bit on that job; I got more money helping build the bridge than at anything else I had done up to that time. I was using some of it to buy hay and food from the Chinle stores because I had credit there. Those things I took to my wife and family because they did not go up there with me. When the bridge was completed, I started back for my home in Chinle, where I stayed for awhile.

While I was still working for the Franciscan Fathers here in Chinle they told me that a school would be started here soon. In 1910 they started building that school,[16] and I went over there to work on it. I was put in charge of the people who were hauling stones. Horse Herder was one of the men who hauled stones in with wagons from the road that goes to the sawmill on the other side of the place now known as Thunderbird Ranch, next to the Canyon. They also had a quarry over there near what is now García's store.

It seems that Tall Woman and I had been living together for about six years when that school plant was completed. Seya had been born by then and there was another child on the way by the time we finished that building. I worked on that school for a whole winter. It took a little more than a year and a half to finish it. They built just two or three buildings there at that time. The same company also built the old stone Catholic church then. That building is still standing, but it is ready to cave in now. After that building was finished, the company moved over to Rehoboth to build a school or a hospital. I used my wagon and my team to help them move all of their equipment over there. That was the last trip I made for those people. I had worked for them for about two years.

During this time, an infant boy was born to us. He died after about two months, and our family moved back to the Valley. I do not know why he died; I was freighting things to Rehoboth and was not home very much.

I was the only one around here at that time who had a wagon and teams. When I returned to Chinle, I managed to establish myself with things for my future use. The traders from this area wanted me to haul things in from Gallup with my wagon and team. There was a lot of freighting to be done for these trading posts. Since I had a good solid wagon for that and a good strong team of horses, of course I was asked to do plenty of freighting for the local stores. So I started doing work like that for them, going back and forth between Chinle and Gallup. Any time the store-keepers ran out of supplies, they sent word to me saying, "Rush over here, I need this and that." I guess I got in good standing through that, because the traders were willing to let me have credit and I could buy whatever I wanted. I became known to everyone as honest and as a man who would deal fairly with anyone.

So in that way I managed to keep things going well and to take care of the children. I would buy saddles; some of them were better than saddles today; they only cost about thirty or thirty-five dollars. Flour at that time was a dollar and ten cents for twenty-five pounds; sugar was ten cents a pound, and we bought coffee in bags for twenty cents for a pound of beans. Groceries were really cheap then, and you would get quite a lot of food for very little money. Now you spend one hundred dollars for groceries, but when you start to carry them out, there's only an armful. You can put it on the back of your saddle and take it all home on horseback with you. What is happening is that they are just kicking the prices up and up.

I would buy two saddles at a time then and trade those saddles for horses. Some of the people around here had good work horses, really heavy-set, strong horses. I would buy those horses and break them in by hitching them to the wagon. I broke all the horses that I bought. Eventually I had many good teams of strong horses to help with all that hauling.

I did not haul freight all the time. The school had been built here, and they needed fuel to keep the buildings heated. Other people were also using wood for heating their homes. The school tried to get coal over at Black Mountain but did not have too much luck with that. So when I was not hauling freight, I was hauling wood for the school and for others, too. The only place you could get that was from the east; there was no wood to be hauled from the Black Mountain side. We brought it in piles that were four feet long and stacked four feet high. We made ten blocks which were eight feet long. Coal was also brought in from Black Mountain when they could find it.

When I was not hauling wood with my two teams for the school, I was hauling something else with my wagon and team. I was always needed somewhere because I was the only one in this area that had a wagon and a team. I would always be called here and there to haul this or that; I was well-known for my hauling.

I must have continued hauling freight for those stores, and for others, off and on, for about ten years. During that time I saw the first automobile[17] here on the reservation. In fact I kept working like that until cars came into use for hauling freight. I was the first one to start hauling freight with wagons. Finally some other men earned wagons, and several years after I started hauling, they joined me. Then there was a group of us freighting all the time. Just about at the time when more freighters joined us, the cars and trucks began hauling and took the work away from us.

One time, before anyone else joined me in hauling freight, I left here and was going to Gallup to freight for a store. I met a fellow called Son of Tall Singer way up in the timbers on top of the mountain. He had a brand new wagon he had just gotten from the agency. His horses were played out. They had not had anything to eat, and they were hungry. They were resting there in the trees on the mountain when I came by. I stopped and gave part of the hay I had in my wagon to those horses.

Then this man started talking to me. He said, "I recently got this wagon, and I don't have anyone to work it out with me. I'll give you this wagon and you can work it out yourself." He said, "There is a sheep dip built at a place called Sheep Dip, and I have been asked to deliver some wood there, which I cannot do."

So I agreed to that, and then I left him there. I told him to go ahead and drive that wagon on home, and I would come sometime later to get it. After I delivered that wood and came back with the freight for the store, I came home, and a few days later I got a team of horses and rode up to where this man lived, towards Lukachukai, at a place called Rock Spruce. I picked up the wagon there. Then I had two wagons; one of them was brand new.

A bit later, a fellow living here by the name of Soda Pop Man asked me to let him have the whole new outfit complete – two teams and the wagon – for five head of cattle and a horse. I took his offer, but I did not have anywhere to put those animals where they could graze, and I had no one at home to care for them. So I decided I would just sell them over at the Black Mountain store. I started to drive them over there, and one of them just played out on the trip. So we just killed that one.

When others began freighting,[18] I used to work with Mr. Sand[19] quite often. He did not have a team or a wagon of his own, so he used Little Two Streams Meet Man's wagon and horses to do that work. A fellow called Slim Man also had horses and a wagon, but he never did much freighting. John Gorman down here also had horses, and so did his brother Arthur. I freighted with them and with Many Goat's Son, Black Man. A man they called Black Mountain Man was freighting on different roads. He was familiar with the road from here to Fort Defiance, Gallup and Lukachukai and along through this area. A fellow by the name of Man With a Cane's Nephew had a wagon and team and was equipped for freighting. There eventually were a number of people doing that on this side.

Sometimes when we were freighting in a group we would get into some foolishness and do things that were just nonsense. One time we left from here in a group that included old John Gorman. A lot of us would ride into Gallup

From Link 1968:40

FIG. 3. One of the freight wagons used between 1868 and the early 1900s to transport provisions and supplies to scattered reservation trading posts.

all together, and camp over there at the base of the mountain on the way. Of course, John Gorman was a pretty strong Christian and a church member. So we would scheme around.

I said, "Let's get John to dance with us. I have the urge to dance, just for fun, you know." So we got together and lined up for that sort of dance. But without his knowing it, we planned to start singing and then cut off the song all of a sudden to see what he sounded like. So we did that; we played a trick on him that way. We danced there, and we started out pretty strong with a song. Then all of a sudden, we all stopped. And John, he had kind of a funny voice, you know. We listened to him. That was the first thing we did on that trip.

Then we went into Gallup and loaded up our freight wagons and started back this way. Just the other side of a place they call Black Hat now, about fifteen miles from Window Rock and this side of Gallup, we stopped to make camp on the ridge of a hill. The old road used to go by there instead of the way the paved road goes; it used to go direct, straight all the rest of the way to Gallup. We stopped there and unhooked our team for the night.

Then a group of freighters came in, going into Gallup. They all stopped there at our camp. There were a lot of them we knew; they were from Round Rock and other trading posts up along the mountain near Lukachukai. We all got together there; we were coming back this way, and they were going in to get their freight. So we decided that we would just visit there and all camp together and have a little fun, like a kind of reunion. We unhooked our teams, took our horses and fed and watered them, and then had our meal with these fellows who had met us there.

Afterwards, we got to talking, and they said that just a short distance back on the road there was a saloon. You see, it was off the reservation. Somebody said, "Let's go over there and get something to drink and have a little fun." When that was suggested, of course a lot of them wanted to go. I was included, so I went over there on foot. It was not very far away, and we walked over to that saloon to buy something to drink.

When we got there, of course, each one bought what he could afford. Some bought small bottles, others got big bottles. I bought a gallon jug, a clay one.[20] I got that gallon of whiskey and some small bottles besides. We came back to camp, and of course we started drinking and talking and having a good time. We treated one another and kept on all night long.

After awhile, I guess there was so much drinking that some of them just started passing out; they were overdosing themselves. I just kept my seat; I sat there and did not want to move. I tried to keep my mind awake, but later in the night, I guess I had too much in my belly. So I thought, "Well, I'd just better turn in and go to sleep." I got up to walk out a ways, and that's the last thing I remember. I must have stumbled into a ditch or an old rut in the road. I fell over flat on my belly, landing that way, and everything just went black. I guess that squeezed all of the liquor out of my belly. I just slept there like that all night long until towards morning, when I began to feel cold. So I got up, but I could tell I was pretty weak; I started walking around to get limbered up. I walked around for some time before I got straightened out and a little cooled off. Then I went back and got under the wagon.

Well, the next morning the group going to Gallup left, and then we left, after we fixed breakfast and hooked up our teams. Before we had gone too far, this old fellow, Black Mountain Man, just passed out again, before we got on top of the ridge. He must have still been drinking, although I had never seen him drinking that morning. Of course, I had that jug in my wagon, and I was not drinking much, except now and then. So we did not get very far that day. We stopped there near a place called Rock Springs, not very far out of Gallup, to give him time to get sobered up a bit. We unhooked our teams and waited for him, camping there overnight.

The next day, before we went very far, he got that way again. So we had to stop again, over the Divide on the ridge. We could not tell why he was doing that, or whether he was just pretending or whether he was feeling the aftereffects of what he had drunk the night before. We tried going on, and he'd be all right for a short distance, and then he'd pass out again.

We were not making much headway on account of him. We kept starting and stopping like that; we passed just this side of Fort Defiance and we camped again. The next night we must have camped on top of the mountain. Then we started down off the mountain, on this side of Sawmill, and before we got to the base of the mountain, we had to stop for him again. He had another relapse there on the west side of Sawmill Mountain. It was early in the day that time; it was not even noon. We had to stop and unhook our teams again and wait for him to get sobered up. He was one of the drivers. Each time we stopped for him, we had to pull him off the wagon and lay him in the shade to cool off. We did that again at this place.

While we were waiting there, we unhooked our teams and fed and watered them. Then we started making a little pot of coffee for our lunch. We had another fellow, Curly Hair, who had married into the Standing House Clan to which old Black Mountain Man belonged. I was busy greasing my wagon and working around there, and old Black Mountain Man was lying under the shade of a tree. Suddenly I noticed he was sitting up, eyes wide open, sitting there like a sick man just staring at me with bloodshot eyes.

I just dropped everything I was doing and went over to the wagon and reached in there and pulled out my gallon jug. I showed it to him to let him see it; holding it towards him I started the song that is used in the Shootingway to feed the one who is being sung over the herb medicine.[21] Handling that jug, I started singing that song and walking towards him. I walked to where he was sitting while I was singing, and then I started pressing his limbs with it, singing that song: "This that is ailing you, gaze on it; it will cure you, it will put you back to normal."

Of course, I was not supposed to do that, but I did, just for foolishness. The singers always warn the People in general against doing such things. It's common practice for them to say, "You have to respect these songs. Don't use them foolishly because they are bound to come back and affect you some way later on."

Old Curly Hair was sitting over there in another wagon. He said, "That's terrible; it's against the rules to sing a song like that. I don't think you should do those things. You aren't supposed to do that." But all that time, he was just laughing and laughing. I still went ahead. That song is what we use during a ceremony to limber up a person, when he is cramped or sort of paralyzed. They use that song to press the person who is being sung over, to get the circulation going again and get the person back to normal. If you have a sickness and they start performing a ceremony, they will test you, as they tested out that little boy down at that Red Antway with the Bear Man, to see if it's really affecting you. Of course, you are going to become numb and paralyzed, and you have to be put back to normal with those songs. So I suppose I did the right thing.

Black Mountain Man got a little better after that; he even took some coffee and ate a little lunch. By that time, we were running low on food and were out of meat. So after that ceremony, we hooked up our teams again and started continuing our journey. When we had passed the peach orchard at Flat Rock, we had to stop again. After awhile we went on over the ridge from the west toward Chinle.

Then we decided it was not a good idea to take Black Mountain Man back in that condition, since we were all liable to get into trouble because of him. So we unhooked our teams and rested there over the ridge from Good Luck Rock Pile, letting him sober up again. We were over to the west of that place where the single old lady's grave is. There used to be an old lady whom we called, "Single Lady," or "Lonely Old Lady." She died there, and her grave is there.

I started walking around, and I noticed that there was nothing in the area except a hogan. I decided to walk over and see who was living there. So I went to the hogan and started looking around, but there was nobody in sight. Somebody was living there all right, because there was a fire outside, and the fire was about gone, but there was a pot sitting in the ashes. I knew something was cooking there, so I walked over and looked around and still did not see anybody. I walked over to the fire and looked in that pot; it was full of stew; there was lots of fat mutton being boiled there. So I walked into the hogan and got a pan and poured some of that stew out and took it back to my drunken friend. I wanted to revive him, and that is a quick cure for that.

I walked back to where old Black Mountain Man was sitting, and I put this in front of him; I put plenty of salt on it and told him to drink it up. "This will help you get sober," I said. He ate that right up. Then I took that pan back to the hogan and then came back to the wagon.

As I was standing around there I noticed somebody coming back to the hogan. Right away I knew that he would come over and make trouble about what had happened. He started walking around there looking for tracks. When he found out which way they went, he started tracking me, and of course the tracks were leading this way.

When I saw him coming towards our camp, I knew that I probably knew him, although I did not recognize him right away. So I went over to my wagon and pulled out my gallon jug and poured some of that whiskey into a small bottle. I carried that small bottle in my pocket all the time; I think it was a quarter pint; we called those *atééłíí*. Every now and then I poured a little in and stuck it in my pocket, and when I was driving around, I sipped on it. So I started out toward that man, with the bottle inside my coat pocket.

He looked very angry. He said, "There are thieves. Somebody's been around my hogan, and they have taken some of the stew that was boiling outside."

I said, "I did that, cousin; I'm the guilty one."

Sure enough, I knew this man; he was Blinded Meadow Man; he used to be married to a woman called Singing Woman; she's dead now, and so is he. I told him, "The reason I did that was because it was an emergency. We have a man here who is pretty drunk, and I thought that that broth, that fat, might sober him up a bit. That's the reason I went over there and, when I didn't find anybody home, helped myself." I told him that I went and borrowed one of the pans from the hogan to put that broth in, and then I took it back.

Then I said, "Here, in payment for that, is a gift for you. You can drink this." Then I pulled out the bottle and gave it to him. That man sure grabbed for that bottle and drank it. It changed his expression right away; he had looked angry, and after that he had a beautiful smile spread all over his face. He asked how much of it he should drink, and I said, "Just go ahead and finish it if you want to." And so he did.

Afterwards, he invited me over there for some more stew, so I went behind the wagon and put a little more whiskey in that bottle and gave it to him. Then I got myself one of my own dishes and had some stew. Then we left there; I didn't want to hang around there because of Black Mountain Man's condition.

We started off again, and old Black Mountain Man was somewhat sobered up at first. But by the time we were coming by the rim of the Canyon here, he started slipping back again. I didn't want to fool with him any longer, so I just took off and left him behind. I went on down to John Gorman's trading post in Chinle and unloaded the freight I was carrying for him and got my pay. Then I left and went home. The others came home too.

Later I heard that Black Mountain Man came over and stopped under the cottonwood groves. Reid Winnie's father-in-law was living there then with his family, and when Black Mountain Man stopped there, he walked around and finally passed out. People started looking around for him, and they finally found him. He was lying there. They thought, "Well, what's the matter with him? Perhaps a ghost attacked him." So these people carried him home and gave him a blackening ceremony.[22] That is what I heard about that.

While I was freighting for the stores, some more children were born here at home. After that infant boy who lived only two months, there was a girl. We called her, "Girl with a Light Complexion"; that's Agnes. After about two more years, another girl, Ruth, was born. She was nicknamed, "Woman with a Light Complexion" and later, "Mama Ruth." Following her about two years later, another boy was born; he died in infancy. Then we had a girl, who was known as Pauline. She lived through infancy but died when she was about eight at the old Chinle school building. She died from measles and pneumonia which she got over there. Only the auditorium of that school is still standing; it became an office building across from the present post office. Following this girl, another boy was born; that was about 1920, and he was known as David.

Agnes went to the Chinle School and then on to Fort Apache and elsewhere to learn to be a nurse. We kept Ruth home here with us. The Bureau of Indian Affairs schools were overcrowded then. Schooling was still the law, but it was on a first come, first served basis. Delegates were sent to Washington to ask for more space; the law was not enforced then. So we kept Ruth home, and later we kept David home, too. One reason was trouble with sickness among the children who were sent off to school. We also liked having somebody home with us. David helped with the work around here; Ruth herded the sheep and goats and helped her mother with the carding and spinning of the wool. When I was home, I would put in the crops, and when I was not here, the children would hoe and weed the fields.

One summer I put in my corn here in the Chinle Valley, and when the plants were up and had started to get tassels, a stray burro, a strange burro, started coming around, getting into my field. This burro had a habit of coming there as soon as the corn was high enough to be chewed on. Of course, in those days, we didn't have any barbed wire fences to put around the cornfields. It was all open.

This burro got into the habit of coming into my cornfield while I was asleep. He seemed to know just when to go there; towards morning, after midnight when we were all asleep, he would come into the cornfield and start to feed on the corn. He knew how to go about it; he got filled up on the corn, and he got to know just when to leave. He would do that every night. In the morning I could see his tracks and his manure scattered around in the cornfield, but I never could catch him.

That went on for some time until one morning I was surprised to see him right by the cornfield after the sun was up. I guess he forgot to leave before it was daylight, and so he just stayed there. It was an old burro.

So I took a lariat down there and caught him. I led the old burro here to my place and put a rope around his legs, tangled him up and threw him down on the ground. He was lying there all tied up with the rope. I looked around for a piece of wood or a post, brought that over and laid it under his tail; then I got an axe and gave him one whack and chopped his tail off at the base. Then I went and got my knife and cut his ears off right close to his head, both ears. Then I turned him loose. It seems as though that cured him, because he never came back any more.

Well, fall came and we harvested our corn and put it away for the winter. Then I heard there was a Yeibichai Dance down here somewhere. My horses were all wagon horses; they were not saddle horses or riding horses. I was ashamed to saddle one of those wagon horses and go down to the dance. I thought, "I'd like to go, but I don't have a decent-looking horse." Then I remembered the man whose burro I had trimmed. He had a few good saddle horses around there that were decent-looking. I just happened to get the idea of going down to ask that man to loan me a horse because his were good-looking; they were fat. Of course, I never thought about what I had done to his burro.

I saddled up and went down there to ask to borrow a horse from this old man, who was called Belching One's Son. When I got there, the old man was lying around in the shade. He had some granddaughters, young girls. So I went over there, and he was friendly. I sat down and got to talking with him for some time. His granddaughters were around there too, listening in. After some time, I said, "Grandfather, I came to ask to borrow your horse. You've got a good-looking horse that I'd like to borrow. With that intention, I came to you to ask to borrow your horse. I'll give you some kind of a fee for the use of it."

The old man answered right away; he said, "Sure, sure; I have a horse; yes, I have a horse, my grandchild. That horse is over the hills here somewhere. The one that you trimmed, cut his ears off and his tail, that's the horse; you're welcome to use it. You go ahead and use it to go to the dance. Put your saddle on and ride it down to where there's a lot of people to look at it. See how they look at it and what it looks like."

When he said that, then I became embarrassed. When he said that to me, of course his granddaughters, the young girls, started giggling about it and cracking jokes. They said, "I wonder what it would look like if you rode that burro in there without any ears or any tail? I wonder what the People would think? He'll have a rounded-off horse!"

I was so embarrassed that I didn't want to say anything more, so I just got on my horse and took off and came home. I don't care to talk about that any more, because it isn't anything nice.

While I was hauling things for the stores, gradually I began to feel that my back was paining, that it was bothering me. I had not had any sicknesses after that first injury when I wrestled with my cousin, until later, after I had started raising a family. Sometimes I would sit down and I could not get up. It began worrying me; I wondered what was causing that. So I asked these hand-tremblers to find out for me. They said, "It is something to do with Beautyway that is ailing you. That's what you should have for it."

So I went and got old Curly Hair and Gene Begay. Curly Hair was the main singer, and they sang Beautyway over me for five nights, with the fire inside every morning for purification by sweating. I had that after the Chinle School was completed and opened. My father was still alive then, and I had about six children of my own.

I don't know how much help I got from that first singing, maybe a little bit. But since I did not take care of myself, working too hard doing lots of heavy work, that ailment just came back again. The hand-tremblers diagnosed my case again and said that it was a Ghostway ceremonial that I needed. So I got Sickle Moustache to sing over me for five nights again.

When you get a hand-trembler and they do that over you, they say, "You did this or that in your early life or in the past, and that is what is ailing you now." Then you freshen your mind on your past life. A lot of times they will tell you things you have no idea about; you cannot remember that you even did such a thing, but still they tell you that you violated this or that. But if it happens that it comes back to your mind that you really did do that, then, of course, that gives you the idea that you'd better have that ceremony to remove the effects.

That first sing, the Beautyway, had to do with the Snake People. When those hand-tremblers performed over me, they said, "Well, you did something you shouldn't have to a snake," which I knew was true. Sometimes I just chopped snakes up in half and let the head run off and leave the tail. Those were the things causing the ailment. So of course I had to have that restored.

The second singing I had, the Ghostway, pertains to violations of rules concerning dead persons. I knew I had done a lot of things that I should not have done here, too. For instance, when I was in school, if somebody died, we did not bother keeping the observances we were supposed to when we were home, like erasing our tracks at the grave or not spitting there or not speaking to each other. Those are the things that are forbidden when you are burying a dead person.

And when the school started, wood was used to run the power pump. We would haul wood from the hills, just picking up any kind of wood we could find. Sometimes we used a lot of wood from hogans which were abandoned because of death in them. We are not supposed to use or touch that wood, but we did not bother with those things because we did not know. Those were the things that caused these ailments. Then, too, I had to help with the burials of my mother, my sisters, my brothers and my own children. Because of all of these things I had to have this Ghostway.

Some of my close relatives were hand-tremblers. My father-in-law was one, and my mother did that occasionally.[23] Also Curly Hair Skinner and my older brother, Jimmy Mitchell, who died when he was still a young man. Those are some of the ones I remember who worked on me. Jimmy, of course, did that for me when I was much younger.

For my back, the Beautyway was first, and the Ghostway was about five years later. After the first sing, of course, I felt the effects of it. But, like I said, I was careless; I just went back to doing a lot of heavy work, and the pains gradually came back on me again. So the second ceremony was performed over me.

With the Ghostway, the common practice is to do it in just two performances; the five-night sing and the one-night, because the first five-night's singing concludes with the blackening, and the one-night ceremony requires just red ochre paint. Now, with the Holyway ceremonials, such as the Beautyway, the custom is to have them four times: five-night, one-night, five-night, and one-night. The reason for that is the stripes on the body; they switch the color of those four lines. They have the black, the blue, yellow and white; they maybe start with the white and go until they've started with each of the colors.

I went through that Ghostway, but it did not have too much effect on me. I got some relief, but I really was not cured completely. That was because when you have this Ghostway, they forbid you to do certain things; you cannot have anything to do with dead people. You must not handle them or be in a place where a dead person is. But I could not help that because soon after that ceremony I had to help with the burial of our baby boy who died. I had to handle him because there was no one else to do it. It was forbidden to do that, but I could not help it. I also had to support my children, which meant doing heavy work to get a little income.

After a while I had the Male Shootingway, Holyway. The reason I had that was because one time while I was working at the sawmill, I was designated as foreman for a crew that was cutting logs. I was just a boss and was out in the woods with them. I was marking the trees that were to be cut, since I had been taught what kinds they should be. I did not do any chopping myself.

One day when I was out there with the crew, I found a tree that had fallen over and was lying up high. I got on that log, laid back and got sleepy; the men were busy chopping, and I fell asleep. Somebody felled a tree, and it made a big noise. I jumped up, and when I did my hair stuck with pitch on that tree. Then I found out that the tree had been struck by lightning; the bark had peeled off, and the pitch was there. No doubt I left some of my hair sticking over there where it got caught.

When the hand-trembler came, he said, "It appears that you did something with lightning. You struck something. I don't know what it is, but you violated something pertaining to a lightning-struck object." Then it came back to my mind that I did that at that time when I fell asleep on a fallen tree which had been struck by lightning. So for that reason I had this Shootingway for five nights.

It wasn't really just this, my falling asleep on this lightning struck log; that Shootingway was held also on account of what happened right here. You see, one evening there was a sing going on across the wash, and I wanted to go over there. So I got on my horse bareback; I wanted to hobble him over there across the wash so I could bring him back home in the morning. At that time, the current of the stream was right next to the bank here. I went down to Nazlini Wash; there was not much water running, and just shortly before that there was supposed to have been a woman who came across there on foot.

So I started, and before I knew it, there was a lot of water coming down. In spite of it, I went on riding across; the first thing I knew, my feet were in the water. Gradually the water got deeper and deeper, and finally I doubled my legs until I was sitting on my horse on my knees. Then I noticed that the horse was just about ready to tumble over. When it did, I just wrapped the bridle rein around my hand, because I didn't want to let go of it.

So that's the way I hung on, and that horse and I floated down the wash all the way past Woody's place down there. Once or twice I tried to get on my feet, but the water was too deep. It just kept throwing me, you see. I hung on to the horse, and the horse was not even walking either; it was swimming. I hung on until we got across and then turned around and came back this way where the water was safer, where it was a little shallower. I hung on and I tried to walk, but I couldn't. My clothes, my shoes and everything were just full of sand. I had a headband that I wrapped around and tied under my chin before I started to cross. It's a good thing I did; that's what saved my face.

So mostly on account of that I wanted to have this ceremonial. You see, where you float or where you almost drown by floating, that Shootingway is used for that, too. That was the main reason I had it. Of course, the sleeping on the log was part of it, too. I floated down the wash after I was living around here, after I had returned from working at the sawmill. Herbert Mitchell's stepfather, Bead Singer's Son, who was also called Yoe Begay, did the singing. So that made three times I had ceremonials done for me around that time — Beautyway, Ghostway and Shootingway.

I had that Male Shootingway performed once. The singer died before I decided to ask him to come back and do it over again in the one-night version. Another reason that I waited to have that one-night done was that the pain was still in my back, and the ceremony had not seemed to help very much. I thought that I might just as well start having different ceremonies done to see if any of them might help.

I was still not altogether well, and I wanted to get over it so I could do some work to support my children. So I had a Chiricahua Windway performed over me not very long after the Shootingway. That's a one-night affair; it was performed three times on me. Naschili's Son from Black Mountain was the main singer, and Sand Man who was also called Bead Singer's Son, Yoe Begay from down near Valley Store, helped with the singing. Naschili's Son sang all three of those one-night ceremonies for me. That ceremony was advised by the hand-tremblers too; they said that I had violated something pertaining to the Chiricahua Apache Windway. Those Windway singers used a cactus to press the one-sung-over.

When I was living with my father while he was living with Woman with Goats, they moved the family. The wife of Tall Water Edge Man was just a small girl then, and she and I herded sheep together. I saw a lot of these Chiricahua Apache Windway singers perform, and I knew what they did. So when we were out herding sheep, I would go and cut a cactus and just fix it up any way; I would play I was a singer and she was the one-sung-over. When we were out herding sheep we used to carry that cactus around, and whenever we got time to spend while the sheep were grazing, why she'd be the sick person and I'd be the singer. That's the way we played. Then without untying any of those things, I just threw them away. No doubt there were a lot of them scattered all around here. The hand-tremblers said that was what was causing my illness.

I had that ceremony done three times for me; there was only about a month between the first two times, and then I let it rest for a couple of years. Then I had it done the third time. I wanted to have it completed, to have it the full four times, but something else came up in the family that prevented completing it. The reason it is supposed to be performed four times is because of the drawing on the body; there were lines drawn on my body, and whenever the one-sung-over is painted with figures like that, it requires four performances to complete it.

They say you have to have all four of them done to get the full benefit of that ceremony. But the singer passed away before I had a chance to ask him to do the last of those, so I just had three of them performed. Another singer could have done the last one, but first I would have needed to have an Evilway blackening ceremony to get rid of any bad influences from the singer who had died. We wanted to clear it all up and remove those spirits so the ceremony could be renewed with a new singer. Those ceremonies just take a couple of days.

The singer in the Chiricahua Windway usually gives the one-sung-over a little turquoise bead called a Windway bead. You are supposed to keep that bead with you at all times, and whenever you have another Windway done, all you have to do is take that bead out. If the same singer is performing the ceremony, the same bead can be used over and over again until four performances are done. But in my case, the new singer would have had to throw the old bead away because it was made by a singer who had died. The singer would have to make a new bead for me. It is the same in all of the larger ceremonials that take five nights or more. In each of them, we get a special bead that is tied on the top of the head in the center of the string. When a singer passes away, a new singer must throw the old bead away and put a new one in its place.

There is no bead like that for Blessingway or for Nightway or for Beadway, though you would think there would be for a ceremony with "bead" right in its name. Mountaintopway does not have a bead like that either, but I guess the rest do.

You are supposed to have the ceremony four times, but it is not really necessary to have all four performances right away. It takes a lot of things to have any ceremony, so I had one and then later in the year I had another one after I had gotten prepared for it. At that time, I felt fine. If you have a ceremony and you think that it really has an effect on you, that it relieved some pains you had before it was performed, then the best thing to do is to have a one-night sing done right away just to release you from that much more pain. After that, the other two performances can be done a little bit later, when you get ready for them. I am still thinking about having the others done, but it will take time to prepare for them. They are expensive.

During the time when I was hauling goods for the stores, one other thing happened that I remember. This was when I hauled a mummy out of the Canyon for some men who were digging there in those ruins.[24] I don't know exactly when that was, but the Chinle school had been constructed and white people were starting to move into the area. I was still the only one here with a wagon and a team to use for hauling when those men came around.[25]

I only hauled the remains of the cliff dwellers one time when I was a young man. It happened that there were some white people who came out here, digging in those ruins. About five white men came to the school and made inquiries; they wanted to go into the Canyon and do that work. They wanted to get someone with a wagon and team to take them up there. They were told that I was the only one with a team, a wagon and equipment to do that. One day somebody came to me and asked if I could do it. This man inquired about my equipment and said, "I hear that you have a team of horses and a wagon and that you can take us into the Canyon. We are going there to do some work in the ruins." I told him I would charge by the individual, so they could figure out how much it would be. He said that they would pay me well.

So I took them as far as Antelope Ruins, up in Canyon del Muerto, and I camped there. They went to a ruin at the foot of the wash, not up in the rocks. I stopped there to unload them across the wash from the ruins. I told them, "I will unload you fellows here, and since you are going to spend some time here digging around, I'll go back, and if you tell me when to come back for you, I'll be back here then."

I thought I could come right back, but I guess they did not trust me because they said, "No, don't leave us. Stay here and watch the camp and we'll pay you for your time for watching things here while we go over to the ruins and dig around."

So I stayed there at the camp; I just took care of the horses and the camp. And these white fellows, as soon as they were through with their meal, would go over there and dig. I forget exactly how many were in that party; I think it was five men. I don't remember just how long we stayed, maybe four or five nights.

One day they went over there early in the morning and I was just sitting there in the camp; after they had gone over there, sometime later in the morning, one of them came rushing back. I guess they must have found something over there. He came in and said, "What are you doing?" I said I was just sitting there watching the camp. He said, "We'd like you to help us a little over there." Then he said, "It's just a small job that we'd like to have you help us with." He was taking out materials to use — brushes, like paint brushes, white cloth and a collapsible frame with handles on it, like the stretchers they use in hospitals. He went back over there, and when he rushed back again to get that frame, he asked me again to go along. He said it wouldn't take long, just a little while. After he left, I went over there.

When I got there, I saw the skeleton. That dead body was all dried up. The skin was dried up against the bones; it was not rotten, just dried up. That body had no clothes on it; it was completely naked with nothing on it whatsoever except the hair. Part of that had turned to dust, but there was still some on that man's head. I could not tell what color the hair was because it was full of dust. Those men were using brushes to clean off all the loose dirt still on the body. I had a good chance there to take some of that hair for a scalp, but I did not do that.[26] They handled that body very carefully; it was so brittle that it could have broken easily before they put it on the stretcher.

They were kneeling around that body, brushing the dirt off the fingers and all around here and there, all over the face. I could smell the odor of that dirt, and it really smelled, but these men were not bothered by that. They were sniffing around it. When they got the whole thing brushed off, they lifted it up inch by inch and got the sheets under it. That skeleton was quite tall, even taller than I am; he must have been almost eight feet. He had no moccasins or anything. The place where he had been lying down was padded with some kind of grass or reeds. Of course, it was away from where it could have got wet, so it was all perfectly dry.

All of that brushing and getting the sheet under the body took almost the whole day. Those men were careful about that because they did not want to break anything. Then they laid the stretcher alongside the body, and, very carefully, we placed it on the stretcher. Then they placed some kind of covering over that body and tied on some tags. Of course, I do not know how any of those things felt because I did not touch anything.

Then they asked me to go hook up the team, because they were going to start home from the ruins. Those ruins were right there at the base of the rocks, not up in the cliffs. So I went and hitched the wagon and brought it over there. They put the stretcher in the wagon, and then we all went over to the camp and loaded all their things in the wagon. They made something like a bed for that body, and then I started hauling all of them and those things out of there in my wagon.

Those men were very happy about what they had found. Sometimes they would get off the wagon and walk alongside while I was driving. They kept telling me to be very careful; they did not want that body to bump around. They told me how to drive, not to go through those rough roads or over those bumpy places through the mud. When we got back to Chinle, they had a car waiting. They wrapped the body up some more and put it in something like a box; they covered it all up so it could not be damaged. Then they put that in the car and paid me. After they left I went back home and washed and scrubbed myself all over. I never saw those men again, and I do not know where that body is now. I suppose it is put away somewhere. It was still in good shape.

When you are hired, you are getting paid to do something you have been asked to do. You don't think about being afraid when you agree to work for someone like that, regardless of what it is, you agreed to do it and you have to go through with it. From the beginning of that work to the time they dug this corpse out of the grave, I was not there. I was there only after they took the body out. All I saw was a kind of shawl that the mummy was on. I did not handle that body at all. All I did was help lift it onto the stretcher.[27] I did not refuse to go there with them because I was getting paid for it, but otherwise I probably would never have gone there because at the same time I was afraid of doing that.[28]

After that happened, there was talk against excavating ruins. Curly Hair was the one that started that talk, because we found out that such things were being kept and shown to people at Mesa Verde. We had not known what they were doing with the remains before that. Once, when I was down near Phoenix, I saw a place where a lot of digging was going on.[29] They told me that they were digging down there trying to trace things. Lots of the ceremonials came from those ancient people. They were here before any white man was in this part of the world. White men were still across the ocean at that time, when these ancient people were living on this land here. The Navajos did not come from across the ocean; it seems as though we have been here for centuries.[30]

I have seen ceremonial things that have been dug up so I guess those people way back then believed and lived the same way that the Navajos do today. They must have been some of our ancestors from long ago; those things probably got carried down to the present generation. I do not know how long those people inhabited those places. It must have been an awfully long time ago.

Now, at Mesa Verde, you can see the excavated ruins there. All the dirt has been cleaned out of the buildings. There are signs there explaining things. The rooms are in a circle with a raised seat around the edges, around the base of the walls. Over there, in one place where they excavated the ruins, there's a tree that has grown out of the center of the room and gone dry. It was a cedar tree. They sawed that off, and they estimated the years by the rings of that tree. That showed that those ruins are pretty old.

Down around Phoenix, near the state penitentiary in Florence, there's a museum[31] where they keep the relics taken from the ruins. They are hanging in showcases with signs explaining them. Some of the ceremonial things there are like what the Pimas are using today in their ceremonies. And some of those implements that I saw there resemble the things that the Navajos use in Shootingway. The arrows, for instance, are only a little different. The feathers that are used in fletching these arrows are not split. Like the things over at Mesa Verde, lots of these museum things resemble those used in ceremonies by Navajos today. One of them was the yucca leaf drumstick used for tapping the basket.[32] Because of that, I figure that there's some truth in the idea that these things have been handed down from the old people of the ruins to the present Navajos, somehow. Of course I do not know exactly what the connections are.

The rangers in those parks tell you what they know about the origins of a lot of our ceremonies. They say that they originated in these areas from the ruins. That seems to be according to our legends. The rangers tell us that we Navajos are still in possession of these different ceremonies that the ancestors must have used. That is why they are preserving and protecting these things there in the museum.[33] Of course, before we learned that, we never thought

about tracing it. Now from what I heard from these rangers, I can see that
there is some truth in it.

The ranger told us that these things are being preserved under the
supervision of the government in Washington because a lot of people, like the
missionaries from some Christian denominations, do not want us to continue
our religion. They want us to forget all about that and follow their beliefs
instead. Their aim is to get rid of the pagan ceremonies practiced by the
Indians and to have us join their churches. Maybe eventually they themselves
will all belong to one church.

But after the ruins began to be dug up and investigated by different
people, the government told church people not to bother us. They said, "Let
the Navajos practice what religion they want, what beliefs they have, since
from all indications, those things have been handed down from one
generation to another since the time of these ruins." The church people are
supposed to follow the government rulings; this is a country where you can
practice any religion you believe in.[34]

While I had been freighting for all the years I've been telling about, Man
Who Shouts and his wife were growing old and were getting more sickly.
They were living at the foot of Black Mountain at that time, and Man Who
Shouts had been sick for two or three years before I stopped hauling freight
from Gallup. When he got worse and finally reached the point where he could
not get around, I decided to come home. So I quit freighting and came back
to my family and started working over there to help my wife and her people.
I started helping with their farm and their livestock. Man Who Shouts was a
well-to-do man, with cattle, sheep and horses, and I just started taking care of
those things for him.

By this time, I was getting interested in learning the Blessingway. But
before I got serious about that I was still doing some foolish things. One time
there was a Squaw Dance going on near the rim of Canyon del Muerto. After
the dance was over, a big group of boys, most of whom spent their time
loafing, were there playing cards and gambling. They had made their camp up
there and were gathered away from their hogans down here. I came upon this
whole group; in that group were Edward Francis' father-in-law, who was
known as Son of Yucca Fruit and also Gach'ilni. They are both dead now.
They were lying down asleep there.

It seems these boys had been playing cards all night long, and they were
tired. They were sleeping with their heads almost touching each other. They
resembled each other; they looked as if they were twins. So I walked up to
them and sang the Blessingway song about the pairs of corn plants that were
mated to become humans. The song that tells about that is a very, very sacred
song. Of course that was just for foolishness that I did that. I started singing
there, standing over these two boys who were lying together there, about
pairs being matched together to become the human race. I sang that, and

everybody there started laughing. That was another time that I did something I was not supposed to do. The refrain means "Lying in Pairs."

There were other people who did things like that too. In my earlier days, while I was helping my uncle do silversmithing, something like that happened there. I was working the bellows for him, blowing on the coals while he was pounding on the silver. A fellow by the name of Nadíí'áani came by and started watching us while we were doing that. That old crazy man just sat there and kept looking at me. The way he was looking was a sign that "I don't like you." Girls will often do that to boys who are trying to flirt with them. They will make faces at them. That's a sign that the girl does not like you.

Well, all of a sudden this crazy fellow fell over and fainted. He did that quite often; he'd faint all of a sudden, just pass out. So he did that there. There was another visitor, Naat'áani Nédíłne, there at that time too. When my uncle was ready to go to the hogan for something to eat, this old crazy man was lying there, still unconscious. The other man stood up over him and started a song that belongs in Shootingway, one of the Buffalo songs. The words in that song have a meaning; they are very sacred and should not be sung just for fun. While he was singing that song, he started to work on that man, pressing him. He was not using the regular words in the song; instead he was just making up some words.

According to the story, this song was created at the time that Holy Young Man killed a lot of buffalos. When he got through, of course, he could not leave them there dead. He had to pull the arrows out of their bodies and then use the arrows to restore them to life. That is what the song is about. It is a very sacred song and should not be sung just for fun, but that is what this visitor was doing. He was changing the words, using Nadíí'áani's name in the part of the song where buffalos are mentioned. In the rest of the song he used the regular words. The song goes something like this: "I killed the buffalos with the tail-feathered arrows, and I pulled them out of their bodies again. I used the arrows again to press them, to restore them to life. The only thing left there was the blood spots. That is the sign that I am the guilty one, I am the one who did that." The words in the song are about that.

There were any number of songs like that which some of those foolish men would use on such occasions. They would take the regular words of the song, and then where the song keeps repeating like a chorus, use different words. A lot of times those Buffalo songs from Shootingway would be used in connection with horses that had saddle sores. In a case like that, one would start scraping those scabs off the horse's back and would sing those songs. They were about the buffalos that were wounded and the wounds that had scabs grown on them.

Saddle sores were very common in the past. Many of the People had just one horse, which they would use all the time. They would abuse that horse and let it get sores on its back. Some of the older people would take care of their horses very carefully. When the horses had just been watered, they would not let them trot; they would make them go slowly. They trained their horses themselves, too, but there were different ways of doing that. My uncle liked to get his horse hardened up. He would tie it up all night and mistreat it. Then in the morning, he would get on it and make it run, so that it could stand hard usage. Other men would do just the opposite; they did not want their horses to be abused; they handled them like babies. Those kinds of horses could not stand much strain or a lot of punishment.

You always had to be careful about sores on horses. My uncle told me once about a time when he borrowed a horse to ride someplace. After he had saddled that horse, he started out from the hogan and was just going over the ridge from there when the owner started yelling after him. My uncle wondered what he had forgotten, and so he went back. The other man asked, "How about your saddle blankets? Are they clean?" You know, the saddle blanket from a horse that has those sores can spread the sickness to other horses. You have to be very careful with such things.

There was one man in particular who used to be known for making fun of sacred things. That was old Sacred Bundle Man. The People used to tell all kinds of stories about him and the way he had no respect for his songs. He knew twenty-four different ceremonials, and he had twenty-four different sacred bundles, one for each. He was almost totally blind; the only way that he could tell one bundle from another was by feel and smell. He had something like a cellar dug in the hill, and he kept the whole row of sacred bundles in there, each in its place. If you came to him for a Female Shootingway, well, the only way that he could distinguish between the Female and Male Shootingway bundles was by how they felt and by the smell of the herbs in them. He would go along and feel each bundle until he found the right one by smelling. He did the same thing for the Mountainway bundle. That was the way he would distinguish them. He was always making fun of his songs. The People say that he was finally murdered by his wife. They say that he was breaking the rules about those things and doing that is bound to bring bad results.

Fellows like that and probably others, too, used to make fun of those sacred songs, especially when they were not around the singers. They would just do that for a joke, you know, and sometimes other people would just laugh about it. Sometimes they were very serious about this and told them not to sing those songs like that. The singers say that we should be serious about those songs and not sing them at the wrong time or disrespect them in any way. If singers are sincere with their songs and their ceremonies, they do not do that. But that is the way things are, you know; some people are disrespectful. But I have not heard of anyone ridiculing the Blessingway songs, except that story I told you about when I sang that song while two fellows were sleeping together lying side by side. Other than that, I do not know of any incident like that.

Once I started practicing Blessingway as a singer, I never ridiculed it or any of the other ceremonies. At no time have I ever disrespected it. You see, in the instructions we get from our teachers when we are learning these songs and prayers and other parts of the ceremonies, we are told to have high respect for these things and to observe them very carefully. We learn that these prayers and everything that goes with them belong to certain Holy People who are no longer visible here on earth. They have gone to holy places out of our sight, but still they are aware of what is going on around here. It is just like that kind of church that says God is everywhere; although you cannot see it, still it is there. So it is with us, too. If I should start misusing my Blessingway, the Holy People would know about it from where they are. It is like when you are listening to a radio; something may be going on out of your sight, but still you hear it, you hear what is happening. So therefore, you must be very careful.

We are told by the singers who teach us that these Holy People, although they are no longer visible on earth, are still aware of how we are conducting ourselves here, and if we are in trouble, they are there to protect us from misfortune. They are aware of our actions, whatever we are doing.

As soon as you are hired to perform a certain ceremony, they know right away that you have been asked. If you have no reason to refuse to do that, then they know that. If you do have a reason to refuse, then they know that, too. They know that you should refuse sometimes because of the rules they have laid down. Under certain conditions you should not try to go through with certain ceremonies. If you do that in spite of those rules, then the holy beings know it, and you are bound to be affected. Doing that may bring on sickness or some other kind of misfortune, even death, to you or members of your family. You may be punished for breaking those rules. So in order to remedy those things, you have to fall back on the ceremonies that will remove the trouble.

It is similar to arrangements nowadays for law and order. When you break a law, the police come and get you and you face a judge, and he gives you a sentence for punishment, either a jail term or a fine. Those are the things that cure you, purify you. Well, it is the same way with these things in the ceremonies. You have to find remedies by prayer offerings, by jewels and prayers and songs.

Even if little children break these rules without knowing any better, still it has an effect on them later on. Through these hand-tremblers and star-gazers it will come out; "It looks like he did this," or "here's where she broke the rules, therefore this illness has come on him or her." Even when a child is unborn, such things can have an effect on it. If a pregnant woman violates something that she should observe while she is carrying the child, like killing a snake or looking at a dead snake, or looking at an eclipse of the moon or sun, anything like that is going to affect the unborn child. After it is born, it is going to get sick. So there are ceremonies to remedy those things too.

EDITORS' NOTES

1. While contemporary residence practices vary among Navajo couples after marriage, in Frank's time it was customary for newlyweds to live with the wife's mother and her family. A husband usually moved his flock and other possessions to this location over a period of time and began assisting with the planting and other work in his wife's extended family. Traditionally a rule known as mother-in-law avoidance existed whereby a son-in-law was not to look upon or speak directly to his mother-in-law. Today, fewer of the People observe this rule.

2. Here, Frank stopped and added as an aside, "That band of sheep is still in the family's possession; it's owned by Garner's widow. That lady is one of my grandchildren; she lives up on Red Mesa. The cows have just disappeared."

3. To non-Navajo people, Tall Woman is known as Rose Mitchell; around home she is known as *shimá*, "my mother," and *shimá sání*, "my grandmother."

4. See Chapter 4, note 17, for a history of hospitals on the reservation.

5. See Appendix A for Frank Mitchell's and Tall Woman's conjugal families and other genealogical information, as well as comparisons of the variable census materials.

6. If the dates on the Chinle Mission birth records are followed for the children of Frank and Tall Woman (see Appendix A-4), it appears as if the couple probably began living together in 1906.

7. One of the reservation's natural resources is marketable timber, including ponderosa pine, spruce, Douglas fir, white fir, pinyon and juniper. As a resource, the timber has been protected by the Navajo Agency Branch of Forestry since 1929.

As described by Young (1961:178-184), two sawmills seem to have been in operation on the reservation in the 1880-1907 period. One of the first pieces of equipment brought in by the new railroad was a portable steam-driven sawmill. This sawmill, which Underhill (1953:225) says was ten-horsepower, was set up in the Fluted Rock area, southwest of Fort Defiance, and ox teams hauled logs to the mill which provided timber for the agency, school and mission construction. On October 14, 1880, Agent F. T. Bennett of Fort Defiance reported that the sawmill was in operation and that the stone needed for the construction of the Fort Defiance boarding school was also being quarried (Link 1968:34).

The second mill, which Young (1961:179) describes as semi-portable, was located northwest of the sawmill used by the tribe until 1963. This steam-driven mill provided timber needed for construction of agency buildings at Chinle, and from Frank's description, seems to be the one at which he worked.

The Sanostee-Toadlena area also had a mill from 1907-1935, which provided materials needed by the Shiprock Agency. This mill burned in 1935, and the equipment was moved to fifteen miles northwest of Fort Defiance, at Sawmill, Arizona. Construction of a mill was started in 1935, and the sawmill placed under the operational control of the Navajo Agency Forester on July 1, 1936. After financial difficulties, the mill became self-supporting in 1944. Several equipment changes were made in 1946, and this mill remained in operation until May 1963.

The present tribal sawmill is located about thirteen miles northeast of Fort Defiance near Red Lake, at a place now known as Navajo, New Mexico. Construction was started on it in 1958, when Navajo Forest Products Industries was also created; the mill became operational in September 1962 (see Young 1961:178-184, Link 1968:90-93, and the *Padres' Trail* for February 1973).

8. Usually in the summer Navajos bring their sheep to places on the reservation where sheep dips have been constructed. These dips consist of a series of holding pens and chutes which lead into trough-like dipping vats, which hold liquid medication. The sheep are herded into these vats; once there, they swim through them, being supervised by various people who use crooks to guide the animals. The dipping serves to reduce ticks and other parasites as well as to remove some of the dirt from the wool. As part of the procedures, sheep are counted, branded and possibly vaccinated before being dipped. These practices were instituted after concern for overgrazing and land erosion led to the Stock Reduction program of the 1930s and 40s. Related to the latter are the relevant development of range management and animal husbandry programs and the issuance of grazing permits which limit the size of individual flocks (see Downs 1964:44-47).

9. Additional comments about conditions at home during Frank's work at the sawmill have been provided by two of his daughters, Mary and Augusta, and one of his sons, Seya. According to Mary and Augusta, during these years Frank was gone most of the time. Here is their narrative:

> We were living with our grandfather, Man Who Shouts, and his wife. They had plenty of sheep, and they always had plenty of meat and wool. Our grandfather always made a big garden where the soil looked good; in those days there were no fences, and he would plant lots of corn, beans and squash. We would use that down to the last piece; we even dried it out and saved it for winter.
>
> Man Who Shouts was so patient; he never scolded us, but just talked nicely to his grandchildren and encouraged us. His wife's name was Tall Woman; she was very tall when she was young. We herded sheep for them in the summer, and our grandfather herded them in the winter.
>
> Our grandparents taught me [Mary Davis] and my sister Mary (who died after going to school in Albuquerque) lots of things, like how to weave, make all the parts of the loom and put it together. They taught us how to put up the loom; they showed us how to make a little loom first and how to carry it around while we worked on our rugs.

Our first rugs were just awful; they were all out of shape and everything. But our grandfather did not scold us; he just said to keep trying. As we learned how to weave, he helped us make bigger and bigger looms.

When we finished our rugs, Man Who Shouts would help us take them off the loom, and then he would put another loom up for us. We did not know how to trade at the store or how to count money, so Man Who Shouts and his wife would take our rugs to the store with them in their one-horse, two-wheeled buggy and trade them for us. They were the only ones around with a buggy like that. When we went with them, they would always tell us to buy food with those rugs, not candy, and that is just what we did. When they traded them for us, they would always bring us each back some big treat. They kept the goods purchased with each rug separate so we could see what each was worth. Man Who Shouts was very patient during all of our learning to make rugs; he used to put up the looms and take them down without ever scolding us.

Our mother, who was also called Tall Woman, worked very hard from the beginning. She wove a lot and exchanged her rugs for food. She also took care of the children; by then about three of them had been born. There was always enough; when Frank would come home with his check, he too would buy food. Food was cheap then, and it seemed to us that in those days rugs were worth a lot of money and they brought in a lot at the trading posts. When Frank was home, we usually did what he told us to do right away. He never punished us with a whip, but he did whip Howard and David several times as they were growing up. He would control us mainly with his talks; he was very stern, and we were scared of him. We spent most of our time then living across the way, where I [Mary Davis] do now. There was water in the Canyon wash much of the time, and we were always sent to bring it home in containers. We usually did that right away when he told us to.

Man Who Shouts and his wife taught us lots of other things too. My sister Mary and I used to watch the two of them making pottery. They would let us come into a separate hogan which had to be used in making that pottery and let us sit in there and watch the whole process. We would gather the sheep dung for them for the firing. Man Who Shouts would go and bring in pine pitch and just bake it into that pot. When that was done, they would boil some water in that pot and then kill a lamb or a goat kid and cook it in that pot. Then that pot was ready for everyday use. Our mother also knew how to make pottery, and she used to help our grandmother and grandfather with that when we lived with them.

While Frank was gone much of that time, our mother, Tall Woman, just followed what her father said. She never planned ahead or stepped ahead of her husband at any time during her life; she always depended on him for advice and for the planning. When he was home, they never argued. She was always just concerned with her babies and raising her children. She followed her father in the same way; she never scolded us children or anything like that; that was probably because she took after her father.

Our grandparents also knew how to make paper bread on the Navajo grill stone. They made that cooking stone from a white rock that Man Who Shouts used to haul in all different sizes. He showed my sister and me how to grind that rock down so that it was smooth on the surface. He did that with stones which had been smoothed in the water for a long time. When it was ground down, he put pitch on the top of that. During this time, the rock was sitting in a burning fire. He and my grandmother would heat this rock to burn off that pitch. Then Man Who Shouts would get a pine branch and go over that rock, burning off all of that pitch and cleaning that stone with a pine brush. Then they put sheep fat on it and let it heat into it. When that was done, the stone was taken off the fire and set aside to cool. By then, it was as smooth as ice.

Our grandparents also taught us how to make the paper bread on that stone. We both learned a little bit about making baskets from them too. But they told us that making baskets took many days' work and that it was really hard to do that. They taught us about the different herbs and plants that were used for the inside and the outside. Now they just use those commercial dyes.

There were always a lot of people around my grandparents' place while we were living with them. Many of those people gathered around Man Who Shouts' hogan to hear him talk about his Blessingway ceremony. Sometimes Frank's father, Water Edge Man, used to stop by our place too. This grandfather would come and go during those days, and sometimes he would live with us for a while. Most of the time, he stayed up around Steamboat at a place called Pointed Red Rock. When he was moving around like that, he always left his livestock with the family of Tall Water Edge Man, the cousin Frank wrestled with. He stayed in Canyon del Muerto for awhile too, but much of the time he was at Pointed Red Rock, where Tall Water Edge Man's brother, Pointed Red Rock Man, was learning Blessingway from him.

* * *

Seya Mitchell gave a different picture of these years:

Frank gambled a lot during his years at the sawmill and the years when he was freighting. He would be gone for a whole year at a time sometimes, hauling freight and gambling. There was never enough food, and I learned very early from that what hard times are like. That is why I left home. Frank stopped wandering around like that when my grandfather, Man Who Shouts, died.

10. The Windway, in either its Navajo or Chiricahua Apache form, is used to cure any disease caused by wind infection, particularly heart, lung and head disease. See Wyman and Kluckhohn (1938:27-28), Kluckhohn and Wyman (1940:111-154) and Wyman (1962) for further information.

11. The Navajos have very strong taboos against contact with dead people (*ch'iindi*) or items, such as dwellings and personal possessions, which were associated with them. Traditionally the People burned hogans in which death had occurred or abandoned them, relocating at least one-half mile away. For further information, see Frank's discussion of burial taboos in Chapter 7, as well as Franciscan Fathers (1910), Haile (1917), Kluckhohn (1944 and

1948), Kluckhóhn and Leighton (1946), Reichard (1963) and Ward and Brugge (1975).

12. In the process of translating this section, Frank and Chic got into an interesting semantic discussion, the content of which is also applicable to translations of song texts which use the idea of "servant," or "slave." Chic Sandoval explained the concept as follows:

> When the term *naalté* is used in a song, it does not refer to a captive or prisoner of war. The servants in this case can be either men or women, who have been hired to work around the place of a rich man, in order to help with the chores and keep the standard of living up. They are not slaves because they are compensated for the work they are doing. When one acquires wealth, jewelry, soft goods, livestock, sheep, horses, cattle, mules and other things like that, someone has to tend to all of those things. So people are hired to do that. How they are compensated depends on the financial standing of the family and the work that the servant does. It is up to the boss. In most cases, the servant is given part of the things that he is tending; he is given a share of that and told to take it for his own; he is given instructions on how to care for it. If a servant is not working to the boss' satisfaction, then, of course, he does not get as much as one that does better quality work.
>
> The Navajos use different terms for those sets of black slaves. There are also war prisoners captured by the People, and they are used as slaves. If you are referring to one, then you use, *naalté*; for more than one, *na'nil*. Frank Mitchell does not agree with me on the use of those words. He says that *naalté* means a slave, a person who has been captured in a war and brought home and works without drawing wages. That person is just ordered around like the southerners used to do with the Negroes. Frank says that *na'nil* means a servant, one who gets some compensation for working. But it is my understanding that *naalté* means one servant, and *na'nil*, more than one.
>
> When your relatives go different places and help their kinsmen herd sheep and do other work, they are not classed as *na'nil* because they are members of the family. They are doing their share of the chores. If they went off to work for someone they were not related to, that would be a servant, or one who works under an agreement or contract for a certain length of time. If those people do not work to the boss' satisfaction, of course, the boss can just terminate them anytime. Or the person can just take off. But with a *naalté*, or slave (according to Frank), that's different. The slave has no liberty.
>
> When the Navajos had slaves, the slaves changed hands just like the Negroes did in the South. They were bought and sold by the bosses of the slaves. There is only one case of that that I know of among the Navajos; that was a man called Hastiin Chǫ'. He was a slave of a man over here. Another man went and bought him, and then he was his slave. When that second boss passed away, why that slave was free. Nobody else claimed him, so he went on his own then.

Interestingly enough, Father Berard Haile (1951:259, 266) gives the following information on the terms for slaves and servants: *naalt'é, naal'a'í* = slave; *yisná* = captive slave; and *naal'a'í* = servant. For further discussion about slaves, see Brugge 1968:117-134.

NOTES TO CHAPTER 5

13. Fort Defiance Agency Letter Books suggest that wagons were among the "seeds and agricultural implements" to be made available to the Navajo people by the government according to the Treaty of 1868. The construction of the Atlantic and Pacific Railroad through the Southwest facilitated the issuance of government supplies. In 1880 (Underhill 1953:207), eleven Navajos received wagons for use in farming; however, all wagons were disassembled by their owners for the iron they contained. In 1881, Manuelito requested and received a wagon from Agent Eastman, and Ganado Mucho was given a used spring wagon. Underhill (*Ibid.*) says that Manuelito was the first Navajo to learn to harness and drive, and that he made hundreds of dollars hauling supplies for the traders in the early years of the railroad.

By 1890, "there were some farm wagons and harnesses but not nearly enough," available from the agents. "By that time, however, many Navaho were prosperous enough to buy their own tools. They were sending east for expensive saddles and harness. Slowly the covered wagons which the People use today made their appearance. Sometimes the Navaho worked for these at the agency and sometimes bought them for themselves" (Underhill 1953:226).

Fort Defiance Agency Letter Book No. 26 (10/20/1898-9/4/1899) contains a letter (pp. 154-155) from Hayzlett to the Commissioner of Indian Affairs in Washington, D. C., showing that Navajo enthusiasm for wagons was a major factor in increasing school enrollments. Evidently, at least some agents were dispensing wagons, as well as axes, hoes, utensils and other items, to Navajos who enrolled their children in school. Fort Defiance Agency Letter Book No. 27 (9/6/1899-8/23/1900) shows that wagons were also being given by the agency to Navajos who hauled twenty to thirty-five loads of wood (1/25/1900 letter, p. 217). Letter Book No. 28 (7/1/1902-4/11/1903) contains information (pp. 19, 21) which indicates that on 7/19/1902 and 7/21/1902, buggies were valued at $110, spring wagons at $125, double harness at $40 and two horses at $200.

As Kluckhohn, Hill and Kluckhohn (1971:100) point out, the Franciscan Fathers' records of the early twentieth century confirm the mid-nineteenth century introduction of the wagon to the Navajos. As the Franciscan Fathers (1910:151) indicate, "Harness and wagons of any kind were not in use by the early Navaho, but are of quite recent introduction. They are issued by the Government, though many prefer to purchase a better grade of wagons and harness, including light rigs and buckboards for driving. The farm wagon is used for freighting, hauling wood, and often for travelling."

No specific information is available on the number of wagons owned by Chinle Navajos at this point in time. Chic Sandoval (Hoffman and Johnson 1970:251), however, refers to the team and wagon owned by the Franciscan Fathers at the mission, which he used in 1911 to haul trash away from the B.I.A. school construction site, for $2.50 per day.

14. In 1963 the wheels from Frank's first wagon were still at the Mitchell homestead, as shown in Fig. 13. They continued to provide a source of pride for Frank until his death.

15. As Appendix A shows, Frank and Tall Woman had a total of 12 children, 2 of whom died in infancy and 3 others who died before reaching adulthood.

16. See Chapter 4, n. 23.

17. See Chapter 4, n. 28. According to Chic Sandoval (Hoffman and Johnson 1970:252) the first automobile that came to Chinle belonged to the B.I.A. Boarding School construction contractor. He arrived in Chinle in his car upon completion of construction in the summer of 1911. Frank and other sources gave the date as 1910.

While non-Navajos began coming into the New Mexico-Arizona area in large numbers after the completion of the Atlantic and Pacific Railroad through Northern Arizona in 1881-82, the number of non-Navajos in Chinle remained sparse. Camille García, when recalling the early 1900s in Chinle (McNitt 1963:215), said, "not many tourists came to Chinle in those days — no cars and bad roads." The scarcity of outsiders was responsible for Lorenzo Hubbell's decision that his second post in Chinle would never be financially successful and his subsequent sale of the post to C. N. Cotton in 1917 (McNitt:*Ibid.*).

18. More specific details from Navajos about the identity of the Navajo freighters during this time, their employers, the routes they followed, the cargo and freighting costs are currently unavailable to the best of the editors' knowledge. McNitt's *The Indian Traders* does, however, provide excellent information from the trader's viewpoint.

By the 1870s freighting was being done for the agents under contractual agreements. "Indian traders themselves ordinarily freighted their own supplies and goods taken in trade, oxen and mules both seeing service until gradually retired during the 1890s by horses" (McNitt 1963:112). In the 1880s (*Ibid.*:81), traders were paying 50-75¢ per hundred weight for a four-horse team and wagon to haul freight the twenty-five to thirty miles between Fort Defiance and Manuelito.

In the 1880s the Atlantic and Pacific Railroad's route led to the establishment of Ferry Station seventeen miles west of Gallup. This spot became a terminal for trading posts to the north and west as well as for the Navajo agency. The station was a mile or two east of Manuelito. Freight headed for the agency was hauled by wagon north from Ferry Station through Manuelito Canyon into Ciénega Amarillo and on to Defiance, about twenty-eight miles (*Ibid.*:249).

By 1900, twenty-four traders were on the reservation, and they as well as government agents were sending ox carts to the freight station (Underhill 1953:208). Letter Books Nos. 26, 28 and 29 from the Fort Defiance Agency refer to the shipping that was in process by C. N. Cotton from Gallup, New Mexico, to Ganado, Arizona, at the turn of the century (Letter Book 26: 10/18/1899), his paying Indian freighters 50¢ per 100 pounds for hauling shingles (Letter Book 29:371) and some of the unfair trading practices of the period, wherein traders were forcing Navajos to transport supplies for 40¢ per

100 pounds (Letter Book 28:177). That Navajos were turning to freighting as an occupation also is reflected in the Franciscan Fathers' (1910:510) statement: "At present the Navaho are employed in hauling freight, carrying United States mail, as couriers, etc., and are usually willing to undertake anything for which horse or wagon may be of service."

McNitt (1963:214, 220, 257, 340, 343) conveys the dependency of traders on freighters during these times, as well as some of the working conditions. Likewise, he reveals agreements traders had with each other, the existence of the Hyde company freighters and freighters employed by Progressive Mercantile Wholesale and other wholesale stores, as well as the horse-drawn stage and freight service inaugurated by Lorenzo Hubbell in the spring of 1915, which operated from Gallup to Saint Michaels, Fort Defiance, Ganado, Chinle, Keams Canyon and Oraibi for varying fees. The passenger service ended long before the freighting, which continued until 1945.

19. Chic Sandoval said that Mr. Sand was Frank's stepfather, but this appears doubtful unless Hastiin Tsei was one of Star Gazer's Son's multiple names. Further clarification was not possible from family or clan relatives in 1971.

20. This gallon jug is called "partial white" by the Navajos. The jug is brown on the top and white on the bottom.

21. Although many Navajos know ceremonial songs, these are apt to be mainly for "good luck" and protection in their personal lives. The fact that Frank already knew a highly esoteric song seems to indicate that his interest in ceremonial materials and his ability to retain them in his memory developed earlier than his narrative implies.

22. In a subritual of ceremonials such as Enemyway where the purpose is protection from ghosts, witches or other dangerous powers, the one-sung-over is blackened with charcoal in order to be disguised and concealed. The blackening also conveys the powers of the substances that were burned to produce the charcoal and renders the blackened person frightening to ghosts (Reichard 1963:196; Franciscan Fathers 1910:371-375).

23. Although Kluckhohn (1964:92-96) found that the women of Ramah with whom he worked in the late 1930s had a limited knowledge of ceremonial matters, Navajo women as well as men can be diviners and ceremonial practitioners. Traditionally women were restricted from practicing ceremonials until after they had reached menopause.

24. Reference to Frank's work for the archaeological excavation team at Antelope Ruins was not included by him in the 1963 undirected version of his life history. Both editors had heard about it from Augusta and so asked him about it in 1964. Seya did not know anything about it because Frank never had mentioned it while he was home. Mary Davis knew that Frank had gone over there in his wagon, that the whole body of the mummy was there,

that the white people had dug it out and that it was solid and hard. She also knew he had helped roll it in a sheet, place it in a box which was then put in his wagon, and drive it out to the mission, where those people had transferred it to a case. Mary said she had once asked her father for more details about the incident and he had started telling her, but Tall Woman came in and scolded him for talking about it. Tall Woman had made him stop his whole story, and he never finished it.

Tall Woman continued to maintain throughout Frank's life that the fact that he had helped transport the body from the ruins would probably make him very sick, and that he would make it worse by talking about it and joking around about it. Mary remembers Tall Woman's mother also telling Frank that that was wrong because the event had occurred when Tall Woman was most likely pregnant with one of the children.

25. Attempts to identify and/or date this Canyon de Chelly excavation have been unproductive, at least to date. That it occurred after Frank earned his first wagon and before others in Chinle did the same seems certain from his story. This would place the dig between 1909 and 1915. The few of Frank's children who ever heard him talk about the incident can only add that Frank "probably did that soon after he married our mother [Tall Woman]; he was very young then and wasn't scared of doing anything. At that time he was doing just about everything under the sun." Augusta and Mary say that Frank was "the only one in the area who had a wagon when that happened," and that "those men were white men from Washington." Seya suggests that it may have happened while the Chinle school was under construction (1910-11), since Frank was in Chinle at that time with his wagon.

A date closer to 1915 is suggested by the fact that the archaeologists packed their findings into an automobile, which they had waiting in Chinle. A terminal date for the possible time of occurrence would be 1930. The initial discussion of the possibility of a National Monument in Canyon de Chelly took place on July 7, 1925, during the Tribal Council meeting (see Navajo Tribal Council 1925:34-35 and Brugge and Wilson 1976:7-17). The idea was originally introduced by H. J. Hagerman, commissioner to the Navajos. During the eighth Annual Navajo Tribal Council Meeting, July 7-8, 1930 at Fort Wingate, New Mexico, the Council voted to adopt a resolution approving the bill authorizing the President of the United States to establish Canyon de Chelly National Monument within the Navajo Indian Reservation, Arizona (see Navajo Tribal Council 1930:65-73 and Brugge and Wilson 1976:7-17).

A careful review of archaeological site report data does not illuminate matters further. David Brugge brought Frisbie's attention to the Dr. F. M. Palmer dig at Antelope Ruins in 1906. Sponsored by the South West Society of the Archaeological Institute of America, Dr. Palmer, the curator and director of the excavation, arrived from Los Angeles and worked at Antelope Ruins in 1906. An album of fifty photographs taken by Virgil Huff White documents this excavation. The album, which has been donated to the Park Service Museum (catalog #3282, #17), includes pictures of Arizona, California, Chinle, Canyon de Chelly, Antelope House, Navajo crewmen and a burial. The Navajo guide for the expedition is shown alone in several photographs, and is identified as "Hastiin Nez, son of Chief Hastiin Yaza." This guide is also shown in a dark group photo with other unidentified and unidentifiable Navajos. Upon viewing the photos, Augusta said there was no chance that Hastiin Nez was Frank; her identification was based on the single subject photos and the fact that no other Navajos assisted the archaeological crew to which Frank refers in his story.

Another lead, again provided by David Brugge, was to Don Morris of the Arizona Archaeological Center in Tucson. An exchange of information and further discussion with Morris, who was working at Antelope House in 1971, led Frisbie to further research. One of Morris' suggestions was that Earl Morris may have directed the dig on which Frank assisted. A letter written by Earl Morris to the Superintendent of Canyon de Chelly refers to Morris' photographing of pictographs at Antelope House on 6/3/1923 (MS: Canyon de Chelly National Monument. Field Notes, C. L. Bernheimer, pp. 14-15 through Don Morris, personal communication, 1972).

Subsequent research showed Earl Morris worked in Canyon del Muerto in 1922, 1923 (Mummy Cave), 1924, at White House in 1926, Tseahatso, and Antelope Cave in del Muerto in 1929. As reported by Ann Morris (1933), mummy bodies were uncovered from Tseahatso Cave in del Muerto, Mummy Cave, and from a rock shelter up-canyon from Antelope Cave in del Muerto, where the burial became known as The Tomb of the Weaver (see Lister and Lister 1968:139-141). Morris headquartered at Cozy McSparron's trading post in Chinle in 1923, and described the town as consisting of a government Indian school, a church and two trading posts (Morris 1933:142). Cozy's is described as a "hotel, restaurant, supply center, post office (including rural delivery for telegrams via Indian pony), employment agency for Navajo workmen, and general contact point with the great outside world" (*Ibid.*:144).

The fall 1923 dig used a wagon and four mules, although the following year Morris was experimenting with taking cars into the Canyon, and the 1923 crew included five Navajos, among others. Morris preferred crews which combined white, Zuni and Navajo workers, and he found the Zunis steadier and less temperamental than the Navajos. That Earl Morris was well acquainted with the Navajos is illustrated by Chapter XI, "The Irrepressible Navajo," in Morris (1933), and the numerous photographs of Navajos within this same account. None of the Navajo crewmen are identified in the photographs or the text, however, and nowhere, either in this publication or those of Earl Morris related to finds of this period (Morris 1925, 1938, 1948) is there any indication he ever used only one Navajo assistant. The possibility that the notes of Earl Morris housed in the University of Colorado Museum might facilitate further identification of his Navajo workmen remains open.

Don Morris of the Arizona Archaeological Center also suggested that a review of the field notes of C. L. Bernheimer who was working at Antelope House in 1918 would be appropriate. Such a review, however, has not yet been possible, but a 1923 publication by Bernheimer was checked and found to be topically unrelated to the problem.

Don Morris also suggested that Frisbie contact Chauncey NeBoyia, a Chinle Navajo who worked with Earl Morris and other archaeologists for about fifty years. The materials were sent to Chauncey, who replied, through Augusta Sandoval, that the work that Frank ("a close relation of his") had done must have been before the time of Morris, since he had never heard of it in all of his years as Park Service guide. Chauncey joined Morris in the fall of 1923 at the age of twenty-four (Steve Jett, personal communication, 1975).

Among other approaches attempted was that of reviewing the work of the Sam Day family (Trafzer 1973:259-274 and Brugge and Wilson 1976:3-4). When Sam Day, Sr. arrived to begin trading in Chinle in 1902, he was immediately impressed by the archaeological remains as well as the beauty of Canyon de Chelly. One son, Sam Day, Jr., was reportedly the first to enter Massacre Cave in 1902, and the collection which resulted from this visit was sold to the Brooklyn Museum where Stewart Culin was curator. On 6/1/1903 another son, Charles L. Day (who was guide-interpreter for Edward S. Curtis), was appointed custodian of the canyons de Chelly and del Muerto (Fort Defiance Agency Letter Book 29:28). Part of his job was to prevent further unauthorized excavations; "nonetheless, illicit diggings continued" (Trafzer 1973:265).

Whether the group Frank assisted was among those doing "illicit" digging is unknown at present, although the excavation techniques Frank describes hardly sound like those of pot hunters. It is possible that a review of the Collection of the Day Family papers, housed at Northern Arizona University Library, Flagstaff, Arizona, might provide further illumination.

In summary, research to date has not provided further clarification of the single archaeological episode in Frank's life story. Future reviews of Bernheimer's field notes, the Earl Morris papers and the Day Family papers may provide answers to some of the remaining questions. Likewise, it is also hopeful that a book on Canyon de Chelly by Campbell Grant (in press at the time of this writing) and continuing archaeological investigations at Antelope House may eventually lead to further clarification.

26. In Enemyway, a bit of scalp or some other part of an enemy's person or clothing is used ritually to represent the enemy ghost. See Haile (1938) and McAllester (1954).

27. Later in Frank's life his participation in this excavation was cited by a hand-trembler as one of the reasons he was ill and in need of an Enemyway ceremonial (see Chapter 10).

28. See note 11.

29. Here Frank is probably referring to Snaketown.

30. The Navajos are Athabascan speakers who migrated into the Southwest from a homeland in Alaska and northwest Canada sometime between 1400 and the late 1600s A.D. Adapting cultural traits from Great Basin and Plains groups during their journeys, the People later had much contact with the Puebloan groups who were already in the Southwest. Intermarriage and much borrowing of traits resulted, but the Puebloan people were not actually the

ancestors of the Navajos as Frank states. Archaeologically we know that the Navajos were well established in Canyon de Chelly by the mid-eighteenth century (see Hester 1962).

31. Frank was probably referring to the Heard Museum in Phoenix.

32. In Shootingway and certain other ceremonials, an inverted basket is tapped rhythmically to accompany the singing. The drumstick is made of plaited yucca leaves. See Matthews (1894).

33. Despite his interest in preserving ruins, on Sept. 8, 1930, Frank Mitchell was one of between sixty and seventy Navajos who attended the Chinle Court day and signed a petition against the proposed bill establishing Canyon de Chelly as a National Monument. The petition arose from a fear that the boundaries would be more extensive than originally thought and that the Indians would lose their grazing, agricultural, wood-gathering and other rights in the area. On October 2, 1930, Special Commissioner Hagerman sent a letter to Superintendent John Hunter commenting on the petition he had received. Hunter attended the Chinle Court day, October 8, 1930, and explained the matter extensively. The result was a new petition retracting the earlier one, signed by 152 Navajos including Frank Mitchell (see Brugge and Wilson 1976:13-14, Chinle Navajos 1930a and b, Hagerman 1930 and Hunter 1930).

34. Coincidentally, right at this point in the story-telling, a pair of Mormon missionaries arrived at the Mitchells. Frank requested that the tape recorder be shut off and then said, "That's why I don't like these Mormons who come running around the country here, roaming all over the place serving people."

6. In the Beginning

*Frank tells a myth of Navajo origins: coming up from the
underworld, the contest in the water . . . origins of the mountains
and Mountain songs, the first hogans and Hogan songs, the
Earth's Surface songs, first Placing of the Mountain songs and
other Mountain songs, a prayer to rectify mistakes . . . the People
inhabit the country: how the clans started . . . the animal
protectors, fight with the Arrow People, guardian animals return
to their homes . . . clan origins from places and people . . . the
People are taught ceremonies.*

I do not know who the ancestors of the Navajos were.[1] They probably
originated from some other Indians. After I started to learn the Blessingway, I
began to pay attention to those stories. According to what I learned, a group
came up from under the earth — they must have been some kind of
supernatural beings. They were given this area of land within the four sacred
mountains.[2] It was in this area that the Navajos had their beginnings.

The whole place was covered with water at that time. Then the water
was removed so something could be planted and grow on the earth. The water
was all removed to the ocean, perhaps. And from there the first songs and
prayers of the Blessingway had their start. They were for the planting of
crops. The first thing the Holy People did was to make a song and a prayer
for the plants on the earth so the earth would be fruitful. That was the first
song and the first prayer to be performed, and they were the first ones that I
learned. They were the most important ones that I had to learn, right from
the beginning of the ceremony.

It is through this that we have summer and winter. In the springtime
everything comes up from the ground just the way it happened in those first
days, when it was all made in the beginning. In the wintertime the plants all
die and are buried under the snow, and then late in the spring they all come
back up again to make all the crops in the summer.

This whole surface where we're living now was under water, and when
people appeared on this earth they encountered some kind of water beings or
water animals; I don't know what they were. They drained the ocean from all

this region and made the land appear so that the people could come on this land and use it. From the story we were told, since this was all under ocean water at one time and then drained off, that kind of water should not be brought back here and used again on this earth. The water that has been made available since that time, springs, rivers — natural sources of water, not wells that have been dug or anything like that — those are the waters that we use for ourselves. So, according to the way I have been taught, we do not use water from the ocean for any purpose.

But shells from the ocean we do use.[3] I value them very highly. Like abalone shells, for example — we have lots of uses for them. But not the fish that live inside them. They belong in the ocean, whatever things are inside those shells, and they should not be brought out here.

The old people were before the time of the Navajos, because we never saw them. The only thing we know about them is that they must be the Holy People we talk about in our legends. The First Man and the First Woman in our stories were the leaders of these people, and they inhabited the lower world, the world below us.[4] We have no idea what kind of people they were; all we know about them is what has been handed down in the legends about how they lived. It used to be said that they were desperate people, always being moved along from one place to another. The reason they were always moving was that they were being forced to. When they came up from the lower world to this one, they found the surface of the earth all under water. And the water was full of creatures living on the water and under the water, too. They were dangerous: they ate people.

All I know about the story is that the old people just moved about, the way ants do. Ants dig out of the ground and come to the surface. When the old people came up from the bottom to the surface of the water, the first one was the locust, and he started building some kind of structure there, rising up out of the water. When the locust came to the surface of this earth, above the water, some of these water beings came from the four directions and met him. They questioned him as to where he came from and what he was doing there, and he went ahead and told them that his people were being pursued by a flood of water and that they were coming up from down below.

Then the locust told these beings that even though the place was all under water, they would like to settle down somewhere so that they could live there. These beings told the locust they would not permit him to settle there because it was all owned by somebody already. But the locust kept on asking and said they were being pursued by a flood of water coming from below. "We have no other place to go!" he said. He insisted that they be allowed to settle down there.

Of course they exchanged words back and forth for some time. Then one of the water beings, there in the water, showed the locust that he had tail-feathered arrows with him. He thrust one arrow down his mouth and the other up through his anus and pulled them right through in opposite directions. Then he tossed them to the locust. "Now," he said, "If you can do as I did, we might permit you to stay."

So the locust picked up the arrows and said, "That's easy, you already had an opening at both ends there. That's not difficult. But if you can do what I do, then we won't move up here, we'll stay down in the underworld." And he took the two arrows and thrust them sidewise through his chest from opposite directions and pulled them on through like that and tossed them back to the water being.

Of course he knew it was impossible for the water being to do that. That is where his heart is, so he just swam off. That was done four times. The first water being came at him from the east, the second from the south, the third from the west and the fourth from the north. There were four of them that came to him, and there were four tests like that. He just showed them what he could do, and after it was all over they just left him.

The next thing that came was a bald eagle. There was something he placed on the top of his head to gouge out trenches so that the water ran off in different directions. Of course the water all ran off that way and settled where it is now, in the present oceans. So that is where the first people settled, and according to that, I do not think we Navajos were in existence at the time of the flood.

Then after that was all done, the next thing was for the earth to produce all kinds of plants. Because of that the people were puzzled. They did not know how to get any growing things started on earth. So that is why leaders were created at that time. Then of course everything was made according to their planning. That is why they are called the leaders, the planners, the chief planners. It was similar to our present arrangements. We have Chapter officers for the various communities, grazing committees for the districts, and then we have land management committees, land use committees — different ones for different things.[5]

About the mountains, too: they were in existence in the lower world. They did not have any sun down there. All they had were lights that came up every so often in the four directions, which gave them light to go by. There was white in the east, in the south it was blue, over in the west it was yellow and down there in the north it was black. There were beings lying inside those curtains of light, lying flat on their backs. And right over their mouths was something containing pinches of dirt. Those are the pinches of earth that were picked up there and brought up here to this world. That is what formed these mountains up here. The pinch of earth picked up at the east curtain, at the east side, was used to form the east mountain in our present country. And the one in the south was used to form the mountain in the south. And the one that was picked up in the west was to be the west mountain. And from the north, the north mountain. That is where they started singing the Chief Hogan songs. They were being used to make those mountains holy and strong.

The original hogan, the very first hogan that was built, was put up at the edge of the Emergence Place. After that a place was fixed for Changing Woman. It was formed in the shape of a hogan, and it was also marked with the sacred marking of cornmeal. That was the hogan in which Enemy Slayer was to be born, and it is where Changing Woman had her coming-of-age ceremony performed.

There were only two styles of hogans in the beginning. The one that was built at the edge of Emergence Place is the type with the uprights set in the ground and with a flat top. And the one where Changing Woman was living at Fir Mountain,[6] that is the kind with the main poles forked together. Those were the only two styles of hogans at the beginning. Of course, as time went on they changed the styles and made them in all different ways, you see.

Nowadays we have songs about that. The first song says: "It's being talked about. . . ." those are the words of the first song: "It's being talked about, it's being discussed." Then later songs say: "It's being set in position. . . ." and so on. There is a song for each action as the house is being built.

You see, the main ones involved in building the first hogan were First Man and First Woman. And besides them, there were other people who have taken the form of animals now, but in those days they were humans, as we are. When they arrived on the surface of this earth, there was no vegetation of any kind. Of course it was all under water when they arrived here. When the water was drained off, then of course the earth was dried, and after that is when the vegetation started to grow. But even before that some of those people had in their possession different kinds of materials for building. The beaver had wood, for instance, and the mountain sheep had wood, too, and the various other animals had other things. They used these materials: we do not know exactly what they were.

They did not start these songs we sing now until after the hogan was completed. The songs mention these different individuals, like Earth Woman and Water Woman and Mountain Woman and the Corn People. Everybody helped build it, all the people who had come up from the underworld. First Man and First Woman were the first couple. They were the ones who were the head of the family made up of all those people. That is the reason they are mentioned in those songs, too. I do not know what language was being used when that first hogan was made, but the words in the songs now are like the language we speak today. So here are two of those Chief Hogan songs[7]:

Heye nene yaŋa,
One is thinking about it, one is thinking about it,
One is thinking about it, one is thinking about it, *holaghei.*

Its main beam, Earth is to be made the main beam,
    One is thinking about it,

Its main beam, Wood Woman is to be made the main beam,
  One is thinking about it,
Now *Sạ'ah naaghéi, Bik'eh hózhǫ́ǫ́*[8] are to be made the main beam,
  One is thinking about it,
One is thinking about it, one is thinking about it,
One is thinking about it, one is thinking about it.

Its main beam, Mountain Woman is to be made the main beam,
  One is thinking about it,
Its main beam, Wood Woman is to be made the main beam,
  One is thinking about it,
Now *Sạ'ah naaghéi, Bik'eh hózhǫ́ǫ́* are to be made the main beam,
  One is thinking about it,
One is thinking about it, one is thinking about it,
One is thinking about it, one is thinking about it.

Its main beam, Water Woman is to be made the main beam,
  One is thinking about it,
Its main beam, Wood Woman is to be made the main beam,
  One is thinking about it,
Now *Sạ'ah naaghéi, Bik'eh hózhǫ́ǫ́* are to be made the main beam,
  One is thinking about it,
One is thinking about it, one is thinking about it,
One is thinking about it, one is thinking about it.

Its main beam, Corn Plant Woman is to be made the main beam,
  One is thinking about it,
Its main beam, Wood Woman is to be made the main beam,
  One is thinking about it,
One is thinking about it, one is thinking about it,
One is thinking about it, one is thinking about it, *holaghei*.

* * *

Heye nene yaŋa,[9]
Howowo 'aiye ye! It is a sacred house that I have come to,
It is a sacred house that I have come to,
Howowo 'ai yeye 'aiye! It is a sacred house that I have come to,
It is a sacred house that I have come to,
Howowa 'ai ne! It is a sacred house that I have come to,
It is a sacred house that I have come to, *holaghei*.

Now I have come to the house of the Earth,
Now I have come to a house built of wood,
Now I have come to a house built of all kinds of soft fabrics,
Now I have come to a sacred house, the sacred house of *Są'ah naaghéi,*
    Now, of *Bik'eh hózhǫǫ.*

Howowo 'aiye ye! It is a sacred house that I have come to,
It is a sacred house that I have come to,
Howowo, 'ai yeye 'aiye! It is a sacred house that I have come to,
It is a sacred house that I have come to,
Howowa 'ai ne! It is a sacred house that I have come to,
It is a sacred house that I have come to.

Now I have come to the house of Mountain Woman,
Now I have come to a house built of wood,
Now I have come to a house built of all kinds of jewels,
I have come to a sacred house, the sacred house of *Są'ah naaghéi,*
    Now, of *Bik'eh hózhǫǫ.*

Howowo 'aiye ye! It is a sacred house that I have come to,
It is a sacred house that I have come to,
Howowo 'ai yeye 'aiye! It is a sacred house that I have come to,
It is a sacred house that I have come to,
Howowa 'ai ne! It is a sacred house that I have come to,
It is a sacred house that I have come to.

Now I have come to the house of Water Woman,
Now I have come to a house built of wood,
Now I have come to a house built of all kinds of gathered rain waters,
I have come to a sacred house, the sacred house of *Są'ah naaghéi,*
    Now, of *Bik'eh hózhǫǫ.*

Howowo 'aiye ye! It is a sacred house that I have come to,
It is a sacred house that I have come to,
Howowo 'ai yeye 'aiye! It is a sacred house that I have come to,
It is a sacred house that I have come to,
Howowa 'ai ne! It is a sacred house that I have come to,
It is a sacred house that I have come to.

Now I have come to the house of Corn Plant Woman,
Now I have come to a house built of wood,
Now I have come to a house built of corn pollen,

I have come to a sacred house, the sacred house of *Sạ'ah naaghéi,*
    Now, of *Bik'eh hózhǫǫ.*

Howowo 'aiye ye! It is a sacred house that I have come to,
It is a sacred house that I have come to,
Howowo 'ai yeye 'aiye! It is a sacred house that I have come to,
It is a sacred house that I have come to,
Howowa 'ai ne! It is a sacred house that I have come to,
It is a sacred house that I have come to, *holaghei.*

Four Holy People were chosen to be responsible for the four main poles of the hogan, and they were supposed to mark these poles: one in the east, the west, the south and the north.[10] The first pole, to the east, was marked with the dawn by Earth Woman. The next pole was the one in the west, and it was marked by Mountain Woman with jewels. Next was the pole in the south. It was marked by Water Woman with cornmeal. The reason that these sacred materials were used in marking the poles is that they are the things that would be used ceremonially in there later on. Soft fabrics are used in the hogan, and jewels are used in there. Water is used in there, too, and so is corn pollen.

After everything was completed, the Holy People brought all their belongings into the hogan. That is when they sang the songs for building the hogan. There were thirteen songs and then a fourteenth one to conclude them, a sort of blessing song to finish off with. It was First Man who was the leader of all this. It was his idea to have the songs follow the steps of building the hogan, about preparing it and putting it into use for a dwelling place.

Marking the house in the four directions was according to what was done below in the lower world where they came from. You see, down there they did not have any sun to give them light. There was a dawn curtain in the east that moved up to give them light. Then in the west they had a curtain of evening twilight for the same purpose. In the south they had the sky blue, and in the north was the darkness. And there was something like the dew, or the moisture, of each of these curtains of light that was used in marking the first hogan.

At the beginning they marked it crisscross – east-west and south-north – and the words in the songs went accordingly. Now we go sunwise: east, south, west and north. The pole on the east side was marked with the dawn – therefore they use white corn today, the meal of white corn.

The second hogan was put up for the purpose of planning – it was the "chief's hogan," the "planner's hogan." This was done under the instructions of Changing Woman from her home in the west. The present kind of wood was used then, and the four main poles were marked. For the conical-shaped hogan, the east pole is the one that comes up from the south side of the doorway, facing the east. Then, of course, there is a pole coming up from the south, the west (that is the main pole) and the north. Those are the ones that were marked, but we do not know who did the marking. Even those two boys who were carried off to the west to be instructed as to where this holy hogan was, not even they were told who it was who marked the second hogan.[11]

Fir Mountain is a hill in the shape of a hogan. Then Mountain Around Which Traveling Was Done is the home of Monster Slayer and Born for Water, and is built for war. He was the one who did away with the monsters that inhabited the earth. Fir Mountain is mostly for peace, the peaceful way of life. According to my father, Fir Mountain was the first one to be built of those two. He named that in his songs as being the first, before Mountain Around Which Traveling Was Done. But my other teacher, Man Who Shouts, had it the other way around. According to the story about that, he said that Mountain Around Which Traveling Was Done was the lung of the earth and the other mesa, Fir Mountain, was the heart of the earth.

The two boys were told by Changing Woman in the west, "When you build homes in which you are going to live, you must mark them in the four directions, just as was done for my home on Fir Mountain." That is what she told them. They were told to do the marking with cornmeal. That was after corn was created by placing jewels in the ground. They grew up into a cornstalk, and Talking God was performing a ritual over it as it grew up. When it matured it had twelve ears. Six ears were kept by the Holy People, and six ears were for the use of the human race.

When the earth was established with the vegetation on it, there was still no life. So, for all these things, souls were created to make them come to life. The souls were placed alongside those things on the earth: that is what you call "placing the pairs." And then a Twelve-Word song comes in that is called the Earth Surface song.[12] It tells about when the earth was in place and all the plants were there and the souls were put into them.

'ai- nai- yaŋa,
Her grandchild, *ye,* you are, *yeyi,* really, *ye,*
Her grandchild, *ye,* you are, *yeyi,* really,
Her grandchild, you are, *ye,* you are, *yeye, neyowo.*

Now, Earth, *ŋaŋaleye,* its indwelling one, *yiyi' neye,*
    Her grandchild, *ye,* you are, *yeyi,* really, *ye,*
    Her grandchild, *ye,* you are, *yeyi,* really,
    Her grandchild, you are, *ye,* you are, *ye, neyowo,*
Now, Sky, dark, *yiyi ɫeye,* its indwelling one, *yiyi' neye,*
    His grandchild, *ye,* you are, *yeyi,* really, *ye,*
    His grandchild, *ye,* you are, *yeyi,* really,
    His grandchild, you are, *ye,* you are, *yeyi' neye.*

Now, Black Belt Mountain, *yiyi*, its indwelling one, *yiyi' neye*,
    Its grandchild, *ye*, you are, *yeyi*, really, *ye*,
    Its grandchild, *ye*, you are, *yeyi*, really,
    Its grandchild, you are, *ye*, you are, *ye*, *neyowo*,
Now, Tongue Mountain, *yiyi łeye*, its indwelling one, *yiyi' neye*,
    Its grandchild, *ye*, you are, *yeyi*, really, *ye*,
    Its grandchild, *ye*, you are, *yeyi*, really,
    Its grandchild, you are, *ye*, you are, *ye*, *neyowo*.

Dook'o'oslííd, yiyi deye, its indwelling one, *yiyi' neye*,
    Its grandchild, *ye*, you are, *yeyi*, really, *ye*,
    Its grandchild, *ye*, you are, *yeyi*, really,
    Its grandchild, you are, *ye*, you are, *ye*, *neyowo*,
Big Sheep Mountain, *ŋaŋa yeye*, its indwelling one, *yiyi' neye*,
    Its grandchild, *ye*, you are, *yeyi*, really, *ye*,
    Its grandchild, *ye*, you are, *yeyi*, really,
    Its grandchild, you are, *ye*, you are, *ye*, *neyowo*.

Turquoise Boy, *yiyi 'eye*, his indwelling one, *yiyi' neye*,
    His grandchild, *ye*, you are, *yeyi*, really, *ye*,
    His grandchild, *ye*, you are, *yeyi*, really,
    His grandchild, you are, *ye*, you are, *ye*, *neyowo*,
White Shell Girl, *yeye deye*, her indwelling one, *yiyi' neye*,
    Her grandchild, *ye*, you are, *yeyi*, really, *ye*,
    Her grandchild, *ye*, you are, *yeyi*, really,
    Her grandchild, you are, *ye*, you are, *ye*, *neyowo*.

Abalone Boy, *yiyi 'eye*, his indwelling one, *yiyi' neye*,
    His grandchild, *ye*, you are, *yeyi*, really, *ye*,
    His grandchild, *ye*, you are, *yeyi*, really,
    His grandchild, you are, *ye*, you are, *ye*, *neyowo*,
Black Jewel Girl, *yeye deye*, her indwelling one, *yiyi' neye*,
    Her grandchild, *ye*, you are, *yeyi*, really, *ye*,
    Her grandchild, *ye*, you are, *yeyi*, really,
    Her grandchild, you are, *ye*, you are, *ye*, *neyowo*.

Są'ah naaghéi Boy, *yiyi 'eye*, his indwelling one, *yiyi' neye*,
    His grandchild, *ye*, you are, *yeyi*, really, *ye*,
    His grandchild, *ye*, you are, *yeyi*, really,
    His grandchild, you are, *ye*, you are, *ye*, *neyowo*,

Bik'eh hózhǫ́ǫ́ Girl, *yeyi deye,* her indwelling one, *yiyi' neye,*
   Her grandchild, *ye,* you are, *yeyi,* really, *ye,*
   Her grandchild, *ye,* you are, *yeyi,* really,
   Her grandchild, you are, *ye,* you are, *ye, neyowo.*

   Her grandchild, *ye,* you are, *yeyi,* really, *ye,*
   Her grandchild, *ye,* you are, *yeyi,* really,
   Her grandchild, you are, *ye,* you are, *ye, neyowo.*

After that in the Blessingway come the Mountain songs, where those four sacred mountains were placed in their positions. The way these should be sung, the Mountain songs begin with the mountain of the east, then the south, then the west, then the north, and then it goes to Mountain Around Which Traveling Was Done and ends up with Fir Mountain. That is the way my father told me, but according to Man Who Shouts, my father-in-law, the words in his songs went the same way except that he switched the last two mountains: he mentioned Fir Mountain first and then ended with Mountain Around Which Traveling Was Done. As for me, I use it either way.

     Leader Mountain, see it over there, rising up,
     Leader Mountain, see it over there, rising up.

Black Belt Mountain, *haŋa hea'ahe,*
White Shell Mountain,
Dziłnanita, decorated with *Są'ah naaghéi, Bik'eh hózhǫ́ǫ́,*

Tongue Mountain, *haŋa ho'a'ahe,*
Turquoise Mountain,
Dziłnanita, decorated with *Są'ah naaghéi, Bik'eh hózhǫ́ǫ́,*

Dook'o'oslííd, haŋa ho'a 'ahe,
Abalone Mountain,
Dziłnanita, decorated with *Są'ah naaghéi, Bik'eh hózhǫ́ǫ́,*

Sheep Mountain, *haŋa ho'a 'ahe,*
Black Jewel Mountain,
Dziłnanita, decorated with *Są'ah naaghéi, Bik'eh hózhǫ́ǫ́,*

Fir Mountain, *haŋa ho'a 'ahe,*
Soft Fabrics Mountain,
Dziłnanita, decorated with *Są'ah naaghéi, Bik'eh hózhǫ́ǫ́,*

Mountain Around Which Traveling Was Done, *haŋa ho'a 'ahe,*
Hard Jewels Mountain,
Dziłnanita, decorated with *Sǫ'ah naaghéi, Bik'eh hózhǫ́ǫ́,*

Leader Mountain, see it over there, rising up,
Leader Mountain, see it over there, rising up![13]

The people in those villages got to multiplying so fast they were
crowding each other. And they were getting so closely populated that there
was a discussion about what to do for a solution. They were ordered to move
to various places like the mountains, to the holy places in the mountains,
holy places in the rocks, holy places where the waters are, where the springs
are. They were told that they would disappear into those locations and would
live there without dying off. They would just continue on with no births and
no deaths. Those people who went to live in all those holy places would have
everlasting life, it seems.

But it was said, "Some of you who are left here behind, after all these
other people have gone into these holy places out of sight, you will still have
death, and you will have to have births to replace the dead. Like the plants,
they grow up from seed and mature, and they die off when the time comes.
They dry up, but they have produced the next crop of seed. That is the way
you will be, also."

When they went away like that they still had ways of communicating
with each other. Just like your electrical instruments here. I used to wonder
how they could talk to each other like that without being near each other,
but now I understand. The white people were the ones who figured it out.
Now, regardless of where anything is going on, whether it is on the other side
of the world or far away elsewhere, they will hear it, just as though it were
here before us.

And so, therefore, I know that what I have been saying has already
been heard in those holy places by their means of hearing things. That is the
reason we are told not to say anything we should not say. That is the reason
whenever you say a prayer or sing a song, at the end of it you always say a
prayer of your own. You say, "Well, my Holy Beings, I don't claim to know
everything about what I did. I was just doing as well as I could with what
knowledge I have of it. I hope it does not displease you or anger you, because
I know I am not expert in all these things."

At the end of prayers you always say something like that in your own
words and ask for understanding from these beings. Of course they listen to
you; they hear you. They hear what you say and the words of your
performance. And you plead with them and say, "May I live on into life
continually renewed, according to which blessing is everywhere." Those are
the final words in your prayer.

I do not know what killed those early people off, what kind of epidemic might have come among them and wiped them off the earth. I asked Curly Hair, and he said he had an answer for it. He said that a big cyclone, a tornado, got them. That was his answer. At the present time all we see is the ruins, the remains of their homes. That is all that is visible to us. We do not know what happened to them at all. When I asked Curly Hair about that he said they were wiped off the face of the earth by a strong tornado or a cyclone. Then he turned around and asked me what I knew about it. I said, "I don't know anything about it, but this is what I heard," and I told him just what I repeated here. My father told me this different story, that they vanished because of water or rain. He thought it must be water because you see all those water marks in Canyon de Chelly and it is below the water marks that you see some of their ruins.

Now all these different chants, like Male Shootingway, Female Shootingway, the Navajo Windway, and in fact all of them down to the small rituals, all these originated with these people and holy beings who used to live in the ruins. This is my late father's account of it. Well, that is the reason I am very careful of it. I do not want to tell anything I did not hear from others, those who taught me. I have to watch what I say so that I do not make any error in any of these things. So that is another reason that I would like to have all this recorded for the future. Of course I am going to die of old age some day, if I live that long. That is the order that was laid down for us, that we would be dying off.

So the belief is that any singers, those who use any ceremonies or any stories, are not entirely gone when they pass away. Their stories are still here for the future use of the People. It is like the plants, like corn and beans. When they mature you pick the seed and you plant it again. It comes up again and produces some more seeds. So it is with the human race.

Each clan has its own story of origin and how it is related to the others. Many people among the Navajos go into these matters about the clans in great detail, but my father said, "This does not go with the Blessingway songs that you are learning, so just ignore it. You're learning the Blessingway ceremony here, so stick purely to that. It's too complicated. It's pretty hard to go into, and it has nothing to do with the Blessingway ceremony anyway." It is confusing, and that is the reason I never got all the details about each clan.

You see, when I was learning the Blessingway from my father, he told me to just forget about those things. But on the other hand, my father-in-law, Man Who Shouts, had a little taste for warfare in him. His uncles and other relatives probably participated in raiding; he used to have a lot of interest in talking about such things. So there was a difference, you see; one of my teachers said to ignore everything else, and the other encouraged me to be interested.

So here are some of the things Man Who Shouts told me about the clans. Changing Woman (or White Shell Woman) used to live in Fir Mountain before she went to the West. It is in the shape of a conical hogan. Mountain Around Which Traveling Was Done is a flat-topped mesa in the style of the kind of hogan with uprights supporting the door.

Changing Woman moved to the West and was told by the Holy People to create human beings. She rubbed her right breast and made a female, and she rubbed her left breast and made a male. They became the Bitter Water Clan. That is the reason they speak of a man as the side that holds the bow, and a woman as the side that holds the stirring stick. So when they are having the blackening ceremony, they mark the woman on the right cheek with three spots and two spots on the left with sparkling black powder. They reverse it for a man.

Then Changing Woman rubbed her back; a man came from the right side and a woman from the left. The pair that came from this became the Standing House Clan. That is the reason they speak of a man as having his left side exposed to the enemy and a woman as having her right side facing the fire. Then she rubbed her arms; the upper part of her right arm made a man, and the underside of it, all the way down to the waist, gave material which became a woman. The sayings are the same for these people. They became the Near the Water Clan. Then she rubbed her left arm; from the under part of it she formed a man, and from the upper part of it came a woman. They were the Mud Clan. Because she switched around like this in the way she created people, she caused confusion. That is why people today argue about certain customs.

Then she made four pairs by rubbing skin from various parts of her body. She matched them: the woman from her right breast was matched with the man from her left arm. They were not clan relations, so they could marry. She laid them down as man and wife: Standing House Woman with Bitter Water Man; Bitter Water Woman with Standing House Man. This is why there is all the argument over so many things. In one instance the man was made first and the woman was made second; at other times it was reversed. Therefore there is always dispute about customs.

We observe these rules even today. In the beginning people were matched outside their related clans. There was no relation between them because Changing Woman's body was between them. The front two were related and the two from her back were related. Changing Woman said that none of the clans that were related could intermarry. Today they can only match with unrelated clans. The offspring of the first matching are related to both clans. They may not marry into their father's clan or their mother's clan. Now this is being ignored with the children in school and everything.

Then Changing Woman put life into them in a ceremonial way. She kept them until they matured. She intended to direct them back to her original home, where she had a cornfield. They were to live there and raise corn there. When they were ready to leave, she gave a basket, images of talking prayersticks and canes all of white shell to the Standing House Clan. To the Bitter Water Clan she gave a basket, images of talking prayersticks and canes all of abalone. To the Near the Water Clan she gave the same things, but they were of turquoise. To the Mud Clan she gave similar things, but they were of jet.

The People were not named with clan names when they were formed. Their names came later, when they started using their canes to get water by putting them into the ground. The Bitter Water Clan put their abalone canes into the ground and got bitter, salty water. The Standing House Clan got clear, crystal, sweet water. They did not get their name until later, when they arrived at the village of Standing House. Then they were named the "People of Standing House." The Near the Water Clan put their canes, which were turquoise, into the ground and got water before going too far. Therefore they are called "Short Distance to Water People." The Mud Clan put their jet canes into the ground and got muddy water, so they were named the "Mud People." This took place on the surface of the ocean in the west, where Changing Woman was living. The People had no means of going to land. They had to use little bugs, water-striders, to get there. These were the forerunners of boats that float on the water.

When the People got to dry land, they noticed that something was coming out of the ocean. They grabbed it; it was a human female of some sort; she was on the edge of the water, or the shore. This is the origin of the Water Edge Clan. That girl they took from the shore of the ocean was what they call a *Ttéhostsodi*. It is hard to say just what that is: some kind of creature that lives in the water, some being that inhabits the ocean – a whale or an alligator? In the story it is just called *Ttéhostsodi*, which means "creature that pulls you in." It grabs you from the water. Our understanding is that we have these different beings like people that live in the ocean, in the deep water. They are people just like we are. They can talk with each other so we understand. The people in the skies are the same way. When we see them we do not see them in their natural shape; they imitate other forms.

So the People started on their journey to the cornfield. After they got to the mainland, Changing Woman gave them animal helpers. The Bitter Water Clan got a bear cub to protect them and give warning in time of danger. The Standing House Clan got a turkey, which was to be for food. The Near the Water Clan got a mountain lion, and the Mud Clan were given a porcupine. These were given to them by the Holy People at the request of Changing Woman. She is in communication with other beings along the mountains and on the shore; she told the animals to help the People who were starting back to the old country near Fir Mountain. Today, things are happening much the same as in the beginning: when there is disobedience in relation to certain things, suffering for it comes afterwards.

From there on, I cannot go step by step because most of that story has been forgotten. How many days it took them or where they went each day is not known. But west of *Dook'o'osliíd* somewhere, they passed a settlement which consisted of flat-topped hogans. They sent two scouts over there to see what kind of people were living in them. They went over there, but they only found quivers lying in the four directions, all full of arrows. No people were there. The scouts came back and reported this. Later they found out that this place was inhabited by Arrow People.

After the scouts had returned, two of these people came to visit. The Arrow People questioned them as to where they were going and by what way. They went back and told the other Arrow People that there were human beings going across the country all dressed in jewels. The Arrow People gathered and said, "Let's kill them and get the jewels."

When they camped one night, the Arrow People came. But the People had their watchdogs: the bear in the east, the lion in the west, the turkey in the south and the porcupine in the north. Several nights, early in the evening, the bear started growling, indicating that someone was around. The lion did this, too. The turkey's duty was to arouse the People early in the morning, like a chicken. I do not know what the porcupine did. It seems as if they were just being watched by the Arrow People, who were waiting for an opportunity to kill them because of the jewel garments they were dressed in.

For four nights the enemy could not get near them. The bear growled a little longer each night; on the third one he growled almost until dawn, and on the fourth the Arrow People must have encircled them because the bear growled all night, even though these people were invisible. The bear rushed out and broke through in all four directions, and then he ran in a circle and killed all of the Arrow People. Then he came home all fuzzy with arrows but, of course, these did not kill him.

When the bear killed those Arrow People, those enemies, the next morning they found a little girl who was the only survivor. The one who was the originator of the Bitter Water Clan is the one who got the girl, and so their descendants became the Arrow Clan. That is how they are related to the Bitter Water Clan.

On the way west, they were not yet equipped with any songs or prayers for their welfare. The lion provided them with food on their way. Once the lion killed a deer. The bear went over and fought with the lion and slapped him. Then the owners of the lion complained. The owners of the bear scolded him and said, "We depend on the lion to get us food."

The bear got insulted. He went back to his place and started singing for his own protection. He sang a long song. After he got through, he said, "This is the only time I will save you. Since you value the lion more than me, I am going." After he had gone, one of the owners tracked him towards the east. Over the ridge, he saw that the bear had made a mountain-shaped mound and decorated it with arrows: he had made four mounds — black, blue, yellow and white. This is imitated in the ceremonies now. Then the man stepped over the mounds and followed the bear's tracks. Before they started on the journey, the People had been told to let the bear return to his original home, Black Mountain. By his tracks they found that he went from Apache Mountain to Tongue Mountain and then to Black Mountain in the Jemez Range.

Changing Woman merely created these people and provided them with these protectors. This is like the Catholic guardian angels; they are invisible, but they are still there.

There is not any mention of what the porcupine did; the only thing is that they used him as food. Of course he had weapons: the porcupine has those quills, you know, to fight with. In case of an emergency he would have stepped in there and used his quills to protect the People.

As for the turkey, when it was time for him to be released, he shook his feathers and dropped some corn kernels out, two times. These became the seed corn to be planted when the People got back to Fir Mountain. They carried that with them as they continued on their journey.

But of those four animals, the bear was one of the most useful. The People have lots of uses for what comes from the bear. The pollen that has touched a bear is used for our protection; you hold this in your hand, in a pouch, and it will protect you. It is said that a person named Man with a Cane pulled a bear out of a cave while it was hibernating and sprinkled pollen over it and then gathered it up. Man Who Shouts gave it to me to use and to support my family with. This pollen will go to my children when I pass on.

When the bear left the People, he never came back. He left them for good. And so as they continued on their journey the mountain lion began to get sulky, as though he felt lonely. They continued on their journey up into the region where Tuba City is now. When they were given this mountain lion at the start of their journey, they were told that he would accompany them as far as that area where there is a place called Wildcat Butte. The People were told to release the mountain lion there because that was his home. So when they got to that area, the story does not tell the exact place, the mountain lion left them.

After they had released the mountain lion, the People had to release the other guardian animals too. They had been told, "Once you get back into your own country, release these animals, since they really came from that area, too." So the bear was originally from Black Mountain in the Jemez Range, the mountain lion was from Wildcat Butte, the porcupine was from the White Mountains, where the Apaches are now, and the turkey, too. *Kiit'ąą' naskid* is the name of that place. *Kiit'ąą'* is the name of a bush with berries that turkeys eat.

From there on the People continued their journey to the east. Somewhere along there they camped again, and snow fell during the night.

The next morning, when the originator of the Near the Water Clan got up, he noticed rabbit tracks around their camp, so he started to follow them. The rabbit had encircled the camp, and so the others joked with him about that. They said, "Why do you circle about us?" So that is where that name of the "Those Who Walk About" Clan started, though in the beginning it was "Near the Water."

After they got this joking name, "Those Who Walk About," they continued on to another place, where they stopped to rest. A Bitter Water man walked away from the camp and was sitting under a tree that provided a little shade off by itself. The others joked with him about that and said, "Now, why do you go over there and sit apart from us under a lonely tree?" So that is why he was called "Lonely Tree Person."

So the Lone Tree Clan is related to the Bitter Water Clan, and so is the Arrow Clan. But the Bitter Water Clan is the main one; those others were just joining on. It is not that outside members were being added but that they were giving each other joking names, and from that new clans had their start, though they were all originally one clan.

Then they continued on the journey until they came to the neighborhood of a point of land on Black Mesa, near Steamboat. That place is called Abundant Fish. At that same place, at the point of that mountain over there where they had their camp, there is a little dripping water there from the rocks. It forms a pool down there, and they found fish in it. That is the reason they call that place "Abundant Fish."

You see, then they continued on their journey. They just moved around in this area all the way back to Kayenta and then east again up to this valley and on to the country around Crystal. You know the Sonsola Buttes — there is a gap there. On their journey the People were carrying chopping rocks that they used to cut up meat for drying. I do not know where they found these stones, but that is what they were carrying, and they left them there. "Stars Lying Down," is what they called that place, and they left a number of those glittering stones right on the main trail there.

Well, then they continued from there on to Washington Pass and over that range to the east side. And along there somewhere, of course we do not know exactly where, they went across country to Crownpoint, where the Crownpoint Agency is now. There is a gap there, and they passed over that gap down into the valley. Down there is an old ruin with a tall house, which at that time they found inhabited by Pueblo people. There they picked up another woman, and from her came new clans related to the Standing House Clan. You see, that place is called Standing House. The original clans were made by Changing Woman. We still know which groups came from her and which ones came from the woman from Standing House.

They continued their journey from there on to the east until they got to the base of the Jemez Mountains. They were gradually drifting back to where they were supposed to stop at Fir Mountain. They camped in one place at the base of the Jemez Mountains and noticed that there were some green meadows over there. Bitter Water Man was the one who went over there to see what was there. He found that there were a lot of deer coming there for water where there was a natural spring. He came back and reported that there was water over there, and then he said, "It is deer water." So they gave him the joking name, "Deer Water."

It appears that as they traveled back to their original home the People began to multiply. The original Near the Water Clan were getting to be so many that one family became known as "Those Who Walk About," after their leader followed those rabbit tracks. It was the same way with the Bitter Water Clan; so, that is another way the clans had their beginning. In the meantime, the People were beginning to move around and spread out. There were some Pueblo villages near, and some of them were coming out and joining the Navajos. Whatever clan they joined, they became members of that clan. So then certain families were named after places, like the Hogan on the Rock Clan. Other clan names also came from place names and from different Pueblos.

So that is how the clans multiplied. Some were named after places, being called the people of this place, or that, and that became a clan name. And some of them were named after their occupations. The Black Sheep Clan is an example of that. After the Spanish came in, some of the People began to raise stock, and so these people were named after the livestock they were raising. They were raising a lot of black sheep, so finally they just got the name Black Sheep Clan.

After that incident when the Deer Water Clan got its name, the People moved back to where they were supposed to go. They were living there again and cultivating their cornfields, and people began to multiply and become too many. Naturally, they began to quarrel with one another and to fight with each other. All that time Changing Woman had some way of watching over them, and she was aware of the condition they were getting into. She called a meeting of the Holy People to discuss the situation with the Navajos whom she had created. "Those Navajos I made and sent back to their original home — they are multiplying over there and beginning to abuse one another. They are also misusing the holy things that I gave them, such as the baskets and the sacred canes."

So that was discussed by her and the Holy People and finally it was decided that it was dangerous for the Navajos to be fighting among themselves. They were liable to ruin those things that were supposed to be kept holy. Then it was agreed that the Holy People should pick up two boys from over there, two young boys. They would pick them up from the cornfields and bring them back to Changing Woman to learn the way to do things. Also, they brought back with them those jewel canes and baskets and other sacred things. These were lifted up with the two boys.

So the People lost those two boys. They belonged to the Near the Water Clan. They were taken to Changing Woman's home for instructions, and they were there for four years. That is where this ceremony, the Blessingway, came from. They were taught all about that. That is why they were taken back there, that was the purpose. She taught them everything about the Blessingway so that when they returned they would know all the actions and songs and prayers to be used.

You see, Changing Woman was created to bring good life for the people on earth. There was nothing bad, nothing wicked about her. She asked all the Holy People who were here to benefit the Earth People to be on her side, and they helped her. On the other side were First Woman and First Man, beings that are sometimes bad. There are other beings like them, too. They were all to go over to the northeast of the Navajo country. That is the reason that, whenever they have ceremonies, they blow to the north. That is to order these bad things not to return to the People.

Among the things the two boys were taught were the four Dawn songs pertaining to the children. There were these two warriors going to their father's house, and that is when they encountered the Darkness and the Dawn. There were fourfold curtains that they had to go through, and at each of these curtains were two boys who met the warriors and gave them these songs. They sang these songs for them. Later, during the instructions at Changing Woman's home, she said, "Those songs shall be used for Dawn songs."

'e- neye yaṇa,
He, from there, *wowo,* they are speaking,
He, from there, *wowo,* they are speaking, *ye,*
He, from there, *wowo,* they are speaking, *ye,*
'e, from there, they are speaking,
'e, from there, they are speaking, *yeye, neyowo,*

He, from there, *wowo,* they are speaking,
He, from there, *wowo,* they are speaking, *ye,*
He, from there, *wowo,* they are speaking, *ye,*
'e, from there, they are speaking,
'e, from there, they are speaking, *yeye, neyowo.*

Now Dawn has appeared, *na,* it is into it, *wowo,*
    They are speaking, *ye,*
Now it is the Talking God Youths, *'owo,*
    They are speaking, *ye,*

Moccasins, white, *ye,* they all have them, *wo,*
> They are speaking, *ye,*
Now leggings, white, *ye,* they all have them, *wo,*
> They are speaking, *ye,*
Wonderful tail-feathers, white, *ye,*
Twelve of them being their head-plumes, *wo,*
> They are speaking, *ye,*
Before them, at that place, being Dawn, *wo,*
> They are speaking, *ye,*
Behind them, from there, being Dawn, *wo,*
> They are speaking, *ye,*

Before them, at that place, being blessed, *wo,*
> They are speaking, *ye,*
Behind them, from there, being blessed, *wo,*
> They are speaking, *ye,*
Now *Są'ah naaghéi* Youths, now *Bik'eh hózhǫ́ǫ́* Youths, being those, *'owo,*
> They are speaking, *yè,*

He, from there, *wowo,* they are speaking,
He, from there, *wowo,* they are speaking, *ye,*
He, from there, *wowo,* they are speaking, *ye,*
'e, from there, they are speaking,
'e, from there, they are speaking, *yeye, neyowo.* [14]

Now, from there on, as the People began to multiply, of course they were being watched over. Game and plants were provided for their food. Sometimes the game animals would lead the people into holy places where they were not supposed to go. Then they would be taken in by the holy beings who lived there in those houses that are now ruins in order to be taught chants like Shootingway and Big Starway and others. Then after such instructions by the holy beings, they would be returned to their homes in order to teach the people there. After doing that, they were taken back to the sacred places and became Holy People themselves. Now they are not dead, and they are not ghosts at all. They are among the holy beings in those places, like the Wind People, the Lightning People, the Star People and all the others. That is how those chants came into use, by someone being picked up that way.

When those boys who were taught the Blessingway left this world to become Holy People, one of them disappeared into a hill over here at Nava called *Hweech'á*, and is still in there. It is a hill with some rocks on it right out in the valley. It is supposed to be the home of the Spider People, and they picked up that boy and took him in there. The other one stayed over at Fir Mountain, and he is supposed to be in there still.

As for the Bitter Water Clan, they were roaming around from place to place and accidentally came upon a place called *Naalyó'ó*. They picked up another member of the group there whose descendants are the *Hóbikebiyó'ó* Clan.[15]

As for my own clan, the way I happened to become a Navajo is that *Tsétlehé* is married into the family. He is the one who went and grabbed my ancestor out of the water at the place known as Two Streams Meet. So, you see, I am really a Water Person, pulled out of the water. Because my ancestor was captured there at Two Streams Meet, I am one of the Two Streams Meet Clan. Because *Tsétlehé* is the one that caught her, that is how he is my relative.

At the place where the rivers join, two fleet-footed men saw a little girl going into the water. *Tsétlehé* grabbed her first; another man named Black Streak of Wood ran and caught her, too. She was caught by these two Navajos; in this way the Two Streams Meet Clan came into being and I have no Pueblo blood in me.

That girl who was pulled from the water was one of the Otter People. They are people who live in the water. *Tsétlehé* was the one who got to take her home. When they got there, the headman in the family wanted to claim the child. He wanted to raise her and use her as a servant for himself. But before she was old enough to do anything, he was struck by lightning and killed. Then somebody else came forward and said, "I'll take charge of her and she will be my servant." But the next thing that happened, he was drowned. Then a third one came in and wanted to claim that girl to be his servant, and soon after that he was frozen to death. So after something like that happening three times they said, "It seems we're not supposed to claim her as a servant. We'll just recognize her and all her descendants as a clan."

So that is the reason that it was decided that those people were not to be thought of as captives to be used as servants, but were to be considered just like anybody else. They said, too, that from here on the Two Streams Meet People will never be injured by water, lightning or freezing, although it seems that no longer holds good, since one of them was drowned here not long ago.

In the early days there was a man who captured a Ute, and this led to still another clan. *Jitháát* was his name; he went on a raid to San Mateo after the Spaniards had settled there. At that village he captured a Mexican or a Spanish girl and brought her home. That was the origin of the Mexican Clan, which is related to ours.

At that time, when these clans were coming into being and certain things were being laid down as rules for us to follow, it was also mentioned that in the future we would not know when a change would take place again on this earth. It was said that changes would come and the earth would respond to these changes and a new way would come into existence. When that time comes near, things that were forbidden formerly will start happening, and that will show that we are approaching a new period. That is the way Changing Woman laid down the rules for us.

EDITORS' NOTES

1. A much more detailed origin myth was given by Frank to Father Berard Haile; see Wyman (1970:343-492). For archaeological and historical information on Navajo origins, see Chapter 5, n. 30.

2. The Navajos consider the area bounded by Blanco Peak on the east, Mount Taylor on the south, San Francisco Peak on the west and the La Plata Range on the north to be the "land of the People." See Fig. 1, p. 13. These are the first four mountains listed in note 6, below.

3. Shells of various kinds are used by the Navajos for jewelry and ceremonial paraphernalia. Abalone shells provide containers for ritual decoctions or sacred cornmeal, for example, and polished discs of abalone shell may be used to ornament the protagonist in the Girl's Puberty ceremony. These shells were obtained in trade from the West Coast from prehistoric times to the present. See T. Frisbie (1975:120-142).

4. For an account of Navajo cosmology, see Reichard (1963:568-574).

5. See Chapter 9 for Frank's account of Navajo political organization.

6. In translating the names of Navajo mountains, two different principles have been followed: where the text deals with poetry, ritual or myth, the editors have translated the Navajo literally whenever possible. Where the text is narrative and deals with recent travels, mountains have been translated with the geographical place names commonly used on maps. The first four mountains listed below are the sacred boundary mountains discussed in note 2, above. The "inner" mountains are the most important of the many sacred mountains inside the Navajo country, especially in the context of the origin story. Thus:

Direction	Navajo	Literal	Geographical
East	Sisnaajiní	Black Belt Mountain	Blanco Peak, Colorado
South	Tsoodził	Tongue Mountain	Mount Taylor, New Mexico
West	Dook'o'oslííd	— — — —	San Francisco Peak, Arizona
North	Dibé ntsaa	Big Sheep Mountain	La Plata Range, Colorado
Inner	Dził Ná'ooditii	Mountain Around Which Traveling Was Done	Huerfano Mesa, New Mexico
Inner	Ch'óol'į́'í	Fir Mountain	Gobernador Knob, New Mexico

7. These are the first and tenth Chief Hogan songs, from the full set recorded by Frank for Frisbie in 1963. The editors have altered the format and translation slightly here from Frisbie (1967:116-117 and 130-131). For a further discussion of the Chief Hogan songs, see *Ibid.*:102-168. Among "those songs" Frank must have included the first of the three sets of songs he always sang *after* the Chief Hogan songs. These eight songs tell of the first chiefs to be chosen by the deities for the Navajo people. The scene is laid in the houses of First Man and First Woman. The Chief Hogan songs, themselves, do not mention First Man and First Woman directly. See *Ibid.*:104-105; 118-121.

8. These phrases contain much of the essence of Navajo religion and philosophy. Frisbie (1967) translated them as "long life" and "everlasting beauty." Father Berard Haile stresses a different aspect of *hózhǫ́ǫ́* when he translates the phrases, "long life," and "happiness," (as in, for example, 1947:98). Reichard (1950:45-48) makes an attempt to convey the more universal content of the phrases with "according-to-the-ideal-may-restoration-be-achieved." The most extensive discussion of the context and meaning of the phrases is in Witherspoon (1974, 1975a). His semantic analysis produces the explicit meaning: "life constantly restored, according to which conditions all around are blessed or made beautiful." The concepts implicit in the phrase are so far-reaching that the present editors have decided to keep the Navajo here.

9. The vocables *Heye neye yaŋa* are a common introduction to ceremonial song texts. They are untranslatable, lexically, but set the mood for sacred chanting. The phrase *Howowo 'aiye ye!* is also untranslatable. Frank said that the "*Howowo*" was the call of Talking God.

10. Marking the hogan poles is part of the House Blessing Ceremony. For a study of this ceremony, see Frisbie (1968, 1970). Though Frank did not specify how the pole in the north was marked, a possible inference is that soft fabrics were used for this purpose. White cornmeal is used for all four poles today.

11. Frank tells this story in detail later in this chapter.

12. The term "Twelve-Word song," refers to the twelve verses. In verse five of this song, *Dook'o'oslííd* is the name of San Francisco Peak, near Flagstaff, Arizona. No translation of the Navajo has been obtainable. This song is the tenth in a series of twelve Earth songs recorded by Frank for McAllester in 1957. The vocables *'ai-nai-yaŋa* are a variant of the introductory formula mentioned in note 9. These and the other vocables are untranslatable.

13. This is the third of four Placing the Mountains songs recorded by Frank for McAllester in 1957. No translation was obtained for *Dziłnanita*. The name of the mountain of the west, *Dook'o'oslííd*, is also untranslatable; see note 6.

Again, the sacred phrases discussed in note 8 are used; the vocables are untranslatable.

14. This Talking God Youths' Dawn song was the fifth in a series of eight recorded by Frank for McAllester in 1957 and again in 1961. In the narration of his life story, Frank said, "The four words in the song were sung by four children to complete the song." We assume that the four children are the Talking God Youths and that the four words refer to the four items of white (dawn) clothing. Note the usual introductory and closing formulae and other untranslatable vocables.

15. This clan name does not appear among those identified by Reichard (1928) or the Franciscan Fathers (1910). We have not been able to find a translation of the name.

7. Learning the Blessingway

*Frank and his brother John start to learn the Blessingway
from He Who Seeks War . . . he begins learning in earnest from
Man Who Shouts, his father-in-law, and starts taking life
seriously . . . the death of Man Who Shouts; Frank inherits the
Blessingway ceremony . . . he learns the Blessingway from his
own father; his father's death . . . trips to the sacred mountains to
make up the Mountain Earth bundle . . . renewal of the Blessingway bundle . . . the lost earloops.*

During the time I was going to school, my brother John was working at Fort
Defiance, and his family was living there with him. I already told about how
he was married twice; that was his first wife he was living with when he was at
Fort Defiance. I lived there with him during the time that I worked at the
trader's place as a housekeeper and dishwasher. There was an old man who
was some relation to my brother's wife. His name was He Who Seeks War, and
he was a singer of the Blessingway.

He used to visit my brother's place a lot, and I guess John learned that
he was a Blessingway singer and started picking up some of the songs, learning
something about them. That man used to give me some instruction in
Blessingway, too, telling me what goes on in the ceremony and how the
Blessingway goes. At the same time I listened whenever I could, trying to pick
up pieces of it. I began learning some of the songs from here and there in the
ceremony, and I remembered them pretty well.

Later on I came back over here because my wife's parents were getting
pretty old and sick. I gave up hauling freight and started tending their farm
and livestock. Like I have said, my father-in-law was a well-to-do man: he had
cattle and sheep and horses. Also, he was a Blessingway singer, and I went out
with him whenever he performed his ceremony. I noticed that the songs I had
learned from He Who Seeks War were the same as the ones my father-in-law
was singing.

Before I began to learn these things, way back before that, I did not
even think about life as being an important thing. I did not try to remember
things or keep track of what happened at certain times. Nothing seemed to

matter to me, I just didn't care about anything, so long as I kept on living. But then when I began to learn the Blessingway, it changed my whole life. I began really thinking about ceremonies. I had heard singing before that, but now I began to take it more seriously because I began to realize what life was and the kind of hardships we have to go through.

Before I started learning the Blessingway, the older people used to tell me that I should think about life more seriously. "If you don't know any songs you have nothing to go by. If a child grows up in a family like that he doesn't know where he is going or what he is doing." That is what the older people told me, that I should have something to live by. It is just like going to school: you are being trained and being told what is wrong and what is right. It was the same way with this ceremony; that is when I began learning about life.

So during that time after I stopped hauling freight and began working more around home, I used to go out with my father-in-law, Man Who Shouts, whenever he was asked to perform the Blessingway. At first I just watched, and then finally I had learned practically everything he was doing, and before I knew it I was helping him with the ceremony. Finally I reached the point where I had learned it well enough so that I had a ceremony of my own.

Man Who Shouts and his wife used to move to the mesa during the winter months. We stayed here because I had a separate home and my own way of making a living. When he got sick I went over to the mesa and took care of him until his end. After he got sick he lived on for about three years. We moved over there during his last days. That is where he called me in to talk to me about the future.

He said he noticed that I was the kind of young man who didn't seem to care about anything. He settled down to talk with me and told me that if I was going to continue being the way I was then, I would never achieve anything in life and would just end up ruining my life, one of these days. He told me that I'd better settle down soon and start living right if I was going to make a living for my children.

If I wanted to get out on the farm and work, if I wanted to be a farmer, he said, it was going to take all my strength, all my heart to do that work. "It takes a lot of work to do that," he told me. "And if you're going to be a farmer, you will probably make a good one if you really put your mind to it. But you can't be a farmer all your life; as soon as your strength starts to go, as soon as you start getting weaker and weaker, that will be the end of your farming life," he said. Then he told me it was the same thing with raising stock. "If you're going to be a cattleman or a sheepherder it's just the same thing; there is a lot of work to it; it takes a lot of energy to do that," he told me. "But then, again, you'll end up just the way a farmer will," he said.

Then he told me, "But if you are a singer, if you remember your ceremonies really well, even if you get old, even if you get blind and deaf, you'll still remember everything by heart, how each part of the ceremony is performed." He said to me, "Even though you are so old you can't ride a horse or you can't even see any more, people will still have a use for you until old age finally finishes you off."

So that is why I chose this way of life. When Man Who Shouts got sick I got seriously interested in learning the ceremony, but I was not too sure yet – my mind was not really made up until just before his death. And now I can see that my father-in-law was right: even as old as I am, unable to get around too much, people still come to have my ceremony done over them. I have it inside my head so well that I remember everything, and even though I can't get around, they come in a wagon or a car for me and take me over to where the ceremony is needed and then bring me back. So I think my father-in-law was right. If I had decided to be a farmer at that time I probably wouldn't have lasted very long.

It was mainly from Man Who Shouts that I learned the Blessingway, by following him whenever he was asked to do some singing. I picked up most of his songs and prayers that way. Whenever he went to Fort Defiance we would go in a buggy. We would stop in Sawmill overnight where there lived He Who Seeks War and his younger brother, who knew the same Blessingway songs. They would practice them, and I would listen. After we would leave there he would explain things to me, and that is how I would learn.

We would spend the night there sitting around talking about the Blessingway until late at night, and then we would go on to Fort Defiance the next day. And then, coming back, we did the same thing. We always stopped there, and I learned a little more again. Just gradually like that I learned all about that ceremony from those two men. He Who Seeks War was related to my wife's father through a niece, or something like that. So they knew each other pretty well.

So I picked up a lot of knowledge like that and finally got to the point where I could do the ceremony all by myself. I did not have a Blessingway bundle of my own, but I was able to help Man Who Shouts and do whatever he asked me to do.

During that last winter we went up there on the mesa with him. He gradually got worse and worse. There were four singers with him all the time towards the end: Red Water Tall Bead Man, Little Many Goats, Nowetałi and Dził Yé'há. They were doing their ceremonials: Mountainway, Shootingway, Flintway and Big Starway in the Ghost Chasing and Evilway forms. The helpers in all this were all the members of the immediate family and his wife's family. Long Moustache was supervising everything. So was Jake Tom. The young boys were told to do the chores around there.

One day I had a sweat bath with the singers. They were all tired after so many days, and Man Who Shouts told me to fix a sweat bath for them, so they could take that and be refreshed a little bit. I went out and cut wood and fixed a sweathouse, and we all got in there. Then I went to my house to eat, and Man Who Shouts requested that I come in and see him. I sat by him as he was lying in the hogan. He told me he did not think he was going to live much longer the way things were. He told me that all these singers had been here so long performing their ceremonies for him, but he could not see that it was doing any good. He felt that his time was coming, and that is why he called me in.

He wanted me to know that he had been depending on me as a strong young man to look after the livestock and the farm when he was away performing his ceremony. Now the time had come for me to take charge of things because there would be nobody for me to depend on the way I could when he was living and strong. He told me that it was up to me at that moment to make up my mind if I was going to carry on the Blessingway ceremony the way he had. He said he had worked hard and had acquired this farm and livestock and a good deal of property to take care of his children and his grandchildren, too. He told me that from there on it would be up to me to carry it on.

He said, "It appears that I will never recover from this sickness. This is my final talk to you. After I am gone, the burdens you and I have been carrying will be yours alone. If you have patience and strength you can do it. If you are the man I think you are, even though it may mean a lot of hardship, you will continue to carry on the work of the farm the way you have since you first started living with my daughter." He said, "If you aren't, if you are going to be the kind of man that isn't too good at anything, then you might leave the whole thing and go away and just let the women do the work. It's up to you right now to decide."

I think the main reason he talked this way to me was that he wanted me to have this Blessingway bundle that he had been using for so long. Then he told me that I had done the ceremony so many times and had been such a good helper with it that he knew I could carry it on by myself. He said, "If anything happens to me, then that Blessingway is just yours." Before he began talking this way, those four singers had come back into the hogan, and he said to them, "If anybody ever questions my son-in-law's right to this ceremony, you men here have heard me say it. You've heard everything I said to him: that the Blessingway is just his, and he is to use it the right way."

At the same time he told me, "If you use it properly, you may live on to a good old age yourself. But if it does happen that you get too old, if it comes to the time where you can't use your ceremony any more, then whatever you do, do not pass it on to the Two Streams Meet Clan; it should go to the Standing House Clan. That is one wish I have that I want you to respect, that this Blessingway should be kept in the Standing House Clan. In these last three years none of my relatives have visited me. Don't give it to them after I am gone. It is not to go to the Bitter Water Clan or the Near the Water Clan, either, even though those relatives of mine come running in here after my property."

This was said in the presence of those singers from outside the family, so it was binding. He willed his crane bills for the Flintway ceremonial to his grandson, Man with a Yellow Face, who is now dead. Even though he did not know any of the songs, he could just keep the ceremonial bundle and later he might be able to sell it. The bundle for the Cutting Prayersticks ceremony was willed to his stepson, Mr. Cottonwood, half-brother to my wife, Tall Woman. He was named for a lonely cottonwood tree that stood on his property.

He had other sacred bundles, too, like the one that my wife still has. That also used to belong to my father-in-law. I do not know what ceremony that is used for, but she still has it. When Man Who Shouts died, that bundle was given to one of my wife's cousins who just passed away last October. He never learned a ceremony for it, but it was willed to him before my father-in-law died.

Man Who Shouts still had quite a lot of property, even though the family had used up about half of what they had during all that time he was sick. You see, for about three years he had been having ceremony after ceremony, and this was using up all their sheep and cattle and whatever little money they had, too. So the number of cattle went down, but there were still some left, and there were still some sheep. My father-in-law said for me to take care of them, that they all belonged to his wife: "She can do whatever she wants with that, it's all hers. The children should not claim any of it, saying that this or that is theirs. They are just to let their mother take care of it until the day she leaves them, too. It is the same way with the cattle that are left; they are to be in her hands, too." He also had a buckboard, and it was left to my wife. There was another wagon, too, that was used for heavy hauling, and I was to use that for the farm in any way I wanted. But this other buckboard was given to my wife for her use alone. "If she ever wants to go somewhere, make sure she is taken in that. Take care of your wife and take care of your children."

He went on talking like that and gave me a good lecture on how I should live and what I should do and should not do and how I should not mistreat my wife. He talked to me about everything.

Finally he mentioned the jewels he had gotten together during his lifetime. He had every known kind of precious stone: abalone, coral, jet, turquoise, all on one string. He had a set of earloops. He also had carved out two eardrops that were buried with him. The rest of the beads went to his wife.

"Fix me up nicely and put me away in a suitable place. That buckskin horse that I've always like so much, I want that, too, because the saying is that people live after their death, and I may need something to get around on. After I'm gone, don't be afraid of me. I want you still to respect me as you do now. Don't call me a ghost."

I said, "Wait a minute, don't go on talking like this. Tell me why you feel the end is near. What is overtaking you?"

He said, "I haven't urinated for the last twenty-four hours. I am beginning to feel it."

I said, "I know that's dangerous." I thought of the doctor in Chinle right away and how they have a way they can help that trouble. "Well, my father-in-law," I said, "be patient and I'll get something to help you." I came down to Chinle on horseback and got there about nine in the evening.

The doctor said he had no way of getting up on the mesa. "But I'll give you the instruments to use and tell you what to do," he said. This took a little time, and then I rushed right back up there.

When I got near the place where they were living, I saw that the people had built a fire outside the hogan and they were all outside there. And when I got there I realized my father-in-law had already died. They had him all fixed up, covered with blankets. I went over there and pulled the covers off and felt for a pulse, but there was no life. I was too late with those things, even though I tried to help him. So I talked to him: "Well, my father-in-law, I was hoping I would get back before it was too late. But whatever you have asked us to do, we'll follow your instructions." That was how he passed away. He was very old, and old age had a lot to do with it, too.

The next morning we prepared him for burial. We put him on a horse and took him away and dug a grave for him. Those of us who put him in the ground were myself, Man with a Yellow Face and his son-in-law. Whoever carries a body out like that has to make the grave according to our customs. A body is supposed to be buried in a deep hole a long way from the hogan, against a rock wall. First we put the body in, then his saddle and saddle blanket. We killed his horse at the grave, and we left the digging tools there, too. We broke them up so that nothing was left in a whole piece. You are supposed to blindfold the horse first and then kill it with an axe or a club. That is according to the old custom, though in later years people felt it was all right to use a gun. The people doing this burying should not be wearing clothes.

If you are obliged to do a burial, you must prepare yourself. When you remove your clothes you tie your foreskin closed with a strip of yucca leaf but not with a square knot. You build a fire some distance from the hogan where the death took place and have a bucket of water heated there so that you can bathe yourself in soapsuds when you come back. From the time you pick up the body until after the bath you only speak with sign language. If the person is buried some distance away, you then remove the furniture from the hogan and burn it down. If that cannot be done, you can bury the person inside the hogan and then pull it all down over the grave. After the burial, you brush away your tracks as you leave the grave. You can do that with anything that acts as a brush.

After all this had been done and we had eaten, my close friend Long Moustache sat down and told me, "After four days you can go back to normal life; until then you must remain quiet. On the fourth morning you should wash your hair and bathe yourself all over. Then the outsiders can all return and try to arrange things according to what he told us about his property. The reason is that now the different clan relatives will be coming in here to claim all sorts of things. You singers should remain, too. You should wait four days until the members of the family have purified themselves, then you can come and get the things belonging to you and take them away." He told the young boys doing the chores around there to come back to help with the old singer's stock. Just the family and those who helped with the burial were there for the four days. After that everything was done as he said.

We had farmland across the wash there. All that farmland belonged to my father and mother. My father had left us for the second time at this point and was married to that woman down here called Those Who Walk About Woman; he was still with that woman when I married my wife. When we moved to the mesa, my father was still in this area here. So when we moved back over here my father used to come and visit me every now and then, and finally it got to the point where he left that woman. Another man took his wife, that old man, White Sinew, who passed away about two or three years ago. So my father just kind of hung around where I was, down here with my children. He went back and forth from here to Tsaile to visit Slim Man, one of his sons by Red Woman.

My father left his livestock with that cousin of mine who used to wrestle with me — Tall Water Edge Man. He only brought his personal possessions when he came to live at my place. My father came and went while I was working as a freighter. He stayed mainly in Canyon del Muerto. He would also go to visit Redhaired Water Edge Man where Tall Water Edge Man's brother lived. Redhaired Water Edge Man was learning Blessingway from him. These were the same songs that I use. When my father was staying with me, I would ask him about Blessingway prayers and songs — all the things I had learned from Man Who Shouts. This way I filled in the gaps in the two versions and formed my complete ceremony. I learned things this way for quite a long while. Some of the time I would be busy, and my father would be visiting other people like Slim Man, who was always asking him about Blessingway, too.

We lived like that for some time here, just taking care of the farm, and finally my father decided to go back to Slim Man for another visit. While he was there he got sick. I got word from there that my father was pretty bad, so I saddled up my horse and went up there to Slim Man's place and, sure enough, he was sick, and they were having a five-night ceremonial for him. I got there on the third day. I spent the night there and the next day and the last day of the whole ceremonial I spent there, too. I stayed there until it was all over with, until the next morning. I think it was a fever that he had, some kind of fever that was going around. He was not sick in any particular place.

So he got all right after the singing was over, and he wanted to come home with me. They told him he should not leave right after there had been this singing for him. They said he should spend at least a couple of nights there before he left that place. So he stayed there another night, and then the night after that and then he came back with us. We went by way of the Canyon. Slim Man took him in the wagon, and I came along with the horses. I rode and drove my father's horses and we got to Standing Cow in the Canyon where some of our relatives lived and spent the night there. While we were there we saw a great many people going up the Canyon, and finally we stopped someone and asked where they were going and if there was something going on up that way. They told us there was a Blessingway and that those people were making a new ceremonial bundle. Right then my father told Slim Man and me to go over there and find out exactly how such things were done. He was curious to know if it was done the same way he was taught. This singer we heard about, Cane's Son, was supposed to be very careful with how it was done.

All that time my father knew all about the Blessingway, but he had never performed that ceremony because he was never asked. He had learned it from his father, Man Who Speaks Often, but during that time so many of the singers had their ceremonial bundles already, and there were not many new ones being made for younger singers learning it, so they didn't ask him to perform that ceremony.

We went over there that night, and when we got there we went inside the hogan. All that took place in the early evening was a prayer, nothing else. Just a prayer, and then everybody went to bed. Slim Man spent the night there, but there was another Blessingway just beyond that place, and I went over there. The singer there was a man by the name of Tall Schoolboy; he was the one that was doing this Blessingway there at his place. This ceremony and what I learned from my wife's father were about the same. I was over there for the last night. I stayed all night and helped with the singing until the next morning. Then I got back over to this other place where they were making the Mountain Earth bundle.

That day they brought the yucca soap and performed the regular bathing ritual and all that. They bathed the one they were making the ceremonial bundle for. He was the main one that the ceremony was for. The bundle was going to be his, so he had to be the one-sung-over. So they brought the soapweed, and they started the regular Blessingway rituals. After the bathing and all that goes with it, they started working on the ceremonial bundle, and they didn't sing any songs during that time. There were just short prayers here and there until the bundle was completed, and they told me that was all there was to it. They just made up the bundle, and there were no songs at any point. We were just there to listen and to watch how things were done.

In the afternoon it was all over with, and we got restless and went back to where we had left our father at Standing Cow. When we got back over there, he was a little ways from the house there, under the trees sitting straight up, all ears for what we had learned. Before I even got off my horse he called out, "Open up your pack of news!" So I told him what happened the night before from the time we first got there, and how things went on and then about the next morning too, up until the time we left.

Before we even finished telling him, my father was not interested in hearing any more. He just moved away from us. Later he told us he knew what I had said was true, that there are some singers that will do crazy things like that just to get something out of it. He knew right away that the way this singer Cane's Son did it was all wrong.

Making up the ceremonial bundle was one thing I had not learned from my father-in-law, Man Who Shouts. I just learned the straight Blessingway from him, so right then and there I got interested in how the new ceremonial bundle is made, and I started asking my father all kinds of questions. I asked him how it was done, and that is when my father gave me all the information; he told it all to me. He told me how the story went along with the prayers and the songs, and I got them all put together until I had them learned. The songs used by those two men over where we stopped are the same ones I learned from my father. I guess they came from my grandfather, and all the people in that area learned it from him. There are little differences, but there is no place where the differences are large enough to say that it is a different version of the Blessingway. The prayers and the songs are the same, too.

I really got interested in it from there on. I asked my father all the questions I could think of about the way that ceremony goes, and I started learning it. First he told me all about the story of it and the songs and prayers and all that went along with it. It was just about the same as the way I learned from Man Who Shouts. That was how I came to learn the Blessingway.

After we returned to my place, my father gradually got sick. He started having ceremonies for that, using his own property and livestock to pay for them until finally he was left with nothing. Those Who Walk About Woman had married that old man by then, so he didn't even have a wife. He began to feel that it was hopeless. He said, "This is too much of a burden on you. Go to my relatives in Steamboat and tell them I want to go over there. Let's see what they can do." Red Hair Knot and Tall Water Edge Man would come over here to help while I was sponsoring some of my father's ceremonies. His nieces and nephews would come over, too, and they took him back with them in the fall. He wanted to leave his beads and other things with me, and also his ceremonial bundle, but I said, "Take them, you may need them to hire a singer."

My father passed away early the next summer; I was not there when it happened. When he left here he had called me and Tall Water Edge Man in to talk to us: "I don't think I'll ever get well from this sickness. I want to leave two head of cattle and the horse I always use here." And that is what he did. He said to Tall Water Edge Man, "If I don't take them back for my own use before I die, then they are yours."

After my father died, Redhaired Water Edge Man took his Blessingway bundle; he claimed my father had said it was to go to him. It contained a mirage stone[1] that originally belonged to my mother. John Mitchell, being stingy as he was, went over there and got that stone. When he died it was not mentioned in his will, and so it went to Herbert. Redhaired Water Edge Man is still living at that place, where he is a Blessingway and Shootingway singer. He used to be the best Yeibichai dancer in the country.

I was one of those who helped collect the contents of the Mountain Earth bundle from the four sacred mountains. It started way back in about 1925, when Father Berard[2] was out here and I had a chance to go on some of those trips. He put up the money himself for the gasoline and told us we could use the mission car he had available. We wanted to collect earth from each sacred mountain so that we could each have a Mountain Earth bundle.

We had to furnish our own food while we were out camping on those four mountains. The women around here, especially my wife, got all of the things ready to go on that trip. There were still only a few trading posts out here at that time and very little flour. That is why the bread we took was corn bread rather than fry bread.

When a trip like this was to be undertaken we had to plan everything carefully in advance. We had to take a kind of bread with us that represented all the vegetation that is grown on earth, like wheat, whole wheat, corn – all different kinds of corn – and all different kinds of wheat. You can get flour out of barley, and all those other different kinds of wheat that grow around here, including the wild kinds. You can grind that all up like cornmeal, or make it more like flour.

So we ground all that together, all those kinds of wheat with cornmeal and all the other vegetation that grows. We ground it all together into something like cornmeal and made bread out of that to eat during the journey. It was all right to have other food from the store, too, but we had to have this particular bread that is made out of all different kinds of vegetation. Then, when we were going on our way up the mountain, whenever we would stop to eat, the first thing would be some of this bread. There was some boiled meat that we took that we also had to eat first before any other food was taken – coffee or tea, or anything else. After we ate some of those things, then we could eat what supplies we had brought.

I was not on the visit to the first mountain, Blanco Peak.[3] Those who went with Father Berard were Two Streams Meet Curly from Chinle and Slim Curly from Sonsola Buttes, this side of Crystal. Chic Sandoval was the driver. After resting up for a few days, they went on the second trip, to Mount

Taylor. Another man, by the name of Big Cripple, and I went along. His children now live in the Black Mountain area, but at that time he lived over here at Chinle. The driver was John Foley, Sr. He's getting pretty gray, too. Chic wasn't the driver on that trip.

The third one was to San Francisco Peak, and I went with Two Streams Meet Curly. John Foley was the driver again. The last trip was to Colorado, and I went again with the same ones who went the time before. This trip lasted three days and three nights. We also visited two other mountains: Gobernador Knob and Huerfano Mesa. So I have earth collected from six sacred mountains! All the sacred mountains except Gobernador Knob and Blanco Peak belong to me because I prayed there. I made offerings of jewels and sang all the way, both going up and going down again. Some of the mountains have white bears and wolves on them. On others there is nothing like that.

When we would get to a mountain, we would not just go up into it in our ordinary clothes. Besides our food we took a new basket, such as we use in a Blessingway when we bathe the person being sung over. And we took a mirage stone in a little ceremonial pouch. We would go up as far as the first waterhole that we could find. And there at the waterhole we all undressed and bathed ourselves. We did that just as they do during the Blessingway. We dried ourselves with cornmeal and then with the powder from grinding the mirage stone. Then, when we were dry, we got into clothing something like you see on the Yeibichai dancers. You know, when the Yeibichai is ready to dance he is all decorated with silver belts and bracelets and beads. That is the way we dressed on the mountain. We had buckskins thrown over our shoulders, too.

Then we started going up the mountain, and there was always one of the men who was picked out to be the leader. He went before the others, and we started singing before we left that waterhole. I was the leader for the trip to Mount Taylor. When we got to the top of the mountain I gave the directions as to where the earth was to be picked up from.

There is something else that we took when we set out on these trips for the mountain earth — little chips of turquoise and other jewels. The leader took this, and he went before the others; we were all singing just as in the Blessingway. We all followed him until we came to a waterfall. That is where we put the jewels as a gift to Mother Earth for what we were going to take from her. We left the jewels there and in return gathered up some of the earth from the mountain. After we gathered up as much as we needed, we smoothed out the place; we did not want to leave it disturbed. We fixed it up so that it looked just as it had been before, and then coming back we sang more songs until we reached our starting place at the bottom. There we finished with the singing and passed the pollen[4] around so that each one of us could bless himself. Then we dressed in our ordinary clothes and started back home.

On those trips we just went up each mountain as far as we had to go in order to find water. On Mount Taylor we did not find any water until we got clear to the top, but the other ones were not like that; we just had to go a little ways. Most of the mountains I went to had spring water here and there all over. After we made the jewel offering to Mother Earth, we said a prayer up there on each mountain to thank her for what we came for and for the protection that we would have because of that. We were praying for the whole Navajo tribe, because the ceremonial singers are the ones the people look up to for protection.

It took about three years to visit all of those mountains. It took so long because a trip like that requires so much preparation. Another thing that had to be prepared was a buckskin especially made to wrap the mountain earth in. This could not be just any deer that you would go out and shoot with a gun or a bow and arrow that would wound it and make it bleed. This deer had to be roped; no kind of weapon could touch it.

That is why it took all that time to visit those mountains: the preparations like hunting a deer for that purpose. It is pretty hard to rope a deer, and then you cannot shoot it; what you do is put a handful of pollen in its mouth, hold the nose and mouth tight and suffocate it. Then you butcher it, and the skin is used for wrapping up the mountain earth. It takes a long time to get that all fixed up. After you get the deer, then somebody has to tan that hide, and it takes quite a while to do that, too. That is a highly valued thing whenever a deer is killed like that.

In wrapping the mountain earth, we put just a bit into each little pouch, about half a teaspoonful. What we do is cut a little piece of the buckskin and, when it is still wet, push a stick right into the middle of it so the skin is stretched out the other side like a nipple. After it dries that way we just put the earth in there and then fold it back and tie it. You can put a lot of these little sacks together and tie them into one bundle just the right size for holding in one hand.

What we do is put the earth from each of the four mountains in a separate sack and then right in the center put a mirage stone, a nice one, for the center piece. Then we put the earth from Blanco Peak on the east side of it, and from Mount Taylor on the south side of it and so on, all around in the same direction as the mountains. Then you know just how this should be so you can hold it facing the right way. Some other mirage stones or other things that are valued can be put in there, too. You tie it all together that way, and there is something on each of those little sacks so you know which earth is from Mount Taylor and which is from San Francisco Peak. You make sure that the right one goes on the right side of the bundle.

Then at the bottom, before the whole thing is all tied up, a perfect white shell from the ocean is placed. It is shaped like a basket, and it is set at the bottom of the whole thing. Then the mirage stone is set at the center, and the little sacks are placed all around it. Then you fill in all around with other things, such as mirage stones, jewel offerings, bits of various types of vegetation that grow on the earth and all kinds of herbs. Mixed in with all this is the fur, or a little bit of hair or the hide, of all kinds of animals living on earth. That fills up this little shell basket that is underneath everything. The mirage stone stands on an inch or so of all these substances and then those other things are grouped around it.

The people who taught me used to say that the little shell basket resembles Mother Earth and all those materials in it are the things that are growing on top of the earth. Corn pollen is always in that bundle, too, among all the rest of the things.

This bundle is something you have to have to perform the Blessingway. Without it you cannot do Blessingway because that is the most essential property of the ceremony, right there. Not many Blessingway singers have bundles that are put together as carefully as mine was for me. A lot of times I have noticed that all some of them have is pollen, just pollen and nothing else.

There are special songs, Chief songs, that are sung during the time that they are making up that bundle for a new singer. Nobody knows them but me; my father taught me those songs. As far as I know, around here none of the Blessingway singers know those songs. I am the only one. Those particular songs are for tying up the Mountain Earth bundle. There is another reason that most Blessingway bundles are not as properly made as mine: these younger men just ask the older singers a few questions, but they do not stop long enough to find out the real answers; they just want to do it their own way. I know a lot of them who have this mountain earth, but it is not put together the way it should be.

I learned how to prepare a bundle from my father, Water Edge Man; my grandfather, Man Who Speaks Often, was the one that knew it before my father did. It was carried down in the family to me. Another generation back, Man Who Speaks Often's father, would be my great-grandfather. It was his ceremony in the beginning. His name was Thin Man. He was from the area of Wheatfields, and Man Who Speaks Often was from there, too. My father was from Pointed Red Rocks, somewhere over on the road to Keams Canyon.

Those special songs are kept very secret, and they cannot be sung just anywhere. The only time they should be used is when you are performing that particular ceremony. There are three or four different special songs, and each one is sung at a particular time when something is taking place during the making or the renewal of the Mountain Earth bundle. Last of all there is a song after everything is all put together and the last cord is being wrapped around the whole bundle. Even that has a song to go with it.

After it is all put together, it is set in a basket on the floor. Then a pipe is smoked for it, too. We use a special dry herb and breathe out the smoke from it on the bundle while it is sitting there. Some singers make this pipe themselves out of a kind of hard rock, and some of them have found their

FIG. 4. Frank Mitchell holding his Mountain Earth medicine bundle at Chinle, Arizona, in May 1965.

pipes in the ruins where the early people lived. These pipes are usually small and in the shape of an L.

When the bundle is all tied up and set in the basket, the singer lights this pipe, and some of the smoke is blown on the person for whom the bundle is being made or renewed. Then smoke is also blown on the bundle, there in the basket. And then the pipe is passed from south of the door of the hogan all the way around to everybody there. Everyone takes a puff of that smoke. It is just the way they pass the pollen in a ceremony. The tobacco is made of special herbs, and when they use up what is in the pipe, it is just refilled, lit again and passed on. Matches are not used; instead there is a particular lighting stick.

The ashes in the pipe are saved; they are not thrown out. Some of them are put on the bundle and some on the person for whom the bundle is being fixed. This is done just like a pollen blessing, starting with the feet and going on up to bless the other parts of the body. When that is finished, the singer gets up, takes the bundle and puts it in the hands of the new Blessingway singer. Then that person has what is needed to start giving this ceremony.

Last fall, I had a renewal ceremony for my Blessingway bundle. It had been fixed up and everything securely tied for many years. The custom is to untie it, every so often, and inspect it to see if everything is in the right place and in good condition. I had not done that in so long it was beginning to worry me. So I was thinking about who there was around here that I could ask to do that for me. Of course there are a lot of singers around here, but they do not understand very much about this particular ritual. If the singer makes the least mistake it would affect him, and it would affect the bundle and the owner of the bundle. So it has to be done very carefully.

I couldn't think of anyone whom I could ask to do this around here, so I went up towards Lukachukai to get someone to open my bundle, redecorate it and reset it for me. A man by the name of Eli Smith from Nazlini used to come around here visiting now and then. He told me that he had a Mountain Earth bundle fixed for him, so I asked him who did that. He said that it was Slim Standing House Man. I asked what version it was that he used for that. Eli said that Slim Standing House Man had mentioned Waterway Man, and so I knew that this man probably got his version from He Who Seeks War. I wanted to use him for that if he was experienced in fixing up bundles. So I went over there with Slim Man's Son, to look for him. He wasn't home when we got there, so I started inquiring around at his neighbors and others. They said, "We don't know. He never used to do any of those things until lately. He has just recently started doing that, and giving Blessingway, so we don't know."

After learning that, I came back and went over to Tsaile to get another man, Long Bead Man. He said he did not have any voice to do the singing. He had a nephew who could do those things, Old Mescalero Man, but his voice was poor, too. So I agreed with him that when he came he could bring his brother to help him out. Though he, himself, had no voice, still he went ahead and did that renewal of the bundle for me.

Of course I could have renewed my bundle myself with my own songs, but I wanted to see what the differences were between his songs and mine. The trouble with doing it for myself is that at the end, when it is all done it should be placed in my hand, you see, and I could not do that. It is done with a prayer and a song and then I am supposed to inhale the breath of that bundle. In that way it is made new again.

The main songs for that bundle are the Mountain songs. Then there are one or two songs each for the different stages in renewing the bundle, like untying it, then laying it out, then cleaning it, then rubbing it with the fat of deer, mountain sheep, beaver and otter. Whatever is being done, there are songs for each step of the way.

The last of June and the first of July are the right times of year for making the bundle and tying everything up with all the proper ceremony. Another good time is towards the first of September. That is when the dews are plentiful, and that is a good time to gather all the plant material that has to be used.

When we brought the mountain earth back from Mount Taylor, we sifted it so that the fine earth was separated from the pebbles and the coarser sand. When the fine earth had been blessed and put into the bundle, I put that other material in a cloth and tied it up and put it away where I keep the bundle. It does not really belong there, but I just put it away there anyway.

One time I was here in the morning and was searching for something in the trunk and I felt this bag of coarse earth. I had forgotten all about it, so I wondered what it was when I felt it. I opened it and realized that it was the coarse earth that had been separated from the rest. And when I looked at it, it had a strange color like fragments of turquoise.

So I called my children and my wife and told them to come in there. "Look at this," I said. "At the time these bundles were first made we were told, 'The earth in these bundles changes every so often, depending on the time of year. At certain times it will be one color and at other times it will be another.' " So when I opened it up it was all turquoise color, sparkling. My family was looking at it and they all agreed, "It does look like turquoise." Now Mount Taylor is recognized as being a turquoise mountain, so I told my children about that and we blessed the bundle and prayed to it and offered pollen to it.

That same day two Santo Domingo Indians came here at noon about lunch time and we invited them to eat with us. As they were eating, I asked them what they were doing on the reservation, and they said, "We're out here trying to trade."

I said, "What are you trading?"

"Turquoise," they said, so they spread a whole set of turquoise in front of us. I asked them what they were trading for, and they said, "Anything: cash, goods, buckskins, blankets, just anything that has any value."

I was looking over the whole set of beads that they had spread out, and there were two sets of earloops that looked more valuable than the rest of what they had. I was looking at them and I said, "I think those two are the only worthwhile beads you have." So then they got to talking among themselves, those two Pueblo Indians, and I guess they came to an agreement with each other. After some time, one said, "I'm going to give these to you. I want to give them to you as a gift of friendship." And so I accepted them and thanked them. He said, "And certainly I don't expect you to pay for these: this is just for friendship." And so they gave them to me.

Well, we had those beads for some time, and then they accidentally got lost some place around here. There was a Squaw Dance going on down below here, and somebody went there wearing the earloops. Then that person came back and lost the earloops on the trail going over to a rodeo across the way.

I was wondering how to get those back somehow, and I hired a star-gazer to see if he could tell me where they were. He said, "They are lost for good. You'll never get them back." Then I spread the word around that I would pay twenty-five dollars if anyone found the beads and brought them back to me.

So after some time a boy came along here asking, "What kind of beads are you trying to find?" He had heard about this pretty good offer for the beads.

And I told him, "They're very good color turquoise, and the way you can tell that they're the right ones is the jet beads on the tip." You see most turquoise earloops have red shell beads at the tip, but these had black beads made of jet.

So this boy said, "I have them over there." He went back and brought them here. Sure enough, those were the ones, and I got them back that way. And of course I paid for them, I paid the twenty-five dollar reward.

But even though the star-gazer was wrong, I still have some faith in them. We just go by what our elders tell us about how things are and what we should expect. They have told us what the results of our actions would be, according to how we act. The old people have a lot of confidence in these things. They merely say this, "If you do these things sincerely, well, you are going to get some benefit from them."

EDITORS' NOTES

1. A mirage stone is made of aragonite shaped into a smooth cylinder, usually about four or five inches long. The bands in the composition of the stone suggest layers of mist or mirage. The power of the stone is to provide symbolic concealment from danger as in a mist or mirage.

2. Father Berard Haile, noted scholar of Navajo language and ceremonialism, was an active Franciscan missionary on the Navajo reservation from 1900 to 1954. He was a close friend of Frank Mitchell and recorded Frank's myth of the Blessingway in the early 1930s (Wyman 1970:xix-xxv; 343-492). For a brief sketch of his life, see *Padres' Trail* 1961.

3. According to Father Berard's account of this first trip (Haile 1938:66; Wyman 1970:18-20), the date was September 8, 1932.

4. Pollens of various kinds are among the most complexly symbolic substances used in Navajo personal and ceremonial life. Their most common use is as a means of asking for a blessing. A highly treasured personal possession is a small deerskin pouch of corn pollen ready to use in any situation where a blessing is needed or the trail must be cleared for safe travel (Reichard 1963:509-510; 582-584). Corn pollen is the kind in widest use. Cattail pollen represents, among other things, the power of wild vegetation (*Ibid.*:193).

8. Blessingway Singer

The two sources of Frank's ceremony . . . the structure of the Blessingway ceremony . . . uses of the ceremony: renewal, pregnancy, seed blessing, at an eclipse, house blessing, in other ceremonials . . . more on renewal . . . the way particular songs are used . . . how Frank remembers all the material . . . the two sacred words . . . teaching the Blessingway.

The very first ceremony of Blessingway was held at Two Streams Meet. At that time, you see, the Mountain Earth bundle was made for the use of the Navajos, the people on earth. That is the last time the Holy People, the invisible beings, were gathered there. When they got through, that is the first time that they sang the Twelve-Word concluding song. After that, they told the people: "Now, from here on, we no longer will come into contact with one another. We will no longer speak to each other. You are going to inhabit the earth, while we will disappear from the earth into the rocks, into the mountains, into the hills, into the water, wherever we belong. Whenever you want to ask our help for any purpose, go to these spots and deposit offerings for us and we will accept them."

When they were making things for the use of the Earth People, of course songs were sung, prayers were offered. These were for the future use of the People. At one point in the ceremony, where the Mountain Earth bundles were made, then all these songs and whatever else had been done were established in their proper places so that they could be used in the ceremony. You see, in the story it says that whenever anything was established for the use of the Earth People, it required song and prayer. In that way they put it into motion; it became alive, just by the songs, the actions and the prayers. Now with us, we cannot do that because we do not have the power to create anything. If we were singing and praying it would not come to life at all. But we can keep the power alive today by using those songs that were used when the first Blessingway was created.

I think somebody must be responsible for the reproduction of everything, for vegetation and all living beings. Who does it? We do not do it – the human race does not do it. It is something that is beyond the power of human beings. The only thing that I can see that the human race does is create children. It takes a female and a male together to do it, but still they do not do it with their own power. Somebody with a higher power, with more force, must create these things and put them into motion. And we keep the motion going with those songs in the Blessingway.

I have two sets of Blessingway. There is not really much difference between the two, except here and there. Both of these versions go along with prayers. My teacher told me, "If you're going to use one set, don't mix it up with the other one. You should use that one set completely from the beginning to the end, from the Hogan songs to the Dawn songs. Of course the Hogan songs are all alike in each of the sets. But if you're going to use one set, just use that and don't add anything to it. If you're going to use the other set, do the same thing, but don't mix them up. Also, don't get the idea of adding something from other versions that other people use."

So for that reason I have never done that. There are a number of versions; we do not know how they started, but there are quite a number of different kinds. We can only distinguish them by the singers. We can ask the singers whose songs they are using, and they can usually trace them back several generations, as far back as they remember. That's how they can say the song is originally so-and-so's song. For instance, my father's version came from my grandfather, and while they were still living there together there was yet another version of it that was different from theirs. So it is pretty hard to say just how many different sets there are.

But I was instructed not to use certain songs just because I liked the way they were sung, to add them to my set, unless I would go to the man who was using them and ask him to let me do that. There is nothing wrong with doing that. But you cannot just take other people's songs; you must ask and get permission to use them. That is the only way you can use a set of songs from another version of a ceremony.

As for the songs I use, I have told you how I learned one set from my own father and the other set from my father-in-law. Originally they belonged to two different persons: one was Man Who Speaks Often, my grandfather. He learned it from his father, and handed it down to his son, Water Edge Man, who was my father. The other was Kaya, and his son was named He Who Seeks War, who in turn passed it on to Man Who Shouts, my father-in-law. From there on it was handed down to me.

These songs were handed down originally to the Earth People by the beings who had returned to the sky and other places and were no longer visible on the earth. They had gone, just as in your church where you teach about an afterlife. But still their songs and ceremonies are left here. Still, they are remembered; that is how our ceremonies were left to us.

This is the way we think about these things. These deities are living somewhere. They are aware of what we are doing, of how we are conducting ourselves here on earth: if we misuse the songs, that displeases them. It is the same way if we combine two songs that do not properly go together. They know about it there.

As we understand it, the songs were left here by different groups of holy beings. We are supposed to keep them intact and not mix them up. If we do start mixing them up, one with another, they know about it, and therefore, that ceremony is not recognized, it is not honored. It has no effect on the person that you are treating with it. Those Holy People are displeased with you if you start acting like that, and they no longer want to accept your songs and prayers. Otherwise, if you are keeping it up as it should be practiced, it is always accepted. It is understood that the different ceremonials, like Shootingway, Windway and Mountaintopway, are distinctly separate and were left here by the Holy People for the People to use. So, if you are singing Shootingway, you cannot just take songs from the Mountaintopway and add them. That is forbidden.

The difference between my two Blessingway ceremonies is in the words of the songs. The tunes of the songs might be the same, but it is the words of these songs that are more likely to vary. There may be just a few words mentioned in one version and more in the other. Those are the differences. The sets of songs are something like your grades in school; you start with beginners and go on up to twelve grades in high school. The songs are like that, you see.

Every version has the same set of Hogan songs. There are only two sets, the original and the Talking God songs. The Dawn songs are varied. There are certain branches that have a certain set of Dawn songs and other ones that have other sets. But the concluding song, the Twelve-Word song, is always the same, for every one of them.

Those two sets of Hogan songs are all the same. Regardless of what version it is, they are always the same. Except for one thing – I think I told you that one set consists of fourteen songs instead of twelve. From there on, of course, there are any number of songs that can be used all night long. Towards the end of the night, these different versions have their own sets of Dawn songs. Then the concluding song, the Twelve-Word song, is the same. For every one of them it is the same song, except that there is one word that may be done differently, when they mention the corn. Some singers just pronounce it straight: "*naadą́ą́*" and others say: "*ch'inaadą́ą́*."[1] That is the only word in that Twelve-Word song that varies with different singers.

The curing ceremonials – the chantways – most of them have one-night, five-night, even nine-night versions. But the Blessingway has only one version – it usually takes part of a night, the next morning, and all of the next night to perform that.

In the morning the first thing is washing the person being sung over. After breakfast somebody goes after the soapweed[2] and somebody else grinds the corn so there will be cornmeal to dry the one-sung-over, after the bath. Another part of the preparation is soaking a basket so it will hold the bath water, and fixing a small earth mound for the bath to take place on. When that is made and all smoothed out, the basket is placed on the eastern edge, and the soapweed root is put in it, with the upper end towards the east. Then water is ladled into the basket from east to west and back, south to north and back, and then just into the middle until there is enough. During this time the one-sung-over gets into place on the left side of the singer on blankets spread out to the west of the mound.

Now the singer starts the Bathing songs. These were used on those two boys who were taught by Changing Woman at her home in the west, and we use them now. There is no action during the first song, but from the middle of the second one on, the soapsuds are made. The singer rubs the root in the water with both hands until there are fluffy suds in the basket. Meanwhile, the one-sung-over undresses. All the clothes, except for a skirt if it's a woman and a breechcloth if it's a man, are placed on the one-sung-over's blanket which has been put, folded, on the ground just in front of that person's position. Beads, bracelets and other jewelry are kept on.

Next the singer takes pollen and sprinkles it over the suds east to west and back, then south to north and back, then all around the rim of the basket. Then, on the ground to the west of the basket, little crosses are made to show where the hands and knees of the one-sung-over are to be placed. After that the singer sprinkles pollen all around the mound.

The one-sung-over is then told to gather up all the clothing in a bundle, walk around the fire and then back into place behind the basket and stand on the pollen crosses. First the right foot is put in place and then the left. The singer picks up a pinch of soapsuds from the basket, from east, south, west, north and then the middle, and gives a body blessing to the one-sung-over with these. The third Bathing song is sung at the same time.

Now the one-sung-over stands back and kneels on the pollen crosses. First the right palm, then the left, are placed on the other crosses so that the one-sung-over is on all fours in front of the basket. The singer takes suds and puts them in the hair of the person being blessed. After that, bracelets, beads and other jewelry are taken off and put in the basket. They are washed and put on the blanket with the clothes. The third song continues during the hair washing and rinsing, which is done over the basket, with the gourd dipper. Then the rest of the body is bathed by the one-sung-over. If it is a woman, some blankets are held up for her when she removes her skirt for that part of the washing. There are just three songs for the bathing. In the bathing, everything is washed out of you, and then the drying puts it back into you again, sacred and renewed. The basket used has to be a new one; some singers are strict about this.

As soon as the bathing is over, the one-sung-over sits down in place. Helpers empty the last of the bath water on the mound, and all that wet earth is gathered up and put in a sack or a blanket and taken outside. The basket goes to the singer, who puts it away in the west corner of the hogan. The helper takes the soapweed and carries it out with the earth from the mound. The earth is dumped about fifty yards from the hogan, and then pollen is put down before it; the soapweed is also placed there, with the growing end pointing away from the hogan.

In the place where the mound was, dry earth should be sprinkled and a clean blanket spread on top. Then the jewelry should be placed on the right and the clothing on the left; the one-sung-over should sit on the blanket, in between, facing east. A bowl of cornmeal is placed nearby with pollen on the right and before it. Then the singer gets up and starts singing the Drying songs. When the feet are mentioned a blessing is given to them with cornmeal and so on, going all the way up as each part of the body is mentioned, giving a body blessing. Then the singer puts the bowl of meal before the one-sung-over, takes a little and sprinkles his or her back. The rest of the cornmeal is used by the one-sung-over for drying the rest of the body and for sprinkling over the jewels and clothes. All this is done during the first Drying song.

On the second Drying song the same thing is done with pollen. Then some pollen is put on the palms of the one-sung-over to be rubbed all over the body as the second song ends.

Now comes another song. This originated at the time the twin boys were eating at Changing Woman's home. This third song is called the Eating song. As Talking God is mentioned, the singer puts pollen in the mouth of the one-sung-over. This happens again when the song mentions "pollen food." Where "Hogan God's food" is mentioned, again pollen is eaten, and again at "the food of *Są'ah naaghéi* and *Bik'eh hózhǫ́ǫ́*." That makes four times altogether.

The singer's pollen pouch is now handed to the one-sung-over, who does a self-blessing and then blesses the jewelry and the clothing. Two pouches of pollen are then passed around the hogan to everybody who is there. One starts from the one-sung-over to the north on the women's side, and the other starts from the door and moves towards the singer on the men's side.[3] The singer tells the one-sung-over to dress, starting always with the right and then the left, from the socks and shoes on up. The jewelry and bracelets come last. All the clothes are blessed at that time, and any that are not being worn are put aside. The blessed person's blanket is put on; then he or she goes back into place.

Some singers gather up the cornmeal that is left on the blanket from the drying, but I leave it there. The ceremonial bundle is now placed on the east edge of the blanket, and a strip of cloth or buckskin is placed on the west edge. Footprints are made with pollen on the buckskin at the south end to mark the position of the one-sung-over, and crosses at the north end on which the singer is to stand. Then pollen half-circles are made to show where each will sit down. The prayer is usually done standing, but in the case of a crippled person, for instance, the one-sung-over is allowed to lie back, in place.

Now the one-sung-over goes around the fire and back to place. The singer passes over a pollen pouch, and after a self-blessing, the one-sung-over sends it on, around the north side of the hogan. At the same time another pollen pouch goes sunwise around the south side. After this pollen blessing for everyone there, the singer tells the one-sung-over to get up and stand on the footprints, putting the right foot in position first.

Then the singer gets up and takes the Mountain Earth bundle and stands before the one-sung-over for another blessing, pressing it to the body from the feet up. After that, the singer places a pollen pouch against the bundle and, keeping the pollen towards the one-sung-over, puts the two into that person's right hand. The left hand is underneath supporting the bundle. After that the singer goes around the one-sung-over on the south side, to a position on the crosses at the north end of the buckskin. Now come the Prayer songs. There are four or five different prayers possible here, and the songs would depend on which prayer is to be used.

The first prayer has a lot of words. It may be eight, twelve, or twenty-four verses in length, and, among other things, it names all the mountains. After this, there is another prayer asking the Holy People for protection and blessing. Here is where the way of blessing comes in for everybody, including all their possessions, such as sheep and horses. At the end, pollen is placed in the mouth, and then more is sprinkled outwards and you say, "Everything will be well, everything will be blessed," four times.

After that the singer opens the pollen pouch, inhales from it four times and then goes back into place on the right of the one-sung-over. Once there, the singer tells the one-sung-over to imitate the inhaling. Then the singer puts away the first pollen pouch, takes another one and does a body blessing for the one-sung-over. Next comes the sprinkling of pollen from the singer's mouth towards the smoke-hole of the hogan, four times. After that, the one-sung-over is told to look as far as can be imagined towards the east while loosening the whole body. After that the singer goes back into place.

Now the one-sung-over may go out. The singer gathers the materials on the blanket and puts them all away. The cornmeal is gathered up and placed behind the rolled-up bedding of the one-sung-over there at the ceremonial position. The singer calls out, "Bring in the food, it's the ceremony's day now!"[4] The time will be around eleven o'clock or noon.

If there is to be a drypainting, it will be made on the mound when everything there is being prepared. If it is a figure of Pollen Boy or Big Fly,[5] you would take a pinch of the pollen from the feet, knees and every body part of the drypainting and put that into the cornmeal before the drying. This represents the body of the one-sung-over. You have to pay extra if there is a drypainting. Some use different things for this, but I make it of pollen.

After the noon meal there is a break in the ceremonial until evening. The one-sung-over can go anywhere around the place, but not to places like the store or off to work.

In the evening everybody eats; then it is time for things to be blessed — pouches of sacred things such as pollen and other things such as jewelry, clothing, blankets, bridles and weaving tools. These things are put out between the singer and the one-sung-over, and the ceremonial bundle is put on top of this. Then everybody is quiet, and somebody blesses the hogan with pollen. It is taken around and rubbed on the roof beams in the four directions. The one-sung-over then goes around the fire and back to place for a pollen self-blessing. After that, the two pouches of pollen go around for everybody to use. When the pouch on the men's side has gone all the way around, the singer is the last to make that blessing.

Now come the first twelve Hogan songs — Talking God's Hogan songs about Changing Woman's home in the east. They were sung on the Mountain Around Which Traveling Was Done by him. Then there is a prayer of thanks to Talking God, just in the singer's own words. After that come twelve more Talking God Hogan songs; these tell about the home built for Changing Woman, floating on the ocean in the west. The last one is called the Circling song. At the end of the song the one-sung-over goes out and then comes back in, representing the time Changing Woman went out to calm the supernatural beings disturbed by Enemy Slayer's killing of the monsters. After the one-sung-over comes back in again, anyone can go out. Up to that point people could come in, but no one was supposed to leave.

Now come the "Songs with Which Things Were Fixed in Pairs," twelve of them. These are about the sacred things given to us to be used by the Holy People: the heavenly bodies, Earth Woman, Mountain Woman, Water Woman and the four sacred mountains that are the boundary of the Navajo country and that provide the Navajos with sacred herbs. These were guarded by the Holy People, and they are probably still doing it now. They are in charge of all these things. The last two songs are different from the rest; they have the sacred words about long life and blessing in them.

The next five songs are Earth songs, or "Songs by Which Pollen Is Applied." The blessing is given with pollen, white crystal and cornmeal. You cannot leave these out. This is the time the one-sung-over is made holy again with all these blessings. Pollen is applied with each of these songs. At the beginning, when these were first sung, each of the holy beings mentioned in the songs was there and received a pollen blessing.

The next thing is the Twelve-Word song of Blessingway. This is the connecting link between the first part of the night and the rest of the ceremony. All the songs so far must be in order, and no other songs can be put in between them, anywhere. At the end of this song all those in the hogan take a pinch of pollen and say a prayer in their own words. This concludes the first part of the night. It is about midnight, now, and food is brought in. It may be brought in several more times from now on.

Next are groups of different songs about the beginning of the world, putting the sacred mountains in their positions. First come ten Mountain songs, mostly about the creation of the mountains, putting them in their places, giving them names, giving them something to smoke and putting a spirit into them. Then there are six songs in two groups of three about when the mountains are in position and protectors are placed inside of them. It is like when a person puts on a Yeibichai mask and starts dancing with it. You are supposed to take care of these masks; in the same way, when the mountains were placed, they had to be cared for. The twin boys were taken up on the mountain to learn these songs. They went up on Black Belt Mountain, and from there they could see Tongue Mountain. From Tongue Mountain they could see *Dook'o'oslííd*. They used rock crystal to look through, the way you use a telescope; from each mountain they could see all the others.

There are quite a few of these songs. Those two boys circled the mountains four times, and that is where they learned them. If you sang all of these, it would take all night. So you just do a few from each group. It is the same way with the Earth songs and the others, just a few from each group are performed. The main root of the whole ceremony is in the first part of the night up to the Twelve-Word song. After that it spreads out; you can use different groups, you can twist it around for different performances, and that is the way you complete the ceremonial. For example, you can use "*Ts'ídá haazdi'i*,"[6] when a person has returned from war. It all depends on what is needed by the one-sung-over.

There are two other songs in here — the Songs of the Follower Pair — and there are prayers, also. On the second round of Mountain songs, prayers are included. You could call them Mountain prayers. These could be used when that prayer is made standing on the pollen footsteps. I cannot tell you now which songs would be used on this part of the night. I would just do it without thinking about it when the time came.

There are three groups of prayers with these songs that are used after the one-sung-over has been bathed. The sacred mountains used to send words to each other. I don't know how they did it: they must have had a radio. One of these prayers has eighteen verses. This is used especially when a ceremonial bundle is being prepared or renewed. Any time after the Twelve-Word song, food may be brought in. It can be brought in three or four times after that, depending on the cook. In all this singing I prefer not to have any interference, so I usually do not have any other singer in to help me.

Next it will be time for the Dawn songs, eight of them. Then, at the last, is another Twelve-Word song. This is for all the groups that went before, it is the leader of them all. When I get to the tenth word[7] I get up, take pollen and give a body blessing to the one-sung-over and pinches of pollen to be eaten four times. During the day pollen was rubbed on the outside; now it goes inside. Next I sprinkle a pollen trail from the one-sung-over to the door around the south side of the fire to the door and then back to the ceremonial position. The one-sung-over takes the pollen pouch and goes outside by that trail.

If you are the one-sung-over, you go out about five yards and stand facing the east. You take out the pollen, sprinkle it towards the dawn and scatter it from north to south. Then you inhale the dawn four times and give a prayer to yourself, the dawn and everything that exists. Everything is to be made holy again. When you come back in, you pass in front of the sacred materials all laid out there and go back to your place. Now the pollen goes around the hogan again, and then the singer puts away the sacred bundle. The household things that were brought out to be blessed are put away, too, and the singer takes the materials that were put there as part of the payment, rolls them up, puts them back and leans on them. Some of those things are given by the singer to those who have been helping through the night with this ceremony. The ceremony is completed.

Food is brought in, and after everybody has had something to eat, somebody goes for the singer's horse. They saddle it, tie the bundle on it, and then the singer leaves. The one-sung-over is supposed to keep quiet all day but should not sleep until night comes again.

It is a custom with the People that even though everything may be going all right with a family and nothing is wrong, that family still may say, "Well, let's have a Blessingway to freshen things up, to renew ourselves again." So they do. Or sometimes they might have acquired some valuable goods, if they have been off trading or something, and have brought them home. Then the things that they brought in from other places, well, it is on their minds — "That's what we're blessed with in this family." They might feel they need the Blessingway because you do not wait until some misfortune happens before you have it. That is the reason it is called the peaceful way, the healing way, the blessing way. There is no specific time limit; it depends on the family. If they feel that they should have it, then they do it, just an ordinary Blessingway.

Of course if you are able to have that ceremony, if you have the means to put it on, well, then you should do it. But if you have not, then, in that case, you just keep putting it off until you are able to bear the cost.

Now to go back to the time when I was being instructed in the Blessingway ceremony by my wife's father and my own father. I was told that when you are learning and after you have completed your instructions, you have to have this ceremony performed over you in order to make it holy.

After I learned the Blessingway, my teacher told me not to go beyond four performances without having the Blessingway performed over me. Every four times that I did the Blessingway I was to have it done for me because I was told that in that way you renew it every time, it is as good as new again.

In those days, of course, I was pretty well occupied with those performances, so it was not too long between times when I had this Blessingway done over me. I would ask anyone who I knew was a sincere singer to do that ceremony for me. It could be one of my relations, and of course you can use your teacher for that too, time and again. Of course, the custom is to have this ceremony performed over you by your teacher at the beginning. You are blessed with the same songs that were given to you for your use.

You see, my teacher asked me this: if you go beyond four performances of the Blessingway without renewing it, then what set of songs are you going to use? You see, if you use the first set of songs for the first time, the second set of songs for the second, the third set of songs for the third, and the fourth ... you see, there are about that many sets available that I could use. These are Mountain songs, Woman songs, Talking God songs, and songs of Returning Home. Those last songs are used in case the one-sung-over has been a prisoner of war. Like in your case: now, your home is not here, your home is somewhere else, but you are here for some reason. Now if you were a Navajo in such a case, when you got home those songs of Returning Home would be used, about your journey: that you had a wonderful journey, been where you wanted to go and returned peacefully home. That is what those songs are about.

Blessingway is used for everything that is good for a person, or for the People. It has no use other than that. For instance, when a woman is pregnant she has the Blessingway in order to have a good delivery with no trouble. It is also done so that she and her child may have a happy life. In case of bad dreams, they are a kind of warning that there are some misfortunes ahead of you; in order to avoid that you have the Blessingway so that you will have happiness instead. Or if you are worried about something, your family will want to get you back, to get that out of your mind, out of your system, so that you may have a good life. It is the same for any other things that could cause you to worry, to feel uneasy about yourself. That is the sort of thing it is used for.

As for the prayers, you say, "Beauty shall be in front of me, beauty shall be in the back, beauty shall be below me, above me, all around me." On top of that you say about yourself, "I am everlasting, I may have an everlasting life. I may live on, and lead an everlasting life with beauty." You end your prayers that way.

I have heard that there is a ceremony concerning the blessing of seeds,[8] but I have never done it. I have never been taught how to do that, so I do not know what songs, prayers or ceremony is used. They call it the Blessing of the Corn. It is also called the No Sleep Ceremony for Corn. I have been told that in the songs used for that there are always some Corn songs, songs having to do with vegetation, like Harvest Fly Girl songs and Corn Pollen Boy songs. Of course they have the Hogan songs in there, too. Those are the foundation of it. You can use either of those two sets of Hogan songs; they can be the original ones, the Chief Hogan songs, or the Talking God Hogan songs.

What I heard was that when a family in the old days had a good harvest they would bring in all the corn, you see, all the five colors of corn: white, yellow, blue, gray and striped. The best ones, the best ears were brought in to this one place, and they would be blessed there by the ceremony. They are arranged in rows, you see. The corn, jewels and the collection of different kinds of food made from corn, like mush, dumplings, cake and other things were all brought into that one place. There a regular one-night Blessingway ceremony was done to bless the corn and the collection of food.

After the Hogan songs and other sacred songs are sung, then the collection of different kinds of food is removed, after small amounts from each bowl are set aside. These small amounts are taken four times. These are blessed, too, and of course the rest is eaten by the people who are participating.

That is what I have been told, although I have never done this myself. The corn that is left is used for seeds in the future. The collection of food is used to bless the food of the families attending the ceremony. They take a pinch of it and put it in their own food. Everything that is in there has some purpose. That food has other ceremonial uses. In the Nightway when the masks are being blessed, they use that food to feed those masks.

That food has to be kept in there to be eaten in the hogan. Nothing that is left can be taken out, and naturally there is bound to be some left. So they just keep it in there until it is all used up. It is kept all night long because they cannot take anything out of there once they have brought it into the hogan to be eaten.

The main songs used are the original Hogan songs, the Chief Hogan songs. Those are the ones that were made first, and they have to do with all growing things. The Talking God songs are used for human birth and growth. Actually, the Hogan songs are sung when the one for whom the ceremony is being given walks out and then returns to the hogan. After that, the corn pollen is passed again, and then it is offered for different things that are there to be blessed. People pray in their own words to the beings who have control over these growing plants.

Of course, in this Corn Blessing they usually use the Dawn Songs of the Child, the Dawn songs that are used in the coming-of-age ceremony. For the blessing of individuals, the Talking God Dawn songs can be used. There are only four of those Dawn Songs of the Child. There are eight of the other ones.

The seed-blessing really was not performed in creation times. It is just that the rule was made then for how it should be conducted. That was after Changing Woman moved to the West. According to the story, there was a stalk of corn that had twelve ears. After the two boys were taught at Changing Woman's home, the Holy People kept six ears for themselves; the other six were for the use of people on earth. Talking God is the one who performed that ceremony, blessing this stalk of corn, and when he did that there was no singing. He is the one who blessed that stalk and made it grow twelve ears.

The way the story is told, when the white shell beads were put in the ground to grow up to be corn, Talking God blessed them by running up to that place from the east and from the other three directions. When he finished those motions, then the stalk of corn appeared, grew up and produced twelve ears on one stalk. In the same way, Hogan God blessed all other vegetation. Talking God is the one that blessed the corn, but Hogan God blessed vegetation of all sorts. So that is the reason we mention that in the ceremony; first we mention the corn, then we mention the other vegetation. In the words of the song it says "upward." Then "coming down" refers to the rain. The rain comes down on the vegetation, and the vegetation grows up out of the ground.

The main two uses of Blessingway songs outside the ceremony are for an eclipse of the sun or the moon. Those are the only two that I know of. The songs used during the eclipse are those having to do with the sun: the making of the sun in the beginning, the creation of it. It is the same way for the songs used for the moon. If there were a ceremony going on where a lot of people were gathered, then all those present would join in the singing. In the case of a family not being visited by any outsiders, the head of the family would do the singing. In case nobody knew the songs, they do not have to have that. The only thing is that they should not sleep and that they should not eat. Those are the restrictions at the time of an eclipse; you do not do anything, just sit there patiently and wait for the sun or moon to come back. Nowadays most people do not observe the rule about abstaining from food.

When you are singing the songs you do not have to keep singing all through the eclipse; just sing through the set of songs. The songs that deal with the creating of the sun in the beginning are used for that purpose, starting with the time that it was decided to make the sun. It is similar to the Hogan songs, you see. The songs tell about all that happened up to the time that the sun went into the sky to the west and disappeared. I myself do not know these songs and have never used them.

Another use of the Blessingway is for house-blessing.[9] Most of the people who are really Navajo are still practicing this except for those who have become Christians. It is only recently that they have been blessing public buildings. For instance, when they built that central hospital at Fort Defiance in the late 1930s, that was the first time a public building was blessed here.[10] Pete Price was the one who did the singing and the prayers, with the help of some others. I suppose it was on account of Chee Dodge's advice that it would be good to do that. He said, "All of these buildings are placed here for the use of our own people, and they should be blessed, and should be marked, and prayers offered for them so that they may be good for the use of the People."[11]

When I do that, I do it according to my own stories, the way things were done in the beginning. That is where my ideas about what to do come from, and I use those ideas when I bless public buildings as well as our own hogan. As for Pete Price, the Blessingway songs that he used were the same as my songs; we both learned from the same teacher.

At the blessing of the high school last winter, my granddaughter Geneva was the one who marked the building. I did that according to my own ideas. I felt that it was good that this house, where our children would be kept to learn, should be blessed and made holy. So I used the prayer called the Hogan Prayer. I know that Pete Price did not use any prayers, only songs. Nobody else helped me except my granddaughter.

The song that I used was the song of the Sun's house in the east. It is not a Blessingway Hogan song. It is a different song that was used over there at the house of the Sun. The prayer is the Hogan Prayer. I used the most central room in the whole place, a classroom. I was at the entrance on the east side, and we did the marking first, exactly the way I do my Blessingway ceremony. Before anything else is done, somebody gets up and marks the hogan in the four directions. Then, of course, the ceremony starts; after the marking you start the songs. That is the way I did it at the school.

Of course, when you are marking the logs in a hogan you use cornmeal. But in this case, we used corn pollen. Geneva just sprinkled it along sunwise: east, south, west and north. When I blessed the boarding school plant, the B.I.A. school, Isabelle helped me with it. Over here at the high school, Geneva was the one who helped.

At those ceremonies we did not pass pollen to the people because there were all kinds of people there as spectators. A lot of them did not belive in the Blessingway, did not respect it. So, for that reason, we just sprinkled it over their heads. We sprinkled it in the four directions, then sang the songs and did the prayers. Of course, after the set prayer for that purpose, you can just say something in your own words: a prayer addressing the invisible holy beings and asking that this house may be of benefit to the People.

The reason I blessed the high school is because I was asked. The principal there is the one who asked me to do that. I do not know who told him or how he found out that I do that. Of course he paid me a fee for one song and one prayer.

The only other school blessing I was asked to do was at the Cottonwood School. I was reluctant and said, "Well, you have plenty of other singers who can do this ceremony over in your area. Why don't you get one of them?" I kind of refused, and I imagine they got somebody over there to do it from that locality. I think they must have gone through with the ceremony.[12]

At the time they completed the new Law and Order Building here in Chinle, they asked me to mark it and have a blessing, but I refused that one, too. I said, "I don't know why I should mark that and bless it; I can't see what good that would be because it's a house of punishment." Schools and some other buildings are houses of well-being for the future, but I didn't want to bless the Law and Order Building because it was a house of punishment. That was my opinion, so I refused. Some priest or missionary blessed it.

Another use of the Blessingway is in certain ceremonials that have Blessingway at the end. After the main ceremony has been finished, they conclude with a Blessingway. In the early days, of course, there was a special kind of Blessingway that they used, but I do not think anybody uses that any more. It has all been forgotten; the regular Blessingway is used for this purpose now.

The Mountaintopway ceremony has to do with the Eagle People. It is used for skin eruptions, itchy skin and troubles like that. They make sandpaintings for four days. After the four days are completed, they finish the ceremony with Blessingway.

Red Ant Holyway also uses Blessingway, but not at the conclusion. The first night is when they have it. Then Nightway has it at the blessing of the masks when they are halfway through the ceremonial; it does not come at the end. Mountaintopway, with the Corral Dance, has it and so does the nine-night Shootingway, Holyway. Some of these nine-night chanters do not even know Blessingway; they have to ask somebody else to do it for them. But, no doubt, in the beginning, when all these nine-night ceremonials were laid down for the use of the People, every one of them had a Blessingway included. Those Blessingways were used to bless the sacred things, such as the masks and other objects, that were used in each ceremonial.

After I stopped hauling freight, I was in daily contact with Man Who Shouts. But Son of the Late Little Blacksmith was a neighbor of ours when we settled permanently in Chinle, and so I would also get together with him quite often. Son of the Late Little Blacksmith was very friendly with me; lots of times he would ask for my assistance while talking to the People. So I used to step in and help him. Of course, in that way, I learned too. Another close friend of mine, Long Moustache, also used to help Son of the Late Little Blacksmith.

One of my clan uncles, Two Streams Meet Curly, was also a respected talker among the People. I began to get pretty close to him too, and since he was a relative of mine, naturally I sided with him. I got some more ideas on how to speak to the People from him. I went around with him quite a bit, too, helping him out. He was one of the leaders in the community here while I was helping him. Finally the People elected him as the first councilman from this area, when Chic Sandoval helped spread the word urging the People to vote for him.

In this way, I started going around with these leaders. I merely helped them along in their dealing with the People. Of course, I was still doing little odd jobs myself, whenever I had the chance. All of that traveling around and helping I did with those leaders was voluntary on my part; there was no pay for that. Through these experiences, I began to understand what the future plans were for the People. Of course, in this way I gained experience in dealing with the People.

My father-in-law, Man Who Shouts, had been known as a headman, a peacemaker and a spokesman for the People for quite a long time before I met him. He had been selected to be headman for this community, and he had a paper indicating that he was to be recognized as a headman, or peacemaker. This paper was from the superintendent of the agency, and every four years, I think, he took that paper into the agency to have it renewed. In cases where a new agent or a new superintendent would come in and another would leave, Man Who Shouts would go over to Fort Defiance with his paper to have the new man sign his name to it, too, to renew it.

Man Who Shouts kept this position until he died. When he passed away, the People knew that I had experience in helping these men. I was approached by different ones who suggested that I have that paper renewed for me. They said, "Well, you seem to get the best information on the things to be explained to the People. It is clear; we can understand you much better than a lot of the other leaders."

Some of the leaders were hard to understand; it was hard to figure out what they were talking about. But the People always told me that whenever I talked, it was always clear. They understood it right away. Some of the others talked a lot better than I did, but the People could not understand what they were saying. That was one reason that they started asking me to come to different meetings. Whenever there was a dispute in a family or among other people, the talkers would be called on to find out about that right away. My clan uncle and I did a lot of talking, and eventually I just started talking to the People myself. So on account of that, the paper that my father-in-law had was rewritten in my name and given to me, indicating that I was his successor.[13]

The agency appreciated the fact that we were out here helping in any way we could because the government needed help in preventing trouble. That was the main thing the white people had in mind at that time. They were so scared that the Navajos might raid the whole country again. There was only one man out here from Washington during those days, and about all he did was bring in the news about what the government had planned for the Navajos in the future. He spread the news to the headmen, who then told the People about it. We did not have a Tribal Council at Window Rock or Chapter houses in those times. There were no records of any of these meetings at that time, either.

After the headmen had met, they would come back and bring the news they had collected. Some of them were not too good at getting all the news. They would come home and start to talk, but they could not make things understandable to the People, and then the People were confused about things.

In those days the People were spread far apart all around the reservation. There were not too many headmen at that time, just a few in the different areas. Not many of us were recognized as having influence or being able to guide the People. Many just did not have the knowledge needed to instruct the People. Some of the leaders then were Chee Dodge, Silversmith and Charlie Mitchell, and over on the eastern side Bicenti Begay, Left Foot Man's Son, Red Moustache's Brother, Tall Big Water Man and two others by the name of John and Many Horses. There were a few others, too, but none of those were educated enough to inform the People about the plans of the government.

The headmen used to get together with the superintendent in Fort Defiance. Sometimes he would come out here himself, and at other times all of the headmen would go into Fort Defiance to meet there with him. The headmen would find out the news, and the superintendent would ask them if they were willing to go along with the plans that the government had. We were told that in the future we would get more experienced than we had been in the past, and that the government would gradually turn things over to us. The responsibilities of the Indian agent to oversee our affairs would be ended.

In Washington, they looked upon us as children, or minors who did not have a mind of our own. But, when the Window Rock Agency was established, gradually Washington started turning things over to us. That was right after I had that paper put in my name. We were told to use our best judgment to make plans for the People. But the government also had plans for us, and they wanted us to put them side by side and compare the plans to see which would be the best. In this way, we would gradually get the foundation for our planning system. By hearing those things, I gradually began to understand the various ways that the white people used in government, and I began to compare them with the ways of my own people.

By the time I had that paper renewed in my name, being a peacemaker did not seem to matter to some of the People anymore, because all those leaders did was talk. You really did not have any power. I was hesitant about stepping out in public telling the People that I was a peacemaker, since there were a lot of people there who were higher up than I was. I did not always feel like getting out and talking that way. The People would ask me to give a talk at gatherings, like at a dance or a meeting. But I was not always too anxious to do that. Being a poor man, I did not feel like getting out there and trying to talk to the People. Well, they would insist on it, and so to satisfy them, I did it now and then.[14]

In those days there was only temporary work, and it was hard to make a living. Of course I had a wagon and a team, and I had chances to do some work for white people and earn a little money. But it was never mentioned that these things would be permanent or that there would be any benefit in them for me in my future. All of those jobs were temporary; they just lasted for a little while and then they were over. Being a Blessingway singer, of course, was different; it was something that I could use for my entire lifetime to earn a little food for myself and the children. By this time most of the People knew me because of my singing, and they were always coming to me to perform ceremonies. So as I became a leader of the People, I was combining two things together for my job, because I was also practicing the Blessingway. That was my occupation, going around singing, going around talking to the People, and every now and then, also working for others, helping them build hogans and assisting them in other ways.

When I started talking to the People on my own, I became more aware of my Blessingway ceremony at the same time. It seemed as if the songs and prayers became clearer to me. The more I talked to the People and the more I learned about that, the clearer the Blessingway became to me. I began to see that some of the stories connected with that, such as how there had always been good and bad people right from the beginning, were true. It was like I was completely lifted out of the mind that I had when I was a young boy. All of the nonsense that I used to think about when I was young started to disappear, and all the things that I was never too clear about started to change. I began to realize that some things were very important, and my whole way of thinking was changed.

It no longer was hard for me to talk to the People, and it was not hard for them to understand what I was telling them. I found out that I was not afraid to get up and talk; I knew what I was going to say, and it was easy for me to say those things. I guess the People found out that I was like that. A lot of them told me they could understand what I said very easily. You had to talk to them in the simplest way possible so that they could understand; some of the other leaders used some of the Navajo words from way back, and the People would not understand what they meant.

Many people, including government officials and others who worked with the Navajos, began to take notice of me. Even some of the foremen on projects would approach me and ask, "Do you have any knowledge of what is going on?" and I would say, "I do to a certain extent." Then they would ask for my cooperation. I always had answers for their questions, and that is how they got to know me pretty well.

When I was learning Blessingway from Man Who Shouts, he told me that if I was going to learn it, there could be no lying or wrongdoing during the time when I was learning. He also said that later in my life people would come from near and far because I was recognized for the Blessingway. It would be that way if I did it right from the beginning. If I did this, the Blessingway would bring me good blessings, and I would live a long time to see things.

Man Who Shouts must have foreseen my white friends way back then; he must have known that you were going to come and sit here in my hogan and talk about these things. It is because of these things that I believe we must practice ceremonies correctly and keep them holy. This is what my father-in-law told me, and I learned it the right way. I did not add anything later. I have practiced the ceremonies correctly, and I have become known by others who call upon me for advice, just as he predicted.

A singer who does a five-night curing ceremonial — say, for example, Flintway — he is not supposed to perform that more than four times without renewing it. If you performed a ceremony for a man who was very sick and this man got well, then his family would like to have the one-night version done right away. There are supposed to be four performances in all. If they are all done and the man has completely recovered, you would know right away that the ceremonial did some good.

So, to renew the whole thing, you are supposed to have Blessingway done for yourself and for your ceremonial bundle. Then you would be able to do another five-night singing, and the whole thing would be fresh and strong. This is why Blessingway has that name; it blesses the whole thing and brings it back to life.

It is just as if you had tools that you were working with all the time. The blade would get so dull you could not do much work with it, so you would have to sharpen it. That is where Blessingway comes in. It makes everything new and sharp again so you can do whatever has to be done.

I have used my Blessingway over and over again that way. The first singer whose ceremony I renewed with Blessingway was known as the Crippled One. He performed a great many different ceremonials: Mountaintopway, Shootingway, Ghostway, Chiricahua Windway, Flintway and Blessingway. He did so many, I think that is why he needed them renewed. He was the first one for whom I used Blessingway as a renewal.

Then the second one was Little Many Goats. He was from Many Rocks, over near Black Mountain. He did only the Flintway ceremonial. Blessingway can be used to renew ceremonials, no matter what kind they are. So you see how it is the root of the whole thing; it supports all the ceremonials.

Of course, it is the same way with the Blessingway: you can do it for only so many people and then you have to have it for yourself, to renew it. Nowadays the People do not look at it that way. They just want to perform what they know and get something out of it. They do not even think about how their various ceremonials should be refreshed with Blessingway. The blades are so dull these days they probably will not do any good at all. They are not sharp enough to make people well. These singers do not even realize what they should be doing.

These young singers that are around now never learn from the older, expert singers about how this Blessingway for renewal should be carried out. That is one reason why it is not done much anymore. It takes a lot of experience; there are little things added to the regular Blessingway that a lot of them do not know. I am probably the only one who still remembers all that has to be done. Around this area I do not know anybody else, as far as I can recall, who knows how to do it. Even if they say they know, when they start in doing it I would probably find some mistakes that they make. I am not trying to say that I am the only one who knows anything, but I know the singers around here that claim to do these things, and I know they do not do them correctly. As far as Blessingway is concerned, I learned it from a very good singer a long time back, and I am still carrying it on the way I was taught.

The special thing about the Blessingway when it is used for renewal is the prayers. They are the most important part of the ceremony, and a majority of Blessingway singers do not know the special prayers for renewal. All they know are the straight Blessingway prayers.

This first renewal prayer, called the Talking God Prayer, mostly has to do with renewing Blessingway itself, where a singer has been doing Blessingway too much and wants to have the ceremonial bundle renewed. The next one is for singers who do five-night or any other ceremonials. If they have done a lot of them for men, women and children, and yet at the same time keep losing those people they sing for, even though they do the ceremonials many times over them, then this prayer is the one for renewal: they would have the Monster Slayer Prayer, which is called the Protection Prayer. It is a shield, like a shield that is used in battle. Then after that, they would have the Blessingway ceremony.

These two are the only prayers that can be followed right away by Blessingway. If you use both of them, the Protection Prayer comes first and the Talking God Prayer comes second. Then, on top of that, comes the Blessingway. You could do prayer rituals for two nights and then, on the third day, have the Blessingway with the bathing and cornmeal drying. Or, you could have the prayer before the Blessingway for one night only. After the bathing and drying, there are usually more prayers. That is where this last prayer comes in, the Talking God Prayer, and the singer's bundle is returned for renewal. From there on is what we call "the day," of the ceremony, and what follows is straight Blessingway.

Right after your bathing is over, after the cornmeal drying, then, as a singer, your bundle is put into your hands. While you are holding it, this particular prayer is said again. After the prayers are all finished, you lift your bundle and take four deep breaths from it. Before that, because of singing your ceremonials so much, your songs had all come out; you did not have any more singing left in you. When you breathe in from the bundle, four times, that is a sign that you are getting all your singing back inside you again. Whatever you breathe in from the sacred bundle is going back into you so that you will have more strength with which to sing. Your songs all go back into you, in a sacred way. Then you can carry on your singing again, all refreshed and sharpened.

In a Blessingway ceremony for a pregnant woman, it is usually the Talking God set of Hogan songs that is used. The reason for this is that when Changing Woman was having her first coming-of-age ceremony, those songs were used. Since it is necessary that there be a man and a woman in order to make a child, these are the two who are really involved in this Blessingway ceremony.

There is no strict rule about which Hogan songs you use, though. It is like my two ways of doing Blessingway: after using one version three times, I switch over to the other one. It is the same with the Hogan songs; I use one set three times and then switch over to the other.

It all depends on the circumstances of the one-sung-over, what the ceremony is for. Is it because of dreams, visions or because someone is worried? Sometimes it could be for someone who has been away to war or away from the Navajo country for a certain length of time and has just returned. It all depends on the situation; you use your own judgment as to what set of songs you are going to sing. When a woman is pregnant you use Corn songs because they are protection songs. If you sing over someone who has been away from the country, like off to war or off to work or school, you use the songs we call the Returning songs, Returning Home songs. For visions you can use either the Mountain songs or the Changing Woman songs.

You use your own judgment, depending on the reasons the one-sung-over has for wanting the ceremony. It is related to what has happened in that person's life. Of course, with the Hogan songs, the singer's welfare has to be considered, too. You think back, "How many times have I sung the same set of Hogan songs?" If you have done it three times in succession, then it's customary to switch over to the other one.

Whenever there is a renewal of a Blessingway bundle or any part of it, or the masks of the Nightway are to be blessed, then you must use the Chief Hogan songs. It is up to you to decide when to use certain sets of songs for certain things. It depends on what the circumstances are, and why you are hired to do this. Of course, I am talking about the times when they were very strict about those things. Nowadays people are careless and do not bother. They may use the same Hogan songs all the time, and some of them do not even know the Chief Hogan songs. The only ones they can use are the Talking God Hogan songs.

The Earth songs tell how the pairs of plants were placed and how a beam of light brought them to life so they could be of use to the People. All this took place within the sacred mountains: the mountains of the east, west, south and north. It was within the boundaries of these mountains.

All those beings were placed there for certain purposes. Darkness, for instance, was told, "You're responsible for the time when people rest." Dawn was told, "You're there to awaken people." And with the Sky and Sun, "You're placed there so that there will be light for people to go by." That is the reason they come in pairs, you see. They were placed there in order to be responsible for certain things.

It is like the way your country is arranged where you have one supreme head and also somebody there as an alternate to step in if the main one is disabled or anything. Of course it is required that the songs go without a break all the way up to the Twelve-Word song. That includes the pairs and the souls of those pairs. In Planting songs, the plants are mentioned first, before the inner beings which give them life are placed inside them.

In the story of how everything started, the first ceremonial was held at the edge of the Emergence Place, where all these things were put in position for the future use of human beings. There was no Blessingway there, no songs for the pairs were made there. It was not until after the two boys were picked up, taken back to the west and taught there, that these things came into being. And so, from the beginning up to the Twelve-Word song, that is all one story.

Of course it is the story that tells us the order of the songs all straight, the story of how the songs began. That's why it is simple to remember all these songs. It is just like your history, your American history. You always remember who is the first president and the second president; who invented this and who invented that. Of course you have those facts in books; you do not memorize them, and you do not keep them in your mind. But with us we have all that memorized, you see, in the story. People who do not know the story have no way to remember those songs, and that is the reason they get confused.

That's why a lot of singers hesitate to do their ceremonies in the presence of others who do know the stories. The story is like a trail. You see, a trail runs in certain ways, and if you have gone that way more than once, you know every little thing that is on that trail. That is the way you think about these songs. As you are going on, sometimes you skip – you take a shortcut and skip some parts of the trail and then go on, and that is the way these songs go, you see. The rows of songs on one side and the trail alongside of it: that is how you keep those two things in mind. And if you want to skip two or three songs, why you skip that much of the trail and continue from a point further on.

There is a set phrase[15] to be used at the end of each song, by which it is made more holy and more lasting so that anything that is accomplished will have no end. "And according to this, everything is blessed." That is the phrase that comes at the end of the song. Sometimes it comes at the end, and sometimes it comes in the middle. It is there so that anything that is created here for the use of the Earth People will be everlasting. Each time you sing a song you cannot complete it until you bring those words in. You can bring them in, in some songs, after each verse.

The phrase is used mostly in Blessingway songs, starting with the Hogan songs and ending with the Twelve-Word song. In the Twelve-Word song, after each verse is sung, the phrase comes in. The most important songs all have that. Some ceremonials do not have it, but Blessingway does.

In the very beginning they did not have those words; they were not part of the songs in the beginning. But after they were passed on to the Navajos, we were told to add those two terms to the songs and to the prayers. This was ordered by Changing Woman. Those words represent the ones who created all the different beings and then disappeared from the earth into the invisible places, the holy places. They are the ones who are everlasting; they are the ones who are still in existence and always will be. With them there is no suffering, no sickness and no hardships. Therefore, with them it is blessed. When you sing those songs you will be saying: "I am, according to the renewal of life, blessing everywhere." The words are *Sǫ'ah naaghéi Bik'eh hózhǫ́ǫ́*. That is what you would be singing. In order to make your songs more holy, to add more strength, that is the reason you use these words.

This is the Twelve-Word song from my Blessingway:

Haiya naiya yana,
   I have come upon it, *yo,* I have come upon blessing, *wo,*
      People, my relatives, *yowo laŋa,* I have come upon blessing,
      People, my relatives, *ya,* blessed, *na'eye laŋa heya 'eye,*

   I have come upon it, *yo,* I have come upon blessing, *wo,*
      People, my relatives, *yowo laŋa,* I have come upon blessing,
      People, my relatives, *ya,* blessed, *na'eye laŋa heya 'eye, holaghei.*

[1.] *Neya,* now, Darkness, *'iya,*
      He comes upon me with blessing, *wo,*
   Behind him, from there, *ye, Sǫ'ah naaghéi,*
      He comes upon me with blessing, *wo,*
   Before him, from there, *ye, Bik'eh hózhǫ́ǫ́,*
      He comes upon me with blessing, *wo,*
   Before him, it is blessed,
   Behind him, it is blessed, *neya 'eye, laŋa heya 'eye, holaghei.*

[2.] *Neya,* behind her, from there, *ye,* Dawn, *'iye,*
      She comes upon me with blessing, *wo,*
   Before her, from there, *ye, Bik'eh hózhǫ́ǫ́,*
      She comes upon me with blessing, *wo,*
   Behind her, from there, *ye, Sǫ'ah naaghéi,*
      She comes upon me with blessing, *wo,*
   Behind her, it is blessed,
   Before her, it is blessed, *neya 'eye, laŋa heya 'eye,*

I have come upon it, *yo,* I have come upon blessing, *wo,*
    People, my relatives, *yowo laŋa,* I have come upon blessing,
    People, my relatives, *ya,* blessed, *na'eye laŋa heya 'eye, holaghei.*

[3.] *Neya,* behind him, from there, *ye,* Afterglow, *woye,*
    She comes upon me with blessing, *wo,*
    Behind her, from there, *ye, Sǫ'ah naaghéi,*
    She comes upon me with blessing, *wo,*
    Before her, from there, *ye, Bik'eh hózhǫ́ǫ́,*
    She comes upon me with blessing, *wo,*
    Before her, it is blessed,
    Behind her, it is blessed, *neya 'eye, laŋa heya 'eye, holaghei.*

[4.] *Neya,* behind him, from there, *ye,* Sun, *'iye,*
    He comes upon me with blessing, *wo,*
    Before him, from there, *ye, Bik'eh hózhǫ́ǫ́,*
    He comes upon me with blessing, *wo,*
    Behind him, from there, *ye, Sǫ'ah naaghéi,*
    He comes upon me with blessing, *wo,*
    Behind him, it is blessed,
    Before him, it is blessed, *neya 'eye, laŋa heya 'eye,*

I have come upon it, *yo,* I have come upon blessing, *wo,*
    People, my relatives, *yowo laŋa,* I have come upon blessing,
    People, my relatives, *ya,* blessed, *na'eye laŋa heya 'eye, holaghei.*

[5.] *Neya,* behind him, from there, *ye,* now Talking God, *'iye,*
    He comes upon me with blessing, *wo,*
    Behind him, from there, *ye, Sǫ'ah naaghéi,*
    He comes upon me with blessing, *wo,*
    Before him, from there, *ye, Bik'eh hózhǫ́ǫ́,*
    He comes upon me with blessing, *wo,*
    Before him, it is blessed,
    Behind him, it is blessed, *neya 'eye, laŋa heya 'eye, holaghei.*

[6.] *Neya,* behind him, from there, *ye,* now Calling God, *'iye,*
    He comes upon me with blessing, *wo,*
    Before him, from there, *ye, Bik'eh hózhǫ́ǫ́,*
    He comes upon me with blessing, *wo,*
    Behind him, from there, *ye, Sǫ'ah naaghéi,*
    He comes upon me with blessing, *wo,*

Behind him, it is blessed,
Before him, it is blessed, *neya 'eye, laŋa heya 'eye,*

I have come upon it, *yo,* I have come upon blessing, *wo,*
People, my relatives, *yowo laŋa,* I have come upon blessing,
People, my relatives, *ya,* blessed, *na'eye laŋa heya 'eye, holaghei.*

[7.] *Neya,* behind him, from there, *ye,* Coming With A Turquoise Boy, *'iye,*
He comes upon me with blessing, *wo,*
Behind him, from there, *ye, Sạ'ah naaghéi,*
He comes upon me with blessing, *wo,*
Before him, from there, *ye, Bik'eh hózhǫ́ǫ́,*
He comes upon me with blessing, *wo,*
Before him, it is blessed,
Behind him, it is blessed, *neya 'eye, laŋa heya 'eye, holaghei.*

[8.] *Neya,* behind her, from there, *ye,* Coming With A Corn Kernel Girl, *'eye,*
She comes upon me with a blessing, *wo,*
Before her, from there, *ye, Bik'eh hózhǫ́ǫ́,*
She comes upon me with a blessing, *wo,*
Behind her, from there, *ye, Sạ'ah naaghéi,*
She comes upon me with a blessing, *wo,*
Behind her, it is blessed,
Before her, it is blessed, *neya 'eye, laŋa heya 'eye,*

I have come upon it, *yo,* I have come upon blessing, *wo,*
People, my relatives, *yowo laŋa,* I have come upon blessing,
People, my relatives, *ya,* blessed, *na'eye laŋa heya 'eye, holaghei.*

[9.] *Neya,* behind him, from there, *ye,* White Corn Plant Boy, *'iye,*
He comes upon me with blessing, *wo,*
Behind him, from there, *ye, Sạ'ah naaghéi,*
He comes upon me with blessing, *wo,*
Before him, from there, *ye, Bik'eh hózhǫ́ǫ́,*
He comes upon me with blessing, *wo,*
Before him, it is blessed,
Behind him, it is blessed, *neya 'eye, laŋa heya 'eye,*

[10.] *Neya,* behind her, from there, *ye,* Yellow Corn Plant Girl, *'eye,*
She comes upon me with blessing, *wo,*
Before her, from there, *ye, Bik'eh hózhǫ́ǫ́,*
She comes upon me with blessing, *wo,*

Behind her, from there, *ye, Sǫ'ah naaghéi,*
She comes upon me with blessing, *wo,*
Behind her, it is blessed,
Before her, it is blessed, *neya 'eye, laŋa heya 'eye,*

I have come upon it, *yo,* I have come upon blessing, *wo,*
People, my relatives, *yowo laŋa,* I have come upon blessing,
People, my relatives, *ya,* blessed, *na'eye laŋa heya 'eye, holaghei.*

[11.] *Neya,* behind him, from there, *ye,* Pollen Boy, *'iye,*
He comes upon me with blessing, *wo,*
Behind him, from there, *ye, Sǫ'ah naaghéi,*
He comes upon me with blessing, *wo,*
Before him, from there, *ye, Bik'eh hózhǫ́ǫ́,*
He comes upon me with blessing, *wo,*
Before him, it is blessed,
Behind him, it is blessed, *neya 'eye, laŋa heya 'eye, holaghei.*

[12.] *Neya,* behind her, from there, *ye,* Harvest Fly Girl, *'eye,*
She comes upon me with blessing, *wo,*
Before her, from there, *ye, Bik'eh hózhǫ́ǫ́,*
She comes upon me with blessing, *wo,*
Behind her, from there, *ye, Sǫ'ah naaghéi,*
She comes upon me with blessing, *wo,*
Behind her, it is blessed,
Before her, it is blessed,
Beneath her, it is blessed,
Above her, it is blessed,
All around her, it is blessed,
Everywhere, it is blessed, *neye 'eye laŋa heya 'eye,*

I have come upon it, *yo,* I have come upon blessing, *wo,*
People, my relatives, *yowo laŋa,* I have come upon blessing,
People, my relatives, *ya,* blessed, *na'eye laŋa heya 'eye, holaghei.* [16]

In the Twelve-Word song at the end of my Blessingway, I mention the Darkness coming to my relative. Right after that comes *Sǫ'ah naaghéi* and right after that *Bik'eh hózhǫ́ǫ́.* That has to do with the Darkness, not the singer, who only pronounces those words. It is what is in the song that is *Bik'eh hózhǫ́ǫ́.* But in another song, for example, the Returning Home song, you say, "I am Talking God." You say, "I am," you do not mention anyone else and you say, "*Sǫ'ah naaghéi*, I am," and "*Bik'eh hózhǫǫ*, I am." That is the way you say it. Then you are referring to yourself, not what is in the song. That is the difference between the songs: a lot of them are like that, you see.

So for each verse in the song, you say, "*Sǫ'ah naaghéi, Bik'eh hózhǫǫ.*" The phrase is a holy being. You see, these songs, when they were turned over to the Earth People, were to be used in a certain way. If you leave out those words, then the holy beings feel slighted. They know you are singing, they are aware of it. But if you omit those words, then they feel it and they are displeased. Then, even though you are singing, whatever you are doing over the one-sung-over has no effect.

If you forget to mention those holy words in one song, and in the next song you think of it, then you will mention them. That makes up, somewhat, for their having been left out before. That is the reason that at the conclusion of your songs, you will say a prayer in your own words. You ask the holy beings to help you and to go through these songs with you; that also helps to make up for what you may have left out.

One time my late father-in-law was having a Blessingway performed for him. Since he was the one-sung-over, there was another singer doing it for him. They started with the Hogan songs. Well, at a certain point, my father-in-law[17] started a song that skipped over a number of others. It was not time for that one yet. They stopped him, saying, "No, you can't do that, you've made a mistake." So they just sat there for a while and finally the singer said, "I'm not the one who skipped it, the one-sung-over did. He shouldn't have done it. Well, we'll just ignore it this time and continue the way I've been doing it." Cases like that will happen. Of course my father-in-law did not do that intentionally.

There's a man who has given me a string of beads as payment for someday making a Mountain Earth bundle for him. But I don't think he would be capable of learning everything that is involved in making a new bundle. So I am not going to try and teach him that at this point.[18] He has a long way to go before he is ready. All I am going to teach him is the songs. I will go ahead and do that for him and later on make him a separate bundle for himself.

The reason is that I know that one of these days I am going to die of old age or something, and then I will not be around to do the Blessingway for my children. So if he at least learns a plain Blessingway, my children will have him for that. That way my grandchildren will at least have somebody around that they know was taught by their grandfather a long time before. They will know he is the person to call whenever they want that ceremony done.

Whenever I am hired to do this Blessingway ceremony, he usually comes along, and he seems to be interested. I encourage him to learn the whole thing, but I give him a test now and then. I start a set of songs and tell him, "Go ahead, now you lead them." But he does not lead them very well, he hangs back and hesitates. As long as he is following another singer he is all right. He knows the beginning, from the Hogan songs up to the Twelve-Word song. But from there on, you see, it branches out. The songs may go this way or that, depending on what is needed in a particular case. He has not been taught that yet. Though he has paid me something for that bundle already, there are certain rules that we have to go by. It cannot be made just any time; it has to be made at those certain times of the year I already told you about. And then you have to go by the condition of the moon, whether it is full or not.

If he is really interested and wants to get his own bundle, the Blessingway will have to be done for him, and at the same time the bundle will be made for him, too. The date we have set for that man is sometime in September after the sixth. We have to go according to the moon, and it will not be full until after the sixth or perhaps the tenth. When the moon is full, I will do that for him; I will sing one or two of those Chief songs then.

We could also do this with just an ordinary Blessingway. In this case, we would just have the prayer the night before, and the next day all we would do is get the bundle out and start fixing it. Just as soon as it is finished, it can be given to the man it's being done for; then there are more prayers and songs.

I have not even seen that man lately, so I don't know if he still wants to have that done. Perhaps it will be on a weekend when he has some time off. What takes time is preparing the things that are going to be used for the bundle, as I told you earlier.

Of course I've told him about all those materials that are required. After you decide to do it, you have to go around and get all those things together. After you have the materials collected, then you have to pay a singer to make up the bundle for you. But this man said, "Well, I don't know what is required. Suppose you go ahead and get those things collected, and I'll pay you extra for the materials to be used. And then about the mountain earth to be used in the bundle, I will pay a separate fee for that." He asked what time of year it is supposed to be done and I told him.

Of course, if anyone else is interested in learning my ceremony I can use my own judgment, learn about the person's background and then act accordingly. If I think it's just a case of curiosity, I know what to do: I refuse to do it. But if I think the person is reliable, dependable and sincere, well, I can go ahead. Also I could teach it to my own offspring, my grandchildren and other children on the maternal side. I can teach it without hesitation to my own clan, Two Streams Meet.

My father said the same thing, "If any of my clan relations ask you for it, do not hesitate to do it for them. But some of the songs in there are very sacred. In that case it is up to you. If you want to teach them, that's all right. But if you want to keep those hidden from them, well, that's all right. That's up to you to decide."

My father-in-law kept the Corn Bundle songs from me. He asked me to learn them from someone else. He said that if I took everything from him, he would not be able to survive on earth. That is the same reason we hesitate to tell about our ceremonies to strangers who come from some place outside the reservation.

There are certain songs in my ceremony that are looked upon as more sacred than others. Of course, the Blessingway in general is very widely practiced. Anyone can listen to it. But there are certain special sets of songs that are very sacred, and we do not want to sing those in public.

Once you learn Blessingway, you have to perform it in the presence of your teacher. After it's decided that you really are sincere and are going to perform the ceremony correctly, then you have the privilege of asking your teacher for those especially sacred songs. You do not learn those right at the start. They are extras used for special purposes and are not part of the regular Blessingway.

When you are learning the regular Blessingway ceremony and you suddenly begin asking questions about the secret songs, they always put you aside and say, "No, I can't tell you that. You're not ready for it. You are not prepared for it. I haven't seen how you conduct your ceremonies."

Isabelle got interested, and so did Ruth. So they asked me to teach them some songs. I got them in here one day and just to test them out I gave them a very short song called, "What Was Used by the Sun in Midsky." It is just a short one that is used so that your neighbors will respect you. The song is concerned with that, you see, that people will be friendly with you and treat you courteously. So I sang that for them, but they couldn't do it; they could not remember the way it goes. That is an extra song, you see, a special song. It is used for a special purpose; of course it has some connection with the Blessingway, but it does not come in the regular ceremony. But they gave it up. They said they could not learn it, so they gave up. In spite of my efforts they do not seem to be able to learn my songs.

I cannot say about my grandchildren. I do not know what their attitude is. I don't know whether they might be quietly learning some of my songs at a ceremony or not. But to openly come to me and ask me for advice, they do not do that. They hesitate to do that, they are backwards about it. That is the way with all my family, including my wife.

People are talking about my recording my Blessingway songs on tape. But I do not want you to think that I mind recording for you; it's just these other people talking like that. It is not coming our of their mouths; they are not singing it themselves, and it is all right for me to be doing this with you.

Someday I would like to have somebody here in the family get a tape recorder, and then I would be willing to record some of these very sacred songs I hesitate to let go of. I would like to record those and just keep them in the family.

I remember all that I know about the Blessingway because I had those years of study to get it all in my head. And from my experience of learning I understand that it is not just my ability that makes it possible. I believe there is a spirit that really is answering my prayers, because all these years I would not have been able to learn so much if I did not have such help. I could not do it by myself, so there must be something beyond human power helping me. I really believe that is what has been behind all this.

EDITORS' NOTES

1. *Ch'inaadą́ą́'* apparently is a combined form, adding the word *ch'il* (plant) to the usual word for corn.

2. "Soapweed" refers to yucca. The root is cleaned and pounded, and the juice thus obtained makes a soapy lather in warm water (Kluckhohn, Itill and Kluckhohn 1971:314-315).

3. A Blessingway is usually attended by the immediate family and a few other relatives. There may be only a dozen participants. The women and children are seated on the north side of the hogan and the men face them from the south side.

4. *Bijí*, "its day," refers to the concluding rituals which usually begin sometime after noon on the last day of a ceremonial and end the following morning.

5. Pollen Boy, usually paired with Pollen Girl, is "the power by which we and all things live," a symbol of life and fertility (Reichard 1963:668). Big Fly is a mentor and intermediary between humans and deities. He may ". . . 'sit in the ear' of a person who needs instruction and . . . whisper answers to questions or forecast the future." (*Ibid.*:64).

6. "Truly, returning has been completed."

7. In this context, "word" usually refers to "verse." Frequently verses are almost identical except for a new key word in each one, usually expressing a progression of ideas. See Reichard (1963:291-300).

8. Little has previously been known about the Seed Blessing Ceremony except that it is one of the rites abstracted from Blessingway (Wyman and Kluckhohn 1938:18).

9. See Frisbie (1968, 1970).

10. This building was dedicated on May 10, 1938. Others interviewed during field research on the House Blessing suggested that a variety of other public buildings were blessed earlier than the Fort Defiance Hospital. See Frisbie (1970:186-201).

11. Frisbie (1970:200). Frank conducted three public dedications: Chinle Chapter House-6/20/59; Chinle Boarding School-5/19/61; and Chinle High School-2/29/64.

12. In total, Frank refused to bless three structures: the new Chinle jail and two public structures in communities outside Chinle, namely Many Farms and Cottonwood. For further information on reasons Frank and other singers gave for refusing requests to perform House Blessing ceremonies, see Frisbie (1970:204-208, 209-211).

13. According to Frank's letter to Reuben Perry on 2/9/31 (Chapter 10, n. 3), Man Who Shouts was a recognized headman in the Chinle area from 1890-1922. Frank replaced him in 1922 and seems to have served as a *naat'áani* or headman, until being chosen as a member of the Constitutional Assembly in 1937.

14. In addition to carrying news and opinions between the agent and the local people, and serving as a spokesman at public gatherings, early community records at the Franciscan mission in Chinle indicate that Frank also contacted the agent and others concerning complaints of the People, requested meetings, witnessed marriages and helped arbitrate disputes while serving as a headman.

15. See Chapter 6, n. 8.

16. This is the song with which Frank concluded his Blessingway. It was recorded by Frank for McAllester in 1957. There are the usual vocables with no lexical meaning.

17. The one-sung-over and other participants in a ceremonial are expected to help with the singing when they are able. There are favorite songs where many people join in to create a powerful chorus.

18. For further information on the teaching and learning of Navajo ceremonials, see Chiao (1971).

9. Public Servant

*Frank learns to talk to the People . . . an installation
ceremony for leaders . . . working for Father Berard Haile . . . the
trouble over Charlie Mitchell's death . . . a visit to Chee Dodge . . .
Frank as councilman: trip to Washington, the tribal constitution,
stock reduction . . . Frank becomes a judge: his training, practice
and special cases involving ceremonial bundles.*

I have told you how during my earlier years, when I was working at the
Chinle Mission, I went around with Son of the Late Little Blacksmith, who
had been sent there as peacemaker. I learned what he was doing by staying
with him and listening to how he talked when he held meetings with the
People. His talks were mostly about the white man's government and orders
from Washington.

In those days I myself did not really talk; I just went around with Son
of the Late Little Blacksmith as his partner. I would listen to what he
was saying and how he spoke each word. At times he would question certain
individuals. It was really interesting to see how Son of the Late Little
Blacksmith knew what kind of person he was talking to. There were times
when he would be talking to some young boys who thought they were smart.
They would say smart things without thinking; Son of the Late Little
Blacksmith would just sit there, listening to them. He would be able to tell
what they were thinking in the back of their minds; without them saying
anything more, he could tell them what they were thinking.

Son of the Late Little Blacksmith told me that you can always tell
about people by watching them and listening to what they are saying and
the words they are using. If they know what they're talking about, the words
will always have order to them and will make sense to you. But if they are
just going along, making up sentences or using words incorrectly, you can tell
right away that they have something more on their minds than what they are
telling you. He told me to listen to people's conversations, and I would learn
to almost read their minds. With time, I learned that that was true. I just
watched people who were talking, and I got so I could figure them out. A
person who is respectful will respect others, especially older people. Those

who are not will show by their actions and their ways of talking that they have no respect.

Son of the Late Little Blacksmith used to tell me that you could always tell people who were getting into trouble by gambling or drinking or stealing. Those people would always try to talk their way out of that or to find a sneaky way around that when they came to face the law. But if a person is honest, never lies or cheats, and just concentrates on tending the household or the livestock, such a one will not know how to fool people or to lie. That person will be taken advantage of by crooked people. I used to remember that when I became a judge later in my life; when there was a dispute between a sneaky person and a quiet one, it always came out the way Son of the Late Little Blacksmith had said it would.

In the Blessingway story, it says that these things, like telling lies and doing bad things have been with us from the very beginning. People started out with those things, and they will continue to live on with them. There will always be good and bad people. I realized that was true when I started talking to the People.

After I started living with Tall Woman and began to get to know her father, Man Who Shouts, I began listening to him, as I told you before. Because he was a headman[1], he, too, gave talks to the People and instructed them. Man Who Shouts used to talk mostly about how one should live in the future. He would tell the People that it was hard to make a living unless you really tried. If you gave up easily, you could not manage. Man Who Shouts also talked about how to get along with your relatives. He used to tell the People not to forget those who were their clan relations, and to help each other. He also talked about how to care for livestock, like horses and sheep. He would say to set your mind on it. If you were going to farm, set your mind on doing that and nothing else.

He would sometimes talk about things that Navajo people should not do: wrongdoing such as drinking, gambling, getting into fights and stealing. He would tell the People that they should stay out of trouble as much as possible, and that it was not worth doing something wrong because that would always lead you into further trouble. Once you got into trouble, you just went deeper and deeper into it, and before you knew it, you ended up in a big mess that you could not get out of. Those were the things that my father-in-law, Man Who Shouts, used to say when he talked to the People.

In Navajo religion there are prayers for certain purposes. I found out from my own father that in Blessingway there were some songs for headmen, and I learned them from him. I think that this is another reason why things came easily for me when I was talking to the People. It may be one reason that I was recognized for being a talker and a leader among the People, why I became well known as a headman and even eventually ended up on the Tribal Council.

Old man Curly Hair used to know those songs that go with being a leader, too; one time we compared them and found that he had the same set that I used, with a few different words in several places. I think that is why he could come out and talk to the People. He had those songs in him, and whenever he started talking, he got the best out of people. Those songs gave him power to give his speeches in the right way.

Now, these songs are only used when you are preparing to go to talk. The way you learn them is by heart, by yourself. They are within you once you learn them, and whenever you are asked to make a speech somewhere, to go before the People to talk to them or to come forth on some big occasion, you can do that without being scared. After I learned these songs, every time I was called to a big meeting, all I did was sing two or three of those songs while I was on my way over there. Then when I got there, I knew just what I was going to talk about and that I was not going to end up like the man who drew two lines and mumbled something. With those songs within me, I am not afraid of anything; they take the fear and the shyness out of me, and I just get up before the People and start talking, and they always understand what I am talking about.

When a man has those songs, he does not get stage fright standing up before the People. I used to wonder if that were true until I heard a story about one man who was elected to a Chapter office. When the People first started Chapter organizations,[2] they used to elect people who were called together at Fort Defiance for a meeting. Of course at that time, the People in general were backward about getting together in a group, in the white man's way, in a room, with the speaker up front before them. When we used to talk to the People, we did not gather in meeting houses or auditoriums as they do now. When we talked in the old days, the People were just scattered around, a few here and there; they were never all in a group, sitting in rows facing you. Now when you go before the People, all eyes are on you, and that alone is frightening.

The story I heard said that there was a man who was elected to office. I don't know what area this man was elected from, but when the People finally agreed and asked him if he were willing to take office, he said yes, and everything was settled. Then he was asked to get out in front of the People and give his opinion on how he was going to lead them while in office. He was told that the people in the area knew him and he knew them and they understood him, and he was told to come up on the stage there at Fort Defiance and give his opinion.

When he got there, he found that everybody was looking and staring at him; it frightened him so much that he did not know what to say. He lost his speech; he just stood there, stamping his feet on the floor for a long time; finally he just fell over backwards, but his leg was still sticking up in the air making that stamping motion. All you could see was the sole of his shoe.

When they got him up he was soaking wet; he was sweating all over and mumbling and almost crying; he could not say a word, he was so scared. So those people just appointed someone else to that job.

I imagine that that man did not have those Chief songs within him. That is what makes me know that it is the Chief songs that have given me the power to talk to the People without getting tongue-tied halfway through the speech, or having everything go blank. That is also why I think that some people who are elected to be speakers in some capacity get sick; they are not immune to those things because the songs are not within them.

Those songs, the Chief songs, are also used when you fix up a Mountain Earth bundle and bless it. I cannot sing these Chief songs[3] for you right now; they can only be sung before you go to give a speech, for installing a chief or while fixing up a bundle. Right now there are lots of rumors going around about me. The People are talking about me letting you come here, and some of them do not like the idea that I am recording my Blessingway. They are criticizing me for giving away my sacred songs and my secrets to outsiders. But it is not up to them to decide; the songs are my own and I have the right to do whatever I want to with them. If you could help us when we get ready to make a new medicine bundle, then we could have that ceremony right here at our hogan, and you could record those songs then. I would like them recorded and left here in the family before my memory fails me too much. Then, even after I pass away, my family will have something to go by.

Judging from the way things are going, I know that although I know some of these songs and some of the requirements in connection with them, I am not in perfect health anymore. I do not feel physically well anymore. I guess the reason that I have not become seriously ill from anything yet is that I possess some of these Chief songs. Probably I can get by because I know something about these protections.

Maybe one reason I feel sick is because when I was put into office I was not blessed with the ceremony for installing leaders. If I had been, I would not be sick now; I would be perfectly well. I do not know how long ago the People stopped using that ceremony, but as far back as I can remember I never heard of any ceremonies like that being done to install leaders. The only way that I even know about it is through my grandfather. He used to talk about how they did things in the past. I do not think that my grandfather ever performed that ceremony, though.

You see, in the old days, whenever they selected someone to be a speaker for the People, that ceremony was performed. By equipping him with moccasins called Chief moccasins, and garments and everything else that he wore, and by putting something in his mouth so his talks would have more of an effect on the People, he was blessed. There was a second kind of ingredient that was used to anoint his lips. Whenever he wanted to get up and talk to the People, he would put that on his lips; I guess that is just like a lady's lipstick.

When a leader was blessed with that, he was made immune from any witchcraft. The ceremony was a one-night sing, and all of the things that the leader might want to use in his capacity as chief were blessed with him during the Blessingway ceremony. Of course the songs and prayers were a little different from those in an ordinary Blessingway, but still that ceremony was a Blessingway ceremony. The People could use the Chief Hogan songs in that, and there were lots of other songs pertaining to that ceremony to be used when they installed a new leader. Probably one reason they do not use that ceremony anymore is because the People are picking up just anybody around here and putting them in positions where they must lead. Who wants to perform that ceremony for such people?

There are lots of songs that go with being a headman or leader. They start out from the beginning, way back with the first people. The story starts with how it was planned at first and how the first people decided who were to be the chiefs. After these chiefs were elected, the songs go along describing how they were dressed. They tell about all of the things they were wearing, their shoes, leggings, sashes and skirts, belts, wristlets and beads, their head plumes and everything up to the last thing, that which is put in their mouths from which their speeches are known. The last thing is like the power to speak; it was put into their mouths so they could have the wisdom to say wise things and so the People could understand them.

There are enough of those songs to sing them all night without sleeping. The songs are used in a series, but they are not just to be sung any place. You can only use them when someone is going to be a chief, a good leader; they can have the songs done for them. There are so many songs in that series that you could almost have a Blessingway done with them; there are just about as many songs involved in that as there are in the Blessingway itself. The story and the songs are just like the Blessingway right from the beginning – how the earth was first formed, how the mountains came up. The songs go on like that. It would probably take a little longer to do that than the regular Blessingway; it is just like Blessingway except that the ceremony is mostly just singing. Almost all of what takes place is the singing of the Chief songs.

The Chief Hogan songs started even before the first hogan was built. After the songs about building the hogan, step by step, then that home is complete, and the People move in there. They built that hogan to install leaders who were to instruct and to lead the People. These songs also talk about the garments that the chiefs should wear and the things they should use when they step out and talk to the People. All of those things were made holy in the first hogan. That is the start of the human race on earth.

Even today we have good examples to show that without a hogan you cannot plan. You can't just go out and plan other things for your future; you have to build a hogan first. Within that, you sit down and begin to plan. It is similar to the way it was in the beginning. When the first people appeared on earth here, they did not have anything. They did not have any hogans, they had no dwelling places where they could gather together and plan. So they had to build a hogan where they could meet and discuss things for the future. That is the reason *naat'á* means to plan ahead and *naat'áani* means the planner, the one who plans for the future. In English, you say king, president, dictator; we say planner. I guess the word "dictator" would be closest, since that is a person whose orders people must obey; a *naat'áani* is similar to that.

At the present time we really do not have any substantial foundation that holds us together with a leader. We are somewhat selfish; we want to plan for ourselves individually without bothering about the next person. You white people settle down all in one place and you have a system. You start building something, cultivating a field; pretty soon somebody else comes next to you and after a while, there is a community there. But you always have some form of government that allows you to live peacefully and orderly. But we do not have such a system; we used to, but we no longer use it. Instead of us doing the planning, well, you people are the ones doing it with your system of government. You operate so that even if your leader dies, there is always someone else to replace him. With us, it is just the other way; they die and that is the end of it; we do not have anyone there to replace them.

If you look at the conditions the way they are now, they are like the universe, the earth and skies and things like that. There is change: it's summer one time, winter, another. There is always a change from one to another. I guess it is like having hot and cold, night and day, or two parties in the country, the elephant and the donkey. I guess it is good that there is a change in conditions. As we go along, we begin to understand how these things operate and to discover why there are such changes. There is some truth in all those things.

After I had learned my father's Blessingway ceremony, I heard that Father Berard Haile, the Franciscan missionary at Saint Michaels, was working on the ceremonies of the People. I happened to go over to the Catholic mission there at Saint Michaels at one point, and I found old man Curly Hair over there talking with the priest, telling him the story of his ceremony. I guess it was Curly Hair who told Father Berard that I knew that Blessingway ceremony, too. As soon as Curly Hair got through telling his ceremony, the Father called for me to come over there and talk with him. So that is what I did; I went over there to tell him my story about that.[4]

A few years after I had told my Blessingway story to Father Berard, we got word that Charlie Mitchell was sick and wanted us to visit him. At that time he was living around the Canyon area, in Tsaile and Lukachukai, and the Franciscan Fathers had already settled here in Chinle, Lukachukai and Saint Michaels. Of course I was already well acquainted with Son of the Late Little Blacksmith and Curly Hair by then, and Charlie sent word through Curly Hair that all of us should come over to Lukachukai. So we went up there to see him. When we got there, we learned that his troubles began when he had been treated roughly by a man who was working at the mission, taking care of Father Marcellus' house and helping around there as an interpreter. I guess that man had hurt Charlie in some way and he had gotten sick from that. He never recovered from that.

When Charlie called us over there the first time, he said that he had complained to Father Marcellus about what this man, Roy Kinsel, had done to him. They had gotten into a fuss over that and had exchanged some harsh words on that account.

Charlie said to us, "I want you to know about it. Old age may have something to do with my illness, but still I do not like the idea of a young fellow like Roy Kinsel pushing an old fellow around like he did. If they are going to do these things to the Navajos, then I am not the only one whom they will abuse like that; they are liable to abuse others. In case I never get over my sickness, I am going to blame the mission for it. This kind of thing was not included in the understanding we had with the missionaries in the beginning. After all, it was Chee Dodge, Silversmith and myself who allowed the first Franciscans to come onto the reservation. I do not think they should have somebody working for them who treats Navajos this way. I want all of you to know about this and to do what you can about it. What I would like you to do is to go up and see Father Marcellus and tell him that he had better remove Roy Kinsel from his job. He is not the only one around here who can do interpreting."

So we went up there and saw Father Marcellus and told him that we would like to discuss something with him. He said, "Yes, but it has to be some other time." Then we came home.

A few months later we heard that Charlie was getting seriously ill and that he wanted to see us again. So we went back up there; he was really sick; he was dying that time. He told us that he was getting worse and if he should happen to pass away, Roy Kinsel was to be blamed for that. He said, "Don't forget that." He told us the same thing again; he still blamed that man for mistreating him and causing him to become sick. He said that if anyone in the future was treated that way by the Franciscans or someone who worked for them, then the People should not keep the priest who is in charge. Charlie thought they should send Father Marcellus back; even though it was not the Father who had done this, he should have had enough sense to talk with the man who was working for him.

We came back from there and sometime later we heard that Charlie had passed away. So then Curly Hair and I went up to see Father Marcellus to talk to him about that. We remembered what Charlie had told us. Curly Hair told Father Marcellus, the one they called the Tall Priest, that ever since Roy had wrestled with Charlie, Charlie had been ill and now he had died from that and something should be done about it. But the Father said, "Charlie is dead and gone now. How can we discuss that now?"

When the Father said that, Curly Hair got mad and started talking harshly to the priest. He said, "You did not come here of your own free will. It was through persuasion that the People consented to your having missions. You had no place to stay, and we were kind enough to give you a piece of land. You did not come in here for things like that, to injure the People and not to talk about it. You are supposed to be in here to pray for our protection and our welfare. If you refuse to discuss it or to do anything about it, I will see that something is done about it myself, and you will end up back east where you came from." At that time, Curly Hair's hair was really white and naturally curly. It was kind of hard to keep it down, and when it was dry it stood out, bushy like. Curly Hair was a man who just came out and told people what he thought. He did not care who you were; he would just tell you off. He often would pound on things when he talked like that, and some of the younger people used to think he was fierce-looking and be scared of him.

While Curly Hair was saying those things, Father Marcellus just sat there not saying a word. Curly Hair said, "What are you just sitting there not saying anything for? You might as well pack up and leave here." Then Father Marcellus said, "Well, I am not free to go where I want to. If you feel that way about it, if you feel that I should leave here, go to Saint Michaels and see the Superior, the head of the Franciscans. See what he thinks about it."

So we left and came back over here and got ready to go to see the head at Saint Michaels. That is when we got the Son of the Late Little Blacksmith and John Foley, who lived down at Many Farms, to join Curly Hair and myself. John was probably the only one capable of interpreting at that time for the Navajos, so we took him. He had a car, too, and we hired him to take us over there and to interpret for us.

When we got to Saint Michaels, we went first to see Frank Walker. He was the interpreter over there at the mission, and he had a place to stay there. We stayed in that building overnight. We told Frank Walker why we were there and he became angry about that. He just started cursing, saying, "That is the way it is with these new people around here. They are taking advantage of the People. You just have to go after them and kick them out." He used a lot of swear words while he was talking. "The priests did not come here because we asked them to. They pleaded with the People and made lots of promises which they did not carry out. Then after they got established here, then they begged for money. They said it was for welfare, for the sake of the Navajos. That is how they got money donated to them."

That night Frank Walker told us we should get together in a secret meeting with the Superior. We should not let anybody else come in and listen because this was an important matter and we should not broadcast it. He thought we should meet behind closed doors to discuss it. So the next morning after we had breakfast, we were taken upstairs into the second story

FIG. 5. Frank Mitchell with a group at Saint Michaels Mission between 1926-30. Seated left to right: Unknown, John Foley. Standing left to right: Father Jerome Hesse, White Singer, Father Emanuel Trockur, John Brown (the Policeman), Frank Mitchell and Father Leopold Ostermann.

of that rock building. I don't remember the name of the Superior there at that time, because I had not been going over there often enough to know him personally. I know it was not Father Berard. The Superior[5] spoke Navajo and could understand a lot of things, but he did not talk back to us too fluently. We told the Superior what had happened to Charlie, about the injuries he had received from Roy Kinsel and how those injuries had killed him. Curly Hair told the Superior about our conversations with Father Marcellus and the answers we had been given by him, and how that had made him lose his temper and use some pretty harsh language to the priest, which he should not have done. He said it was on account of all of these things that we had come over here to talk with the Superior.

Then the head priest said, "There is no use talking about Charlie now; Charlie is gone. He is dead and there is nobody to speak for him, so what can be done about that?" Again, Curly Hair got angry. He raised his voice at the head priest; he shook his fist, his hair stood on end and his eyes popped out. I guess that head priest got scared; he just sat there and let Curly Hair do all the talking. At the same time, John Foley was interpreting, and he was going kind of easy on the interpreting of what Curly Hair was saying. Frank Walker was also in there with us, and every now and then he would pop up and tell the Father just what Curly Hair had said. I guess John Foley was kind of scared to interpret the whole thing in detail, so he was leaving out parts of what Curly Hair was saying. But Frank Walker just popped up and told those parts, too.

Curly Hair said, "What do you mean by that? I am here. Charlie was my brother and I am talking in his place. You priests did not come in here because you wanted to. You did so with Charlie's permission. You got these sites picked for you. You did not come in here to abuse the People this way; you were supposed to protect the People and pray for them, for their welfare. That is something that is good. You did not come here to abuse us and fight with us. You came in here with the understanding that you would teach something good to the People, that you would be teachers to the People. From back in the early days, you have been abusing people. We know in the history handed down from generation to generation that when you first started establishing these missions in the Pueblos, you started abusing the Indians and making slaves of them. Finally they got disgusted with you, and that is why they went and murdered a lot of your priests."

While Curly Hair was saying all of these things, the priest did not answer him; he just sat there and listened. I was doing the same thing, just sitting there listening in. Finally I spoke up and said, "I wonder what the head priest's opinion is on this?"

Then Curly Hair turned to me and said, "What is your opinion on this? What is the next move that we want to make?"

I replied, "You know what Charlie said; he said that what he wanted was for the mission to discharge Roy Kinsel and also for Saint Michaels to have Father Marcellus moved somewhere else. He should not be stationed in Lukachukai any longer."

After I had reminded Curly Hair of what Charlie had said, he spoke again. He said, "I am not demanding that you pay damages for Charlie's death or that anybody else pay damages. We are not here for any kind of reward. All that I am requesting is that these two men be removed from their present positions. If you do not do that, the others who follow will think they can treat the People the same way. We just want this thing corrected by removing those two men, one way or another. That is all we ask."

The Superior answered, saying, "Well, I cannot say one way or another off hand, but we will think that over and discuss it and see what we can do about it. After that has been decided, we will let you know. We will get together again on that."

Then Curly Hair said, "If you comply with our requests, I thank you for your action. You are the authority here, you are head of this organization and whatever you say has to be complied with; that is why I am asking you this favor." Curly Hair was still very angry; his eyes were bulging out because he was so mad.

The Superior said, "Well, I thought a lot of Charlie, I respected him. I still respect him, although he is dead and gone. It is true what you say about him being one of the main ones who gave us permission to establish these missions. There is no doubt that on his advice, his talking to many of you, you joined us."

So then everything cooled down; even Curly Hair's hair stopped standing on end. We had a long friendly talk, and then the meeting ended. We went out and saw Frank Walker in his room. He told us to stay another night because it was already so late and because he wanted to talk with us about the past history of these church people who came into contact with the Indians years ago. He wanted to refresh his mind on what all of the agreements were. Frank Walker was pretty well informed on the beginnings of the mission and all of those things; he even knew about the Franciscans before they came to the Navajo country; he knew a lot about their past history.

Well, we decided to stay that night, and when we were retiring, Frank Walker came into our room. He started to tell us something that he had heard; he said that it was not definite yet, but that he had heard something pretty drastic had almost happened to Chee Dodge in Gallup. Before he went on with that, he asked us what our plans were for the return trip, whether we were going directly back to Chinle. He said that very often when people came in here, they went home by way of Chee Dodge's place in Crystal to visit with him. We said that we had no reason to go back that way, but if there was something that we should talk to Chee about, of course we would do it. Otherwise, we told him, there was no reason for us not to go right back, since we just came here about the incident involving Charlie Mitchell.

Then Frank Walker started telling us what he had heard about Chee Dodge; he always just called him Chee. He said, "I don't know how true it is, but I heard that Chee came into Gallup and went on a drinking spree. You know he looks more like a white man than a Navajo, and he is well known by a lot of white people. They know that he stands up for his tribe, and they take him into their houses and give him drinks and things like that. I guess he was bumming around like that, going from place to place and getting drinks until he had had too much. He did not know where he was going. He had his car with him but he did not know where he had parked it. So he started back across that old bridge across the little wash, the bridge that gave Gallup its name.[6] I heard that he missed the bridge and fell down off the bank there into the mud in the ditch.

"There was some water in there, and the water had made that mud like quicksand; that ditch bottom was not lined with concrete or anything. I heard that he struggled to get out of there but just got covered with mud from his head to his toes. He kept getting in deeper and deeper, and he could not get out. It was very late at night when this happened, and I guess he struggled for a long time.

"Finally Chee gave up because he was so tired and was not able to help himself. Then he started yelling for help. There are houses all along there, and some Mexicans lived in the house right on the other side of the bridge. They heard somebody yelling, and a man went out with a lamp and looked in the ditch, and there was Chee Dodge down there in the mud. So he pulled him out and took him back into his house, peeled off his clothing, gave him a bath to clean off all of that mud, and put him into bed with a dry place to sleep.

"Shortly thereafter, the water came down through the wash at full speed; it roared as it came down the arroyo, and immediately, everything was flooded. It was raining somewhere up above there at that time, and that rain caused the wash to start running. If Chee had not yelled and this man had not spotted him and helped him out of the mud, he probably would have drowned. Then the People never would have known what happened to him.

"It's frightening to think about this. This is the first time I or anybody else has heard of Chee Dodge doing anything like that. The People look up to him; he is a very good man and a leader. To have to hear things like this about him is not good, and the People are worrying about that. That is why I am just sick about it. I want you to go and see Chee on your way home and ask him if this is true or not. If he is man enough he will tell you all about it in the right way. If he is foolish, then he will not."

After Frank Walker had told us that, we realized what could have happened and we knew that it was important enough to go by Chee's place to talk to him about it on the way home. So Son of the Late Little Blacksmith and Curly Hair decided that all of us would go back that way and see Chee. The next morning we got ready to leave. Then the priest with whom we had met to talk about Charlie Mitchell came out with a suit of clothes for Curly Hair and gave it to him. In those days, the missionaries got only a few clothes from different places to give to the Navajos. It was seldom that they got something like a suit.

Curly Hair turned around and in a real high tone of voice asked, "Is this the reward for Charlie Mitchell? Is this what you're paying me with for Charlie Mitchell's death? Is this what Charlie is worth? I didn't expect to take any rags for that." Curly Hair used to speak loudly as his natural way of talking; he always sounded like he was scolding you.

The Superior started getting scared again; he immediately said, "No, it is not for that. It is just a friendship gift. I am giving you this by my own choosing."

Then Curly Hair thanked him for the gift and said, "This is just a friendship gift. This is the way we are going to continue our friendship as long as we are in this world, for the good of our people." Curly Hair also said that he was glad that he had stayed, and that all Franciscan Fathers should act the way the Superior was acting if they wanted to stay on the reservation.

After we left the mission, we went by way of Fort Defiance to Chee Dodge's home in Crystal. When we arrived, there was nobody home but his children; his car was there, too. We asked them where he was, after awhile, and they told us that he was taking a sweat bath with a visitor. They told us that the sweathouse was just a short distance away, so we decided to go over there.

We left John Foley in the car, and the three of us went over there to the sweathouse. When we got there, Chee had already gone in; the curtain was down on the entrance and nothing was stirring. So Son of the Late Little Blacksmith just leaned back against the sweathouse, and Curly Hair and I propped up our feet on a tree there. After awhile, one of the men who was visiting with Chee came out; he was a young man. Then Willow Man's Son came out and finally, Chee Dodge.

Son of the Late Little Blacksmith was lying against the sweathouse right near the doorway, and when he looked up and saw Chee, with his white hair, coming out of the sweathouse, he said, "A great big old man with white hair like yours shouldn't be taking a sweat bath without a sound. You are supposed to be singing in the sweathouse."

Then Chee answered, "We heard somebody on the north side of the sweathouse, and when anyone is over there on the north side, we are not supposed to sing. That is the direction towards which we blow away evil. We could not sing because after each song you are supposed to blow the evil toward the side where you were lying. If we had done that, we would have caused something bad to happen to you."

I guess Son of the Late Little Blacksmith and Chee were always joking with each other. Anyway, Chee came out and we all shook hands. He invited us in for a sweat bath, so we all went in.

Then Chee asked us where we were coming from, where we were going and for what reason we were here. So we told him about Charlie Mitchell, our trip to Saint Michaels and all of the things that had happened concerning that. I guess Chee had heard a little about Charlie Mitchell already, but he did not know for sure if that were true, since he was always up around the Plateau in his own area and near Fort Defiance working with the People. He did not have much time to come out toward Lukachukai to find out if what he had heard about Charlie Mitchell was true.

When we finished talking about that, it was late in the afternoon. We walked back to the house, and Chee gave us rooms to stay in at his place. He told us to wash ourselves, and he told his cook and children to fix a good meal for the visitors. Chee had a big house; he already had electricity from his own generator. He took us into the kitchen, and we washed up. Then a table was set for us.

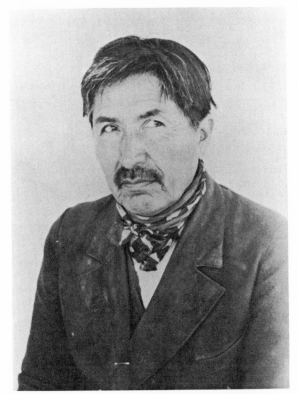

Garnett Bernally, photographer

FIG. 6. Frank Mitchell, c. 1935

It was there that Son of the Late Little Blacksmith did something pretty funny. He had never been to a place like Chee's and I guess it kind of frightened him. When he started to eat, he spilled the food all over his place. Of course, I was acquainted with things like forks and plates because I had learned to use them at the mission. It was a small table, and by the time they put the plates, cups, saucers and everything there, there was hardly enough room to move around. Son of the Late Little Blacksmith was kind of shy about that.

Chee sat down to eat with us at the table. After awhile, he got up and went to the cupboard and took out a can of plums. He opened it up and put some in small dishes for us. Son of the Late Little Blacksmith kept pushing his dish toward himself as he was eating. Finally he pushed it too close to the edge and then just upset the whole thing; the dish tipped over and the whole plate of plums spilled on his lap and on the floor.

Now Chee had put the can of fruit back in the cupboard after filling our dishes because there was some left in it. As he was turning around, Son of the Late Little Blacksmith upset his plate. Chee teased him and said that he had given him those plums to eat, not to throw on the floor. Son of the Late Little Blacksmith replied, "I did that because you still have half a can left there." Chee filled up his dish again and said, "Now, don't spill that. That is all there is." They just laughed about that.

Chee had the whole house for himself. He was no longer living with his wife; they had split up and were living separately. So he slept alone in the big house, and he invited all of us to spend the night with him. The kitchen and dining room were separate from his own quarters, and he took us down the long hall which had rooms on each side to where we were going to spend the night. The first room on the left was Chee's, and on the other side, there was a room like a rug room. Chee had lots of Navajo rugs and buffalo hides piled up in there. I guess he knew that older men preferred to sleep on the floor. He had some people working there for him on the farm and in the house, and he had them fix beds up nicely on the floor, with mattresses and sheepskins. But John Foley and I were given a room down the hall where there were beds. Chee told us that we two younger men could sleep on the beds and that the older two should make themselves comfortable on the floor.

Before we went to sleep that night, we sat in Chee's room and talked about many things. Chee did most of the talking, relating what had happened in the past, how the People had lived in the old days, the hard times that they had had to endure, the wars and fighting and other things. Then he went on to say that the People were beginning to get along with white people peacefully. But there were exceptions, like what we had said about Charlie Mitchell. These things happened. Then Chee started talking about the agreements that had been made with the church people, the understanding that they had made with the People when they asked for mission sites. Abuse of the People was not to be permitted. Chee said, "I think that you are right in demanding that this man be removed from his job because the ruling is like that in any job. If someone does something he should not do, then that is the cause of his dismissal."

After we had talked about those things, we asked Chee if what Frank Walker had said about him were true. Chee admitted that right away. He said that everything we had heard was true and that he was sorry that that had happened. He was sorry he had done a thing like that, but he had learned his lesson the hard way. He promised us that from then on the People would not hear any more things like that about him. And we never did.

The older men, Son of the Late Little Blacksmith and Curly Hair, were just terrified thinking about what could have happened to Chee. They also said that some Mexicans might have killed him because he was well-to-do and had money. They could not forget that Chee could have ended up somewhere in the wash without anyone knowing about it. Chee said, "I know that it was foolish. Nobody would have ever thought of me getting myself into such a thing and I was so embarrassed that I did not even want to talk about it. I did not want it to be known, but you already have word of it. So there is nothing that I can do but say that I feel sorry that such a thing happened. I thank you for coming to me to talk about this. From here on, I'll try to stay away from that and live a better life."

When you talk to a person face to face about things, you feel better. You know that you have the truth; it's better than talking behind a person's back. Chee was thankful that we had talked to him about this incident.

Then he told us that we should always look into things like Charlie Mitchell's case right away and try to correct them. If the People did not think they were being treated correctly, they should do something about it. He said he was glad we were doing this because he himself could not be all over the reservation to see if the People were living right everywhere. He told us that we would be welcome to come back at any time and talk with him and spend a night or two at his place.

That night I heard a lot about other things, too. Chee talked about the old days when the People went to Fort Sumner and all of that. He was able to tell the People about the way things were then because he was a boy then. He remembered it all clearly and told us everything about that. I learned a lot about how they went over there and came back and how they were treated. Chee said he himself had learned a lot from that Long Walk, too.

Finally we went to bed; after the lights were turned out and everybody had quieted down, Curly Hair and Son of the Late Little Blacksmith kept kidding each other. They called themselves cousins, and I could hear them talking late into the night. Curly Hair said, "Hey, cousin; I have my words confused on what you told me in secret one time. You, you are the one who told me that secret."

Son of the Late Little Blacksmith said, "I don't remember telling you any secret. What are you talking about?"

Curly Hair said, "It was about the wolf skin. You said when you want to make yourself a man wolf,[7] you use some kind of song or prayer or whatever it is to tie the skin between your ears."

I guess Son of the Late Little Blacksmith did not know what to give him for an answer. He did not want to say anything; he hesitated and then he got mad. "What are you talking about? Are you crazy? What do you mean asking me questions like that in a place where you are sleeping? This is a beautiful house; it is like a holy being's home, and here you are, talking nonsense like that. You shut up and go to sleep. How can you talk about foolish things like that and think about silly things in a place like this? Are you crazy or something?"

These two men used to tease each other a lot, and I guess Curly Hair was teasing Son of the Late Little Blacksmith about being one of these wolf men and putting on the skin and then using a spell before taking it off. After Son of the Late Little Blacksmith said that, the two men started laughing about it. I guess they knew it was just a joke.

We all slept that night and about dawn, Chee Dodge was already up walking around. He went into the room where Curly Hair and Son of the Late Little Blacksmith were still sleeping and said, "I didn't know you men had some other stories to tell. Why didn't you tell me last night when we were doing all the talking that you had something more to talk about when you got back in your private room? We were all trying to pick up some of the old time stories; why didn't you tell us that one last night? I heard you from next door."

Son of the Late Little Blacksmith said, "I don't know what he was talking about; I thought maybe he had gone crazy." So they all just laughed about it. Then we washed up and went to the dining room. After we had been given breakfast, we left and went home.

While I was working in the community here in Chinle as a headman, we did not have a tribal council. There were no regular sessions; we would just get together with other headmen on the reservation at various places and also at Fort Defiance to get the news from the superintendent. The councilman business did not start until sometime in the 1930s in Window Rock. As I mentioned, I became interested in what the leaders and talkers of the People were doing and saying, and I joined them. When Curly Hair and Chic Sandoval became councilmen, of course I got to working with them, too. When these two men left the Council, I was put in there as a councilman.[8]

After I became a member of that Council, I learned more about what the government expected us to do, about how we should operate our own government and things like that. I found out that a lot of men on the Council were inexperienced. They did not know what they were there for; they simply went there without first understanding what the purpose was. Others, of course, understood those things beforehand. While I was on the Council, the first woman to serve was also there.[9]

In my early days, I found that I could remember things very well. Even though something did not concern me, when someone was carrying on a conversation, I used to memorize the things that they were talking about. When I became a member of the Tribal Council, I had a pretty sharp mind. I could understand easily what was being brought up for discussion before the Council. While others did not seem to catch the meaning of what the subjects were, I was pretty well known for understanding things.

Once I was placed there as one of the councilmen, I began to be asked to do different things. One of the things that there was a lot of talk about during this time was education and the need for building schools on the reservation. We also talked about hospitals and preventing outsiders from moving in with different things like industrial plants. We did a lot of work, and I concerned myself with all those things.[10]

I was very interested in the schools, in putting up a public school for Indian children. At that time there was only the school at Fort Apache and

B.I.A. Collection, Window Rock, Arizona

FIG. 7. The hand-picked Navajo Tribal Council, 1937-38. The following have been identified: Front row, left to right: Chee Dodge, Charles Shirley. Second row, left to right: third in from left, Long Moustache; sixth, Frank Mitchell (with black fur cap); bearded man, Old Man Arviso; last on right, Judge Jim Shirley. Third row, directly behind Frank: Eli Smith.

another in Colorado, and the only others were a long way from the reservation. Lots of times the People would send their children there, and they would get sick. Sometimes those schools would never notify the parents until the child was seriously ill, and lots of times the child died away at school. We did not like the idea of sending our children away and never seeing them again. That is how I lost one of my daughters. They brought her back here when she was in critical condition, and she lasted only four or five more days after that. So I went through that experience myself, and I wanted to see schools on the reservation. We talked about that a lot on the Council, and we decided to ask for the schools and also hospitals and all of those things from Washington.

Several of us were then appointed to go to Washington to ask that these things be granted.[11] I went over there with several other men. We went before those people and asked for a school and a hospital and other things. Henry Taliman, the tribal chairman; Howard Gorman, the vice chairman; and Red Moustache's brother were some of the others who went over there too. We were asked to fly there, but most of the delegates were afraid of going in an airplane, so we went on the train.

While we were there, we were given sight-seeing tours around Washington. I got to see the White House, Arlington Cemetery, the Unknown Soldier's Tomb and other places. One of the delegates got tired when we were near the Washington Monument. He wanted to rest, but he could not find a place to sit down. So he took off his moccasins and laid down on the grass in front of the monument. He was wearing half-socks like the ones I used to knit for myself.[12] This man went to sleep, and while he was sleeping, a crowd gathered around, looking at him. When he woke up, he asked me, "What are all of these people standing around here looking at me for?"

I said, "My younger brother, they are waiting for you to get up to see what kind of a creature you are. They are wondering whether or not when you get up you will crawl on all fours, like a bear."

He replied, "You bear; you would say that!"

These two men, Henry Taliman and Howard Gorman, understood English very well; I went with them before these people in Washington and I asked that a hospital and schools be built on the reservation. That was my request. Another delegate requested that we be well cared for in the future, that farming land be taken care of and that the crops that we plant be taken care of in the case of some insects or something else destroying them, and that Washington help with sprays and other things.

We were asked by those people how the white people who were among us at that time, like those at the Fort Defiance Hospital and the government schools there, were working out. Howard and Henry had been in and out of government service in the past, so they had a bit of experience in working with white people. They answered that some of the white people were not too easy to get along with and others were fine. They said that some of them carried on their jobs well and treated the Navajos well.

The two who were interviewed about how the white people were treating the Navajos out here were told at that time that the People as a whole were not ready to get out on their own yet, because they were still like little children. They had to be trained and brought up just like children. That is what they were told. The people in Washington told us that they were not going to tell the Navajos what they were supposed to do or what they could not do; instead, they were just going to go along very easily with them until the day that they in Washington knew that our people were able to carry on our own affairs. They also talked about other things, like not saying harsh words to Navajos because they get mad right away and might scalp people. In the days of Fort Sumner, the People would not take any kind of rough talk from a white man; they would just shoot him with a bow and arrow. Even when we were in Washington, there were people on the reservation, especially those who had parents or relatives who had been to Fort Sumner, who were still hurting in their hearts over those things.

From that trip I learned many new things that I did not know before. After that experience, I was capable of filling other positions. I found out things that were going on outside the reservation. I learned that you cannot pick up these things in a short time; you just keep on learning something new all the time. Even if you are Navajo and can talk Navajo and make speeches, if you do not have the experience of knowing what is going on outside your own country — what other people are doing, how they are living — you do not know how to talk to your own people.

Through this Washington trip I learned quite a few things that I had never known before. I would tell the People about these experiences when I talked to them. I would also tell them other things, too, like it was not worth gambling. Again, because I had gone through that experience myself when I was working on the railroad, I had learned that it was not worthwhile. I just gambled every penny I earned there and finally, even everything I had. That was another of the lessons that I had learned through my own experience that I told the People about when I talked with them at meetings, dances and at gatherings.

Another thing that came along while I was on the Council was the constitution. I was among those who helped work on that. But that constitution was never accepted. I have often asked about that since that time, but I have never been able to find out why that was not put into effect.[13]

The biggest thing that came along while I was on that Council was the stock reduction. Both Chic Sandoval and I were on the Council at that time. The People were in trouble because their land was being overgrazed, and they were told to decrease their stock. Earlier, none of us had stock permits. We just had all the sheep we wanted. Then we were told about permits by the government, and each one was issued a permit. Mine allowed only ten head of sheep. So that is why we have just a few around here now. Each year they have little ones, and those furnish us with meat. That is what happened. The People all around here did not like those of us on the Council on that account. They kept accusing us, saying that we had urged the government to reduce their livestock and not ours, and that the reduction would ruin the livelihood of the Navajo people in general.

There are lots of reasons why I never really went into big sheep business as I had always wanted to. At one time, I had many head of cattle and sheep but nobody to look after them. Both of the boys were in school and most of the girls were there, too, so I could not very well look to them to herd the sheep. I thought it would be best for the children to go to school and just let it go at that. My wife was sick almost all of her life from this and that; if she had not been sick, we probably would have had lots of stock; I probably would have been a big sheep man.

Another thing was that I was gone most of the time working in tribal affairs by that time, and I always had a job to do. There was always something coming up. They would have a meeting and I would go to that; I was always on the go with those things, and I somewhat lost track of what was happening with my family. My mother's family was almost gone by then, and I did not have much time to be here herding the sheep myself. I would be asked to give talks at schools, Squaw Dances and other gatherings. There I would talk about conducting the ceremonies in the right manner and about trying to get along living together. I would always tell the children to remain in school to get a good education.

I want to make all of this clear because I have a lot of friends in other places, not just white people, but some other Navajo friends I know from way back. They probably wonder when they come to visit me why a man like me, who has knowledge of making something out of himself, did not raise sheep or cattle as some of the other councilmen did while they were on the Council. I know that I have been in various tribal offices, like the Council, the judgeship and serving as a Chapter officer and all of that. But the way it happened was that we were all issued permits and mine came out with only ten head like that. There was nothing I could do about it from then on. Some of the People have a lot of sheep. Some of them did not get a permit for sheep; they just got permits for horses and had to get rid of their sheep.

During those days on the Council, of course, I was also out performing Blessingway for different people at various places. I would be taken outside of Chinle to do this ceremony, and I would be gone from home two or three days at a time. That, too, made it kind of hard to be a cattleman or in the business of raising sheep. Putting all of these things together, it just did not work out for me. You have to be a free man, free from everything to raise sheep.

Look at the big owners: they look like hobos. They do not eat meat as we do; they just suffer from hunger. They do not even butcher because they want to raise more and more sheep. When you visit them, you think that they will have mutton on hand. The first thing they do before talking is to hurry off to tend the sheep. They lose interest in people; they become more of a sheep themselves through that. I saw that happen with my brother John. That is what I found out.

They do not care for their stock in the same careful way that people who have a small flock do. I found that out, too. They ask for so much, but they are not fat. I did not like the thought of going into that business. It is a waste of time; you suffer in the wintertime with the sheep and in the summer with the heat. Every sheepherder dies of thirst. You get careless about yourself; it will be months since you last washed. I made up my mind to be a Blessingway singer and to leave sheep-raising alone.

I was councilman from this area for awhile, but I lost my term after the first one was up. I ran for another term, but I lost that vote. Later on I ran in another Council election, and I lost in that one, too. So I was out of the Council.[14] Chee Dodge was tribal chairman when I lost that first vote, and I

FIG. 8. An outdoor meeting at Many Farms, Arizona, April 11, 1942. At microphone, Howard Gorman; directly behind him, Frank Mitchell. Front row: girl on left, Sally Neez; boy on left of man with concho belt, James Atsitty.

guess he was looking over the group of councilmen to see which ones were getting the most out of that experience. After I lost my vote, Chee told me that he hated to see me go because it was more than likely that I was getting more out of it than the rest. He said that I would be the man to do some more work. So, instead of just letting me go, he talked to the Indian commissioner, Mr. Fryer, and John Collier about it.[15] I did not know that at that time they were talking about making me a judge. So when Chee Dodge came out later and asked me to do that, I did not know anything about it. He said that they figured that I was understanding things while some of the others were not. So I was the one who was asked to take the job. I told them at that time that I did not know if I would be able to carry on that duty.

I guess some of them had been watching me closely while I was on the Tribal Council. They knew that I could talk to the People and that I was recognized as a leader. They also knew that I had a good memory. I could remember everything that was said at meetings I went to, and once is all that I ever had to be told anything to remember it. With others on the Council, no matter how many times something was repeated, they could not get it into their minds. So we were told things over and over and over again on that Council, and some of them still could not get those things into their minds. I am losing my memory now because I am getting old. When you are young, you should remember things; if you start losing your memory before you get old, there is something wrong with you or you have been doing something like sleeping with your cousin. I guess the People knew that I could remember all of the old laws that were made a long time ago. I think that is the reason why I was made a judge in the Indian courts.

The reason I said I did not know if I would be able to carry on the duties of a judge was mainly because I knew that to be a judge would mean the majority of the People would be against me. At that time I believed in witchcraft, and I thought that the People would apply that to me and take my life. So I decided to ask Chee Dodge if there was any truth in this witchcraft and if it would really affect a person. I knew that Chee had gone through many experiences from way back, so I wanted to ask him if the People really could use witchcraft on one another. I kept asking him, "My cousin, you have been here a long time; you have been in contact with the old people and the white people. What do you know about this witch business?"

Chee told me that witches originated with the hand-tremblers after the Long Walk, when many other foreign rituals were brought in.[16] They brought in the ceremony of trembling where people trembled, just like the Holy Rollers. The trembler goes to work and tells you that you are being bewitched. A person who is ill will try anything; that is how these things get going, and that is where the sucking ceremony comes in, too. The singer will suck something out of a person and then ask the hand-trembler, "Whose weapon is that?" Then he will ask them to shoot it back into that person.

So Chee told me that after the Long Walk they started murdering lots of people who they thought were witches. It got so bad that the army came in and investigated; they told the People there was no truth to that and to stop killing each other. So Chee said, "Do not believe that you can injure another person like this. There is no such thing as witchcraft." Chee told me that I would die sooner or later, even if I did not become a judge. He just kidded me about that, saying, "Just because I have recommended you as judge, you are scared to handle these cases."

Chee also gave me this advice. "You will be here a long time. Keep your eyes open and find out about things." So I did; I watched and listened all the time up to the time of John Collier and Fryer. The People had very bitter feelings towards those two because of the stock reduction and everything that happened to them then. So I told the People, "Here is your chance, you witches; put a bean in them and put one in each of us on the Tribal Council who supported that." That did not happen, and because of this experience, I do not believe in witches anymore.

A physical being is subject to many illnesses. Any number of these can hurt the body, so why blame the illness on a bean? Some of those bean shooters are alive, and they blame John Collier still for their troubles. He is living close by, so they have their chance. Maybe the reason that John Collier is hard of hearing now is because he has been wounded by one of them.

The younger generation is outgrowing this belief in witches because they have no reason to believe it. But the old people still feel this way and still believe in it because it has always been a part of their life. When you take the Navajos as a whole, it's like a goat that has grazed with sheep. They are all bedded down together at night, but the goat just will not lie still: he will be shuffling around all night long, listening for every little noise. He will be alert, and suddenly he will jump up and scare all the sheep. The Navajos are like that; somebody gives the alarm and they all stampede. But this witchcraft thing is just a false alarm, and yet the People will stampede that way.

I also asked Chee Dodge about werewolves, the man wolf, about beans and putting poison on a stick and causing paralysis by touching a person with it. I asked him if these things went together. He told me that nobody can shoot beans into another person; nobody can do this. Chee said the origin of this belief is that in the early days, the singers claimed they could do this. They did it to get young girls. They would tell the family, "If you do not let me have her, I will shoot a bean into her or somebody else in the family." So the People got afraid and began to believe in that. It started with somebody bluffing the People.

Regarding the coyote, Chee told me that nobody can change into a coyote or even squeeze into a coyote's hide, no matter how hard they try. This idea originated in the early days when the Navajos were poor. We had no stock then, and somebody got the idea to carve up a coyote, take its paw and tie it to a moccasin. Then such a person would go and steal sheep, drive them away, and when safely in a rocky place, remove the paw. People would come along and see the print and think a coyote had taken the sheep. Then the coyote print would disappear and there would be the moccasin print.

Now, about putting poison on a person with a stick; that originated with some people who were weak-hearted. They were not strong, not altogether normal. Well, they liked to come among the People at gatherings and then faint or pass away. This kind of person would always be overcome. Then the People would say that somebody had poisoned this person. You know you never heard of somebody being poisoned alone, individually; it is always in a crowd. And that is why it is.

Hearing Chee tell me these things, I also realized that when I learned about the Blessingway, I was being taught about the origin, the beginning of things. And of course in all those stories and songs there is no mention of any kind of witch at all. So therefore, I knew that Chee was right, and I decided that I would be willing to take on the job as judge. So I told the tribal councilmen that I would be willing to do it. Then I asked them this question, "Just how do you be a judge? How do you carry on your duty as a judge?" That was the first question I asked.

Then Chee Dodge told me that they would give me a book to go by, the lawbook that they use in the court. I would be given one of those, and someone would go over all of those things with me. So after that was done, I was called back to Window Rock. A man from Washington had come out; he was a young man. It might have been Norman Littell, who later served as general counsel to the Tribe — I don't know. Anyway, the man was a lawyer, and he had been sent to train all of us who were going to do that job. There were several others who were given that duty too, so we all went in from here and spent some time at Window Rock, and that man went through the book with us. He had an interpreter with him who interpreted the whole thing in Navajo for us. That schooling lasted about a week; I guess all of us who had been judged as those who were getting the most out of what we were doing on the Council were there. When that whole week was over, they picked me out of that group.[17]

I guess Chee Dodge was right about those witches, because in all the time I was a judge, the People never really tried witchcraft on me. They did, however, often tell me that I was not going to be around to talk with them, that I was not going to be living too long when I sentenced them and they did not like it. I would hear them clearly saying those things right from their mouths as they talked to me. But those things never upset me, and I was never scared because I knew the Protection Prayer and the song that went with it. In private I would just say those prayers and songs and ask to be protected from what these people were saying.

Of course, in the days when I was being asked to become a judge, talk about witches was not as common as it is today. In recent times, the Peyote cult[18] has come into the Navajo nation. The People who are practicing that are getting all kinds of visions by eating that cactus. They, in turn, are doing things which appear to be like witchcraft. So it is pretty common again, and a lot of people have started thinking about it and talking about it.

I never had a case involving witchcraft, but there have been some since this Peyote came on the reservation. The peyote people operate like that, saying that witchcraft is the case. All the time it is really a group of people using peyote who get together and do those things. They plan in advance to pick up pieces of clothing, hair, or something from their sheep or horses or from around their homes; they pick up those little pieces and gather these things together and then go and bury them near a person's home or in a grave or somewhere like that. Then when the person is ill, they say to call on one of the people in that peyote group to do the hand-trembling. Then the trembler says that only this one singer can get everything cleared up, and indicates another one of the people in that group.

I guess cases of witchcraft can almost always be explained away like that. I found this out for myself through my experience with Hairy Mexican from Tuba City. He was well known for taking these things that the peyote people put in graves and elsewhere. While I was a judge, some people complained about this man, and he came before me. But first I talked to a man at Window Rock who knew the law and could tell me what the situation would be in a case like this. He knew all the laws and what their violations meant. This man told me that he would need to know what the situation was, that he did not think this man was really trying to take those things in the ground. If he were trying to dig up a grave to get the valued things buried with a person, that would be one situation, and he should be sentenced to a full term. But this white man did not think that there was any of that involved in this case. If it were a new grave that had been disturbed, it would matter. An old one, though, would probably not be of any use.

So when this man who was accused came to court I asked him how old that grave was. He said that another singer had told him during a ceremony that several things were buried in a grave at a particular place. So he had gone out there at nighttime and dug it up, and all he had found there was a piece of bone. It was not a human bone, and he had not gone into the grave or disturbed the body. So it turned out that he was not doing anything wrong; he was just doing something to get a little money. There was no ceremony involved, even though the people in his area were worrying about witchcraft. That man was trying to tell the People that these things buried in the grave were causing illness because of witchcraft; all the time there was nothing there. The one who came to court had just made up this whole thing all by himself.

So I found out that the grave was very, very old. Since this man had just dug on the surface and had not gone down clear to the bottom where the ghost was, I sentenced him according to what the white man had told me. I told him as long as he was doing a ceremony it would be all right, providing he did not use anything connected with peyote or grave-digging. If he was going to do ceremonies, he was not to dig up any more graves or to tell people that they were being witched, or put their clothes in the grave and start digging around. I told him he could do ceremonies without disturbing the dead or the graves; I just warned him. I also told him that if the People in his area ever found out that he was doing that again, they would report him. These people would keep a close watch on him. And if they ever found him doing that again, he would be brought right here, and next time we would deal harshly with him.

When a singer uses materials from old ruins, like arrowheads, shells or things like that, that's different. Those things come from our ancestors way back; they are not Navajo things. But still, now they tell us that we should not go digging around in those ruins, either.

Before the courts were established, there were only a few fixed rules and laws. As we were brought up, we were just told not to do this or that; most of the disputes we ever heard about were those between the Navajos and the white people. Sometimes, though, the headmen would have problems, like adultery, brought to them to settle. This continued even after the Indian courts were started.[19]

In the early days, when it was a question of a fight, it was more important who started it than who inflicted the most harm. The headman would give talks to all of the People on how to live, on how to grow up and live correctly. Some of the problems, like telling untrue things about others, did not cause us too much trouble in the early days. At that time, the children were kept around home, and that helped prevent some of that. When those kinds of problems did occur, though, usually they were settled at a meeting. The person who was talking like that was made to promise four times to stop saying those things. Nowadays, when you hear that an individual has something against you, the usual practice is to go and find that person and try to settle whatever the problem is. If that does not work, then you can take the whole thing to court. Around here we don't consider it better to drop things, and we don't try to be noble about these kinds of things, especially in public. People who act like that must not know that we now have courts to settle those things.

Before the courts were started, a payment was expected to be made in the case of a murder. The relatives of the murdered person complained to the murderer and demanded a property settlement. Usually the murderer was expected to fill a ceremonial basket completely to the rim with jewelry and things like that. It did not matter what that person's reputation was; the expectations were the same. If a man was too poor and unable to pay that, he might ask his relatives to help him get those things together. If he did not pay, a relative of the murdered person would just go and kill the murderer.

Of course, there was no such thing as murder in the beginning; when the six original clans came from the west and the Pueblos came in from the east and the Navajos and Pueblo people started living around here, there was no such thing as murder. Today, when that happens, it goes to court, and there a person's reputation and intentions can make a difference. But even now, sometimes the courts will decide to settle it one way and the community will still demand that the murderer make a settlement with the relatives of the one murdered.

If you murder someone or if you commit incest, it will affect you inside yourself. Our belief about those things is similar to your Christian belief. Those things hurt you inside. In the case of incest, it goes to your head. In the old days when that happened, you had to use herbs and have a ceremony to remove the effects of that. Crooked Neck was one who did that with his sister. If you commit suicide, some people feel sorry for you. Around here we knew about one man who did that because of the stock reduction program. If a suicide occurs in your camp, you are supposed to move the hogan, just as you do if someone dies there from some other cause.

There was not much trouble with stealing, either, in the early days. The People had only a few horses and cows, and the owner would usually catch the person who did the stealing; the owner would just track that thief down. We did not use hand-tremblers to discover who that person was in the early days. There was some belief in witchcraft at that time, and if you thought that that was being used on you, you could kill the person you suspected. There were many cases like that which were eventually turned over to the federal government, because there was a lot of trouble from that in the old days. People used to threaten witchcraft in order to get others to do as they wanted. It has been said for a long, long time that if you ask a Navajo something four times that person has to answer you. That is in the Blessingway story when the clans were originally established. There is nothing in there that says if someone does not answer you it is because that person is afraid of being witched.

During that training the group of us had, I found out something I had never known before. When you are a judge, you cannot settle things or make decisions according to your own way of thinking. You have to go according to the regulations and laws that are written in the lawbook. If someone is accused of some crime or misdemeanor, you have to use your lawbook as a guide and pass sentences according to that. It's like price tags on goods that you are buying; it tells you how much it costs and things like that. It's just the same way with a person who is charged with something. It means so many days in jail, no less and no more. You go according to the limits of those things. You have to be careful not to overstep yourself in these decisions, because they go on records which are turned in for inspection. If you go ahead and use your own judgment without consulting the rule book and pass sentences according to the way you think, you may be partial to some party and prejudiced against someone else. Then the ones who are checking your decisions will call your attention to that. If you make a mistake, they will ask you, "Well, how come you passed a sentence like that? It is not this way in the book."

The limits that are on certain things are very similar to the ceremonial performances. The care you take in fixing up the stick for the Squaw Dance, and the care you show in putting it where it will not be damaged, all of that is like a person going to jail. You go before a judge to get a trial; then you are sentenced to so many days in jail. You must serve your term or you are told that your people can pay a fine instead. When you are sentenced, you either serve out your term or pay the fine for what you have done. The fixing up of the stick in the Enemyway is just like making a payment for wrongdoing.

All of the rules tell you just what you can do; the ceremonies are designed like that, too. They must be performed in certain ways and not others. If you disregard the rules, the Holy People who are watching over these things will become aware of it. If you do not observe these rules that govern the ceremonies and perform them according to your own notions, then naturally you are going to suffer the consequences and have some misfortunes. So I compare these two things, being a judge and being a singer, to each other; they are about in the same position; in both of them you have to be careful not to overstep any of the limits.

You remember that in Washington they told us that as a whole, the Navajo nation was looked on as a little child that was just learning to start to walk. So when we were being taught about the law, they told us that we would follow the white people's law. Their law is not limited; it was set up by people who were educated and who had studied the laws and knew what they said; the laws covered the whole length.

The Navajos are not educated; they have a long way to go in learning things about the law. So the laws for them were made to cover just part of the white man's full length of the law. That is where the difference comes in; instead of sentencing a Navajo to a full time like a white man would be, a Navajo is sent away only for a short term. When the day comes when we all learn what the laws say, then we will probably be sentencing people to full white men's terms. After time goes on, the whole Navajo nation will become educated, and we will have our own law just like the white people. The people are already progressing little by little now, and so are our laws.

Before I became a judge and early in the time when I was serving as one, the People were given light sentences. When they did wrong, they were in their right minds, and the judge would just talk to them. He would give them a preaching to, and then most of them would say that they never realized that they were doing wrong. Most of the time they were never seen in the court again. At that time, these short sentences were all right. But with time, and as I worked at being a judge, the whole thing was affected by liquor on the reservation. I blame the white people for bringing that in. With those conditions, I don't know if it is a good thing to sentence people to just a short term when they do something wrong when they are not in their right minds.

I wish they had never had liquor on the reservation; maybe then the People would be able to use their judgment as they did in the early days and not continue to do wrong after the first time. Now it is very hard to get people to go straight. You see the same faces over and over again in court. This drinking is also killing a lot of people. Sometimes two drink together, and then they fight; many times they hurt each other very badly, and sometimes they even kill each other. There are always things like that coming up now, and it really is not the People's fault.

Douglas Mitchell Collection

FIG. 9. Frank as a judge, March 1949.

It is all right for the whites to drink whiskey because they take it right, and it does not hurt them or make them go crazy. But even before this whiskey, the Mexicans were here with their wine. That also upset things. The majority of the People do not drink whiskey now; they drink wine because it's the cheapest thing they can get that is full of alcohol. Half of them die from it, and they do not realize that it is injuring them in that way. So, as a judge, it is hard to say whether a person who is under the influence of liquor should be sentenced to the full extent or just given a short term.

Most of the cases I had as judge involved liquor and disorderly conduct. The way I handled it was like this: when the person came into court, first the complaint was read. Then I asked if what was stated on the complaint was

270 9. PUBLIC SERVANT

true. If it was, then I just remembered under which law and which section this particular case would come, and I knew what kind of a sentence to give. But if I knew this particular person from a long time ago, or if I knew that this person had a family and had been a good person up until the time of the drinking, I would consider that. I would ask how many times the person had been in court. If this was the first time, then I would usually think about it. If I knew that the person was nice, polite and helpful towards other people, then I would give a light sentence instead of the full one, since it was a first offense. So I had to use my own judgment at times. If the person had been in jail a number of times, then I would impose the full sentence.

If it was a case involving property ownership and there were family people arguing about it, it always would be sent before the Chapter officers first. Anything concerning property, livestock, jewelry and things like that goes before the Chapter first. If it concerns land or stock, it goes before the Land Operation Committee or the Stock Committee outside of court. If those groups cannot get it straightened out without trouble, then it comes back to court and the judge settles it.

If you had a case where a woman died and both her husband and her daughter claimed her sheep, whatever the woman owned would be kept separate from all the rest. The sheep that the man owned would be shown by the mark that the Navajos put on their sheep in the spring and by the permit. Those things show that the sheep belong to particular individuals. The man would have a permit for his sheep, and the daughter would have to have a permit made out for any of the sheep in that flock that are hers. The sheep that are left would be those that belonged to the woman who passed away. Then if any other children were involved in the family, we would give some sheep to each of them.

In doing this, of course, you have to judge who will be the one to take good care of the sheep. You cannot give a lot of sheep to someone who will not care for them. If there is a crippled child in the family, however, you cannot give less, because actually that person needs a little more than the rest. If there is some child in the family who really knows how to take care of these things, that one, too, deserves more than the rest. All of these things are up to you to judge. If the man is just a young man, someone who is not old enough to get married, he should get a separate permit, because later on he may want to marry and start his own flock. Records are kept about all of these things: the Chapter officers, the councilmen and the stock committees have these decisions in their records. Then, if these things come up again they will know who got what and not have so many arguments about it in later years.

While I was a judge, there was no law about how to decide cases involving a sacred bundle. Several years ago, when they were making a code for the Indian court, they consulted me a number of times about sacred bundles.[20] The younger people did not know how these bundles started or what the rules were about them. I told them all the procedures you have to go through.

It was never absolutely decided and recorded how a deceased singer's bundle would be passed on. There is no set ruling on that. It was just decided that we should follow the old custom: when a person dies and the bundle is in dispute, it should stay with the clan relations because they have gone to a great deal of trouble and expense. A lot of people do not know that this is not written down, so when someone with lots of ceremonial equipment dies, they all rush in to grab those things. I guess those feelings are caused by the question of expense and the fact that our people are not learning to be singers these days.

Because of such disputes, one time Charlie Mitchell, Chee Dodge and Old Man Silversmith got together and talked about that. They decided that when a singer dies without making a will concerning who is to get the medicine bundle, it should go back to the family if they helped support the learning of the ceremony and the making of the bundle in the first place. If the singer was a man and his family had not helped him in any way during the time he was learning, and if his wife's side and his children had helped him meet those expenses, then it should go to his wife's children. If neither side had helped, there would be nobody in the family who knew how to use the bundle. If there is somebody on either side who knows how to use it, then it is theirs. But if nobody learned, these three men decided that the medicine bundle would go back to the wife.

The reason for that was that it belonged to her husband and he supported her with the little income he got from its use. So it should go back to the wife, and from there on it is up to her to do what she wants with it. If she wants to sell it, it would be all right to go ahead and do that. If she has a close or a distant relative who she knows would use that bundle in the right way, if that person does not have a bundle, then she can go ahead and bestow it there. But that person cannot expect to use it without making payment. Whatever the singer gets for doing a ceremony using that bundle, half of that — money, materials or other things — should go to the woman. They also decided that the woman would have the right to take the bundle back at any time if this person did not use it correctly. She could also take it back if she were not getting her half.

In many cases, the People just sell these things. The ceremonial bundle is a small thing, but it takes lots of money to make it and lots of time studying how to do that. So it's probably better to sell it if you can get a good payment for it.

The reason that Chee Dodge, Charlie Mitchell and Old Man Silversmith got together to make a decision on that bundle was that there was a case about it that came from around Crystal. A long time ago, a man by the name of Laughing Singer died without a will; he was a Nightway singer. His wife had died some years previous to his death, and so there were just his children left. But most of them were Presbyterians and would have nothing to do with ceremonials. So these three men got together and had many meetings about who was going to get that bundle. First they decided to just go ahead and give it to somebody who knew how to do that ceremonial. But Chee Dodge and other singers did not like this because a ceremonial bundle has to be made for you before you can own it. Or if it is not made for you, it can be willed to you. But to just have it given to you would not be like having it be your own. So those three finally decided that they would leave that sacred bundle over at the Franciscan Fathers' mission at Saint Michaels. They told the Fathers that anyone who wanted to use it could come by and pick it up and then return it afterwards. It was left there for the use of those who really knew the ceremonial.

A lot of singers who knew the Nightway used that bundle, and after a few years some of the pieces in it began to be missing. Every time it was loaned out, it would come back with more pieces missing. Father Berard Haile was over there then, and he did not like that. He had written down the story of how Laughing Singer became a singer and how his bundle had been made, and how it was used. Because of his interest, he was distressed about the missing pieces. So he told the People that he did not like the idea of lending out this sacred bundle anymore. It was all right when the singers took care of it and brought it back in one piece, but now some of it was missing. So the same three men met again and talked about it some more. Finally it was decided that since Father Berard had the story that went with what was left of that bundle, it should be put in a museum in Santa Fe. So that is where Father Berard sent it, to the Museum of Navajo Ceremonial Art.[21]

Once after I had finished being a judge I was called over to the court to talk to three current judges because of one of my earlier decisions about a bundle. When I had been judge, I had ruled that a deceased man's bundle should go to his wife. I did that according to what had been decided earlier when that sacred bundle was left with the Franciscan Fathers. It was then that it was decided to give it to the man's wife or whomever had paid or donated most to have it made. I had followed that procedure in this particular case, but when the man's wife died, the people brought the whole thing up again and started arguing over it.

When I talked to those judges about this case, I asked them if there were any new laws about how to handle that, and they told me that they still did not have any. In this case, the in-laws were trying to get it away from the wife's side. But since it was the wife's side that had originally gone through all the expenses of paying for the food and having everything else done so the bundle could be made, the judges just went according to the principles that Chee Dodge and the others had established earlier, and the ones that I had used, and gave that bundle, again, to the woman's side.

B.I.A. Collection, Window Rock, Arizona

FIG. 10. Pictorial ballot photo, used during election of 1951-54 Tribal Council.

When I was a judge, I don't think that I made any blunders. I don't think that I made any mistakes or bad decisions, because even now the People still mention me and say at times that I was a good judge. These things are said by people who are in position to know something about the laws and the white people. They have complimented me on those things. So I think that I did a pretty good job as judge. Of course, I am still trying to do a good job with my ceremonies. People still mention that now, and they also say that I used good judgment while I was in that position as judge.

EDITORS' NOTES

1. See Chapter 2, note 7.

2. A system of local community organization known as the Chapter system was developed in the late 1920s by John Hunter, superintendent of the Leupp Agency 7/1/27-12/31/28, and of the Southern Navajo Agency 1/1/29-9/30/34. Started as a way of improving communication between the Navajos, their tribal leaders, federal government, health officials and others, the Chapters rapidly became popular. As Frank said, "Gradually the old spokesmen were done away with and in their places, three Chapter officers were established: president, vice president and secretary. That is the way it is now." After a halt in their development (1932-1950, when they were often centers of agitation because of stock reduction and range-control politics), they were revived and expanded on a reservation-wide basis until there were well over a hundred Chapters, each with its community house; social, recreational and educational facilities; elected officers, etc. Frank served as an officer of the Chinle Chapter in 1944, 1951, 1952 and 1955. See Chapter 10, note 5. Also see Link 1968:76-77; Shepardson 1963:15, 16 ff.; Williams 1970:33ff.; Young 1961:335-340.

3. See the Franciscan Fathers (1910:422-424) and Wyman and Kluckhohn (1938:19) for short descriptions of the Chief Blessingway. Although Frank willingly recorded Chief Hogan songs and subsequent related sets (Frisbie 1967:102-168), his hesitation about recording the Chief songs was real. It was obvious that like the topics of burial practices, witchcraft and detailed explanations of when to use which variants in Blessingway, the Chief songs were special, and not to be discussed. He never did record these songs for either of the editors before his death. There are some Chief songs in Slim Curly's version of Blessingway (Wyman 1970:152-154), but as n. 132 (*Ibid.*:152) indicates, they are sung to serenade Talking God and are different from "another set of six songs" which "may have ... been employed at an earlier time for speakers or for initiating new headmen."

4. Frank recorded his version of the Blessingway for Father Berard Haile in 1930, according to two of the holograph notebooks. Haile, however, dates it as 1932 in his Introduction to Version II of Blessingway (Wyman 1970:xxiii).

5. According to mission census records at Saint Michaels, Charlie Mitchell (#54860) died on July 15, 1932. The Superior at Saint Michaels c. 1931 was Big Priest, or Father Arnold Heinsman. Frisbie sent a copy of this part of Frank's story to Father Emanuel of Saint Michaels in hopes of further clarification from mission records. None was available, however; Father Marcellus appears not to have kept a diary, and Father Clementine, who was in charge of the Lukachukai Mission in 1928, had never heard the story. The Franciscan Fathers, therefore, remain curious about the entire incident. The only additional information available was that Roy Kinsel died in a fire in his

hogan on 7/17/66, and there was much local talk about witchcraft. For further information on Charlie Mitchell's interaction with the Franciscans, see Wilken (1955) and Trockur (Personal Communication 10/2/74).

6. Gallup is known to the Navajos as *Na'nízhoozhí'*, "extended across," after the bridge which spans the Rio Puerco in the center of town.

7. Fieldwork from 1963-1971 suggests that at least among some Navajos, belief in werewolves is still quite common. Strange tracks, noises, glowing eyes in the night and sounds of rocks being thrown on the hogan and rolling off the roof at night directly before Frank's death were among the phenomena and events attributed to werewolves by several members of Frank's family. For further information on the Navajo belief in werewolves, see Morgan (1936) and Kluckhohn (1944).

8. In 1921, there was a "General Council" to deal with oil and gas discoveries. In 1922, the Bureau of Indian Affairs instituted a new arrangement, the "Business Council," which consisted of Chee Dodge, Charlie Mitchell and Dugal Chee Bekiss and was in charge of negotiating leases. When the legality of this council was questioned, Commissioner of Indian Affairs Charles Burke drafted his "Regulations Relating to the Navajo Tribe of Indians" (1/7/23), which called for one delegate and one alternate from each of the six superintendents' agencies (see Young 1961:393-395 for document). Other regulations, however, were approved by the Secretary of the Interior on 4/24/23 and went into effect 7/7/23 (see Young 1961:395-397). These established a Council of twelve delegates and twelve alternates from six jurisdiction areas, with the chairman being elected separately, and the vice chairman being one of the delegates. The Indian commissioner was in charge of calling meetings (generally totaling two days a year).

With Henry Chee Dodge as the first chairman, the tribe used this 1923 system, with several amendments (Young 1961:397-400) regarding length of office and succession rules, until 7/10/34, when it changed to a Council of twenty-four delegates. Prior to this change, in 1933 the delegates from the Southern Navajo Agency (where John Hunter was superintendent) and their alternates had included Henry Taliman (Jim Shirley), Albert G. Sandoval (Chis Chilly Taahglooni), Black Moustache (Leo Parker) and Frank Cadman (Denet Tso) (cited in letter from John Collier to John Hunter, 5/22/33 on file in Tribal Council Organization Committee file, Saint Michaels Mission).

In the 1930s problems increased; grazing policies and stock reduction were needed, and the gap between the elected officials and the Navajo people widened. Jake Morgan and the separatists represented one of the factions, and the chairman, Tom Dodge, resigned on 3/30/36 to become assistant to E. R. Fryer (superintendent of Consolidated Navajo Agency 1936-42). On 11/24/36 the Council passed a resolution calling for reorganization and was then declared defunct. The members of the executive committee were charged with canvassing the reservation to identify local leadership, explain the purpose of the Council and learn the choice of the local people for delegates who would meet at Window Rock as a constitutional assembly for the purpose of considering, drafting and adopting a constitution and bylaws for the Navajo people.

Father Berard Haile, who served as adviser for the canvassing, described the process and results in a 112-page typed manuscript dated 4/19/37 entitled "With the Reorganization Committee of the Navajo Tribal Council 1936-37," on file at Saint Michaels. The canvassing committee included Henry Taliman (former chairman), Marcus Kanuho (secretary), Fred Nelson, George Bancroft, Nalnishi, Allan Neskahi, Chee Dodge, Dashne Chischilliege and Jim Shirley plus Father Berard (Haile 1937a:7).

The meeting in District 10 (Chinle, Salina Springs, Rough Rock, Nazlini and Frazeis) was held on 12/15/36 and was described as follows (*Ibid.*: 16-18):

> Addresses [were made] by Jim Shirley and nesk'ahi, while Henry Taliman, Jim and Tóaheedliini answered questions. Some of the younger men from Frazeis desired special meetings and even suggested to take a vote among themselves at various local meetings and send the names into the Agency. Others, especially ciishch'ilí from lower Chinle Valley and Ben Gorman, objected to these suggestions, as did Frank Mitchell, while the committee refused to consider the proposition. Finally ciishch'ilí tó'aheedlíini was proposed and seconded by most of the Chinle contingent. Reed Winney (zhił ł'ahni łichíi) was mentioned by John Gorman. (This hardly a serious candidate.) Finally Ben Gorman (Hatałin binálí) who spoke fairly well on making the nominations at this meeting.
>
> For tók' eh hasbį'í (Black Mountain Store), hastiin nééz ts' ósí was mentioned as the choice of that district by residents and Frank Mitchell who vouched for him. But bídáya nneezí seemed to have a strong following there (preferred t'iis yáázh łání). Zhíili tso — (?) and · Walker Norcross (boγwósh-gizhi biye') (John Brown preferred dáγanneezí as representative of entire district. He has apparently no use for tóaheedlíini and Frank Mitchell and spoke well of tsiishch'ili of Frazies). Another man occurred to Jim and Henry Taliman as we drove along the rim of Nazlini, namely tsiish chi'ilin biγe' (known as hastiin tsé'élká'í at the lakes in Chinle Valley). We felt that these men could be substituted at Window Rock for some of the inferior men suggested at Chinle. Reed Winney's remarks, that the committee were crooks and contradicted statements made at the Senate Committee hearings, were resented.

The canvassing of the reservation was completed 3/9/37, and seventy members were chosen by the committee on March 10. In District 10, the Haile manuscript (1937a:101) shows the following choices:

1. Ółta'í (Frank Mitchell, Chinlee)
2. bilį dalbáhí cé łání (Salina)
3. adilóhí biγe' (Eli Smith, Nazlini)
4. bináá'łabáhí (John Foley bik'is of tsé' ch'ízhí, Rough Rock)

When the latter did not appear, bídáya nneezí of tó k'éhasbį'í, Black Mountain Store, was substituted.

The Constitutional Assembly was called to meet 4/5/37. On 4/9/37 it met; [members received their red ribbon counselor's badge] and [the group] declared itself the reorganized Council. Henry Taliman was elected chairman, Roy Kinsel, vice chairman. Taliman appointed J. C. Morgan, Frank Mitchell of Chinlee, Jim Shirley of Sawmill, Roy hashk'aan of Gray Mountain and Robert Curly of Leupp to constitute a committee for drafting the constitution. The chairman appointed Morgan the committee chairman (Haile 1937a:104, 106). (For another account of this, see Parman 1976:162-167.)

Tribal minutes available at Saint Michaels show that Frank was a member of this Tribal Council in 1937 and 1938, and that he served on the Constitutional Committee, the Executive Committee and the Grazing Committee.

The Secretary of the Interior issued "The Rules of Tribal Council Constitutions" on 7/26/38, which established a Council of seventy-four delegates with four-year terms to be elected from within land management districts by ballots identifying candidates by colored ribbons. The first election was held 9/27/38, and Frank did not return to Window Rock when the newly organized Council convened on 11/8/38, under Jacob Morgan as chairman and Howard Gorman as vice chairman.

The Tribal Council has continued to function with the 1938 structure, with the addition of amendments regarding pictorial ballots, voter registration, salary increases and increase of meeting days per year, among others. For further information on the Tribal Council, see Young (1961:371-429) and Shepardson (1963).

9. The first woman who ever served on the Tribal Council was Lilly J. Neil. According to her daughter, Ruth N. Bridgeman, who now lives in Kayenta, Arizona, and who was located through the assistance of Augusta Sandoval, Lilly served as tribal delegate from 1946-1950 while Sam Ahkeah was chairman. She was reelected in 1951, but was seriously injured in an automobile accident on her way to a Council meeting. After forty-seven days of unconsciousness and subsequent brain damage, she selected a man from her community to take her place. Lilly and this man, Tyler Harrison, worked together (Bridgeman, Personal communication, May 5, 1972). Although Frank says he served on the Council with the first woman delegate, it appears that he was a judge during Lilly's term, and was defeated in his attempt at reelection in 1951, when Lilly was successful.

10. Robert Young, University of New Mexico, provided the copies of the minutes of the meeting of the Tribal Executive Committee 5/2-3/38, which are included in Appendix D-1. A perusal of these gives insights into Frank's functioning as a political leader, and when these are considered in retrospect, it is possible to see that a number of his useful statements and recommendations later found their way into the election system. The same is true of some of his statements regarding the future need for singers, made to Clifford Barnett on 5/17/62 and discussed in Chapter 11, n. 1.

11. For a brief account of this trip which occurred shortly after June 17, 1937 and what ensued, see Parman 1976:170-172, especially note 22.

12. Frank learned how to knit these socks from his brother John. He continued making them, using pieces of umbrella ribs for needles, until 1966.

13. The Constitutional Committee, unwillingly chaired by Jacob Morgan, finished its work on 10/25/37 and sent the proposed constitution to the Commissioner on Indian Affairs. (See Young 1961:400-407 for document.) The Secretary of the Interior refused to approve it, evidently because of tribal conflict and dissension. The "Proceedings of the Navajo Tribal Council and Executive Committee, 1/17-20/38" (p. 147) show Howard Gorman remarking that the Navajo Constitution was so complicated in some places that it should be remodeled with the solicitor (Felix Cohen), Superintendent Fryer, and the Constitutional Committee working together, since it would govern next summer's election. The Council then voted to keep the Constitutional Committee working until the new draft was finished. However, the document "Rules of Tribal Council Constitutions," issued by Secretary of the Interior Harold L. Ickes (see Young 1961:407-411) superseded any further developments, and the constitution was never adopted. For additional information on the proposed constitution and the political reasons for its failure, see Parman 1976:160-192.

14. Although Frank ran for reelection on 9/27/38, he was not reelected. In 1951, he again ran for the position of Tribal Council delegate from District 10. This election was the first one to use a pictorial ballot, and Frank's ballot photo appears as Fig. 10. Copies of ballots provided by Lee J. Correll and Saint Michaels Mission, and a "Report on Navajo Tribal Election, March 3-5, 1951," provided by Robert Young, show that in District 10 the results were: Joe Carroll-203; Walker Norcross-86; and Frank Mitchell-61. Hence Joe Carroll served as the District 10 delegate 1951-1954 (and later as well in the 1950s).

Interestingly enough, among the very few of Frank's papers still intact at the Mitchells in 1971 were copies of Tribal Council minutes from 7/22/53, 7/23/53 and 7/31/53, along with a copy of the report on the delegation to Washington, dated 2/10-21/62. When asked on 8/3/71 if Frank had served as an alternate for Joe Carroll in 1951-1954, Augusta Sandoval said no, but that he often had received copies of minutes of meetings and borrowed the same from others, since, although he lost his bid at reelection, he remained actively interested in political affairs and attended as many important meetings as he could.

15. The Courts of Indian Offenses were established in the 1930s, with the six judges in charge of them being appointed by the Commissioner of Indian Affairs and confirmed by a two-thirds vote of the Tribal Council. According to the Department of Interior document "Law and Order Regulations," dated 2/15/37, #85143, one or more chief judges with regular and permanent duties were envisioned; these would be aided by two or more associate judges

called to service upon request, and eligible for per diem compensation. All judges were to hold four-year terms and were eligible for reappointment if they were members of the tribe under the court's jurisdiction, and if they had never been convicted of a felony, or, within the past year, a misdemeanor (see Appendix D-2).

The minutes of the Tribal Council for Nov. 20-21, 1939, contain interesting discussions of law and order (pp. 67-74, 102). The minutes from the same body for July 10-13, 1945, show a discussion regarding salary increase for Navajo judges and policemen (pp. 32-36), with an annual income of $1,500 and $5.00 a day being proposed for judges and associate judges, respectively. By 1945, district councilmen were being polled for recommendations, which were then received by the Tribal chairman and general superintendent, both of whom actually chose the judges. Page 35 of the July 10-13 minutes shows that the 1945 judges (appointed in 1938) had non-renewable terms as required by law. Jury trials on the reservation were also requested seemingly as a way of requesting action on the Law and Order Regulations of 1934 and 1935, drafted by Tom Dodge, Mr. Mueller and Felix Cohen.

During the 1951-59 period, first five, and then, in 1954, seven judges were elected to office and were included on the ballots used for tribal elections; tribal courts were at Shiprock, Fort Defiance, Chinle, Tuba City and Kayenta. In 1959 the Tribal Council created a judicial branch, and since then six judges and a chief justice have been appointed for life after successfully completing a two-year probationary term and training by the Council's legal staff. For further information, see Shepardson (1965a:250-253) and Young (1961:284-287, 417, 429).

16. The period directly after Fort Sumner was a time when many new ceremonies were introduced on the reservation. Frank told Clifford Barnett (Barnett Fieldnotes for 5/17/62:5) that the greatest number of singers developed right after Fort Sumner, because "the Chiricahua Windway ceremony was picked up from the Apaches down there and it spread like a craze all over the reservation. It was at this time that you gradually had people picking this up and using it for all kinds of illnesses and everybody was becoming a singer. Of course, they only knew this song, but everybody then became singers. Also at this time there was a hand trembling craze. I think that during my childhood, and perhaps the twenty years after Fort Sumner was the time when there was the greatest number of singers on the reservation."

17. No documents could be located to confirm Frank's remark that he alone was chosen from the group of trainees. Although no clarification was possible from tribal records, the years of Frank's judgeship have been specified by Mary Shepardson (Personal communication 9/28/71), who has records of cases handled by him and signed with the following dates: 1946, 1947, 1948, 1949, 1950, 1951. A possibility that Frank was a judge earlier exists in a 1942 report by John Boyden and Walter Miller on law and order conditions of the Navajo Indian Reservation. These authors mention six judges in the

Courts of Indian Offenses, but cite sample cases revealing the identity of only five of them: Sam Jim, John Curley, Slowtalker, Clah and Sidney Phillips. These men served while Fred Croxen was chief of Law and Order, and Phillips, Jim and Curley had sei ved earlier under Charles Ashcroft's leadership of Law and Order, when there were five judges (these three along with Jim Shirley and John Rockbridge). Possibly Frank was the sixth judge under Croxen; his own account, and Augusta Sandoval's comments that he was a judge at the same time as the five specified for Croxen's leadership suggest his years as judge began earlier than 1946.

The Mitchell family provided the following dates for Frank's judgeship: 1946, 1947, 1950 and 1951, respectively confirmed by Agnes' return from overseas, Howard's departure date for Wyoming, Frank's refusal to take a case involving Seya, and a $10'' \times 14''$ pictorial rug woven in brown with black letters by Isabelle, saying "February 8, 1951, Frank Mitchell, Judge, Chinle."

It seems evident that Frank's years as a judge ended in 1951, when he tried unsuccessfully for reelection as a Tribal Council delegate from District 10. He was not on the 1955 ballot in either capacity, and the Tribal Council minutes of 3/2/54 (p. 45) concerning Father Berard Haile's request that the Tribe publish his manuscript of the Blessingway (unapproved and later published by the University of Arizona, see Wyman 1970) show Father Berard referring to Frank with, "he used to be one of your judges." Thus, the only question remaining concerns his possible years of service between 1938-1946, as the sixth judge during Croxen's leadership of the Law and Order division.

Department of the Interior Document #85143, "Law and Order Regulations," dated February 15, 1937, was most likely the "book" used by the lawyer to teach the Navajo trainees. This was also probably used as a reference by Frank, who could not read English but could have asked his children to help him with the sections in question. The document appears as Appendix D-2 of this book.

18. Peyote was introduced to the Navajos by the Utes in the 1930s (see Aberle 1966 for further details). One of Frank's granddaughters, Mae, reported (7/2/71) that Frank had told her he once took peyote but that it had made him vomit violently, and that snakes and wolves had come out in that vomit, so he never tried it again.

19. This and the next four paragraphs are from Mary Shepardson's interviews with Frank during the fall of 1965 (Shepardson 1965b).

20. The recall of earlier judges for consultation on specific cases is not an unusual practice among the Navajos. For example, on 8/29/64 a man came to the Mitchells to ask Frank to go up near Lukachukai in a few days to settle a question about a grazing permit. According to Frank, an old woman's sheep were at an illegal place, and he had had the same case earlier when he was a judge.

21. This particular reference to Father Berard Haile's work with Laughing Singer has not been possible to document. Although Frank says this Nightway bundle was sent to the Museum of Navajo Ceremonial Art, the museum has no record of its acquisition. In view of the time and the ceremonial affiliation, it is quite possible that Frank is telling his version of the story recounted in Haile (1947:80-89). The Nightway paraphernalia discussed by Haile ended up in the museum at the Franciscan Saint Francis Seminary, Mount Healthy, Ohio.

10. The Wider Ceremonial World

Births and deaths in Frank's family . . . ceremonials for Tall Woman: Mountaintopway, Shootingways, Ghostway, Beautyway, Windway, Blessingways, Chiricahua Windways, Mountaintopway, Flintway . . . ceremonials for Frank: Navajo Windway, Flintway, Female Shootingway, Flintway, Female Shootingway, Enemyway . . . John Mitchell's death . . . more ceremonials for Frank: Male Shootingway with Sun's house, Blessingways, minor ceremonies . . . his children's ceremonials: Mary – Ghostway, Shootingways; Seya – Shootingway, Blessingways; Agnes – Protection Rite; Ruth – Shootingway; Howard – Enemyway, Shootingway; Augusta – Blessingway; Isabelle – Mountaintopway, Shootingway, Navajo Windway, Protection Rite and Blessingway, Ghostway.

While I was a judge, I would be called to go to Tuba, Leupp and various other places, like Crownpoint, Two Hats, Fort Defiance, Shiprock and Teec Nos Pos. The government car would come to our place, and I would go off in that when I was called. When I was home, I would be asked to go around doing my Blessingway ceremony. Sometimes I would be called to do that ceremony while I was waiting for the government car; if it did not come, I would just take my sacred bundle and go off to do the ceremony. I carried on like that for a number of years. Because I was on the go so much, I sometimes lost track of what was happening around here at that time. [1]

While I was serving as headman for this community and before I started to work with that Council, several more children were born here at home. [2] There was Howard, whom we nicknamed "Big Man" and "Kǫǫzhi"; he was born in 1922 and went to the Chinle school and then to Saint Michaels. He worked with his brother Seya after that, and then a baseball accident ruined one of his eyes; the operation and ceremony we had for that did not cure it. He has had the Enemyway and Shootingway performed for him and was interested for a time in learning my Blessingway. Much of the time, he is off the reservation doing wage work in other places.

Another girl, Augusta, whom we called "Lili," was born about two years after Howard. She went to school in Chinle, then Saint Michaels, and then she went to Saint Catherine's in Santa Fe before her marriage to Cecil Sandoval. Another girl, Isabelle, came along after Augusta, in 1926. This girl, whom we called "Small Woman," never went to school but just stayed home and helped around this place. She is my youngest.

The other children were all moving around during these days. Seya went to school in Albuquerque until I had him moved to Fort Apache so he would be closer to us. Then he did odd jobs at Lukachukai around the school and at the mission. He did the same here in Chinle before he started raising a family with Della. Agnes trained as a nurse and later, during the second World War, went to the South Pacific area in the service. She met her husband in San Francisco, California, and then settled off the reservation. Another girl, Ruth, began raising a family with Leo Shirley, who was farming, herding and doing wage work for others. He left for work at Sawmill and married another woman. Some years later Ruth had more children with Wilson Yazzie.

These years were also full of more deaths in our family. Of course, Man Who Shouts died in 1922, the year Howard was born. Then our second oldest girl, Mary, whom we also called "Go Yázhí," died after becoming ill at the school in Albuquerque. She was brought home from there unconscious, and she died here without recovering. We never knew why she died, but the hand-trembler we had, after she was brought back here, said that she must have smoked something to make her crazy as she was. When she came back here she just talked and talked about smoking. One lady who knew her at school told us that she stayed with Mexicans and Navajos there, and many people thought she probably got some kind of weed from them and that that had killed her.

I demanded that Reuben Perry come out here and explain to me why I had not been informed of her condition.[3] He did come to a meeting, and Chic Sandoval did the interpreting for that. I told him that the government was treating our children like they were trash to be disposed of whenever the government felt like it. Mr. Perry apologized to me and said that they would see that it never happened again.

Before this girl died, one of my wife's brothers died. Then Mary passed away, and then the wife of Man Who Shouts passed on, too. While she was still alive, we used to live where my daughter Mary Davis does now; we had that whole big field. Most of our land came from my wife's people, and after we were given that land, I gave that part of it to Mary.

While my wife's mother was living, she used to visit us all the time, and she would also go around visiting others. When Augusta was five or six years old, she used to go around with her. That old lady would just walk in the heat with a towel over her head. I used to tell my children not to be scared of old-age people, those who were going to die of old age.

This old lady used to love tomatoes, and some of our children used to go over to her place when they were small to see if she were all right and to see if she had any canned tomatoes they could eat. When she became ill, we built her a special structure in which to stay. She was really an old-age person; her hair never turned white, and she never lost her eyesight or her hearing. It was really wonderful; she was really old when she passed away.

When she died in the place we had made for her, we wrapped her up in a blanket. It was late in the fall when that happened, and the corn was just about ripe. The wash was running full, and some of the men around here helped carry her body across. Then the priest from the mission came down and took her body up there and had a funeral for her. She was buried in the old cemetery behind the mission up there, towards the wash. The structure she died in has now fallen down into the wash; some of the children used to play in it before that happened.

After the wife of Man Who Shouts died, Tall Woman and I got all of their stock. Our eldest daughter Mary took care of that. We did not let her go to school, and she used to tease me about this all the time. Father Cormac used to call her Big Schoolboy's daughter, and she used to tease me about this name, which was given her because we would not let her go to school.

Another of my children, David, died after the wife of Man Who Shouts had passed away. David had not gone to school; instead he had stayed around here and done jobs. He got sick here at home. We rushed him to Ganado hospital, where they put him in an oxygen tent. He lasted five or six days there and then he died. He was about thirteen when he died; he was just old enough to handle a man's farming and horse work. We never found out why that happened, although some said he had something called spinal meningitis. He was buried in that same cemetery[4] next to the wife of Man Who Shouts. Seya, Howard, Woody and I helped with his burial, which was in 1936 or 1937.

Shortly after David died, there was a Squaw Dance in the Canyon. At that dance, Seya's wife's father, a man by the name of John Brown, spoke harshly and criticized Chic Sandoval, Curly Hair and me; all of us were councilmen at that time. I was peeved and upset after David died; I had just returned from the hospital. I was so upset that I shoved him around for his talk. Man Who Shouts had told me that I would have to go through life with all of these experiences; he had said that the deaths that you feel the most are those of your own children. I went to that dance on horseback, and John Brown was on foot when that happened. Somebody interfered, and then John went and got the police. He reported that he had been attacked by an intoxicated man. Several of my close friends were with me when John Brown came back with the police. When he came, I lost my temper again. The man I was with grabbed me and told me to leave him alone. The police could see that I was not drunk, so they took John away from me and told him to stay away.

John had been criticizing the three of us for not doing our official duties correctly as councilmen for the Tribe. He had been saying those things while he was in the middle of a crowd. Sometime later, I met him alone. He apologized for what he had said. I told him that I had gotten so angry about that because I had been insulted just after I had lost one of my own children, and I was not in any condition to control myself. So we just let it drop there and have remained good friends since then.

Some years after that, in the middle 1940s, my brother Tom Mitchell died. He lived at Tsaile and used to come down to our place a lot. His hair was long, and he wore it tied up; it was just starting to get gray when he died. Another brother of mine, Jim, passed away a couple of years after that. He died when it was winter; he was living with his own family up in Black Mountain at that time. So during those years when I worked for the Tribe we had to face a lot of deaths and family burials.

We were also busy having ceremonies around here during those years; they were for different members of the family. My wife, Tall Woman, was all right for some years after we had the Navajo Windway for her. That was way back when she was still a young woman and I was working at the sawmill. But as the years passed she began to get sick again. So I went and got Walter Staley from the Canyon for Mountaintopway, Shootingway and Ghostway. The Ghostway is a witch ceremony and goes for five nights; of course I stood the expense of that.

Soon after that time, we were living right here, and we had a patch of alfalfa over there. One day when the alfalfa was high, my wife went out in the field to cut some of it to feed the horses at noon. She grabbed a snake in that bunch of alfalfa while she was cutting it with the scythe, and it bit her. On that account, she had a five-night Beautyway ceremonial which was sung by Fingerless Man.

It was a rattlesnake that bit Tall Woman. We only have rattlesnakes and sidewinders that are poisonous around here; we have no diamondbacks or copperheads, and our other snakes are harmless. That was more or less an accident; Tall Woman grabbed the hay that had the snake in it. Of course if a snake is waiting for you, then it will jump at you from a distance. But this was an accident.

Awhile after that, we were living here in the shed in the summertime, and Tall Woman had a loom set up on the other side of the room there. She had dug a passage by the cross poles. One night she stepped over there with her baby; I think it was the girl, Mary, who died later in school. She was a baby then. I slept away from them with the other children. Early in the morning I heard Tall Woman get up and light the fire; by that time, the baby woke up and started crying. So she went back over there and lay down beside the baby and started nursing it. While nursing, she would stretch out her arm and the baby would rest on it. It happened that her hand was right over that passageway, and a snake bit her. It was no accident that the snake was in that hole there. She jumped up and said, "Something has bitten me here!" So I got up and ran outside, and sure enough, there was a rattlesnake crawling away from the hole. That is the one I tried to split lengthwise on account of that. I killed it. Because of that, Tall Woman had Slim Man sing a five-night Windway for her.

Of course that ceremonial was done after the wound had healed. We used herbs to treat it; after it was no longer an open sore, then we had a singer come. The reason I am certain that it was "Mary Number Two" who was the baby then is because she was the only child we had who had to be fed with a nursing bottle. Since Tall Woman had been bitten by a snake, she had to stop feeding her from her breasts.

I should mention that the evening before Tall Woman was bitten by the rattlesnake, John Mitchell had come over here. You know he lived alone, and he came over to my place in the summertime. He got to asking me about my version of Blessingway, about what was done in the beginning. So we were comparing our legends and discussing things like how the moccasin game was done. He said, "We were told that we should not talk about these things in the summertime when there are bears and snakes out and when there is thunder." It was midsummer when this happened. But he got to questioning me, and we talked about it that evening until about midnight, and then he went back. So that following morning, when my wife was bitten by the snake, I kind of thought that I had done something that I should not have done by talking about these things that belong in the wintertime.

But the understanding that we had was that after she had the first Beautyway ceremonial by Fingerless Man, she would be immune from any more of that. We were told that once you have been attacked or injured by a snake and you have this particular ceremonial to remove the effects, the snakes will respect you, and you have to respect the snakes. Therefore, you are not to abuse the snakes, and the snakes will not bother you. But this time, that snake bit her after she was supposed to be immune from them. So that was the reason we had this Windway performed over her. It is not common for snakes to do that.

Of course, whenever Tall Woman was sick or not feeling well, we also did minor ceremonies for her. In between times, she went to the hospital in Fort Defiance for treatments. It's customary to have a Blessingway whenever a woman becomes pregnant in order to have a good birth, and sometimes her pains or things like that required those ceremonies. I think she had the Blessingway about five or six times.

Of course after those ceremonies, there was the Chiricahua Windway. That was performed sixteen times, counting the last one we had for her. Those were done just to make her feel well. Then about four or five years ago [c. 1959-1960] she had a major ceremonial, Mountaintopway, by Tall Man's Son. We had that for her on the advice of hand-tremblers. They diagnosed her case as needing that ceremonial.

The main trouble with Tall Woman all these years was indigestion. Because of these severe attacks of indigestion, Tall Man's Son performed the five-night Mountaintopway over her. We noticed the results right away. The pains all left her, the aches all disappeared. Therefore, we had a waiting period of only about a week before he came back for the second, one-night ceremonial. In addition, there was one other major ceremonial I overlooked, and that was the Shootingway done by Sand Man. That was some time back.

Tall Woman was sick most of the time when we were having these ceremonials. We were trying different things for her. These illnesses started to come on her after her third child. From then on, she had a good deal of sickness. We thought it might be her appendix or her gall bladder. You see, we have had the same experience with Mary and Ruth and others who have had gall bladder operations. Whenever you get this trouble it does not take long for it to get very bad. In two or three years' time, it is dangerous. But with Tall Woman, I guess it was gradually building up all during those years.

The most frustrating thing was that whenever she went to the hospital, the doctors always said after examining her, "She does not have gall bladder trouble." They could never find anything wrong with her insides. So whenever she came back from the hospital, we would try our own ceremonies again.

Finally last winter [1963] we learned that Tall Woman's problem was gall bladder after all. The doctors did not think it was advisable to operate on her because of her age. But I said, "Well, it is going to kill her anyhow, so let's take a chance and have her operated on." All of the children agreed to that, and that is the last thing we had for her [by 1964]. She did not have any ceremonials when she came back home from the hospital.

Right now, whenever she does hard work or any lifting, she begins to feel those pains. But that is all she complains about. I guess that is the aftereffect of the operation. They took some stones, just little pebbles, out of her gall bladder. That trouble was the cause of her illness for most of her life; maybe its effects were slowed down by having all these ceremonials.

There's no question that Tall Woman has had a lot of singing for just one person. She has been sick all of her life. She has always had pain. So she has been in and out of the white man's hospital too, sometimes staying a month, sometimes a whole year. Then a few years ago, the team ran off with the wagon, and she was thrown out of the wagon and broke her wrist. At that time, Jacob Azye sang Flintway for her. On top of that, he did the one-night ceremonial for her. So that completed half of that for her. She has the other half to think about, I guess.

I myself was also having pains during the time when I was doing these various jobs, such as serving on the Council, and then as a judge. After that, the people I had known from way back talked me into being a Chapter officer in the Chinle Chapter House.[5] In my younger days, I was always in good shape; I did not have many ceremonies done over me then. Up to 1937, I remember that I was healthy in every way; then I was made a councilman and from then on, I have been sick, on and off. I do not remember having many ceremonies done before that; sometimes it seems as if I had a better life when I was not anything important, when I was just out wandering around, gambling and only worrying about the things that could go wrong with that.

I do not really know why doing those jobs made me sick, but I think it was from the fact that I tried to talk to the People while I was a councilman and while I was a Chapter officer. I tried to correct them in various ways when they were doing wrong. Most of the time, the People did not like to hear such talk from me. There were some, of course, who were glad to have my comments and always listened to the advice I gave. Most of them, however, did not care to listen, and in return, they would say things back to me. I figure these things may have had a bad effect on me.

The old people used to say that if you had things of value, like cattle, sheep or things like that, others who did not have them would be jealous. They would try to witch you or get you in such a way that you would not have so many good things coming your way. These people used to say the same thing about the way you talked to others, about how well you could talk to the People. I think they were right about that. When you are good at talking to the People, others get jealous and try to hurt you in any way they can. Not everybody can talk to the People and correct them, and there are only very few who are brought up into high positions like that. I think what the People used to say about getting witched or something like that had a lot to do with it. All of the time when I was nothing, I was all right. But when I got above the People, I started getting sick, and I know it was from those who did not like me and who always said bad things about me.

According to my Blessingway story, the People used to say that there were two groups, good and bad people. The bad people would ask the spirits to harm people whom they did not like. In the Blessingway, you pray to the holy beings and they, in turn, bless you and help everything go well for you. But I really think that bad thoughts from those who didn't like me had something to do with my sickness.

As we know from the story that goes with the Protection Rite, the Twins had to encounter six obstacles before they arrived at their father's home. First Man did not intend that everything should be good, but he did not want everything to be all bad. So instead, he put six good things and six bad things there, and the Twins had to conquer the evil ones. That is the reason that there has always been bad and good; they were equally divided according to the intention of First Man.[6]

When I became a judge, I had to punish people for their wrongdoings; I had to sentence them and fine them or send them to jail. Because of that, I was despised by many of them. They thought that I did that just for meanness, and they would say bad things about me. Maybe all of those things are having an effect on me now, because I am not getting better anymore.[7] People would never tell me to my face that they thought I was a witch, but I think they were wishing me bad things. I have no proof of that, but it is only natural when one person is against another for some reason, that they should want to hurt that person.

As far as I am concerned, I do not believe in these witches. Therefore I have had nothing to do with them. But of course, there are any number of people who believe in them. Sometimes you will have a fuss with a person who says, right to your face, "I hope you die soon. I wish death on you." Well, something like that makes you worry and think about it. I guess in that case you could use the Protection Rite for self-protection. But witches do not fit in any part of the story of the things that the two boys encountered on their way to see their father. That is why I do not use the Protection Rite for that purpose.

If there were a person who wished evil on me or who had evil purposes against me or someone else, I could perform ceremonies using these Protection songs, and that person would be safe. Those evil things would have no effect. You can use these Protection Prayers if someone wishes you dead or sick or injured. You just use them for your own good health; you do not use them against someone or because you have a certain person in mind who may have evil thoughts against you. These Protection songs and prayers are generally used for good health; they are not normally used for witchcraft at all. They are there to protect you against things such as contagious diseases and epidemics that kill people. Now, of course, if the ones that I treat with those songs and prayers are not affected by that, then, maybe I'm the witch.[8]

As far as I am concerned, I personally do not believe in witches. But I have been told by two different persons who were star-gazing that they saw someone bewitching a Navajo. But still they have no proof of that. A lot of those things are exaggerated. It's not as true or as big as the way they tell it. Of course, when I am singing my Blessingway I watch to see what effect my ceremony is having. Some people have been restored to health and are living now. Others did not respond; their sicknesses went on, and finally they passed away.

Now, I cannot say that the person died because of witchcraft. I have no proof of that. On the other hand, I have no proof to say that because I performed these ceremonies, the person who was bewitched was saved and is living now. There are too many things that come into this life, and too many ways that a person can get various kinds of sicknesses. If these things have nothing to do with witchcraft, then why should people be performing ceremonies to get rid of witchcraft? There are just too many other things that can cause sickness.

After I started working on the Council, and began serving as judge, and then later when I was elected to be a Chapter officer, and when I was helping make some of the films for the government and for Hollywood,[9] I started having pains again. They would just stay with me, in spite of the ceremonies I started having. I was serving both the government and my own people much

Mabel Bosch, photographer

FIG. 11. Frank Mitchell, 1957

of this time, and I cannot recall just when some of these ceremonies were done for me. I was always on the go, and when I came home, I would sometimes not feel very well at all, and I would then call on someone to perform ceremonies for me.

After the Chiricahua Windway I already told you about — the one I had for my back pains when I was working at the sawmill — the next ceremony I had performed for me was the Navajo Windway, sung by Slim Man's Son, whom we also call Francis. I had that when my wife was bitten by that rattlesnake when she was nursing the baby. I took the snake outside and killed it. People had told me that in a case like that you should split the snake completely open, from head to tail. So I wanted to do just that. I took some baling wire and tied the snake's lower and upper jaws and tried to split it all the way to the end. But instead of doing that, I just tore it part of the way, and I got splashed by the milklike juice inside of it. So, when I was not feeling well and when my back was still bothering me, I asked the hand-tremblers to come to try to find out what was causing that. They said, "What did you do with a snake? You have done something that you shouldn't with a snake. What did you do?"

Well, I knew what I had done. When I had this Beautyway earlier, I was forbidden to abuse snakes. I was supposed to leave them absolutely alone, but here I had gone and tried to split one open. So, on that account, I went to Black Mountain and got Francis. I wanted some prayers for that; he did not know the prayers, so he and I went and got his father, Slim Man. His father is the singer who does that, and Francis, his oldest son, is the one taking it over now. The old man is completely blind. He could not do Windway for me because some time in the past he performed it for my wife, and it is not customary for a singer to perform the same ceremonial over a man and that man's wife. Slim Man came here and gave the prayers for me, but it was Francis who did the singing during that five-night ceremonial.

I guess that Navajo Windway was done about four years after the other Windways. After that, I was all right until I injured myself by lifting something that was too heavy. I strained myself while carrying a heavy pole that I wanted to set up at the gate of one of my fences. I drove a wagon up to Cottonwood Grove, cut that big log and lifted it into the wagon by myself. I didn't know right away that I had injured myself. I came home from there and Reid Winnie came by; he wanted to use me over at his place for a Blessingway for his wife. So I went over there with him in his car. That night in his hogan, while I was saying the prayers, I began to feel those pains in my chest. I just barely finished the prayers. The rest of that night I was in agony. In the morning, I told Reid that I did not think I could stand the pain anymore and that he had better take me home; I felt pretty sick. So he brought me home.

The people from here went and got White Plant Man's Son from Sawmill Mountain to come over here and sing Flintway for me. He stayed with me for about seven nights. After that he lost his voice and just left. Then we got another man to come and do the singing; that was Yellow Man's Son Number Two. He sang the Female Shootingway. You see, there is a version that is called Female Shootingway, Lifeway. It is the same as the regular Female Shootingway, only they call it Lifeway when it is used for an injury like mine. There are Lifeway songs in it, and that is the reason it is used. He sang over me for about six days, and I felt better. That man is still living today.

Not quite a month later, we went and got the first man, White Plant Man's Son, to come back and sing a one-night ceremony from the Flintway over me; that is Lifeway, too.

During this last singing by White Plant Man's Son, one of my close friends, Long Moustache, came. He was here that night and started singing for me. The next morning after the singer left, he said to me, "My nephew,[10] I think you made a mistake. When you are injured like that and you have this Lifeway curing ceremonial, do not have the one-night singing over yourself until you are completely recovered. Otherwise your injury is likely to become something more permanent."

I think that Long Moustache was right about that. That was the way that the old people usually did things; they would sing over you if you were injured, and maybe get you well again. But even when you were on your feet again, they did not have this one-night, final night over you right away. They usually waited to be sure that the injury was altogether healed; otherwise it might become a permanent illness.

You remember that I told you how singers in the early days stayed with you as long as they thought you needed it. That is what Man With a Hair Bundle did for me when I was sick from that wrestling when I was young. Those oldtime singers would stay with you until they thought that you were able to get about, and they knew that they were curing you, that they were getting you well. Now many singers do not bother about that anymore. They may sing for three or two days, and then they begin to say, "Well, I'm out of voice, I'm getting hoarse." They start making excuses.

In a case like my strained back, it was obvious that I was injured; there was no doubt about it. In cases like that where it is pretty plain that the person has been injured or has a broken bone, the oldtime singers would stay with that person until the bone or the injury healed. But in cases where they were suspicious about an injury or were not positive, they would experiment just to see how the singing was affecting you. And maybe after a certain number of days, maybe about ten days would be the limit, if they saw that there was no effect or change, then they would say, "Well, perhaps it isn't an injury that is making you sick; it must be something else." So then they would stop their songs and leave.

My first Flintway was probably a year or a little more after that Navajo Windway. Less than a year later, I asked this second singer of Lifeway to give me his final night singing. That was a one-night version of the Female Shootingway, Lifeway, that was sung by Yellow Man's Son Number Two. I had that because that sickness just seemed to hang on, even though I was taking care of myself. It is customary that we ask them to finish up the singing with a one-night ceremonial.

Well, that sickness seemed to hang on, and I did not feel altogether well. It seemed as if I would not get over that feeling. In between ceremonials, occasionally I would go to the hospital for treatments; at other times I was busy working as a judge and doing other things for the Tribe and the government.

Because I was not getting over most of those pains, my family encouraged me to have an Enemyway. That was the next big ceremonial I had done for me, and that was the first time I had ever had an Enemyway. That was in 1959. When I was diagnosed by hand-tremblers and star-gazers, I was advised to have the Enemyway.

There was a question as to what kind of scalp should be used. A white school teacher had been hauled in my wagon from Fort Defiance to Gallup after she had died. There was no box to put her in, and she smelled pretty bad. She was wrapped in blankets, but she was decomposed, and I smeared my hand in her blood. There was no car available, so I had to take her. The hand-trembler said that the scalp should be of a white person because of that, so that is what we had for the Enemyway. Perhaps we did the wrong thing; perhaps we should have had it for the mummy that I brought down from the Canyon for those white people. When you have the Enemyway it has to be for some particular ghost, either of a white person, or those ancient people that the remains belonged to, or it could be any tribe of Indians outside the Navajos, or Mexican or Spanish.

Another thing that indicated I should have an Enemyway was something that happened between me and my brother, John. I was hired to do a Blessingway for my nephew's child. Seya came from Beautiful Mountain to John's place with some wine. They went to where the ceremony was being held. I said, "It's good that you came; my voice is not too good. I need help."

During the day, those two kept going out and drinking. Later John came back in and started talking about the past. He said that no one was sympathetic to him or would speak up in his defense. He said that no one had helped him out when he had been called into court.

I caught the hint: I was a judge at that time. But now I said, "I don't like this way of talking. We're here for sacred purposes. I wonder if you are referring to me?"

John kept making worse and worse remarks. I asked, "Who are you referring to?"

John said, "You, yes!"

I said, "You're in no condition to be talking like that; let's discuss it when you are sober."

John said, "You drink, too. Why do you accuse me if you do it too?"

I said, "You should go home and get sober."

Seya took him by the arm and said, "Let's go home, uncle." But John kept talking as he left.

During that night when I was singing, I was helped out by someone who knew my songs. Near the morning, I felt my stomach bloating up. I just made it through to the end of the ceremony in the morning.

When I got through, Seya had returned with a car. I could not stand the ride home because the car could not come straight across; because of all the sand in the wash, it had to go around, and I couldn't stand all that bumping. So I started to walk, and I said, "If I am not home when you get there, bring a horse and meet me." Seya did this, and I arrived home on a horse.

We have a kind of emergency treatment for this kind of thing; we take cedar ashes and water, and it makes you vomit. Finally I did that, but later it was diagnosed as requiring Enemyway treatment. We decided to have one for me, but John never gave one penny to help with that ceremonial.[11] I never really got over that attack of bloating up. Many people diagnosed my case, relating it even to other events in my life.

This Enemyway really has to do with whether you have killed or hurt somebody other than your own people. Like, for instance, white people, or any of those nationalities outside of the Navajos. If you have hurt them in any way like that, their ghost is going to come back and bother you, and that is the main purpose of the Enemyway. I had it done for me because I knew I should not have been hauling those remains out of the Canyon and because of that experience with the dead schoolteacher. I thought those things had a lot to do with those pains I had been getting. And since all those other ceremonials that were performed for me did not seem to help much, I had the Enemyway.

Whenever you are not feeling well and think you need an Enemyway, the reason is you are having trouble from the spirit of somebody. We all have something living in us that is taken out of us when we die. And in the case of each one of us, that spirit has a superior that it goes back to. If we have not been treating someone's spirit right during our lives, after it goes back to its superior it can come back and punish us. That is why, whenever there is an Enemyway to be performed, the person who is having it thinks he has offended some alien spirit, like that of a white person. If he thinks he might have hurt or injured somebody like that in the past, then it might be their angry spirit that is bothering him.

What they do is prepare the rattlestick.[12] They fix it up nicely, polish it, put red ochre on it and then also decorate it with lots of yarn. This resembles the remaking of the spirit that they damaged in the past, the spirit of that outsider; this is a kind of payment for that injury. Fixing up the stick that way is to show that you are trying to make up for what you did. We use this stick for three nights, and then after the Enemyway is all over, we take it back and put it away somewhere where it will not be damaged by anything like fire or livestock walking over it. We put it where it will keep safe until nature gets rid of it.

Since that Enemyway, we have received the stick twice here at our place. That is what you call "bringing the stick over." You cannot have that unless you have had the Enemyway over yourself. After we had the Enemyway right here, then I was just expecting that we would be called on to be Stick Receiver. The first time that happened my granddaughter Linabah was the Stick Girl, and the second time, two years back, it was her sister Marie.

Last summer I received the stick for an Enemyway. I had done that twice before. I have only had one Enemyway done for myself, but I can receive that stick up to four times. Then I must have the Enemyway again. Of course, many times the People do not follow that rule exactly.

During the Enemyway, they give the one-sung-over a special name, a warrior's name. I was given one during my Enemyway. That's a sacred name used only in ceremonials, and I am not supposed to tell it or be known by that in public. In case I have another Enemyway, I'll go by that name again during that. So, you see, I do have other Navajo names besides Big Schoolboy and Big Two Streams Meet Man.

Enemyway was called *nidáá'* until the white people came out here. It was from them that the name "Squaw Dance" came. I think that term "Squaw Dance" came from when they saw the girls dancing. In the story that was told to me long ago, Monster Slayer was the one that was protecting the people. He went out to fight with an enemy called Big God. That is the name of one of the enemies there. The Horned Monster is another one. The third one was Rock Monster Eagle – that was about as big as an automobile, and it had wings. It flew around and would pick up people just anywhere. That is what it fed on; it ate people. The fourth one was Tracking Bear. It was a bear, but it looked more like the lions we have now, only many times bigger. Once it comes on somebody's fresh tracks, it will not stop until it finds you. So that was another enemy that they had here. And Monster Slayer went out to fight all these, and he killed them all. He got rid of them all, and that was where the word *Anaa'jí*, for Enemyway, came in.

Naayéé' means an enemy, or things that are really torturing you, and then *neezghání* means "he has gotten rid of it." So that was where this term *Anaa'jí* came in. *Ana'í* means an enemy that has been gotten rid of. After Monster Slayer got rid of those enemies, he suffered for it later, just like people do now. He was suffering because of these enemies he had killed; their spirits were bothering him. So that is where the first Enemyway was performed. I do not like that word "Squaw Dance." Enemyway makes more sense.

I hope you do not have the feeling that we are going to have an Enemyway because you have been out here visiting us. It is only if someone here has seen many dead white people or helped bury one, or helped with the funeral; that would be something to have an Enemyway for. That is why they do it. As in the case of all these servicemen; they have seen so many dead. Especially the soldiers that were out in front, they may have killed them; in fact I think they just had to kill them.

Shortly after that Enemyway was held for me, John passed away. He had started living alone after that year with that woman from near Sawmill. They had one daughter, Little Left Handed's Daughter-in-law.

About that time, John got the name of Lone Man. He lived on the farmland belonging to my mother and Tall Two Streams Meet Man. He used to stop in there from Fort Defiance and turn over his livestock. John took over that place as his own when Tall Two Streams Meet Man settled down over there with the Coyote Pass Clan. He was always talking about his loneliness and hinting for a woman.

My close friend, Long Moustache, suggested that we go and look around for a woman for John. He said he knew a family where we could get one. We did that and decided on one from below Many Farms. She was the granddaughter of Mr. Left Handed; their family lives below the Chinle bridge.

Long Moustache and John and I went over there and discussed it with them. We got her family's consent and arranged a marriage ceremony for them. We even went down and got Charlie Mitchell to come and perform that ceremony, which was the only time John was ever married in that way. He lived with that woman for three years; they had one child, but it passed away with its mother.

When John got the land that used to belong to Tall Two Streams Meet Man, he put a fence around it and put up a hogan. He tried to add more land that was being used by others, and because of that he got into some fights. But he would take these people to court, where it would be settled in his favor. He was living all alone when he died.

John was like the black sheep in our family; he was different from the rest of us. Maybe it was because he worked in the store; I don't know. I still do not like the treatment that he gave me. We were the only two left of my original family when he died. Now I am the only one.

There is some question as to whether John died naturally or whether he was murdered. But I think that he overdrank and therefore died. The night before he was found dead in the house, he was seen coming from the store on horseback, very drunk. The next morning he was found inside the hogan on the floor. The last person who was with him was Bend of Red Rock Man. He found John and reported it to me early in the morning. It was Bend of Red Rock Man's custom to stay over there overnight, since John took care of his cattle.

That morning, John had taken a tin can containing money; there were eighty-six dollars in there, because Bend of Red Rock Man had counted it and then returned it. He saw John that night coming from the store. He came in there after dark and called to John but got no reply. So he went to bed. Later he woke up and there wasn't a sound anywhere. He got up and lit the lamp and found that John had passed away on his own bed. He started looking for the money, but it was gone.

Then Bend of Red Rock Man came over and woke me up. I told him to go to the police so they could investigate it, but he never did, so it really looks odd. We had to wait for a woman to call the police.

Once before that time, John's house had been robbed of four buckskins, and no clue had ever been turned up for those, either. This is one of the things that he said when he was fussing with me during that Blessingway, that I never did anything to help him when he was in court.

The next morning, Sybil Baldwin came over here to find someone to take care of her children. I asked her if anyone was over at John's, and she said no. I said that the police should have been notified. Sybil said that she had been wondering what would happen to the corn and the peach trees when old man John died. I asked her to help us, and she did. She reported the death to the police and called John's daughter at the Fort Defiance hospital. The police went there and found him dead. They wanted to wait to move him until the investigators came, so those police stayed there watching the place so there would be no disturbance. First, some of them came over here to tell us that they would do that.

Two girls came with John's stepchildren. They were forbidden to go over there, so they came over here to our place. The girls went to Window Rock to get the investigators. Bend of Red Rock Man was over here with me; I was thinking that he was the only one under suspicion. He came in and said that he knew that I thought he was guilty, since he had been the last one there. He hoped that they would not be too hard on him because of that.

I said, "Don't worry; we all know that John drank too much. We knew this before now, and we all told him to stop. Others knew that they could get liquor at his place and that he kept valuables there, too. We told him many times that people might try to kill him over there, but he never paid any attention to what we said."

It was never proven what really happened. The investigators came and took the body to Fort Defiance; down there, the doctors said that John had died of old age. I doubt that, because he was still riding his horse around, his eyes and ears were good, and he was strong enough to do other things. One of his nephews, Billy Mitchell, had already ordered a casket for John once before when he was worried about his health. That casket cost $250. The body was due to come back to the mission here in Chinle for burial.

I went up to John's place; he had told me what property was to be buried with him, what bracelets, set of beads and silver belt. He also wanted a buffalo robe and the horse that he always rode buried with him. His children objected to killing the horse, but I insisted that we go according to his will, and I overruled them. The only thing that the police ever found was that can of money; all of that was recovered.

After John was buried, the will he had made was carried out. I knew that he had made one earlier with Chic interpreting for it. I had asked if I could be present for that, and John had said, "No, I'll count you in." Evidently sometime after that, he made another one and cancelled me out, probably because of that incident when I was performing that Blessingway for my nephew's child and he drank too much and caused trouble. That was about a year before he passed away. When he made that new will, Reid Winnie did the interpreting.

We found out that according to the new will, his surviving daughter, Little Left Handed's Daughter-in-law, got everything — the property in the house, the jewelry, buckskins, land and cattle. John never mentioned his Blessingway bundle in that will; all that it said at the end was that anything that was not already mentioned should go to Herbert Mitchell, whose mother was my mother's sister.

John's money was also not mentioned in the new will; in the first one, he had left it to me, but later, he cancelled that out, too, and did not leave me anything. John had deposited his money with the Catholic mission in Chinle, and eventually that money was split up so that each close relative got about $200. After that had been done, there was still some left. Herbert Mitchell and Emanuel Begay, who were half-brothers from the same mother, were there when that money was being distributed. Emanuel protested on my behalf, and I got $200 because of that.

I thanked the survivors for this cash and told them that I appreciated their action. I was not even complaining about things, and I was a full brother to John. One of his stepsons, Justin Shirley, not his brother Lyn, was complaining a lot, though. He claimed that he was better than the rest, even though he was only a stepson to John. But those complaints didn't work. John had said in his will that Justin had planned to build him a home in the Big Lake area to look after the cattle from on the flat. John had previously said that that would be fine, but in the will, he cancelled that because the house had not been finished before his death.

While these things were happening, my back pains continued without relief and so, about two years ago, I had Gray Man do a nine-night Male Shootingway for me; he did it with the Sun's house screen and all.[13] I had that done because I wanted the bead renewed. You remember that I told you how they give you that bead you are supposed to keep until you have had four performances. Well, Bead Singer's Son had died, and so I threw away that bead and had a new one made. Gray Man advised me on that. You have to throw the bead away when the singer dies. Gray Man also said that when I had had the Shootingway done by Bead Singer's Son, he had used a prayer, but Gray Man did not know that prayer. He said that even White Singer did not know that prayer. So I told him, "All right; suppose you do this: combine all these things with some other prayer." So that is the reason I had it done in the nine-night version. It includes all the five-night and one-night and two-night singing.

I have been telling you about the big ceremonials that have been performed over me, those that were more important and more expensive. Of course, in addition to these five-night and nine-night ceremonials, I have had the Blessingway done for me many times. That is not altogether separate; it comes between each one of these big ceremonials. While I was singing the Blessingway, I was also having minor ceremonies done for myself for various purposes. I have not talked about these because they are just small, just a few hours of ceremonies and prayers.

When Mary was a child she was in good health and had no need of any ceremonials. Of course she probably had some little illness now and then that I usually took care of. After she got married to Woody Davis, she had various short illnesses but did not need anything more than just small ceremonies, like sandpaintings or prayerstick cuttings and things like that. But some time back when old Curly Hair Skinner was still alive, he sang a five-night Ghostway over her with May Holtsoh's daughter.

Then the next one that I recall is when we were all living together there where their home is now. They were drying corn outside there by the small fence, and lightning struck there and also struck the cornfield down below there. On account of that she had a Shootingway, since it has to do with lightning or things that are struck by lightning. That was done by Sand Man, the Son of Bead Singer, before he died. I cannot recall everything that happened to her, but I know that recently she had another Shootingway by Ella Niyaji's brother, Little Man's Son.

Seya had only one big ceremonial, Shootingway. That was recently, after he returned here with his wife and family. He went back over to his old place to look after some lumber that he had set aside. They brought him back here and had this ceremony for him and restored him. Of course he also has had other small ceremonies performed over him, such as one-night Blessingways.

Of course when Agnes was leaving for the service, we had the Blessingway Protection ceremony; that is customary. Of course she is a pretty strong Catholic, but according to the Catholic missionaries, they look on the ceremonial performances as more of a medical treatment than a spiritual matter. That is the way they look at it. It does not concern the soul of a person, it is merely a matter of the welfare of the physical body. So they consider that religion is not involved in the Navajo ceremonies. A lot of them look at it that way, and so do some Navajos.

One time I went with Agnes over to the mission. She saw the statue of the Blessed Virgin standing there. She walked up to it and made the sign of the cross and said some prayers and walked on, so from that I know that she has strong faith in that religion.

Ruth had only one large ceremonial, and that was Shootingway, done by Bead Man's Son. The reason for that was when Mary was down there having her Shootingway, they deposited some prayersticks on the edge of our hayfield, where they were overgrown by weeds. I guess Ruth and Isabelle were burning brush or something and accidentally set a spark there; the prayersticks got burned up. One of them rolled out with some of the plumes still attached. The rest got burned up, but there was that one that did not burn, and that is how they found out.

My son Howard worked off the reservation, and when he came back he was not well. Woody Davis sang a five-night Shootingway over him. He told us that while he was off working, lightning struck near him and he inhaled a lot of the odor of that lightning. So, we had a Shootingway for him.

I sang a Blessingway over Augusta before the birth of her son Augustine. Her labor started quickly, and the baby was born right after I had finished the bathing. Because of that, I waited to complete the Blessingway until that night. According to my teachers, if a woman's labor starts before the bathing, she can go to the hospital for the birth. But if the bathing has already been finished, she should not leave the hogan, unless someone thinks the birth will be difficult and will endanger her life or that of her child.

Isabelle got sick here when she started running off from home and becoming wild and out of control. So we went and got Gray Water, who is now no longer living, and he sang Mountaintopway, a ceremonial concerning bears. The reason we had that bear ceremonial was that Philip Draper had killed a bear up there somewhere in the Canyon and skinned it and brought it down to the Presbyterian mission. They had it spread out on the floor. Isabelle, being a child then, had walked on it with some other children. When she got sick later, the hand-tremblers said, "You've been doing something with a bear hide." So we found out that she did walk on it. Evidently that was her trouble, because as soon as they had that ceremonial she quieted down.

She also had a Shootingway by Bead Man's Son. That was because of what she did with Ruth, burning those prayersticks. She and Ruth had separate ceremonials, but by the same singer. He lived down here, and he was the one that was available all the time here for us to make use of. That was Herbert Mitchell's step-father. In any emergency, we went to him, since he was nearby and we could bring him over. He was a close friend of the family.

Then Francis Slim Man sang Navajo Windway over her. At that time she was coming over here to the hospital because of her lung condition. They had been taking X rays of her lungs, and they said that there was some foggy appearance on them. Her lungs were affected by something. They did not cure it; it kept appearing there in the X ray. And then when she came back, of course we experimented with small ceremonies and finally decided on using this five-night Windway that had to do with lightning. After that was performed, that foggy thing on her lungs disappeared. When she had another X ray taken her lungs had cleared up.

Five or six years ago, I sang a Blessingway over Isabelle about a month before her son Jerry was born. She was having bad dreams at that time, so I did a Protection Rite for her before the Blessingway. Those ceremonies were recorded and filmed here at our place during that time.

About three years ago, Isabelle had a Ghostway by Black Sheep. The reason was that she had to handle a dead baby, Louise's baby, when she had a miscarriage. When it was put away, Isabelle carried it around and had to

FIG. 12. Praying during a Blessingway ceremony, 1957. Isabelle Mitchell is the one-sung-over and Frank Mitchell is the singer.

handle it somewhat. Then, when she did not feel well, the hand-trembler said she had done something she should not have with a dead body.

She remembered that when she was in the hospital over here she had seen all those things from miscarriages from the smallest to a little bigger, that had been kept in bottles. They were kept in the hospital, you see, in order to teach others how these babies are born. She remembered that, when she got sick here, and the hand-tremblers said, "Why of course you've done something, you've seen something you shouldn't, having to do with dead persons." She recalled all that and said, "Yes, I did, I saw all those little bits of things that are born in a miscarriage." That is the reason she was sick, and also because of handling that dead one out there that was miscarried by her niece — Mary's daughter, Louise. All she did was put it in a box. That is the only way she touched it; she put it in a box and took it away to bury it.

EDITORS' NOTES

1. Frank's daughters, Augusta and Agnes (8/1-2/67), provided additional insights on Frank's life during his days as a public servant:

> While Frank was a judge he covered Chinle and Crownpoint, since there was no judge at those places. He spent most of his time in Fort Defiance. He usually held court several days each month at Chinle, but we rarely saw him even then until late at night. There would still be people coming down here to see him about their problems. Our mother would boil coffee four and five times a night and just sit with him. Frank never complained. There was little food during those days, mainly just tortillas and coffee. At the end of the month, they would bring him home in the government car, and he would just have a measly pay check. But he always brought us lots of food. He would just love his children to pieces at those times, joke around with us and call us all by the nicknames he had given to each of us. He was never unkind to anyone.
>
> Whenever he needed a place to stay when he was in Fort Defiance, the Franciscan Fathers would put him up at Saint Michaels. I [Augusta] was there in school then and he often took me on picnics at the Summit during those times. When he went to Crownpoint, he would stay with Garnett while he held court over there.

2. According to Augusta Sandoval (7/17/71), Frank and his wife brought up two children in addition to their own. Garnett Bernally, the first, was the daughter of Tall Woman's sister, who died very young and requested before death that Garnett be raised by her sister. Garnett lived with the Mitchells while growing up; she was older than Augusta, and left for a short time to try living with her father's people after completing the eighth grade. Garnett married Ned Bernally and moved to Shiprock, New Mexico. The second child, an unspecified relative's child, was known as Eva Hashkąą. She called Frank "Grandpa" and eventually married a Hopi man and moved to Tuba City.

3. The Chinle Franciscan mission records, "Old Chronicles – Daily" contains a typed copy of the letter Frank sent to Superintendent Reuben Perry regarding his daughter Mary's death (which was caused by spinal meningitis according to Chic Sandoval). The letter is in an envelope inscribed in Father Leopold Ostermann's handwriting, and he undoubtedly helped Frank prepare it. Another letter in the mission records, written by John Hunter to Perry, 2/24/31, implies that a meeting was held in Chinle on March 9 in response to Frank's query; no further documentation of this meeting has been possible. The two letters follow:

Chin Lee Arizona
February 9, 1931

Supt. R. Perry
Albuquerque, N. M.

My Dear Friend:

I am very much impressed and persuaded to write to you and take up the case of my daughter, who was sent home to me on January 10, 1931. I have learned that [you] did not treat me fair. You have sent my daughter Mary Mitchell back to die in my hands. I know nothing of her case for two full years.

I have come to know you for 31 years. I have had much confidence in you all these years. You have fully learned the ways of our Navajo Indians. You said you are the friend of this tribe and in return we sent our children to your school. With my consent my daughter was sent to Haskell Institute two years ago. Going through Albuquerque you met her and wrote me a letter asking me to enroll Mary in your school, knowing real well you are a friend of this great tribe, the Navajoes. I was well pleased to have Mary under your care.

We, members of the great tribe the Navajoes, had great confidence in Albuquerque School, Santa Fe, and Fort Lewis, because they were the first Indian Schools started for the Indians. I am not the only one making this complaint. A student from Albuquerque School, Harry Lizin walked home the other day, was sent home and his father never knew anything about him until he got back.

We do not know whose fault it is, but we feel that you as superintendant should notify the parents of the children when they are dangerously sick.

We regret very much as a tribe, we had great [interest] in Albuquerque school because the Indians are now very much indifferent, because these things have taken place. We cannot understand why Doctor Richards should not notify the father and mother of the sick children as it comes.

We did not get anything out of Mary because she was entirely out of her mind when she reached home. Many young girls like her work out in summer time, this probably was her case but I did not learn anything of her case. This makes me very unhappy and I decided to write you concerning this matter.

Forty one years ago old man Hosteen Del Woshy was made headman at Chin Lee. He died nine (9) years ago. I was placed in his stead then. Most of my time is spent trying to progress my people to education. We are putting all our trust in those of you who are directors of the Navajo Indians. I feel this is my duty to call your attention to this thing before further steps should be made.

You will find names and signatures below, who are in sympathy with me, who are parents of children in different schools and they demand that hereafter the parent be notified when their children are dangerously sick.

Very sincerely yours,

Frank Mitchell

Mr. Frank Mitchell

* * *

Southern Navajo Agency,
Fort Defiance, Arizona,
February 24, 1931.

Mr. Reuben Perry,
Superintendent Albuquerque School,
Albuquerque, New Mexico.

Dear Mr. Perry:

I wish to acknowledge receipt of copy of your letter to Mr. Frank Mitchell of Chin Lee relative to the death of his daughter Mary. I am quite certain that your letter will be appreciated by him and will be helpful in quieting the disturbed feeling which exists around Chin Lee because of the particular sadness relating to the circumstances in her case. In accordance with our discussion in Albuquerque a few days ago, I have requested Mr. Carruth, the Chin Lee principal, to spread the word among the Indians that you and I will attend the meeting there on date of March 9th. I am sure that we can accomplish a great deal of good by attending this meeting, and am therefore very anxious that nothing will prevent the execution of our plans.

Sincerely yours,

JOHN G. HUNTER
Superintendent

4. On 8/1/71, Frisbie went with Augusta Sandoval and several of her children to the old mission cemetery, located a distance behind the present mission. Few traces were left to indicate this area's use as a cemetery; only several fence posts and scattered pieces of wooden crosses remained. No markers were standing. Augusta indicated where the wife of Man Who Shouts had been buried (lefthand front corner when you stand in cemetery facing the entrance). She said the Navajo basket used to wash her grandmother during burial preparations had been nailed to the cross over her grave, but in the 1940s when Augusta and some friends were trying to locate the graves of

others in this cemetery, only a few pieces of that basket were left on the cross. David Mitchell was buried in the same cemetery. Seya Mitchell reported (8/3/71) that his own attempts to locate the burial spot of Man Who Shouts, who was "buried with his beautiful turquoise" had been unsuccessful.

5. The Chinle Chapter, evidently established in the late 1920s or early 1930s, received tribal appropriations for its present building in 1958. When completed, the building was blessed by the House Blessing Ceremony sung by Frank Mitchell during dedication ceremonies on 6/20/59.

Frank's years of service as a Chapter officer in Chinle are difficult to determine, given the state of local documents. No records were available at the Chinle Agency or Chapter House, and the Chapter records after 1955 on file at the Community Development Department contained no information about Frank. Records at the Franciscan mission in Chinle show that twice in 1944, Frank and John Gorman, who were "Chapter officers," met with people to ease arguments over land settlements. The settlement on July 1, 1944, was made at a meeting with Salina Springs Chapter officers to divide property of deceased Curly Hair's wife (Census #67537), who died on 6/10/44. Frank is also mentioned in a Chapter letter of 1/31/44 concerning land settlements. On 7/8/71, Irene Stewart of Chinle located notes she took as secretary when Frank was Chapter president in 1951 and 1952; she stated that he then left office to be either a judge or tribal delegate (this latter is contradictory to other evidence, but Frank's departure from office may have been correlated with bladder problems he began having at this time and the several operations that followed at Ganado hospital).

Mary Shepardson (Personal Communication, 9/28/71) remembered that Frank was serving as Chapter president in 1955, when she was working in the area.

The Mitchells themselves could contribute little further information about Frank's years as a Chapter officer. Seya said the first Chapter officers took office in 1936, and Frank was on numerous committees at that time, along with John Foley, Reid Winnie, Nelson and John Gorman and Curly Hair.

Augusta (7/6/71) recalled Frank's joking about the possibility that people were witching him to make him sick because he was settling claims as part of his duties as a Chapter officer. She also recalled how a "well-known witch" visited their place during this time, how afraid Tall Woman was of having the man around and how Frank accused this visitor of witchcraft to his face, thereby making Tall Woman extremely angry.

Augusta suggested that Frisbie look through Frank's papers to determine the span of his years as a Chapter officer. She said that Isabelle had these, as well as photos of the Tribal Council in session, Frank's red council ribbon and judge badge. She added, though, that they might have been burned because of Tall Woman's refusal to keep certain things associated with the dead. After securing permission to do so, Frisbie began searching for these papers with the help of Mae Mitchell. However, after two days of searching through suitcases and trunks stored in such places as the cookshack and the corncrib, we unearthed nothing relevant to Frank's service as a Chapter officer. We did, however, locate Frank's sacred bundle, Tall Woman's sacred bundle, Kinaaldá equipment and other Blessingway paraphernalia. We also found Frank's black leather briefcase, with embossed gold fleur-de-lis on the foldover cover. The briefcase contained the Tribal Council minutes (see Chapter 9, note 14) and information on the Social Security program. Later that evening, Frank's son Howard said that none of Frank's papers were left; the big books containing papers about stock reduction had been moved to the log cabin near Ruth's years ago, but were thrown away after Agnes came home from the service. The other things had been burned by Tall Woman after Frank's death. This is where Frisbie terminated her search.

Thus, while we know that Frank served as a Chapter officer in 1944, and as Chapter president in 1951, 1952 and 1955, the possibility that he served at still other times prior to 1955 must be left open.

6. Frank recorded his Protection Rite materials for McAllester in 1957-1958. The materials are on deposit in the Archive of World Music, Wesleyan University, Middletown, Connecticut. In the Navajo origin story, Changing Woman gives birth to the hero twins, Enemy Slayer and Child Born For Water, who were destined to rid the world of monsters. First Man and First Woman were her foster parents. They emerged from the underworld with the pre-Navajo kinds of human beings and established the shape of the present earth and heavenly bodies (Reichard 1963:17-25).

7. Here Frank laughed uncertainly and uncomfortably, seemingly indicating mixed feelings about what he was saying, the potential reactions of the ethnographer to witchcraft or uncertainty about what to believe.

8. Here Frank laughed again, this time in a more relaxed manner. The interpreter commented that Frank learned to joke about such matters from working with white people.

9. Frank was involved in six films in the 1940s-1950s. The first seems to have been a B.I.A. educational film, in color. According to Augusta Sandoval (7/17/71):

> They came down here during the time when Frank was a judge. Our hogan was near the gate at that time, and an old log cabin was right next to the hogan. That cabin was torn down two years later and the wood was sold to the Burbanks, who used it to build the cabin they are living in right now. The government pickup, either green or black with letters on its side, came down here, and those men took shots of Frank coming out of the hogan and getting into the government car. Then they showed our wagon coming down the road (from the north) and turning in at the gate in the barbed-wire fence. Isabelle and the kids were in there, and someone was riding on horseback beside it; either Frank, Isabelle, Leo Shirley or Howard was driving. Frank got out of the wagon and went into the hogan. He came back out wearing his beads, the big white hat he always wore in public, and his coat. Then he got into the government truck. At that time his moustache was full, but his ears were never pierced.

I was also in that, riding my horse, wearing my pink squaw skirt, blue blouse and jewelry. John Brown got in that too, because he came riding in at the gate while they were making the film. He had been drinking and was swinging his whip in circles as he rode his horse.

Frank left for somewhere right after that filming was over, and we never found out anything more about that film. But I saw it in 1947 when I was in high school in Anadarko, Oklahoma. When I saw it, there were some other Navajos in the beginning before they got to the part filmed at our house. I was so embarrassed when people asked me if that was me in there.

Attempts to identify this film have been unproductive. According to the B.I.A. Instructional Service Center, Brigham City, Utah, the scenes do not appear in any of the films now owned and circulated by the Center.

Frank also reportedly had roles in three Hollywood productions partially filmed in the Chinle area in the 1940s. According to Seya (8/2/71) the first one was *Desert Song*, filmed in 1941. Frank and his brother, John Mitchell, played the part of Arabians; Seya's horse, "Smarty Pants," was used in the film, and Dennis Morgan was one of the stars.

The second, *Sudan*, was partially filmed in the sand dunes behind Thunderbird Lodge. Frank and John again were Arabians, and Harry Price led them down the dunes in single file as the sun was setting. The film crew got angry when John's horse fell on him while going down the dunes and John forgot to play dead.

The title of the third film is unknown to Seya and the other Mitchells. Produced during 1944-46, the film featured Guy Madison and Rory Calhoun, and was shot in the Canyon and on the mesa behind Jimmy Begay's place. Woody Davis, Howard, Seya and Tom Tsinajini were also in it. The film company needed Indians to play the parts of Indians and cavalry soldiers. Frank drove a wagon team in that production, using his first big old wagon and driving as part of the cavalry. Woody Davis made Guy Madison some moccasins during the filming of that movie. Seya originally thought it was the movie called *She Wore a Yellow Ribbon* until he saw it.

In 1957, after beginning to work with McAllester that year, Frank made a colored film, *Blessingway*, which was produced under the joint auspices of the Museum of Navajo Ceremonial Art and Wesleyan University. The last film he made was in 1963, when the American Indian Films group, University of California, Berkeley, filmed Frank's performance of a *Kinaaldá* for his granddaughter Marie Shirley. Before it was produced, this latter film triggered off much adverse criticism at a Chinle Chapter meeting, June 26, 1963.

10. Relationship terms such as "nephew" and "uncle" are often used by Navajos as a friendly or joking form of address. The direct use of given names was thought to be impolite and even dangerous.

11. In 1971 Augusta, speaking of this Enemyway ceremonial, said: "During that Squaw Dance, we butchered twenty sheep and two cows to feed everybody. Lots and lots of people came, and all of them said that they had

never seen so much to eat before. Frank always told us to be hospitable and to feed our visitors, even if we only had black coffee." The amount of meat provided indicates that this was a very large affair indeed.

12. The rattlestick is an item of paraphernalia used in Enemyway. It is a juniper staff about three feet long, decorated with symbols of Enemy Slayer, Child Born For Water and other supernatural powers. Two camps or families are involved in the ceremony, symbolizing the opposing sides in warfare. Consenting to "receive the stick" involves a family in a network of ritual obligations toward the people who are "putting up" the ceremony. There are days of hard work and heavy expense. It is a burden, but also an honor to be asked. To undertake this duty is a social obligation. The Stick Girl is responsible for carrying the stick during the Enemyway dancing (known popularly as "squaw dancing") and for its careful handling during the rest of the ceremony. (Franciscan Fathers 1910:366-368). For a discussion of the rattlestick as a symbolic representation of the Navajo people, see Witherspoon (1975b:57-64).

13. The nine-night version of Shootingway is also called "House Chant" because of the extensive use of a symbolic representation of the Sun's house. This is a painted screen of vertical willow rods suspended on a frame. Representations of birds, snakes, winds and heavenly bodies are used with the screen. The accompanying myth tells of a hero journeying to the Sun's house to learn the ceremony and bring it back for the use of humankind. All the supernatural powers helped teach the ceremony.

11. Speculations

Frank's views on education... the value of tradition... the younger generation... the Navajos' condition of dependency... the future of the world... responsibility and other qualities of leadership... current difficulties with the tribal organization.

Since I have had all these experiences as judge, councilman and Chapter officer, some of the outstanding men in the Tribe know me, and they still come to see me about lots of things. They know that I have done a good job. By now some of the things have already come to pass the way they were intended to be for the good of the People.

For instance, education; that was first laid before the People at the time they were at Fort Sumner and it was agreed there that they would send their children to school to be educated. The People did not realize that school is a good thing in the beginning; they did not know what school was for and what good there would be in that for them. Therefore, they opposed it, and on and off there was trouble between the Tribe and the government because of that. I have already related the uprisings that took place because the People did not know what school was for.

Now, however, the People are beginning to realize the value of an education. Now most of the People understand that it is best for their children. So gradually, schools are being established; first it was by the government, and now it is being done by the state and even by the Tribe itself. There is also an effort to inform the older people about the value of education.

Many times, spokesmen for the People have been sent to Washington to ask for more schools and for improvements in the ones that are here. In return, the government sends officials out to look over our situation. They see what improvements are needed, and they go back and report these things. Then changes are made here and there for the betterment of the school system. With the help of the government and the People's own efforts, schools are being located within the reach of everybody so that all children can go. Some are boarding schools where the children stay; others are just day schools where the children come home at night. We also realize now how

FIG. 13. Frank Mitchell in 1963; wheels from his first wagon rest in the background.

expensive the schools are to operate, how much gas they use, the wear and tear on the cars, and the other related expenses. We know that cars break down and it costs money to put them back into running order. Those things are now being done for our school children.

There are other things that the People need; for instance, way out here water is scarce, and improvements are being made in that, too. These are the things that our leaders have been asking from the government. It takes time and money to get them accomplished. It's a big job to build roads to get faster transportation for our children. Those roads have to be kept up. We are still handicapped by the lack of good roads; this is a big problem right now.

Still, our leaders are trying to find ways to accomplish these things. We have seen quite a lot of improvement from the past, but not everything is satisfactory yet. I think we will continue our improvement, gradually.

While I myself stand for the good of the People, right now I am just watching these things. I cannot step in there and try to do some of the things I used to do because I am getting pretty well along in years. So I just sit by and watch. I think about the future; of course, I may never get to see it, but I just wonder how things will be in so many years, what improvements there will be for the benefit of the People. I wish I were young again so I could see more of these things as time goes on. But those are just wishes, and, of course, I do not expect to see those things.

Right now we have schools and law and order for the benefit of the People. But still we have disobedience from our young people. Looking at those things, it's very hard to figure out what the future will be and what the People should do for a better life. I think about that often. It puzzles me because if we continue to carry on the way we are now, there will be no great hope for the future. We will simply come to a stone wall where it all will stop unless the People start planning ahead.

The main thing that I am talking about is the way the People are conducting themselves now. For one thing, they are no longer observing the rules laid down for them to follow. They no longer believe in their ceremonies, their traditions and those things. Besides that, the People are getting into too much mischief, breaking too many rules. The young people are violating a lot of things and now have to be punished for doing that. But it's no one's fault but their own when they do these things. They get themselves into trouble and then they fall behind, instead of going ahead; they fail to get the improvements they should because of that.

For instance, the People are beginning to use peyote. We know that was not made for our use. The People are also using liquor in excess. Those things injure us physically. Our minds are being ruined that way, too. These are the things that are leading the People to the end where there will be no outlet for them to follow.

Of course we cannot expect all of the People to realize these things and to become good people all at once. That is the problem with all people, everywhere, I guess. A lot of them think, "Well, it is no one's business that I am doing such and such; it is nobody's business but mine." That is the way they feel now.

In the early days, the old people were our teachers. They said that as long as we observed the rules laid down for us by the Holy People, everything was going to go along smoothly. But, they said, it would not last forever. Sooner or later we were going to start breaking rules. Then that would lead us to ruin. It is like a seed of any kind, like corn, or beans or anything that you put in the ground. You plant it, and it sprouts and bears fruit and grows to a certain extent. When it matures, you harvest what it has produced; the stalks and leaves wither because their use is past. But you still have the seeds to continue planting and arriving at a new life. That is what the older people taught us. If you do not observe these things, you are bound to ruin yourself.

Now, if people give advice on how to behave, how to live and conduct yourself properly, they are doing that for your benefit. But the young people do not care to listen to that. Then they suffer from their own mistakes. It seems to me that today, more young people are careless. If you start talking to them, they don't want to listen; they don't want your advice. They do not realize that all these things take time and money and that it takes patience to teach the People a better way to live.

In the old days, the leaders talked to all; they did not make any exceptions when they gave advice to the People. They used to take time to talk with all of the People and to try to teach them. But these things are gone now; the older people are disgusted with the younger generation because the young ones do not pay any attention to them. All of the things that used to be done in the past, including the ceremonies, are being forgotten. The young do not care to inquire about them or to ask for advice from the older people.

No one realizes that when you perform ceremonies you can do that to the end of your days. Any of the other ways by which you can seek a living, such as farming, raising stock and things like that, all have an end. But the ones who learn to perform ceremonies, such as the blackening ceremonies and other small ones, use and practice them. They make a living that way until the time they pass away. At the present time, people do not care about those things.[1]

I think the main trouble is with ourselves, with the Navajo people. We are hindering our own progress. We do not try to pitch in and help; instead, we put obstacles in the way of improvement. We want to cheat where we can and live whatever way we want, and the trouble we cause by that is our own fault. We still try to have our own way instead of following the rules that were laid out for us. It is our own fault that we are in a difficult position. We are not trying to help ourselves or to help others to help us. For example, now we have police officers standing along the highways trying to keep the People on the straight road. Even at our public gatherings, our dances and other doings, we have the law and order present in order to keep things under control. All of these things cost money; we now have to have officers around because we do not want trouble or misfortune at these gatherings. Our biggest trouble is trying to keep ourselves in a straight line.

The reason that I do not see any future for the People is that in general, we are disregarding the rules laid down by the Holy People for us to observe. The Navajos themselves have never invented anything for their own use. They have merely depended on the white people for those things. Now everything that we use, eat, wear — it's all produced by white people. We have not made anything to use ourselves. All we look for is something ready to pick up and wear or eat, something that is already prepared for us. Consequently we are not using our minds. We are not thinking about how to make improvements. We are letting the white people do that. Even the tape recorder here was invented by the white people. Of course in the beginning, it was not like this; the white people have gradually been improving things step by step, but the

Navajos have not even started on things like that. We are merely depending on everything prepared by the whites.

We are even doing this with our relatives. At the present time, the old men and women who are unable to support themselves have nobody to take care of them. But the white people are feeding them and keeping them alive. Our own grandfathers and grandmothers and close relatives are handicapped and are living in poor conditions. Yet we do not bother with them because we know they will be taken care of by the white people. In our youth, when they tried to give us advice, we paid no attention to them. Now when they are in this condition, we still do not care about them.

We do not care to help our relatives at all. Instead, we depend mainly on outside help from people who are not our relatives. They raise money to help the poor and also do other things. They do this because they are strong people. But the Navajos are different; whenever we begin living close to each other, we have trouble. We no longer care to help each other, and even when our neighbors are in poor condition, that does not bother us now. We just don't care; we just like to talk about each other and pick on one another.

Because we have had a lot of help donated to us by white people, things have been improving. Before about four years ago, we were just living in ordinary hogans; some were old-fashioned, and some were a bit better with improvements in them. Since then, changes have been taking place. Improvements have materialized through the help of the people planning for us. The homes are improving; you can see this throughout the Navajo country. Houses are being built; of course they are not like white people's houses, but still, we are trying to imitate them to a certain extent.

Taking everything into consideration, we are being planned for by leaders and white people. We now have better hospitals than before. When you go to them, you get all kinds of treatment for different kinds of diseases. I don't know what those sicknesses are; maybe some of them are dangerous. But the young men who take care of you in the hospitals still do not think of you as a stranger or think of that sickness as ugly. Instead, they just go ahead and care for you as if you were their relative. We ourselves do not treat each other that way.

These are my personal thoughts about these things that I am mentioning here. There are many of these things that are worth discussing, but in general, the People do not care to talk about them. We do not care to express our thanks for these things that white people have done for us. It is the white people who plan for our future and try to keep us in good health and do everything for our good. Even some adult men in our Tribe do not care to pay attention to these things or to express their thanks to those who are responsible.

From what I hear now, the white people are getting worried, and there are quite a few disturbances in the world. The feeling among many people is that we are going to have a war. And if we do, they are going to use what they are calling nuclear weapons. I don't know what those things are, but I hear that they are a kind of poison. If that should ever happen, it will affect every human on earth. We too, not just the white people, will be affected by those things. Of course, no one person in the world can control those things.

Another world war is going to start. I can tell because of the way the rocks are starting to split in the Canyon. We saw them when we went in there recently. It is just the way they were splitting before the beginning of the last world war.

I know the world is coming to an end before much longer because we are beginning to see plants around here I never saw before. Also there are birds and animals I have never seen before. I do not believe evil beings will take over at the end like the priests say. These new plants and animals will. There is a prickly vine starting to grow right here by the hogan. I tell the children to leave it alone; it may turn into a big tree and grab them.

Sometimes I wonder what benefit there really is to getting educated. Even if the People do get highly educated, what can they invent that has not already been invented? Things are used on earth, water, under water and up in the air and all of those things have been invented and put to use. What else is there to be invented? Even if our younger generation gets a higher education, all they learn to do is to get a job and make a living by that. That is all they can do. They can't make improvements on things that have already been invented.

We have the Tribal Council that was organized years ago with the best brains of the Tribe, and they have been urging the People in general to go ahead, to make progress and to improve things. But all of that is being done in vain. The younger generation does not seem to bother about those things. With this in mind, I really do not think there is any future for us if we continue to go the way we are headed.

I have no objection to education, and, as I said, I am very much in favor of the policy of children going to school. Of course, when children get higher education that is for their own individual use. To a certain extent they can help their own people through that.

I don't know what to say about the ones who move off the reservation permanently. I think if the family goes off to work, the father goes out for the support of his family, there should not be any objection to having them go for a year or two. But to stay over there for the rest of their lives, I do not know about that. I don't think the People can make a living like the white people who are already there. It's a good policy for the People to go off for just a short period of time to earn a little money to live by here. Even now with a lot of people off the reservation working, work at home is scarce. But to go off and settle there for the rest of their lives, I doubt very much whether they can do that successfully.

Of course, the white people have been doing that for generations and are used to that kind of life. They are in cities, all in one spot. They have rules and some kind of income to live by, and they are used to that, they are adjusted to it. Even if they die there is always a younger generation coming to take their place and keep the fire burning.

When you get put into a position of leadership, that teaches you to have some respect. Even if you have been irresponsible in the past, you now have to behave and lead a good life as an example to your people. Naturally when the People put you into a responsible position, they are always watching for you to make a mistake. They are always looking back into your past life at what you have done. If you have made errors, they like to bring these out into the open to disgrace you.

That is why we were told by the older people to behave and try to lead good lives. These are the things you must go by to lead a good life because you can never tell; sometime in the future, you may be put into a responsible position. Then, if you do not have any bad records, nobody can criticize you. There are any number of people like that who have good records, who are in good standing and are respected by others.

Our leaders are elected to help us and plan for our future. Lots of times, we misjudge the people we put in those positions. We think they are wise enough to advise and instruct and then we find out, when they get into responsible positions, that they don't know what we expected them to know. They get in there and act according to their own ideas; they get kind of annoyed at the People and do not care about them. They just make things more difficult for us instead of trying to figure out ways to improve things. They do not think about the future. We do not accomplish anything by making mistakes in selecting people for office.

People who are better equipped at making a living often do not care to take public office. They want to work for themselves and improve their own standard of living. They do not care about the others. Some of them know what a difficult job it is to try to combine public affairs with one's own private life, and they refuse to be placed in those positions. They feel if they took a public position they would neglect their own affairs or part of them. Some of them will just say, "I don't care to be put in that position because it would mean that I would fall behind in my own affairs."

But others agree to that right away; they say they will work and maybe help the People in general a little. They think, "Maybe if I fill in there for a short while, I'll be remembered for having done something for the People." Of course, certain people who have held public offices and worked for us are remembered for what they accomplished. Those people are not quickly forgotten; they accomplished things for our benefit, like improvements in roads and other things, and they are mentioned even after they are gone.

Then there are others who do not think, who are not wise and who do not plan. These people do many foolish things. They are not forgotten either, because we remember them by the mistakes they made and the foolish things they did. We say, "Well, this young man is taking after his grandfather, or his great uncle; that's the reason he is acting foolishly. His uncle or grandfather was like that."

So there are two kinds of people: one group is praised for what they accomplished, and the other is ridiculed for the mistakes they made. If you show that you are a good leader, of course the People will realize it right away. If you don't have any plans, of course the People will notice that, too. In those cases, you are simply forgotten. The People simply desert you because you do not try to improve things for them. That is what I have learned by my experience.

The purpose of the Tribal Council was to teach the People to improve their standard of living. So far, not much progress has been made. The trouble is when somebody comes in with a good plan, the People go for it and put that person in the position of leader. Then somebody else comes along, who is jealous and fights those plans and ideas, instead of trying to improve them. Well, we cannot make progress that way. It's like a recent situation; we had a good man in there as head of the Council; he was level-headed, and we were going along smoothly. Then here came somebody else who stepped in there with great big promises which he could not fulfill and started to tear down what had already been accomplished by the former leader. So instead of improving on things, they tore it down. In that way there will be no progress.

Now we Navajos are fighting here over the use of the land with our neighbors, the Hopis. I think that there is no sense in fighting over that. We cannot make any progress if we continue to fight among each other like children who get into a fight when they play. If the white people got to fighting among themselves, it would be the same for them; they never would show any improvement, either.

I do not know why the majority of the People voted for this new leader, because he was never among us over here. We never heard what his promises were. Of course, we knew the old leader and what his plans were. So all of us around this part wanted this old leader to stay in office. The People all around who belonged to the new leader's Peyote church believed that he would repeal the law which had been passed limiting the use of peyote on the reservation. Of course, all of the People belonging to that group wanted that and so they voted for him.

Another thing concerns livestock. You see, a lot of us understood what the reason was for the stock reduction. When John Collier was commissioner and Fryer was superintendent, they explained that to us. They said, "We have to do that. We have to cut the livestock down to the carrying capacity of the range in order to preserve our land." But there are people who went against that, without thinking about preserving the land. This new leader knew that a lot of the People had feelings against this program, so he promised them bigger herds. Of course he never spoke about that here to us. He told those other people that he would do away with the grazing regulations and permits, and naturally, they liked that idea.

Ever since this leader started working for that position as tribal chairman, I have not been able to make up my mind to accept him because I do not know him; he is a stranger to me. I do not know what kind of Navajo he is, what kind of life he has been leading. Of course he talks well, but where can he show the People that he did these things so they can follow his example?

The reason I think this way is because I used to listen to old man Chee Dodge. Ever since the tribal organization started, Chee Dodge used to call the uneducated old people together and talk to them. He used to say, "Well, friends, choose men for the Council who you know are dependable and reliable, who are honest in the way they act. Don't just pick anybody because he talks that way and expect that he will do wonders. Size him up; see if he has a good established home, a good foundation. Those are the kinds of men that you want to put into the Council to guide you. You need to consider that about eighty percent of the People are not English-speaking and that about twenty percent are. A lot of those who speak English have not really established themselves on the reservation. So you want to think very seriously when you are choosing your councilmen."

Old man Dodge used to say those things. When I heard about this new leader coming and getting the chairmanship, I did not know him. How could I know him, because I didn't know where he lived or what he had accomplished?

Chee Dodge used to say, "Now you have an organization, the Tribal Council. It is only proper that you should have some kinds of rules, not too complicated for the uneducated ones, and simple enough to understand." The Council started to draft a constitution for the Tribe, and I was delegated to help with that. I don't know why that constitution was never adopted.[2] Still, some of the things proposed in it were put into the code of law and order and are now being used.

We have to have some kinds of rules to go by. The government which is over us makes rules for us to follow. Now the responsibility for planning is being partly turned over to us, and the government is stepping back. Here we are, left like a bunch of children, plain and foolish and fighting among ourselves.

Chee Dodge said, "We don't have anything that can block these agitators. They are going to overrun us and take things into control." Now it seems that that is the case today. There are a lot of talkers who make plans and try to fool the People, and that is the reason they are put in the Council. But what do they accomplish? Where is their home? What improvements do

FIG. 14. Frank Mitchell, 1963.

Isabelle Mitchell Collection; Stanley Bartson, photographer

they have? I do not think any of these agitators have any permanent homes, any farms or livestock to show to the People. They just merely talk.

I think we should stay under government control until we are able to take care of ourselves. We still do not have full understanding of how to operate as an established government. We are just like children who do not know how to plan or to think about the future. That is the way we are. As long as the situation is like that, how can we function as a solid government? Washington is still trying to teach us how to make a living. But most of the People are not interested; they do not understand.

Ever since Fort Sumner, the government has been trying to help us by issuing sheep, farm implements and things like that for our livelihood. People are sent out here to teach us how to use those things. But since we do not understand English, naturally we have had to do everything through interpreters. Since they do not have the command of the language or enough knowledge of how to explain things, that has been a drawback for us.

When the government released us from Fort Sumner, it had in mind that there were some very good things on the surface of the land. The land is valuable, and we were sent back here to learn how to make use of it. But since we were not educated, we did not know how to go about it. The government had to use its own people to teach us. Being uneducated, we were handicapped. The few educated ones who are now on the Council rush the People into modern things that the white people are using. The government is helping us, all right, but we do not have enough education to understand.

I figure that some of our leaders think only of the money they can make; they are only thinking about themselves. They do not think about the welfare of the People; that is my personal opinion. Before those leaders get into the job, they say in their speeches that they are willing to serve even without pay. When they get elected, they immediately demand a raise in salary. That is the reason that I think they are only after the money. I think that any person with self respect would not tell the People one thing and then do the opposite, but would remember what was promised.

I am mentioning these things because I learned them by experience. Now I am just talking from my own experience because I am getting well along in years and everything is being taken away from me. My hearing is defective, my teeth are worn and my strength is gone; all these things that I depended on are worn out. I found out that they are only temporary; they just last a little while, and then they are taken from you. They are just loaned to you temporarily. When you get to that stage, of course you kind of lose interest in things. That is how I feel now. Of course, I have told you how much I tried to help the People. It was only for a short space of time that I did those things. But what little I accomplished for the Navajos has not been forgotten. There are any number of my own people who have great respect for what I have done for them. There are also white people who come and ask me about what I have done.[3] Those things are mentioned time and time again.

EDITORS' NOTES

1. When Clifford Barnett was interviewing Frank on 5/17/62, regarding the effects of modern medicine on Navajo religion and changes in curing practices, Frank formulated some ideas about how to encourage the younger generation to become singers and to carry on the religious traditions. "He made a formal request for me to pass along the information to the Tribal Council with a request that they supply scholarship funds for Navajos who wish to learn to become singers" (Letter from Barnett 10/20/71).

> When you asked me the other day, I had this in my mind. Just as you have some in your generation who are not interested, I have been wondering what we can do to continue these sings, to carry on our customs. This is what I have in mind now. The People in authority in our tribe have no knowledge of what is going on and no knowledge of the old things. I have talked with white people who have come to see me about various things concerning the customs and practices of the People in the past. Now you come and I ask you what do you recommend about this problem. What do you suggest?

Frank agreed with Barnett's reply concerning his ideas that the Tribe could sponsor people to get this kind of education. He had something like this in mind and furthermore, he was not necessarily thinking of people who had not been to school, but of several educated young people who had worked off the reservation and then returned to their people. Frank said, "This is the kind of person I feel would do very well as a singer, if they were sponsored so that the singer could be paid and a sacred bundle assembled for the young person."

Barnett pointed out to Frank that even if the Council acted on this matter, it would not be an unmixed good thing. It would mean that certain singers would have to be picked over others as the ones best able to train people in this type of program. Barnett also pointed out there would be real difficulty and a great deal of argument about this. Frank replied that this indeed might be a problem, but he felt that the positive point of training many more singers or new singers would balance any difficulties in administering such a program. He asked Barnett many times to present this idea to the Tribal Council. Barnett said he was planning an oral presentation of the idea to the Many Farms community at the Chapter meeting later that week and that later a written report would be made to the tribe (Barnett Fieldnotes for 5/17/62:4).

Interestingly enough, *Akwesasne Notes* (Summer 1972:18) reported that the National Institute of Mental Health funded a program from 1969-1972 reportedly begun by Rough Rock Navajos (Witherspoon 1971:1361), wherein six Navajo singers were each paid to teach two young Navajo apprentices "the elaborate ceremonies which often cure the mental ailments of Navajos." According to Dr. Robert Bergman of the Indian Health Service at Window Rock, Arizona, "the program began when reservation leaders decided something needed to be done to increase the supply of medicine men. The remaining men were becoming quite old and few young men were able to assume the economic hardship of several years in training, traditionally in apprenticeship to an established medicine man" (*Ibid.*). Bergman was approached by Navajo leaders for help in obtaining the grant (*Wassaja*, January 1973:18).

The *Navajo Times* (June 7, 1973:A-8) reported a day-long symposium, suggested by Chairman Peter MacDonald, to help singers update their knowledge of Tribal government. The group of over fifty, however, expressed major concern over the future of Navajo ceremonies, urging Tribal officials to take steps to ensure preservation of the traditional heritage. One suggestion included compulsory training for a selected group of young people to relearn ceremonials currently facing extinction. Various councilmen assured the traditional leaders their recommendations would receive action. The re-quested multimillion-dollar cultural center at the Tsaile campus of the Navajo Community College, and the increased utilization of singers as consultants by the U.S. Public Health Service were also mentioned.

Evidently as a follow-up, the *Navajo Times* (July 19, 1973:A-6), reported the Tribal chairman's participation in a Blessingway ceremony, "performed partly in accordance with the recommendations made by medicine men at the recent medicine men symposium held in Window Rock."

2. See Chapter 9, note 13.

3. See Appendix C for a list of scholars and others who worked with Frank.

12. Last Days

A tissue is removed from Frank's stomach . . . comments on unqualified singers, hospitals and white doctors . . . plans for dispersal of land and stock.

There are still lots of people coming around here wanting me to do the Blessingway for them, but sometimes now, because of my physical condition, I have to refuse. When they come to ask, it just depends on how I feel. If I think that I can stand it, then I accept. I don't advertise myself or go around saying that I do the Blessingway for so much and that's my standard fee for the prayers and the songs. It's up to others. They always offer me something for doing that; if I think that it's worth it and if I feel all right, then I still accept them. Last summer [1963] I did the Blessingway several times,[1] even one for that woman in Black Mountain who started labor and had to go to the hospital before I had finished the singing.

But a lot of the time now, I'm not well enough to sing the Blessingway. I can't stand the strain of being in a sitting position for that long, and my voice also gets tired. I especially feel the strain in the wintertime. The nights are long then, and performing that Blessingway is very strenuous, even though we wait to start the all-night singing until pretty well on into the night. Of course, in the summertime, the nights are short. I will do the Blessingway again when I get well and when I think that I am able to do it.

As you know, last fall I had my sacred bundle renewed, and of course a Blessingway was used for that. But even though I had that and all of the other ceremonials I've been telling you about, right now my ailments are still hanging on. I still think that we have not done the complete cure. The doctors do not seem to be able to tell me what the matter is, either. I went over to the Ganado hospital, and they thoroughly examined my body. They could not find anything anywhere that could be causing my troubles.

Finally they decided to take some tissue out of my stomach, just a small piece. I was not really operated on then. The doctor just said that there was no equipment there at Ganado to analyze what they had taken out of me, and that he would send it to Denver to find out what it was. They gave

Margaret Matthews, photographer

FIG. 15. Official participants in the dedication program for Chinle Public
High School, February 29, 1964. Front row, left to right: Frank Mitchell,
Allen Yazzie, Raymond Nakai (Tribal chairman), W. W. Dick (state superin-
tendent of schools). Back row, left to right: Guy Gorman (councilman from
Chinle), Don Kinney (principal, Chinle High School), John Wallace, Jody
Matthews (Chinle school superintendent), Father Cormac Antram (Our Lady
of Fatima Mission).

me some medicine and told me to go home. I think maybe whatever that is is
the aftereffect of my indulging in drinking.

The doctors told me that once they found out what that was, they
would treat it. They did not say exactly when I should come back over there;
they just said, "In awhile, after about two months or so, come back over here
and check on things. We'll see what effect that medicine we gave you is
having." I went back over there once to get my pills renewed and to see what
those doctors had found out. They just said, "We don't know yet what that
is, but as soon as we find out, if we have a remedy for it, why then there is
nothing else that will kill you except old age."

Recently I asked my daughter Augusta to go over there and find out
what they had learned about that tissue they took from my stomach. She did,
and the doctor there did not want to tell her about it. He said, "Just go back
to Chinle and tell your father to come over here himself."[2]

I have not gone over there since they said that. When I do, I know that
they will say they want to keep me for a few days, and then they will tell me
to stay there for at least several weeks. Right now I am getting many visitors,
and I don't want to go back over there.

Another reason I am not going now is that my wife is not at all well yet from her recent sicknesses, and I don't want her to exert herself too much. I cannot desert her. I know that I can depend on Augusta, but she is working much of the time during the day. I cannot count on the younger girls around here to do all that needs to be done, so I am going to stay here. It is not that I am suspicious of my wife and cannot leave her because of that; I trust her and she trusts me. I can leave her here. This jealousy business is not a healthy thing. Once a woman gets jealous, she just starts going crazy. [3]

While I was over at the Ganado hospital and even before I went there, I had a lot of dreams, and most of them were about dead people, those who had already passed away, even women. Those things were beginning to bother me; I was worrying about them. So I decided to have another ceremony. I also wanted to see if I could get some relief from the pains that I was still feeling a lot of the time. So I went and asked Black Sheep from Black Mountain to come over here and perform some of his small ceremonies for me, to see if those could straighten out my dreams and give me some relief from those pains. He came down here and did some Ghostway rituals for me. He said prayers, cut prayersticks, bathed me and painted me with the blackening and reddening ceremonies. You can do those things to find out what effect they will have. If you feel a bit better after those, then you can go ahead and have the big ceremonial.

After he did that, I don't remember having any more dreams. I just forgot all about them. Before those things were done, as soon as I woke up, I would begin to think about what I had been dreaming about. Now I still dream, but I do not remember what those dreams are about. I have felt a little better since Black Sheep performed all of those things for me, and right now I am thinking about calling him back again for a big, regular five-night Ghostway. Then maybe I will go back to the hospital again.

There are a lot of people around who just know small ceremonies.[4] In the past the old people would say to us, "I will teach you some of this ceremony for your own protection and for that of your family and your home. Sometimes you get the feeling that you ought to have a ceremony done because you have done something wrong. So it is a good thing to learn this ceremony. This is only for yourself; it is not to be practiced out there with other people all over." This practice is similar to the priests or ministers who pray; when they go to bed or when they eat or get up, they pray and do a little ceremony. It's like that. We can use it for the benefit of others, but these small ones are really for our own protection and that of our family.

Sometimes neighbors learn that you know those things and then they ask you to do that for them. I think many of the people who just perform one or two of these today started out that way. Now, though, some of them are practicing those short rituals all over, even though they have not been taught enough to do that.

We don't have any special name for those people. You know, some of them are not qualified. There was a man who came here from Round Rock country who would mix up anything – weeds, earth and all those kinds of things – and just give them to people. Finally we learned what he was.

Sometimes people, even whole families, will go to such persons. Some stranger will come in here and claim he has a ceremony for a certain illness. Then the People just go to him for that; they don't even inquire about him at all; they just go. It's the kind of person who is too lazy to make a living, too lazy to do something useful, who goes around doing those made-up ceremonies.

There are very few people learning how to sing today. It is very rare to find that. The People aren't interested in learning. Lots of times we go to the hospital, and the hospital is no help. Then we try a singer.

First we think of a hand-trembler. But then the question always is, "Who is reliable?" People want somebody dependable, someone to rely on. When you make up your mind, then, regardless of the distance you might have to travel, you depend on that person. You have to pick singers very carefully; there are any number who say they can do it but are unqualified.[5]

In the early days, people were often older when they started to learn a ceremony. Often their hair was gray like the hair of their teachers. Older singers are always consulting each other and exchanging ceremonies. That has been the practice for a long, long time.

Some older people used to approach a good singer for their own son or nephew. They would pay a fee to have the younger one taught. After the ceremony was learned, then the sponsor for that would go to work and fix up a sacred bundle for the new singer. There are a lot of expenses connected with that, and that may be the reason that it is not being done very much today. It is often too expensive for anyone to do those things now.

Whether you go to white doctors and hospitals or not is really something each person decides. In many cases, we have our own beliefs about the causes of illnesses. For example, when I was young, I used to hear the older people say that while a young girl was pregnant, she and her husband had to be careful about what they did. The older people used to say that neither of them should butcher sheep and cut the joints of the sheep during that time. They said if they did that the child would be born with that trouble in the joints.[6] If you disregard things like that, it will affect your child. If later on the child complains of pain from that crippled condition, the People will discuss it among themselves and decide just what caused that. Then they will try the ceremony called, "Remaking the Image of the Animal." Adults can have that, too, if they break some rule later in life.

Ever since the Navajos began owning horses, we have had this trouble in the joints. When you castrate a stud horse, you double one hind leg back down and around towards the neck, tying it with a rope while someone cuts the horse. You should not do this while your wife is pregnant because it will lead to the same result. The child will be born the same way, with the cord doubled up just like that rope you used on the horse. I believe that because I've seen that happen. I don't know if there are any stories which explain those things. I never inquired about it, and I just don't know if it's explained in any of the stories about the creation of human beings.

Of course, when the child is newborn, you don't know about the condition of its bones or anything like that. It's only after that child starts to walk that you know that its bones are out of joint, that it's crippled and not the way it should be. You usually know that because the child complains of pain. Then it is decided what happened while that child was in the womb. It is only because of carelessness that you will be punished like that through your child.

If you as an adult are sick for some time, then the case is diagnosed, and you are told what you did. Then you remember that; of course you are the one then who has punished yourself physically. In this other case, you are punished by your child's condition.

A few of the People believe what they hear in the hospital from the doctors and others about those sicknesses instead of what the older people used to tell us. It's up to you what you believe. It's like what Chee Dodge used to say: there's always some goat around alarming the sheep. Some of the People just get suspicious. They say that all the white doctors are doing is making money and that what they are telling you about your condition is not true. Very few of these people have complete confidence in white doctors. I myself trust these doctors and believe in what they tell me, but most of the Navajos are on the other side.

Because I believe that I am not going to get over my present sickness, I have now started thinking about dividing my land between Isabelle and Ruth. Augusta has told me that she would rather work for wages than be tied down to a piece of land; Agnes is living in California, and Mary already has her land. The division is not definite yet because we are waiting for a grandson of Charlie Mitchell's to come out here and stake it for us. He is now working with the Land Claims Department, and they are the people who do that.

All of the land on the reservation is tribally owned, and we do not have individual deeds to it. You can inherit land, but you just hold it in trust for the Tribe. It really all belongs to the Navajo Tribe. If the land is neglected for a certain time, then someone else can lay claim to it in court, in consultation with the original user. If you put any improvements on your land, then these are your personal property. That is one way that you can hold a piece of land, by putting up improvements. If you do not have sufficient land, then you can apply to the Grazing or Land Use Committees of the Tribe for another piece somewhere. The lands can be leased, but that is very different. On the lands that we hold, there is no real-estate tax.

The land across Nazlini Wash has never been used for farming because none of the People were able to irrigate it. The Tribe tried to get a government grant for that, and they got $3000, but no more. The People at

Valley Store wanted a share of that land too, and I don't think that anything was ever done about it.

The land that we consider ours includes the area around our place here over past Nazlini Wash toward the paved highway, and over across the dirt road toward the Canyon in the other direction, almost to the Chinle Wash over there. Man Who Shouts originally had a claim that ran across both washes to Red Mesa and back to the sand dunes in the Canyon. Jake Tom had the next strip. Originally the People were given large sections of land. Man Who Shouts just assigned pieces of that land as new members of the family came along.

The entire big field down near Nazlini Wash is ours. That land goes from the road all the way over to that other road behind Mary Davis' place. From the fence over here where the well is, that fence goes all along the road and up to the end. Up there, it goes east or north and then comes back down this way where there are two more fences. Now our land does not go all the way over to the Chinle Wash, but earlier, it almost did. At one time, that land over there belonged to Man Who Shouts and his wife. Their land also included all of what Mary Davis has now, too. When Tall Woman and I started living together, Man Who Shouts and his wife told us that we could have that place someday. All of us have used that field at one time or another, just as we are still doing now.

Across the road toward the Canyon, we have two fields. Beyond those, there is an alfalfa patch and a corn patch, too. Some of my wife's relatives had a fence put up back in there very close to our land, and while they were doing that, they took part of an acre there from us. They just put their fence way out into our land and then left it like that. We wanted to say something about that, but it only would have meant trouble. Those people were our relatives, so we didn't say anything. The ones who did that were the children of Tall Woman's crippled brother, Man With a Cottonwood. He was the only one left in her family besides two of her sisters who were still living at the time that happened. Last fall, he had a stroke and passed away.

The whole field back there, where that alfalfa patch is, belonged to my brother Jim from Black Mountain. That did not come from my wife's people. I bought that from my brother before he passed away. He used to come out here every summer and camp over there. Gradually, as he became older, he could not come out any longer. The land began to get full of weeds and everything else, and the fence started to fall down, because it was not being taken care of. So I asked him if I could have that land, and he said that I could. After that, I bought it from him and put a fence around it.

On the other side of the road, all of the land from the highway to the dirt road that turns in here from over by the Imperial Mart originally belonged to my brother John. He fenced that in and farmed it; his sheep were over at Fluted Rock. When he died, his last wife, the one he was separated from, remarried and went to live with Charlie Claw in Fort Defiance.

FIG. 16. Frank Mitchell and Tall Woman in 1964.

Down near the wash here, nobody owned that land before I did. That whole area just used to be under water until the Civilian Conservation Corps camp came there and put in the dam. The water used to run differently. We had a large piece of land on the other side, but when they put the dam in, they changed the water so it ran on this side, leaving that little piece on the other side. Now it makes a pasture area down in there. When the water came rushing down at full speed, it would come right up near our hogan, and we probably all would have been washed away without that dam.

After that dam was built, we added jetties in that area right in that line by ourselves. That was a hard job; we did that with barbed wire and great big old poles. We did not have the smooth barbed wire or the skinny poles that we use today. We really worked hard putting that fence all along there, but it was worth it. In the spring, back in there we planted those Russian olive trees that the Bureau of Land Operations got for us. To those, we added some others that we just pulled out of the other wash in the early spring and moved over there. Now there are lots of big trees there.

Years later, I decided that I would fence that whole area and use it for pasture for my stock. Before that, I had put up this other fence and the one on this side up from the wash, too. I had some Ten Days Project[7] workers put that new fence in for me, and finally I had a good fence all the way around that area.

There was always plenty of water around here. We used to dig to get it sometimes for the sheep or for our washing. We did not want to use the same water we drank for washing because it was so hard to get that drinking water. So we would just go down a little ways, less than six feet into the ground, and then we always hit water. In some places you could get it sooner than that, but you had to know where to find it.

I don't know how many acres belong to our family altogether. There are more than five acres alone over there in the alfalfa patch. I know that because one time I asked a man with a tractor to plow that land for me, and we paid him by the acre. He measured that land and figured it was a little over five acres. But around our hogan here, I couldn't actually say because I have not had the surveyors come down here like they should to figure it out.

Nowadays, when Navajos want to set up a household someplace, they go to the Bureau of Land Operations. They have a map of the whole Chinle Valley which shows the parts that are vacant. If there is a particular place that you have in mind for your home, it's all right with them if you put your home there, as long as no one else claims that area. You have to take your case to the Chapter House and put it before the members. Then they have a community meeting and let everyone know that you are asking for that place. If the people vote for you, you can have it. You get the land and your permit right away. They usually allow you about four or five acres or maybe a little less for a home; I am not sure what they do now if you want to farm. If the People vote against you, you are just out. You cannot do anything more about that because it was put before the Chapter and voted on.

Even though this land has been in our family before the Tribal Council began, I would like to have my place surveyed to make sure just what is mine. I want that to be recorded in their book over there so I can get my land permit.

One time my daughter Augusta asked for a piece of land across the wash over there, but it was all taken. It would have made things easier for her to be on the Chinle side of that wash; it's hard in the wintertime for her to cross that wash in all of that mud to go to work. But when she went to the Bureau of Land Operations, they showed her the map. Wilson had a place right over there; he had had that land for three or five years and had not done anything with it. He probably will never move over there, and if he did, it would probably be many years from now. Because of this, Augusta is thinking about asking him for that land.

I plan to give my stock and land permits to Isabelle and Augusta. Ruth already has a permit for five horses, and Isabelle is to divide my stock. Augusta does not have a permit for sheep or horses. On the piece of land that I am going to give Ruth across the road there, she plans to let her daughter Marie build her home.

EDITORS' NOTES

1. Frank continued to perform the Blessingway until late in 1965. Then he became too sick, and ceased to practice for the remaining year and a half of his life.

2. It was during this visit that Augusta was told by the doctor that the biopsy had shown that Frank had an inoperable prostate cancer. She came home and told everyone in the family about it, including her father.

3. At this point, Frank once again told the story of hitting the woman at Saint Michaels with his fist. (See Chapter 4.)

4. The materials in this paragraph and the seven subsequent ones were provided by Clifford Barnett from interviews he did with Frank on May 17, 1962, with Chic Sandoval interpreting.

5. Of the fifty some singers Barnett had identified in the Many Farms area, Frank considered five of them trustworthy enough to use himself.

6. Frank is referring to congenital hip disease found frequently among Navajo women.

7. See Chapter 2, n. 6.

Epilogue: 1966-1969

Increasing illness, recommendations of star-gazers and two short ceremonies... Frank's instructions to his family... baptism and return to the hospital; another star-gazing... Frank dies ... funeral and burial ... family has Protection Prayer ... Frank's sacred bundle is renewed for the last time.

Frank remained active through the late fall of 1965, singing several Blessingways for family members and relatives, and officiating at the Navajo part of the Catholic wedding of his granddaughter Linabah and Franklin Tah. He continued to seek help both from doctors and from Navajo singers, taking numerous kinds of medicine and having ceremonies performed for him. One of these was the one-night version of a Beautyway, which he had sung for him by Charlie Sam from Canyon del Muerto on September 27, 1965.

By shortly after Christmas, however, Frank's health was beginning to fail rapidly, and he was feeling an increasing amount of pain. By February, he was extremely thin and told Frisbie: "I have lost my appetite. That happened

---

NOTE: Frisbie remained in close touch with the Mitchells through 1966 and 1967, when she was in residence for doctoral work in anthropology at the University of New Mexico. The following Epilogue represents a combination of Frank's words, Frisbie's field notes, and observations given Frisbie by Augusta Sandoval, both verbally and in letters. As Frank's condition worsened, he spent more and more time in the hospital. When home, he stayed in bed in his cabin, eating little and responding very little to conversation from even his own family members. At one time, in February 1966, he became interested in recording ceremonial materials, and at that time Frisbie finished some work on Blessingway songs and prayer texts with him. After this, however, he never again cared to record, usually saying, "I don't feel like working today; I feel all right physically but my mind is all mixed up. I don't want to get any of the things I've told you confused because of that."

in the hospital just recently, and now I am just too old and too weak. Then too, I am too drugged from that medicine to get around here anymore. I know that I am dying."

As his condition worsened, the number of Navajo ceremonies done for him, including Blessingway, increased. By April of 1966, various family members believed that just about every possible ceremony had been performed for him; thus they turned to an increasing use of diagnosticians to determine what should be done next. All during this time, the English-speaking members of the family were talking about the terminal cancer, and Frank continued to be in and out of the Ganado hospital. In April, Augusta said to Frisbie, "We contacted several star-gazers and hand-tremblers after practically every ceremony had been done. Among the ceremonies that these men suggested were another Blessingway, the Liberation from Ghostland Prayer and a two-night Medicine Chewing.[1]

"So the Blessingway was done first, and then one of the star-gazers performed two ceremonies, the Liberation from Ghostland Prayer and a two-night Medicine Chewing. In the latter, the medicine had to be chewed by one of Frank's daughters first. Mary Davis did that, and then Frank took it. That made him talk all night and go out of his head for two nights. At the same time, his arms and legs were swollen way up. He called all of his children together and said that this was usually a sign that a person was going to die, but that we should not give up hope. By the time that second ceremony was over, the swelling was gone and he was no longer out of his mind.

"The star-gazers suggested several other ceremonies for Frank, but we have not done them as yet. They suggested Mountaintopway, since Frank also had dreams about mountains, too. That is a lot like the Medicine Chewing ceremony. Mountaintopway can only be done in the winter, since it involves the bear. The star-gazers did not know that ceremony. The other suggestions were another Liberation from Ghostland Prayer and a Protection Prayer."

Describing April 1967, Augusta said to Frisbie, "Toward the end, before he went back to the hospital, Frank called us in while he was real sick and said that he knew he did not have too much longer left to live. He told us that no one lives to the last day with his and her parents. He said, 'This is what I have taught you, that someday you will have to live without me and that you should learn to think for yourselves and to make a living for yourselves on your own. Even if I do get well, it will be just for a short time. Old age or illness will get me.

" 'Do not be hurt too badly when I go; we all have to go sometime. That is life, and no one lives forever. I hope to go where the good people go. Do not cry like a lot of people do for their loved ones. Do not get so carried away that you do not know what to do. Don't talk like that. I have taught you children how to live right and how to live with one another.

" 'Remember, too, that if you cry too much, the spirits say that you are asking for another family member to be taken away. I believe in that, so I want all of you to be strong. Remember that people will be looking at you to see how you are acting, to see if you are acting as if you had not lost someone dear to you.

" 'I want you to care for the stock, the farm. Take care of your mother and be nice to your sisters and brothers. Live happily together in one household. Do not fuss or argue because I am gone; live as though I were still around. I will pray for all of you if I go to where all the good people are.

" 'I am mainly concerned with your mother. Take good care of her. She will be hurt the worst by my going. Be nice to her and be with her at all times. Treat her right so that she does not miss me too much. That way she will know that I have talked with you and that you have listened to me. She won't be so lonesome that way.

" 'I want to stay home and die here. Let me die in the house and do not do anything to it; it is an old-age hogan. I'm not dying of anything that you should be scared of; you should not be scared of those who die of old age. I want to stay here, and you are not to burn up the house, tear it up or do anything else to it after I am gone.

" 'Come and visit my grave. I know that is not usual among our people, but don't be afraid of me when I die. I will not hurt anyone. I am going to a good people's place, where I will be kind to people. You have nothing to fear if you think of death in the right terms; there is nothing wrong with a dead body or the grave.' "[2]

Augusta said, "It was wonderful the way he talked with us; he was not scared to die. It was almost as if he knew when he was going to pass away. The doctor had told me two weeks before Frank called us in to say these things, that he would die within two weeks. I just kept that to myself because I knew it would just hurt everybody even more.

"Shortly thereafter, my mother insisted that Frank go back to the hospital, and he did. Before then, however, Father Cormac baptized[3] both my father and my mother on Good Friday and gave them their first holy communion. Frank was always a Catholic; he was a singer of the Blessingway in the Navajo way and a Catholic in the white people's religion. He sent me to Catholic schools, and he himself was baptized a Catholic while he was at the Fort Defiance school. But there was no record of that, and therefore the priests had to repeat it.

"After we took Frank back to the hospital, we contacted another star-gazer who did the star-gazing over some clothes that belonged to Frank during the last week that Frank actually lived. That man said that he saw my father was very, very sick. He said that it probably was too late to save him, but that he might be able to do a ceremony that would help. However, he could not do that right away because he was waiting to learn where his relatives would hold the funeral of his nephew who had just been killed. If that service were on the reservation, he would not be able to do the ceremony for Frank for at least four days after that. The funeral was held on the reservation, and my father died three days later.

"Father Blase, who was serving the Ganado area, visited Frank several nights before his death in the hospital. The morning of the day he died, the two Fathers from Chinle came down, bringing Ruth and Howard with them. Isabelle and I were already at the hospital, and we were staying there. Ruth and Howard stayed elsewhere.

"The night before Frank died, he talked with Isabelle and me until midnight. He would answer our questions, too. He said that he had no pain and that he wanted no water. Then he went unconscious; he was breathing real heavy and fast. It was as if he had gone into a sleeping spell.

"When he died, his head was on my lap. He went peacefully, and the doctor who was there told us that he had died from the pneumonia that was in his lungs. When he died, I remembered everything that he had said; I remembered it all up to that point. I did not cry. Isabelle broke down, and I told her that her father had said not to do that; I told her to remember what he had said.

"Father Cormac went over to the hogan to tell the others after Frank had passed away. Our other brothers and sisters came in in the morning, and together we washed the body and left it there. Then I started planning the funeral according to when the people, the relatives, and you and David could come to see him."

Augusta called Frisbie at 6:15 A.M. on April 15th to say that Frank was failing rapidly and that she should come to Ganado immediately. Isabelle had taken his clothes to Klagetoh for another star-gazing, as prearranged, even though someone in the family had said not to go through with it. At 7 A.M. Augusta called again to say, "Frank just died very peacefully . . . . He has been in a coma for the last three days and he never came out of it . . . . The doctor said that his cancer had spread but that it was his weak heart that finally just gave out."[4]

After notifying McAllester and several others, Frisbie called Augusta back. Augusta said that they would wait until April 20th to have the funeral so that Frisbie and McAllester could attend. The hospital had told them they could leave Frank's body there until they made plans.

Augusta called on the 18th from Gallup to say that Agnes had just arrived from California by train and that they were in Gallup buying the casket and washing and dry cleaning Frank's clothes. She said that the funeral would be at 10 A.M. on the 20th and that she and Agnes were taking Frank's things to the Ganado hospital on their way home.

Father Cormac had agreed to go down and get the body Thursday morning. Frisbie said she would bring food, and she was also asked to bring

back the ring Frank had given her because the family wanted him to wear it.
She was also asked to bring plastic flowers for the grave.

When Frisbie and McAllester arrived in Chinle, the entire family was
there except two grandchildren — Alfred, who was in California, and Lena,
who was in the hospital at Intermountain and had not yet been told of
Frank's death. All of the women were at home wailing, except Augusta and
Agnes, who were at the church. After coffee, Frisbie and McAllester went
with Seya, Timmy, Howard and Ace to the mission.

The coffin was in the vestibule of the Our Lady of Fatima Mission.
Father Cormac greeted everybody, and then Frisbie gave Augusta the ring.
The coffin was then opened, and amidst wailing, Isabelle put Frank's jewelry
on him: a turquoise bracelet (one of his and one from Ruth) was put on each
wrist, his flower-shaped turquoise ring was placed on his left ring finger, and
Frisbie's ring was put on his right ring finger. His beads were placed around
his neck under the plaid flannel shirt. Isabelle also put a rosary in his right
hand. Frank was dressed in a gray suit and had been wrapped in his two
favorite Pendleton blankets. The coffin was then closed, and the plastic
flowers were arranged on top of it.

The funeral started at 10 A.M. and was a Requiem Mass with
communion. The coffin was wheeled down the aisle to the front of the
church for the service by the pallbearers: Seya, Timmy, Howard, Ace,
Franklin Tah and McAllester. Douglas Mitchell served as an usher, and
Franklin Shirley and Coolidge Martin were altar boys. When the service was
over at 11 A.M., the coffin was wheeled back to the vestibule and opened for
those who wanted to view the body. Frisbie was given the job of holding the
"Abiding Memories" book provided by the funeral home, in which people
had been asked to write their names. Of the approximately 500 people there,
more than 100 signed the book.

All of the Navajos broke down as they saw Frank in his coffin. The
women wailed, and the men cried. Many older people were there; some kissed
Frank, while others held his hand. Outside the church, the speeches started.
First Clyde Tahi spoke, then Chic Sandoval. Frank's family was called in to
say goodbye to him after all others had filed outside. Mary held his hand and
gave an extended speech, telling Frank how good he had been to them and
reminding him not to return. Isabelle spoke only a few sentences addressing
her father before she began to wail. Augusta and Agnes kissed him without
speaking, and Louise talked to him for a short time. Two granddaughters,
Geneva and Ivonne, were close to hysteria and had to be led away from the
coffin by Wilson. Seya and Howard just gripped Frank's hand, and Seya asked
Frisbie to hold Frank's hand while she and McAllester said their goodbyes.

Then the coffin was put in the mission carryall, and some forty cars
escorted it to the Chinle Cemetery in a procession with a police escort. Ace

was leading Frank's saddled and bridled gray horse, Weasel, into the graveyard as the procession arrived.

The grave was blessed by Father Cormac, and the coffin was lowered into a wooden box, apparently the packing case it had arrived in. This had previously been installed in the grave. Then Isabelle gave the pallbearers three blankets to put on top of the coffin: two Pendletons and one plain green one. The pallbearers, who were standing in the grave, nailed the lid of the box shut over the coffin. This was the moment at which the horse Weasel was unsaddled, and the saddle was put on the ground in the grave at the head end of the box. Next, the bridle was put on top of it, and finally the double-weave saddle blanket, Frank's favorite, was draped over that end of the box.

Then those standing near the grave told the pallbearers to come out, and they began shoveling dirt into the pit. While this was happening, more speeches began. Six persons spoke, including Clyde Tahi, John (a friend of Frank's), Franklin Tah, Jimmy Begay and two older men. Jimmy identified Frisbie and McAllester to the crowd and praised their work with Frank.

When an oval-shaped mound had been raised over the burial, plastic flowers were planted there, completely covering it. A candle was put in the mound at the head end and was lit by Douglas Mitchell. Father Cormac then left, and many of the People started to do likewise, wandering around the graveyard in the process, looking at other graves. Some others had started leaving once the shoveling began.

Seya then took a rifle and led Weasel through the graveyard, out the gate and then back along the fence to the point nearest the grave. The horse was killed with four shots and left in the wash where it fell.[5]

Agnes, Augusta, Frisbie and McAllester went back to the church and helped clean it up before returning to the Mitchells. Tall Woman was wailing, and most of the hundred or so people who had gone to the graveyard were there eating. Isabelle took Frisbie and McAllester and several others to the hogan to see the cross that Seya and Howard had made from white cement. Engraved in the cement was: "Our Beloved Frank Mitchell – 1881, 15 April, 1967." They had just started to paint the lettering black and were planning to take it to the cemetery when it was dry.

Geneva, one of Frank's granddaughters, explained during the meal that they could not thank Frisbie and McAllester for the food they had brought[6] because Frank had told the family that the old way was never to say thank you for food eaten after someone's death. That was like saying thank you to Frank for dying. Agnes pointed out that in the old days they did not even eat for four days afterwards. Tall Woman followed this tradition, as did several others there. She also did not go to the funeral because of the traditional prohibitions against viewing a dead body.

Isabelle called Frisbie and McAllester into Frank's cabin, which she said had been given to Howard when the sheep, horses and other things had been divided.[7] Then she gave McAllester the moccasins Frank had obtained for Gene Bunnell[8] and also a Navajo basket that Frank had wanted McAllester to have.

Geneva said that Frank[9] had requested that his children delay the funeral because people would want to come from a long distance to attend. He told them they should not try to get rid of him right away. She also reminded everyone that Frank had told all of them not to cry at his funeral and to be brave. Frisbie and McAllester finally said their goodbyes.

There were three printed announcements of Frank's death. One of these was a mimeographed church news bulletin announcement. This said that Frank "had been baptised December 27, 1965, and had received his first communion this past good Friday. He died well fortified with the Last Sacraments of the Church."

The second announcement was one written by John D. Wallace, councilman and member of the Advisory Committee from Chinle. It appeared in the *Chapter Newsletter*, and read: "The recent death of Frank Mitchell ends an era of leadership and inspiration. Frank Mitchell was truly a patriarch in this community having served as councilman, chapter officer, tribal judge, and as a medicine man highly respected by Navajos and non Navajos alike. Your councilman extends his sympathy and condolences to the Mitchell family."

The third article, which was written upon request of the Mitchells by McAllester as an article for the *Navajo Times* (volume 8, no. 20, p. 5), was printed as follows, accompanied by the photograph which appears on the cover and as Figure 11 of this book:

NOTED CHANTER AND LEADER DIES

By DAVID P. McALLESTER

The Navajo People lost an outstanding leader and exponent of the old traditions when Frank Mitchell of Chinle, formerly a Chapter officer, council member and tribal judge, died at the Presbyterian Hospital at Ganado recently.

Mr. Mitchell's parents, Asdzaan Neez and Hastiin Tabaha, were both at Bosque Redondo and met at Fort Defiance on their return from the "Long Walk." They married a year later and lived with the bride's family, tending large herds that wandered from Tsailee across the Chinle Valley to Black Mountain and beyond. Frank, the seventh of ten children, was born in 1881.

His childhood was that of a typical Navajo of the period, caring for his grandmother's stock, learning the traditions of his people, and learning to love the mountains and wide plains of the central regions of the Navajo country. These were the early days of the white man's schools and many a Navajo family resisted sending children away from home. The mark of leadership was on this tall, sixteen-year-old boy of the Tohedlini Clan, however, and his family decided he should go. He made the long wagon trip from Round Rock to the old school at Ft. Defiance and there he had some four or five years of learning. By the turn of the century he had more schooling than most of his contemporaries and had earned the Navajo name by which he was known thereafter, Oltai Tsoh, or Big Schoolboy.

In his young manhood he worked at a variety of jobs, on the railroad, in building, and at an early sawmill. His knowledge of English led to jobs at St. Michaels and then at the Franciscan Mission at Chinle where he could be near his family. He married Rose, the daughter of a well-known Blessingway singer, in 1904.

By then he was an important figure in the Chinle area. He owned one of the few wagons in the region and had a fine team of horses. He was widely known as the principal freighter for the long haul to Gallup and took the name Frank Mitchell after his noted relative, Charlie Mitchell.

Times began to change for the Navajo people. One sign of self-determination was the establishment of a tribal council in 1923. On an early mission to Washington, Frank Mitchell accompanied such notable men as Chee Dodge, Henry Taliman and Howard Gorman. His was one of the first voices to make the plea for more schools, better roads and other improvements so that the Navajo People could begin to help themselves. This was a time of transition for Frank Mitchell, too. He became seriously interested in the Blessingway ceremony practiced by his father-in-law. As he learned it, the teachings on the Way of Good Hope in the ancient texts deepened his understanding of how people should live together in harmony. He was sought out, not only as a singer, but also as a wise and understanding arbitrator. His voice began to be heard in public affairs and he was chosen to be a Chapter officer and a councilman at Window Rock. On the expiration of his term, in the early 1930's, he was appointed a judge by Chee Dodge and the Commissioner of Indian Affairs, John Collier. For some years he sacrificed his time and personal convenience in the interest of this exacting civic duty.

There is still another dimension of Frank Mitchell's service to the Navajo People. When he met Fr. Berard Haile and sensed his sincere devotion to the preservation of Navajo traditions, he spent many hours assisting that famous scholar in his monumental study of the Navajo Blessingway ceremony. In the 1950's and '60's he again turned his attention to this task. As the result of ten years collaboration with the National Science Foundation and the Library of Congress, the full record of this most important of all Navajo ceremonies is now preserved on tape in the National Archives, for the sake of his family and for future generations of his people. In his own words, "When there is no more Blessingway, there will be no more Navajo People." At the same time he made sure of the preservation of the ceremony, he also stipulated that only those with proper authorization should have access to this sacred material.

A powerful and striking man, still riding his horse at the age of 86, Frank Mitchell could look back on a long, rich life of service to his people. He was the central figure in a large and devoted family, kindly, witty, and wise in the ways of men, a public servant, a religious and moral leader. He exemplified the highest attainments that a man can achieve.

At a certain point in one of the prayers of Blessingway, the traditional verses come to an end and the singer may add prayers of his own composition. It is a fitting memorial to Frank Mitchell, a man keenly sensitive to the beauty of the land where he was born, to quote a few lines of his own poetry:

> Blessed, my country will always be there, this I say,
> Blessed, my mountain ranges,
> With pollen they will be blessed, this I say,
> Blessed, the running waters,
> With pollen they will be blessed, this I say,
> According to these things, I shall live, this I say,
> According to these things, we shall live, this I say!

On May 13, 1967, Augusta said to Frisbie, "About a week or so after Frank's funeral, some of us went back to tell the star-gazer that he had passed away. He surely felt badly about that. He suggested to us that all of Frank's family have the Protection Prayer done for us, as is often done when somebody dies. So we all went over there to his place and had it done, including Woody Davis and his family. That is, everybody went except me, because I stayed home with the children.

"That star-gazer said that the Protection Prayer should be done four times. We have had it done just once so far; we are supposed to have it done three times at the singer's hogan and the last time, here, in our hogan. But that hogan will first have to be moved.

"That man is an excellent singer; he knows things and can talk about them just the way that Frank could. He even knows about the nine-night ceremonials, too."

In 1971, Augusta told Frisbie and McAllester, "We have kept our father's sacred bundle. He told us before he died that it should go to his Two Streams Meet Clan but that he did not want that to happen. He told all of us, his children, that we were Standing House Clan and that he wanted to keep it in our clan. So we are just keeping it. A lot of people around here are starting to say that Doogie,[10] Seya's son, has a voice just like Frank's. They are starting to ask him to learn the Blessingway ceremony from the tapes that Frank made.

"Two years after my father died, his sacred bundle was washed during a five-night Evilway for my mother.[11] During that ceremony, they have the Blessingway for one night. At that time the sacred bundle was bathed in that emetic. We washed the contents like the mirage stone and those things, but not the buckskin covering of that bundle. We did that during the last night, after the sweating in the hogan. First the singer and my mother came out of the hogan, and then they went back in. It was then that the short Blessingway was started. All of those things in the bundle were bathed and dried with white cornmeal; the short Blessingway on top of that was just for Tall Woman.

"It took a lot of work to do that. We had a long white sheet, a blanket spread out with the contents of the bundle on it. Frank had so many things tied up in that bundle in individual pieces of buckskin. The singer who was there knew what most of those things were used for; some of them were not things that were connected with the Blessingway. Those were not washed, and the singer told us to bury them in the wash where the wind and water would take them away. We were told not to burn those things.

"The singer opened all the little things Frank had tied together, like the mixed jewels. He put pollen on each of them and prayed over each one. Then he tied them up the way they were and put them back in the sacred bundle. Those things covered the whole hogan. Each of us was assigned to two or three of those things. The singer told us to hurry up and tie them up and put them back. There is nothing that you can do for the big Mountain Earth bundle, so he just went over it with the emetic and put lots of cornmeal on it. He blessed it with corn pollen and then put it back.

"Then he started singing the Hogan songs from the Blessingway. I started to feel like I was floating up in the air; I got all choked up. That was the first time ever that those songs bothered me. Then I cried out, and when I looked around, everyone else was crying too — Ace, Walter, Woody and all of the rest of the family. The singer told us to let it all out. I think it bothered me that time because I had been handling the contents of that sacred bundle.

"I don't remember that man's name, either his Navajo or English one. He is from Smoke Signal, and after he did that, he finished the regular five-night Evilway for my mother. That was the last time Frank's sacred bundle was renewed."

EDITORS' NOTES

1. *Azee' da'atígí*, literally "who do medicine chewing," is used to designate peyote and its use. See Haile (1950:23).

2. Tall Woman still maintains that Frank's children should not visit his grave on Memorial Day or any other day.

3. Our Lady of Fatima Mission Records, however, state that the baptisms took place on December 27, 1965.

4. Two conflicting reports were given on the length of the coma and the reasons given by the doctors for Frank's actual death after it had occurred.

5. This was the north section of the graveyard. Frank's grave was oriented north-south, with the head to the north.

6. The "Abiding Memories" book showed that two Pendletons were donated by Mr. and Mrs. Frank Claw and one by Mrs. Martin and family. Cash donations totaled $230 and were given by Mr. and Mrs. Coley, Dr. George McClellan, McAllester, the Ted Draper family, Chinle Church of Christ, Latter Day Saints Church, Walter Davis (who had originally planned to donate a pair of moccasins) and Mr. and Mrs. Ned Bernally. Others who helped with finances and supplies donated sixty-eight dollars, mutton, bread, eggs, fruit, milk and other supplies; these included Donna Mae Scott, Adelle Mitchell, Douglas Mitchell, Lucy Begay, Gene Price, Thomas Ethridge and Frisbie.

7. In 1971, Augusta told Frisbie and McAllester the following: "Frank had two old strings of turquoise; one was buried with him, and the other one went to Tall Woman. He also had a revolver an old friend, Tah'nezani Tsoh, who was a Chinle policeman, had given him, but we have not seen that since he died. I had wanted to display it with some tomahawks Howard collected, some old grinding stones which we have and some of my mother's old weaving tools; my son, Dino, was going to make a case for those things. Frank had a lot of beads too, but we don't know where those are, either. Only one set is around now, the squash blossom he gave to his wife about three years before he died. Then too, the four big old deep baskets which I gave him are also gone. I bought them from a trader's private collection for thirty-eight dollars apiece. We haven't seen them around here, either.

"The only thing I got was the long, beaded buckskin gloves Frank had been given by another old friend. He had worn them in the winter so much that they were all dirty; he had even patched them himself. I want to get them cleaned, and Seya says they should be washed with mild soap and worked with sheep's brain to tan them again."

In 1971, Seya told Frisbie and McAllester about "two old drawings that look something like sandpaintings" that were Frank's; "They are either at the sheep camp in an old trunk or at home. I also got my father's cane because my son Doogie wanted that." The drawings to which Seya referred are quite possibly mnemonic devices Frank used in remembering Blessingway. See McAllester (1952) for one of the few illustrated discussions of Navajo mnemonic devices.

8. A student from Wesleyan University who had spent a summer with the Mitchell family.

9. No effort was made by anyone except Tall Woman to avoid discussing Frank or calling him by name. Tall Woman even refused to look toward the hill to the west of their hogan where the cemetery was located.

10. Douglas Mitchell, son of Seya and grandson of Frank, died on December 4, 1972, from a combination of physical ailments. He was given a military funeral at Saint Michaels and buried in Fort Defiance.

11. Isabelle Mitchell sat in as a substitute for her mother, Tall Woman, during the part of the Blessingway wherein Frank's bundle was renewed. The substitution was deemed appropriate because Tall Woman was beginning to suffer from occasional losses of memory. The one-sung-over at this point is recognized as the new owner of the bundle; thus, the bundle was transferred to Tall Woman.

Appendix A

Genealogical and Census Data

The data presented in this appendix can at best be termed incomplete. The genealogies of Frank's natal family are the most problematical. Neither Frank, other family members nor more distant clan relatives who were Frank's contemporaries could recall clear details about people in the great-grandparent generation, be it their single-multiple names, spouses, geographic location area, time span of life or offspring. Even in Frank's parent generation, collaborators remained uncertain as to the number of wives Frank's father had, the number of offspring and his exact whereabouts at different points in time. The same held true for several of Frank's own siblings, who were often unknown to his own children. Perhaps the clearest elements to emerge are the confusion itself and the repetitive emphasis on constant movement, multiple mates who were lived with "without any ceremony," numerous scattered relatives and the unimportance of chronological time to the Navajos.

The genealogical information about Frank's conjugal family is much clearer in many respects. Here, the major problems stem from lack of consistency among several written records which documented birth and death dates, birth order and number of offspring for government, tribal and missionary purposes. Comparative data from Frank, Tall Woman, other family members, the Peter Paquette Census of 1915, the Saint Michaels Mission Census begun by Father Marcellus at Tohatchi in 1915 (Rademaker 1976a), the Window Rock census of 1928-1929 and the latest census available there in 1971, and the birth-burial records at the Franciscan Mission in Chinle are included for Frank's natal family and the conjugal family of Frank and Tall Woman.

Appendix A includes:

1. Frank Mitchell's Genealogy
2. The Extended Family of Water Edge Man and Tall Woman, Frank's Father and Mother

[342]

3. The Extended Family of Frank Mitchell (Big Schoolboy) and Tall Woman (Rose Delaghoshi)
4. Comparison of Available Census Materials re Frank Mitchell's Natal and Conjugal Families
5. Frank Mitchell's Natal Family: A Comparison of Data re Actual People, Birth Order and Birth Dates from Frank Mitchell (1963) (F.M.) and the Saint Michaels Mission Census (S.M.M.C.)
6. Frank Mitchell's Conjugal Family: A Comparison of Data re Actual People, Birth Order and Birth Dates from Frank Mitchell (1963) (F.M.) and the Saint Michaels Mission Census (S.M.M.C.)

A-1. Frank Mitchell's Genealogy

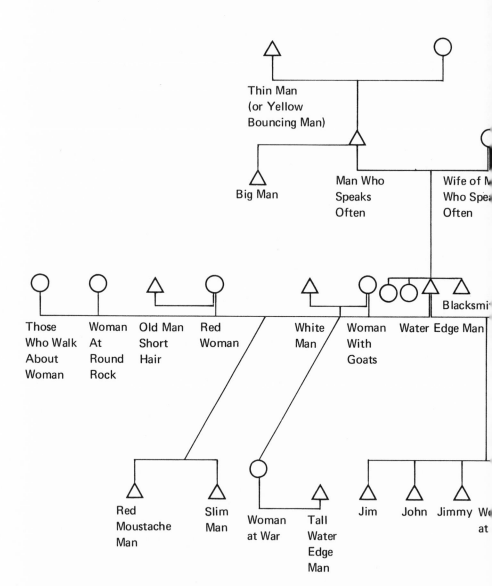

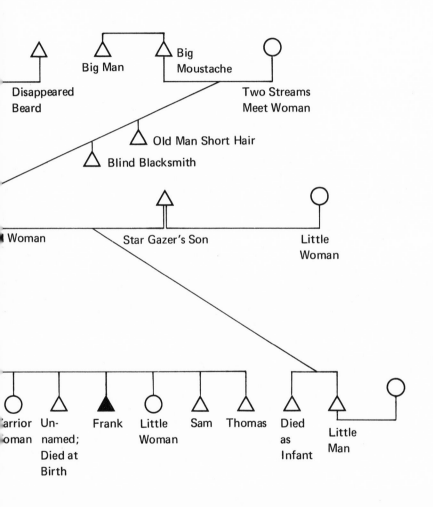

A-2. The Extended Family of Water Edge Man and Tall Woman
(Frank Mitchell's Father and Mother)

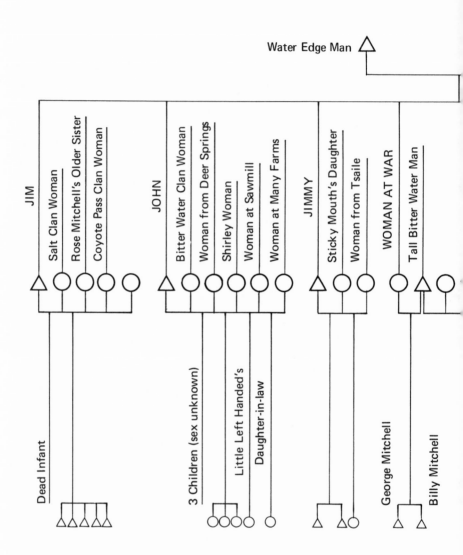

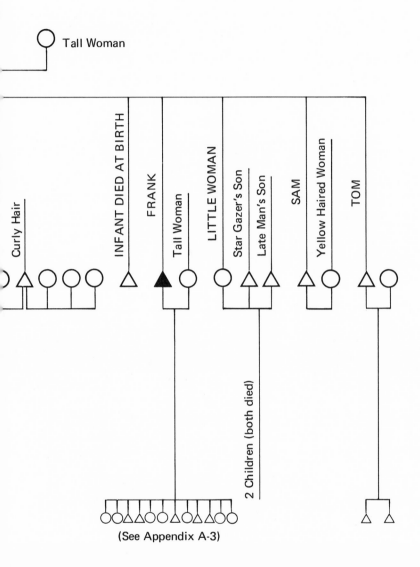

(See Appendix A-3)

A-3. The Extended Family of Frank Mitchell (Big Schoolboy)
and Tall Woman (Rose Delaghoshi)

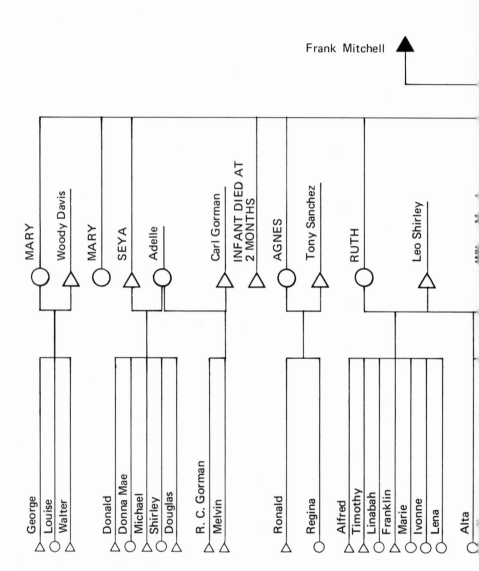

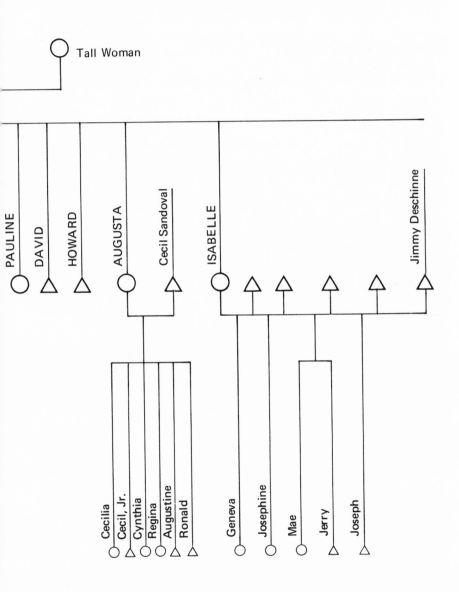

A-4. Comparison of Available Census Materials re Frank Mitchell's Natal and Conjugal Families

Natal Family	Saint Michaels Mission Census	Chinle Mission Birth-Death Records	Peter Paquette 1915 Census	Window Rock 1928-1929 Census	Window Rock 1971 Records	Frank Mitchell 1963
Water Edge Man	died 1922	—	—	—	—	—
Jim Mitchell #66561	b. 1873	#66361 b. 1876, 1873 d. 6/20/48	—	b. 1872	#66561 d. 6/20/48	b. 1870
John Mitchell #50166	b. 1871	#50166 or #67216 b. 1871 d. 9/22/1959	—	—		b. 1871
Jimmy Mitchell	—	—	—	—	—	b. 1873
Woman at War	—	—	—	—	—	b. 1875
Warrior Woman	—	—	—	—	—	b. 1877
Baby Boy	—	—	—	—	—	b. 1879
Frank Mitchell #070048	(b. 1889) —	—	b. 1880	#70048 b. 1887	b. 1889	b. 1881
Little Woman	—	—	—	—	—	b. 1883
Sam Mitchell	—	—	—	—	—	b. 1885
Tom Mitchell	—	—	—	—	—	b. 1887
Conjugal Family						
Tall Woman #070049	b. 1890	b. 1890	b. 1890	#70049 b. 1888	Card #1096 b. 1890	—
Mary Davis	b. 1903	b. 1911	b. 1908	—	b. 1911	b. 1904

Name						
Mary	b. 1910	b. 1911 d. 1/15/31	b. 1910	#70050 1911–1/15/31	—	b. 1906
Seya	b. 6/30/14	b. 6/30/16	b. 1912	#70051 b. 1914	b. 6/30/12	b. 1908 or 1910
Infant Boy	—	—	—	—	—	b. 1910
Agnes	b. 8/20/1918	b. 1918	—	#70052 b. 1916	—	b. 1912
Ruth	b. 1920	b. 1920	—	#70053 b. 1918 Asannie Tulli	b. 1920	b. 1914
Infant Boy	No date	—	—	—	—	b. 1916
Pauline	b. 1917	—	—	—	—	b. 1918
David	b. 1922	#70054 b. 1922 d. 8/21/38	—	#70054 1921–8/21/38	—	b. 1920
Howard	b. 1926	b. 1926	—	#70055 b. 1924 Hastiin Tso	—	b. 1922
Augusta	b. 8/14/1928	b. 8/15/1926	—	#67816 b. 1926 Adaa Tulli	b. 8/14/28	b. 1924
Isabelle	b. 8/6/1932	b. 7/28/1932	—	#70563 b. 8/6/32	b. 7/6/31	b. 1926

A-5. Frank Mitchell's Natal Family: A Comparison of Data re Actual People, Birth Order and Birth Dates from Frank Mitchell (1963) (F.M.) and the Saint Michaels Mission Census (S.M.M.C.)

Name		Sequence of Birth		Birthdate	
F.M.	S.M.M.C.	F.M.	S.M.M.C.	F.M.	S.M.M.C.
Jim Mitchell	Tohadlini Nez	1	2	1870	1873
John Mitchell	John	2	1	1871	1871
Jimmy Mitchell	Jim	3	3	1873	not given
Woman at War	Bazhuaba	4	5	1875	not given
Warrior Woman	Asdzałbaha	5	6	1877	not given
Unnamed infant boy	not mentioned	6	—	1879	—
Frank	Frank	7	4	1881	1889
Little Woman	not mentioned	8	—	1883	—
Sam	not mentioned	9	—	1885	—
Tom	Tom	10	8	1887	not given
Unnamed infant boy — 1st son of Frank's mother with second husband, Star Gazer's Son	not mentioned	11	—	not given	—
Little Man — second son of Frank's mother and Star Gazer's Son	Hastiin Yazha	12	10	not given	1904
Not mentioned	Dine Tso	—	7	—	not given
Not mentioned	Yik'azba	—	9	—	not given

A-6. Frank Mitchell's Conjugal Family: A Comparison of Data re Actual People, Birth Order and Birth Dates from Frank Mitchell (1963) (F.M.) and the Saint Michaels Mission Census (S.M.M.C.)

Name		Sequence of Brith		Birthdate	
F.M.	S.M.M.C.	F.M.	S.M.M.C.	F.M.	S.M.M.C.
Mary Davis — "Asdzáán go'," "Billy Mahi"	Asdza go'	1	1	1904	1903
Mary — "Aheejebah"	Mary	2	5	1906	1910
Seya	Seya	3	7	1908 or 1910	6/30/14
Unnamed infant, died at 2 months	Biye	4	4	1910	died
Agnes — "Girl with a Light Complexion"	Agnes	5	8	1912	8/30/18
Ruth — "Woman with a Light Complexion," "Mama Ruth"	Ruth	6	10	1914	1920
Unnamed infant boy	not mentioned	7	—	1916	—
Pauline	Girl	8	9	1918	1917
David	David	9	11	1920	1922
Howard — "Big Man," "Kǫǫzhi"	Howard	10	12	1922	1926
Augusta — "Lili"	Augusta	11	13	1924	8/14/28
Isabelle — "Small Woman"	Isabelle	12	14	1926	8/6/31
Not mentioned	Asdza Yazhe	—	2	—	1905
Not mentioned	Choshi	—	3	—	1907
Not mentioned	Ateed Ituli	—	6	—	1911

Appendix B

Chronology, 1856-1972

Attempts to establish a chronology for Frank's life history have met with numerous difficulties. While Frank organized his nondirected account of his life story from earliest days to latest events and thoughts, he frequently used phrases such as, "I worked there for five or ten years," or "I was twenty or thirty years old at the time." In an effort to correlate Frank's story with events of ethnohistorical significance to the Navajos, and to delineate time span and setting, Frisbie had to turn to ethnohistorical resources for further clarification.

The chronology which follows is as complete as possible. For genealogical information, Frank is the source; conflicting data from several mission and government census records appear in Appendix A. Other sources include publications on Navajo history; National Park Service records; mission and government-tribal records at Window Rock, Saint Michaels and Chinle; several photograph collections; interviews with Frank's contemporaries conducted by the editors and other anthropologists; and data available from the National Archives and Federal Records Center.

Chronology

4/9/1856
> First post office in Arizona established at Fort Defiance

1856
> Son of the Late Little Blacksmith born

1864-68
> The Long Walk and confinement at Fort Sumner

1868
> Treaty signed

6/15/1868
> Exodus from Fort Sumner begins
> Frank Mitchell's parents start living together

1869-70

First day school started at Fort Defiance

1870

Jim Mitchell born

Barboncito dies

Freighting being done for agents under contract

1871

John Mitchell born

Fort Defiance mission established

1872

Thomas V. Keam, Navajo agent, organizes Navajo Police Force for one
    year

1873

Jimmy Mitchell born

1875

Woman at War born

1876 (or 1878)

Hubbell's Trading Post built at Ganado

1876

Word received about plans for railroad

1877

Warrior Woman born

1879

Infant boy Mitchell born and dies

1879-81

Construction of boarding school at Fort Defiance

1880

Two portable sawmills in use at Fluted Rock and northwest of Sawmill

Eleven Navajos receive wagons for use in farming

1880-87

Railroad moving west from Albuquerque

1880s

Anglo Americans start to come onto reservation in numbers

1881

Frank Mitchell born at Wheatfields. Family located at Tsaile, Black
    Mountain and mouth of Canyon de Chelly

Manuelito and Ganado Mucho given wagons

1881-83

School opens at Fort Defiance

1882

First trading post in Chinle

1883

Little Woman born
Post offices established at Ganado, Keams Canyon, Navajo Springs

1884

Post offices established at Houck and Tuba City

1885

Sam Mitchell born

1886

First license to trade in Chinle issued to Lorenzo Hubbell and C. N.
Cotton

1887

Thomas Mitchell born
Federal Allotment Act
Law enacted compelling all Indian children to go to school

1889

Fort Wingate hospital opens

1890

Tall Woman (Rose Delaghoshi Mitchell) born around Steamboat, on the
south side of Tsaile
Horses begin to replace oxen and mule teams in freighting work
Man Who Shouts begins serving as headman in the Chinle area

1892

Dana L. Shipley is Navajo Agent (Term – 12/19/90-3/31/93)
Trouble at Round Rock (Black Horse vs. Agent Shipley) in October

1893

Manuelito dies
Lieutenant Edward Plummer and group of eleven Navajos go to Chicago
for World's Columbian Exposition – 10/13/93-10/24/93
License issued to Aldrich and Dodge by Plummer for new store at
Round Rock (12/25/93)

1893-94

Frank Mitchell enrolled in Fort Defiance boarding school; returns home
in summer
Lieutenant Edward Plummer acting agent, 4/1/93-11/14/94

1894

Good Shepherd mission established in Fort Defiance

1896

C. C. Manning purchases Billy Weidemeyer's trading post in Fort
Defiance; operates it through 1906

1897

Fort Defiance hospital opens

1898

Saint Michaels mission established in October
Tohatchi post office established

1899

Government giving wagons, plows, axes to induce Navajos to send children to Fort Defiance school
Saint Michaels school starts — 3/19/99
C. N. Cotton is trading in Ganado and shipping in Gallup

1900

Frank Walker goes to Saint Michaels as mission interpreter on 1/23/00
Tohatchi boarding school opens
Charlie Mitchell visits Saint Michaels for first time — 2/21/00
At least twenty-four traders on reservation
First baptism at Saint Michaels — 4/4/00
Charles L. Day granted license to trade in Chinle
Lorenzo Hubbell builds another trading post in Chinle

1901

Hospital, school and mission established at Ganado
Tuba City boarding school opens
Christian Reformed Mission boarding school at Rehoboth opens

1902

Work starts on Saint Michaels elementary school — 3/1/02
First religious instruction at Fort Defiance school by Franciscan Father Leopold — 4/3/02
Saint Michaels post office opens — 9/1/02
Saint Michaels elementary school opens with forty-six children enrolled — 12/3/02
Simpson's Trading Post burns to ground — 12/6/02
Father Anselm Weber, Frank Walker, Miss Josephine Drexel and Sister Agatha visit Chinle to determine feasibility of establishing a Franciscan mission there
Father Leopold begins to go to Chinle in his capacity of Franciscan missionary

1903

Frank returns to school in Fort Defiance and is on fire brigade — 2/20/03
Frank's mother now living with second husband
Chinle post office opens
Franciscan mission site selected in Chinle — 4/16/03

Charles L. Day appointed custodian of Canyon de Chelly and Canyon del Muerto ruins — 6/1/03

Letter sent to Washington requesting land grant for Franciscan mission in Chinle — 6/24/03

Navajo Agency divided into two sections with two superintendents — July

Father Leopold holds first public service in Chinle — 9/27/03

Land granted for mission — 10/10/03

Reuben Perry serves as superintendent of southern part — August or 10/1/03-10/16/06

1904

Frank leaves school and works on the railroad, ending in Needles, California

Frank returns home; family accidentally located near Frank's father and second wife

Father Leopold and Brother Placidus come to Chinle and live in small dugout at store — Summer 1904

Frank wrestles with cousin, is seriously injured, and is treated with Lifeway ceremonial

Frank begins to work at government warehouse in Chinle and then starts to work in Fort Defiance at C.C. Manning's Trading Post with John Mitchell

Frank begins to learn some things about the Blessingway

Frank transfers from Fort Defiance and begins working for Father Weber at Saint Michaels mission

Frank Mitchell starts living with Tall Woman [probably 1906, if birth dates of offspring shown in mission records, Appendix A, are used]

Mary Mitchell #1 (Davis) born

1905

Charlie Cousins goes to Chinle to operate Weidemeyer's store (originally built by Sam Day, Sr., in 1902)

Charles Day goes to Cienaga Amarilla to run Two-Story Trading Post

Site for Franciscan Fathers' residence in Chinle selected by Fathers Weber, Leopold and Ketchum (from Washington) — 10/15/05

Trouble between Chinle Navajos and Superintendent Reuben Perry — late October or November

1905-1906

Franciscan Fathers' residence under construction. Becomes habitable but not finished by January 1906

1906

Brother Placidus dies at Chinle — 2/19/06

Frank leaves Saint Michaels mission and returns to Chinle

Saint Michaels records show a "Francis Mitchell" paid for work there — 4/12/06-5/12/06

Frank works at Franciscan residence in Chinle with Father Leopold until August 1906, when Brother Gervase arrives to replace Brother Placidus

Franciscan Fathers' home in Chinle completed summer 1906

Dr. F. M. Palmer's archaeological excavation near Antelope Ruins

Son of the Late Little Blacksmith comes to Chinle and begins to use mission's grazing lands during his work as peacemaker

Mary Mitchell (#2) born

1907

Father Marcellus comes to Chinle in January — remains until 1915, when he goes to Saint Michaels

Frank begins working at the sawmill

Frank's conjugal family living with Man Who Shouts

Chinle Franciscan Fathers' home raised to a residence — 7/24/07

Shiprock boarding school opens

Another sawmill begins operation in Sanostee/Toadlena area and lasts until 1935

1907-1909

Jimmy Mitchell dies

Sam Mitchell dies

Frank's mother dies

Little Woman dies

1908

Rumors begin about future government boarding school and Franciscan Annunciation mission in Chinle

Seya Mitchell born (Frank also gives 1910 birth date)

Peter Paquette becomes superintendent of Navajo Agency (1908-1925)

Hospitals established at Leupp and Shiprock

1909

Frank earns his first wagon and leaves the sawmill

Leupp boarding school opens

1909-10

Frank works on bridge

Frank hauls stones for Chinle school and mission construction

1909-11

Tom Mitchell dies

1910

Franciscan Annunciation Mission Church in Chinle under construction

Chinle boarding school opens — 4/1/10

First automobile comes to Chinle

Tall Woman begins to have ceremonials

Frank begins freighting (ends c. 1918)

Infant boy born and dies

Frank has Beautyway ceremonial

1910-15

Frank assists with archaeological excavation near Antelope Ruins

1911

Hospital established at Tuba City

1912

Agnes Mitchell born

More cars start appearing on reservation

Leaders in Chinle area include Son of the Late Little Blacksmith, John Brown (policeman), Charlie Mitchell, Man Who Shouts and Bead Clan Gambler

C. C. Manning goes to Gallup

Presbyterian Mission boarding school opens in Ganado

Hospital established at Fort Defiance

Crownpoint boarding school opens

1913

Beautiful Mountain uprising

Toadlena boarding school opens

1914

Ruth Mitchell born

Hospital established at Crownpoint

First World War breaks out

1915

W. T. Shelton, agent at Shiprock

Era of automobiles arrives; five Navajos, including Chee Dodge, Tom Damon, Willie Damon, Hosteen Yazzie, and Clitsoi Dedman own cars. Roads improving

Frank has Ghostway ceremonial

Lorenzo Hubbell starts horse-drawn stage and freight service

1915-16

Father Sextus in Chinle, followed by Fathers Laurence and Ludger

1916

Infant boy born and dies

Charles Day opens new trading post in Round Rock

1916-19

Frank has Male Shootingway, Holyway and Chiricahua Apache Windway ceremonials

1917

Lorenzo Hubbell's trading post in Chinle sold to C. N. Cotton

Frank's father wanders around after leaving second wife; he often comes by Frank's place, which is beside the home of Man Who Shouts

U.S. enters World War I, and some Navajos enter service

1918
    Pauline Mitchell born
    Charles Day killed
    Man Who Shouts begins to get sick
    Frank stops hauling freight and settles permanently in Chinle
    Frank begins seriously learning Blessingway from Man Who Shouts and
        his own father
    Frank starts assisting Son of the Late Little Blacksmith, Long
        Moustache and Curly Hair in their talks to the People

1919
    Chinle school plant still in use in 1976 opened

1920
    David Mitchell born
    Camille García goes to work in Cotton's store in Chinle
    Frank's father dies

1922
    Howard Mitchell born
    Man Who Shouts dies
    Frank assumes headmanship role
    Business Council composed of three Navajos — Chee Dodge, Charlie
        Mitchell and Dugal Chee Bekiss — who meet to act on question of
        oil leases

1923
    First Tribal Council elected; twelve delegates and twelve alternates from
        six jurisdiction areas plus chairman. First meeting — 7/7/23
    Charlie Mitchell active as headman
    Cozy McSparron, Camille García and Hartley T. Seymour buy all three
        stores in Chinle

1923-28
    Henry Chee Dodge serves as first Tribal chairman

1924
    Augusta Mitchell (Sandoval) born
    Frank witnessing marriages in Chinle area as a headman
    Citizenship extended to all American Indians
    Frank witnesses marriage with Hastiin altsi'ichibiye and Father Leopold
        Ostermann — 8/7/24

1924-25
    Father Emanuel in Chinle until February 1925
    Father Marti in Chinle from February until July, when Father Emanuel
        returns to stay until 1928

1925
    Opening of Fort Wingate's school plant still in use in 1976

1925-30

Time of photos taken of Frank at Saint Michaels

1926

Pauline Mitchell dies

Isabelle Mitchell born

Toadlena hospital established

1926-28

Meriam Report on Indian Education

1927

Navajo Agency divided into Northern, Eastern and Southern agencies —
1/1/27-7/1/35

Tall Woman's crippled brother dies

Hospitals established at Kayenta and Tohatchi

1927-28

Chapter Program introduced on reservation

1928

Navajo Indian Congress Program at Saint Michaels — 10/16/28-10/18/28

John Hunter becomes superintendent of Southern Navajo Agency —
(1929-34)

Deshna Chischillige becomes Tribal chairman — 1928-32

1930

Frank records the Blessingway myth for Father Berard Haile   (See
Wyman 1970, Myth version 2)

Large areas of grazing lands are noticeably depleted

1930-31

Tribe agrees to National Park Service supervision of Canyon de Chelly
and Canyon del Muerto

1930-40s

Stock reduction

1931

Mary Mitchell (#2) dies — 1/15/31, burial in Chinle mission cemetery

Frank's letter to Reuben Perry about condition of children in off-
reservation schools — 2/19/31 (See notes to Chapter 10)

Father Arnold Heinsman is the Superior at Saint Michaels

1931-38

Tall Woman's mother, Tall Woman, dies and is buried by mission.
Occurs between 1/15/31 and 8/21/38

1932

Chinle hospital opens

Charlie Mitchell dies at Tsaile — 7/15/32

Frank visits Saint Michaels as part of delegation pursuing question about the trouble between Roy Kinsel and Charlie Mitchell and its relation to Charlie's death

Trips to sacred mountains — 9/8/32 — several trips over a period of time

1932-36

Thomas Dodge serves as Tribal chairman with twelve-member Council (Frank not among members)

Council signs oil leases

1932-50

Chapter Program halted

1933

Franklin D. Roosevelt becomes U.S. president

John Collier becomes Indian commissioner

Reservation reorganized with one general superintendent and Window Rock as new "capital"

Grazing surveys begin

Collier holds his first meeting with Tribal Council in July at Fort Wingate; range problem discussed

Winslow hospital opens

1933-34

First attempt at stock reduction fails

Navajos react bitterly to reduction program

1934

Navajo Mounted Police established

Reservation divided into eighteen land management districts; Tribal Council expanded to twenty-four delegates by 7/10/34

Father Anselm Sippel comes to Chinle, where he remains until 1940

1935

Construction of sawmill started at Sawmill, Arizona. Mill becomes self-supporting in 1944, closing in 1963

Agencies consolidated on 7/1/35; Southern, Eastern, Northern Navajo agencies, Leupp Agency, part of Hopi Agency and Charles H. Burke School joined to form Navajo Agency once again

Chester Faris becomes superintendent — 7/1/35-4/15/36

1936

Navajo Patrol started

Thomas Dodge resigns as Tribal Chairman — 3/30/36

Last meeting of old Tribal Council — 11/24/36

1936-37

> December-March 9, reorganization of Council; reservation canvassed by Father Berard Haile, E. R. Fryer (superintendent 3/16/36-5/31/42), Chee Dodge and Dashne to identify men of merit

12/15/36

> District 10 (Chinle) reorganization meeting held with Father Berard Haile

1937

> Committee picks members of new Constitutional Assembly — 3/10/37; Frank chosen as member
>
> Henry Taliman becomes Tribal chairman
>
> Hand-picked Constitutional Assembly meets for first time — 4/9-10/37
>
> Group declares itself de facto Tribal Council
>
> Son of the Late Little Blacksmith dies on 5/31/37
>
> Constitutional Committee (includes Frank) works on drafting Tribal constitution under unwilling chairmanship of Jake Morgan
>
> Frank participates in trip to Washington, D.C. sometime in late June or early July
>
> Work on constitution completed 10/25/37
>
> Constitution not accepted by Federal Government

1938

> Jacob C. Morgan becomes Tribal chairman
>
> Frank serves on Constitution Committee, which continues to work on remodeling document, as well as on Executive and Grazing Committees — 2/17/38-1/20/38
>
> Government issues "The Rules of Tribal Council Constitutions" — 7/26/38
>
> David Mitchell dies on 8/21/38
>
> Frank argues with John Brown
>
> David Mitchell buried by Reverend Anselm Sippel in mission cemetery, Chinle — 8/21/38
>
> Chic Sandoval and Curly Hair are serving on Tribal Council with Frank
>
> New Tribal Council election held using colors to identify candidates — 9/27/38 or 11/24/38. Frank not reelected. District 10 representatives include Deschinne Nez Begay, Zhealy Tso, Sam Gorman and Eli Smith

1938-51

> Six judges for Navajos are appointed to office by commissioner of of Indian Affairs with Tribal Council approval

1940s

> Frank makes one film for B.I.A. on Navajo daily life (between 1940-47)

1941-46

Frank and other Navajos in Chinle get roles as extras in three separate Hollywood movies, filmed in the area in 1941, 1943-45 and 1944-46

1941

U. S. enters World War II — 12/7/41

Navajo Code Talkers play important role in defense

1942

Chee Dodge becomes Tribal Chairman

Judges in Court of Indian Offenses include Sam Jim, John Curley (who was also a councilman), Slowtalker, Claw, Sidney Phillips and possibly Frank Mitchell

1944

Frank serves as Chinle Chapter officer with John Gorman. Records of settlements of property disputes signed by both on 1/31/44 and 7/1/44

1944-45

Zhealy Tso is Chinle delegate to Tribal Council

1945

Tribal Council minutes for 7/10-13/45 include comments on election procedures for judges and suggestions about wages and sources of pay. Also state that judges appointed in 1938 (and still in office in 1945) have terms which are legally nonrenewable

1946

Sam Ahkeah becomes Tribal chairman

Chee Dodge, elected as vice chairman, dies before taking office

Zhealy Tso elected by Council to fill his term

Saint Michaels mission high school opens

Tom Mitchell dies

First woman, Lilly J. Neil, is elected to Tribal Council. Serves 1946-50 and is reelected. Injured in 1951 automobile accident and picks a replacement

1946-51

Frank Mitchell serves as judge in Court of Indian Offenses

1947-48

Reid Winnie is Chinle delegate to Tribal Council

1948

Arizona and New Mexico give Navajos the right to vote

Jim Mitchell dies and is buried in mission cemetery — 6/20/48

1949

Huge blizzard in January and February

Joe Carroll is Chinle delegate to Tribal Council

1950s

Chapter Program revived on reservation

1950

Reid Winnie and Joe Carroll are Chinle delegates to Tribal Council; Reid may have resigned for health reasons

1950-51

First election using pictorial paper ballot instead of colored ribbons

Sam Ahkeah reelected Tribal chairman (1951-54)

Frank runs for councilman from District 10, province 2, against Joe Carroll and Walker Norcross. Loses to Carroll

1951, 1952

Frank Mitchell serves as Chinle Chapter president; Irene Stewart, secretary

1951-59

Judges elected rather than appointed. Frank ends career as judge in 1951

1950-53

Frank is interviewed once by Ruth Underhill on Western Navajo clans

1952

Cornell University's Medical College becomes involved in Navajo health in January

1952-55

Frank experiences bladder trouble and has several operations at Ganado hospital

1954

First public school on reservation opens at Fort Defiance

Paul Jones elected Tribal chairman; serves 1955-62

Window Rock Area's organizational designation changed to Navajo Agency

1955

Navajo Agency reorganized; five subagencies established with subagency superintendents responsible for certain B.I.A. programs. Subagencies include Chinle, Crownpoint, Fort Defiance, Shiprock and Tuba City

Cornell University's Health Project at Many Farms begins and lasts through 1962

Frank serves as Project consultant

Frank begins work with Mary Shepardson on Navajo legal and political processes (1955-65)

Chinle Chapter officially established; Frank again serves as Chapter president

1956

Many Farms Clinic opens 5/7/56 with Dan Yazzie performing Navajo House Blessing ceremony

Reid Winnie serves as Chinle Chapter president 1956-57 and then resigns

Zhealy Tso appointed as judge for three-year term

1957

Gordon Baldwin serves as Chinle Chapter president

Frank Mitchell begins work with David P. McAllester on Navajo ceremonialism (1957-67)

Frank makes film on Blessingway for Wesleyan University under university and Museum of Navajo Ceremonial Art auspices

1958

Navajo Forest Products Industries started and construction begun on Tribal sawmill at Navajo, New Mexico

Little Man dies

1959

Frank has Enemyway ceremonial performed

Frank performs Navajo House Blessing ceremony during dedication of Chinle Chapter House – 6/20/59

Joe Carroll serves as Chinle delegate to Tribal Council

Judges, including chief justice, start being appointed for life

John Mitchell dies – 9/22/59; buried in new Chinle cemetery

1961

Frank performs House Blessing ceremony during dedication of Chinle boarding school – 5/19/61

1962

Guy Gorman serves as Chinle delegate to Tribal Council

Raymond Nakai becomes Tribal chairman

Frank is interviewed by Clifford Barnett on the effects of modern medicine on Navajo religion and changes in curing practices – 5/17/62

Frank is interviewed by Kathryn T. Coley on Navajo medicine men and politics

Sawmill at Navajo, New Mexico, becomes operational

1963

Frank begins work with Charlotte J. Frisbie on Girl's Puberty Ceremony, House Blessing ceremony, Blessingway ceremonialism, Navajo music, life history (June 1963-April 1967)

Frank performs Girl's Puberty Ceremony, Kinaaldá, for filming by American Indians Films, Inc. from University of California, Berkeley – July, 1973

Film group also films Red Antway ceremonial in Valley Store, Arizona, and other Navajo ceremonials

Frank still actively performing Blessingway

1964-65

> Frank performs House Blessing during dedication of Chinle high school
> — 2/29/64
>
> Frank interviewed on oral history of Canyon de Chelly, during Doris
> Duke American Indian History Project. Interviewers: Sally Peirce
> Harris (10/21/64 and 7/20/65; informant #961, #965, #967); Irene
> Stewart (7/17/65; #965) and David Gorman (7/20/65; #965)

1965

> Frank interviewed by Chien Chiao on learning and transmitting Navajo
> ceremonies
>
> Frank and Tall Woman baptized Catholic by Franciscan Fathers in
> Chinle. Agnes Mitchell Sanchez serves as sponsor — 12/27/65

1966

> John Wallace serves as Chinle delegate to Tribal Council
>
> Frank becomes increasingly ill; prostate cancer revealed to family
>
> Frank increases use of diagnosticians and has numerous ceremonies
>
> Frank in and out of Ganado hospital
>
> Roy Kinsel dies — 7/17/66

1967

> Frank receives holy communion and last rites of church
>
> Frank Mitchell dies — 4/15/67
>
> Frank Mitchell's funeral with Requiem Mass; Our Lady of Fatima
> Church [Franciscan], Chinle, and burial in Mission Cemetery,
> Apache County — 4/20/67

1967-69

> Office of Navajo Economic Opportunity Navajo Culture Project

1969

> Frank's bundle is renewed during an Evilway and Blessingway for Tall
> Woman. Bundle ownership transferred to Tall Woman

1970

> Guy Gorman serves as Chinle delegate to Tribal Council
>
> Peter MacDonald becomes Tribal Chairman

1971

> Final ethnohistorical and interview work for life history started by
> editors
>
> Mitchell family reaffirms agreement about publishing Frank's life
> history

1972

> Frank's grandson, Douglas (Doogie), dies in December

Appendix C

Anthropologists and Others
Who Worked With Frank Mitchell

I. INDIVIDUALS*

Clifford Barnett (Stanford University)
5/17/62   Interview on the effects of modern medicine on Navajo
            religion and changes in curing practices.

Samuel Barrett (University of California, Berkeley; now deceased)
7/63   Interviews in conjunction with Kinaaldá film

Gene A. Bunnell
1965   Interviews on Navajo medicine men, physicians and
            health.

Chien Chiao (Indiana University)
1965   Interview on the learning and transmission of Navajo
            ceremonials.

Kathryn T. Coley
1962   Interview on Navajo medicine men and politics.

Charlotte J. Frisbie (Southern Illinois University, Edwardsville)
1963-67   Interviews regarding Kinaaldá, House Blessing, Blessing-
            way, life history and Navajo music.

David Gorman
7/20/65   Interview on the oral history of Canyon de Chelly (Doris
            Duke American Indian History Project, Informant
            #965).

Franciscan Father Berard Haile (Saint Michaels, Arizona; now
    deceased)
1930   Narration of Blessingway myth which appears as ver-
            sion 2 in Wyman (1970).

_____

*To the best of Frisbie's knowledge, Frank Mitchell did not ever work with
other Navajo specialists, including Leland Wyman, John Adair, Gladys
Reichard, Bertha Dutton, Clyde Kluckhohn, David Aberle, W. W. Hill,
Martin Link, Lee Correll, Edward Sapir, Harry Hoijer, Kenneth Foster and
David Brugge.

Sally Peirce Harris
10/21/64,   Interviews on the oral history of Canyon de Chelly
7/20/65   (Doris Duke American Indian History Project, Informant
             #961, #965, #967).

David P. McAllester (Wesleyan University)
1957-67   Interviews on Navajo ceremonialism, Blessingway, life
             history and Navajo music.

Mary Shepardson (California State University, San Francisco)
1955-65   Interviews on Navajo legal process and Navajo politics.

Irene Stewart .
7/17/65   Interview on the oral history of Canyon de Chelly (Doris
             Duke American Indian History Project, Informant
             #965).

Ruth Underhill (Denver, Colorado)
Early 1950s Interview on Western Navajo clans.

II. ASSISTANCE TO OTHER GROUPS*

Advised Cornell Project staff at Many Farms Clinic, 1955-62.
Drove wagon for unidentified archaeologists near Antelope Ruins,
Canyon del Muerto, sometime between 1910-15.

III. FILMS IN WHICH FRANK MITCHELL PARTICIPATED

Blessingway, 1957 (Wesleyan University, Museum of Navajo Ceremonial
Art; film complete but not released for public viewing).

Kinaaldá, 1963 (University of California, Berkeley-American Indian
Films, Inc.; in 1976 still in raw footage form).

Navajo Daily Life (B.I.A. film made between 1940-47; no further information available).

Three Hollywood feature films (made between 1941-46; Frank worked
as extra; see Chapter 10, n. 9).

---

*Frank Mitchell did not assist with the Tribal Land Claims Project, and he
died before he could be asked to participate in the Navajo Culture Project
sponsored by the Office of Navajo Economic Opportunity (1967-69).

Appendix D

Documents

This appendix includes copies of the following Tribal documents:

1. Minutes of the Meeting of the Tribal Executive Committee of the Navajo Tribal Council, May 2-3, 1938, provided by Robert Young
2. Department of the Interior Document #85143, "Law and Order Regulations," Chapters 1-5, dated February 15, 1937

APPENDIX D-1.
Minutes of the Meeting of the Tribal Executive Committee
of the Navajo Tribal Council, May 2-3, 1938

United States
Department of the Interior
Office of Indian Affairs
Navajo Service
Window Rock, Arizona

TABLE OF CONTENTS

Meeting of the Executive Committee

Chairman — Henry Taliman
Interpreter — Chick Sandoval   Monday, May 2, 1938, 9:45 a.m.

CHAIRMAN: The meeting will now come to order. At this time, I would like
to have all the Executive Committee present take the front seats so we will
know who is present from their districts. We will call roll by districts.

(Roll called by Districts by Chick Sandoval)

        District   1 — Gish ne Bitah
        District   2 — Tsa ad Zeci Begay
        District   3 — Roy Hos Kan, represented by Adolph Maloney
        District   4 — Cla e
        District   5 — Robert Curley
        District   7 — Billie Pete, represented by Pete Totsoni
        District   8 — Hugh Black, absent
        District   9 — Ah de sai Begay, represented by Hosteen Yazzie
        District 10 — Frank Mitchell
        District 11 — Dine Tsosie
        District 12 — Dashne Cla Chischillige
        District 13 — No representative present
        District 14 — Hosteen Yazzie Jesus
        District 15 — Willeto Arviso
        District 16 — Antonio Silversmith
        District 17 — Yazzie Holmes
        District 18 — Chee Dodge
        Canoncito, Puertocito — Jose Mari Apache,
           represented by George Abeyta

CHAIRMAN: I want to say this much to the members of the Executive Committee at this time. The purpose for calling the Executive Committee is to discuss and consider the reelection of the Navajo Tribal Council and, I would like to have the Executive Committee to discuss this matter thoroughly whether they will approve of this suggestion. About two weeks ago we had a meeting with Mr. Fryer and other members of the staff and only two delegates besides myself were called in and we have taken this matter up about the reelection of the Navajo Tribal Council sometime soon this summer. So it is your duty to discuss this thing entirely first thing.

CHAIRMAN: Other matters are going to come up later in the day and if there are other matters that are going to be brought up before the Executive Committee, I would like to have you consider them also.

Now, in the past, you will remember last year that you were appointed as the leaders of the Navajo Tribe, not only for the Tribe, but as the delegates. You are to discuss these matters presented to the Tribal Council for their consideration, and if you don't think it is necessary for them to be considered by the Council, you can approve a lot of matters yourself.

You are the representatives of the Tribe as well as the Tribal Council and this is the reason I make this suggestion, whether you want to discuss this reelection of the Tribal Council and settle it here in this Executive Committee or not, or whether you want to hold a Tribal Council meeting to consider it.

Now in the last Council you know different committees were appointed by myself, such as oil lease committee, timber committee, health and education committee, and other committees, and before Mr. Fryer went east, I took these matters up with Mr. Fryer and Mr. Dodge to see if it would be all right to call in these different committees and Mr. Fyer said to me it would be all right to call in these committees before the next Council.

These committees have considered different matters such as oil, etc., but it does not mean these different committees that have been out to investigate the oil lease and timber five or six places have already approved and given the lease to the oil people, but these committees are supposed to make the recommendations to the Tribal Council and so are the other committees to make recommendations to the Tribal Council.

Same way about this matter of the reelection of the new Council. At this time, I am going to ask Mr. Fryer whether he would like to make a suggestion on this reelection of the new Council to the present Executive Committee at this time.

MR. FRYER: Good morning everybody. I have been away for a long time and this is the first time I have had a chance to speak to the members of the Executive Committee for several months. This meeting was called for several reasons:

1. To discuss the regulations for the election of the new Tribal Council.
2. To renew our acquaintance.
3. To discuss unfinished business.

The most important matter which we want to discuss is the election of the Council, and on that point we should be rather clear. The Commissioner has announced that there will be an election this summer for the Tribal Council. The date has not been set but it will be some time in July, and in this connection regulations have been made for governing the new election, but we suggested that before these regulations become effective that the members of the Executive Committee and the Tribal Council be allowed to make suggestions as to what these regulations should contain, and how the election should be handled.

You will recall that shortly after this Council was appointed, there was appointed by your Chairman a Constitutional Committee. This Committee spent several weeks, several months working on regulations for the Navajo Council and an excellent job was done by that Committee.

In the main, the regulations of the Secretary follow the recommendations of the Constitutional Committee. Before the regulations become effective, you are invited to go over them and make suggestions which might be incorporated in them.

The Washington Office has followed exactly the recommendations of the Constitutional Committee and the Council in the number of delegates that should be elected from each district. There has been no change in the representation of the Tribal Council.

There have been two or three changes made which should be discussed with the Executive Committee and I think recommendations should come from the Executive Committee. One of them is this: In the recommendations of the Constitutional Committee, it was suggested that the Chairman of the Tribal Council be elected by all of the people. The regulations from Washington suggest that the Chairman be elected by the Tribal Council. Now that's one question that the Executive Committee can discuss and make recommendations to the Commissioner.

Another suggestion you might make concerns the composition and the method of appointing the Executive Committee of the new Council. Shall the Executive Committee be elected by the members of the Council from each district, one member from each district, or shall the Executive Committee be appointed by the Chairman, one from each district?

Another matter which might be discussed is this. Both the original recommendations of the Constitutional Committee and these proposals which come from Washington suggest that all members of the tribe over 21 years of age be permitted to vote. Since then, I have been approached by people who claim that women shouldn't vote. I don't see why women shouldn't vote. It seems to me that they take a pretty active part in Tribal affairs. But that's something you gentlemen might discuss here and formulate a recommendation.

A fourth item is whether or not the vote shall be by secret ballot. And a fifth item is the date of the election of the Council.

Now these are the more critical points which should be discussed by the Executive Committee and on which the Executive Committee can make recommendations to the Commissioner. He will welcome any suggestions that this committee has to offer.

We should be clear on the purpose of this meeting. There will be an election of the Tribal Council this summer. The Commissioner has committed himself to that and the members of this Council have committed themselves to the people as a whole.

I think there should be a very free and open discussion and everyone should say just what he thinks, and I hope no one will hold back because we want to make good suggestions to the Commissioner which he can accept.

CHAIRMAN: I just want to make a little remark concerning this new election of the Council. The new election of the Council has been in discussion for a number of times by different delegates here at Window Rock and also different places that I have been.

Now I want to tell the members of the Tribal Council that you have done your part in the middle of a big struggle, in the midst of a big fight, but at the same time, you have done your part towards working with the Government program for the benefit of your tribe. We don't want to come here and try to get cold feet and just throw this thing into the hands of the other people. You all know you have been criticized but at the same time, you should stand for what you have done. You have passed different resolutions which you should try to remember. You should try to remember what you have done because it is important. It is not only you who are in the midst of a big struggle but the white people are the same way with the present administration, and I want to ask you again that you should consider this matter very thoroughly because it means the future improvement for your people and we want to make it improve.

We want to make suggestions to the Secretary of the Interior, and, of course, we all realize that he is in power, and if we don't discuss this matter right, if we just try to fight among ourselves, naturally in time we may never have any more Tribal Council, and at the same time, the Government is in power over the Navajos. They shall continue to do certain things on the reservation and I want to ask you to discuss this matter and I want to have this suggestion for your consideration now.

DINE TSOSIE: The way I look at this new election of the Council is just to let the communities elect their delegates as has been done before and let the delegates meet here in the Council and elect their Chairman. That's the way I look at it. It isn't that we will be scared out of the Council or anything like that, because when we reorganized here we were just to serve, there was no time set for it when we were to sit on the Council. We were to step out any time, so I don't feel that we should be hurt about it because that's the understanding given to us in the beginning.

People think we are getting scared out but that isn't it. Although there has been a lot of talk about stock reduction, the people only keep trying to get as many lambs as they can every spring.

YAZZIE HOLMES: Each one of us has set our mind on the way we shall live. We have taken up the way of living that the Government has given us. We have been making our living that way for years. We can't drop that and take up something else. We have got to continue. Like a child is instructed by his parents and taught the ways of life. He sticks by it.

(At this point there is some confusion among the Committee members as to whether the communities shall continue to elect delegates, rather than having them selected by any other body. They are assured by Mr. Fryer, that selection of delegates by community elections is certain and will not be changed, but the issue is whether or not the Chairman shall be elected by popular vote, or by the members of the Tribal Council).

ADOLPH MALONEY: The Chairman should be elected by the people, not by the delegates, and Vice-Chairman by the delegates.

I would suggest that the people in each district elect the delegates and pick the chief delegate, and let the Tribal Council elect the Chairman.

CHAIRMAN: In your first statement, you suggested that the Chairman be elected by the people. Then you stated that the Chairman should be elected by the delegates that are elected by the districts.

ADOLPH MALONEY: Someone handed me a note, and I read it. That was my first statement, but I suggest that the Chairman be elected by the members of the Tribal Council.

FRANK MITCHELL: I was a member of the Committee who drafted this proposal last summer. In that proposal, we suggested that the Chairman of the Council be elected by popular vote of the people for this reason. When this present Council convened for the first time, we elected our present Chairman by voting here alone and there has been talk all over the reservation by the people. We have been criticized all over the reservation as they say that the Chairman was not elected by the Tribe at all, and for that reason, we propose that the Chairman of the Council be elected by the people and as far as I am concerned, and I am pretty sure that I can speak for the rest of the Committee, we stand pat on that.

I propose there are other members here who want the Chairman to be elected by the Council so I make a motion that we vote.

DASHNE CLA CHISCHILLIGE: I second the motion.

CHAIRMAN: It has been moved and seconded that the Chairman of the Navajo Tribal Council be elected by the people in the future.

All those in favor?   15

All those opposed?   1

MR. FRYER: To continue on from that point, if the people elect the Chairman, then the Constitutional Committee suggested that this Executive Committee of the Council nominate the candidates for the next Chairman. If the people are going to vote, they must have someone to vote on.

The recommendations of the Committee were that this Committee should nominate not more than four candidates, and when the election is held this summer, the people can vote on these candidates.

I bring that up for this reason, that the recommendations of the Constitutional Committee were two:

1. That the Chairman should be elected by the people.
2. That this group should nominate not more than four candidates for the people to vote on.

FRANK MITCHELL: Now last summer, when the Committee worked on this proposal, things like this were discussed by members of the Committee thinking away ahead in the future, how it's going to come out, how it's going along.

We said that since we were living under the Washington Government and its policies are to change every four years and elect its officers and different ones every four years, we should do that. Since that time I have heard rumors, not from the Superintendent or his staff, that this proposal was thrown into the waste basket and now Mr. Fryer has mentioned things similar to that proposal. I want to ask Mr. Fryer if our recommendations were thrown away.

MR. FRYER: These proposed regulations follow almost to the letter the recommendations of the Committee with only this change, that the Chairman be elected by the Tribal Council. But the Commissioner is waiting for recommendations from this Council on some of these points. Whether the Chairman should be elected by the Tribal Council was one of the points.

FRANK MITCHELL: The reason I ask this is that in that proposal, we went into the thing very thoroughly, who should be eligible for Chairman and we said at that time that no one should be eligible for Chairman unless he knew the full circumstances of the Navajo Tribe and of the conditions and who was 100% Navajo and lived the life of the Navajo. And if such a person is Chairman of the Council, there shouldn't be any criticism and that's the reason we made that suggestion in the proposal and because it looks like we must pick up anyone and put in as head of the Council, the people get wrought up about it.

There are people off the reservation living among the whites and they come back here and we just put him up and put him in a responsible place and we find out we made a mistake. We went into that very thoroughly. The Chairman should be someone who lives on the reservation and knows the everyday life of the Navajo.

ADOLPH MALONEY: I have heard, I don't know whether it is so or not, but I have heard that this originated here at Window Rock, that no one was eligible for delegate who was in the Government Service or who has a business interest on the reservation and who was thirty years of age or more. That's just a question from me on that.

If that's the case, do you mean to say that no one who has any enterprise on the reservation can be a delegate unless all they have is their clothing?

MR. FRYER: These regulations provide that no one can be eligible who has interests in the Government or who works for the Government in such a way that he might influence the Council to change their minds. It exempts teachers, judges, etc. But people like Tom Dodge, who occupies a high Government position, cannot be a member of the Council because he might use his high influence on the Council so that the Council would not say what it wanted to say. Judges, teachers, interpreters, laborers, would not be barred because they have nothing to do with making policy.

CHEE DODGE: I am pretty much in sympathy with what Frank Mitchell said about who should be Chairman of the Tribal Council. No one should be Chairman who lives on the outside. I make a motion.

MR. FRYER: That the Chairman should live on the reservation, should have interests on the reservation, and other conditions that you might want to put in there?

CHEE DODGE: Yes.

ARVISO: I second the motion.

CHAIRMAN: It has been moved and seconded that the Chairman of the Tribal Council live on the Navajo Reservation and have business interests on the reservation. All those in favor of the motion make themselves known by standing.

(Vote is taken − 15).

CHAIRMAN: All those that are not in favor of this motion make themselves known by standing. None.

CHEE DODGE: How about the Navajos that are living off the reservation. Are they allowed to vote a delegate?

MR. FRYER: The regulations provide that the Canoncito and Puertocito Navajos have one delegate each, so there would be no change in the representation or delegates.

CHEE DODGE: Are we to understand that this Committee sitting here are the ones to nominate the candidates for the next Chairman of the Council?

MR. FRYER: I mentioned that merely as a recommendation of the Committee who drew the original recommendations. You have done two things. You have provided that the Chairman be elected by the people. Then, that the Chairman live on the reservation. Now, third, you have to provide some machinery to select the Chairman. That's up to this committee.

CHEE DODGE: That's what I mean.

DASHNE: Mr. Chairman, I make this suggestion, that when we have an election we have an election set up at the same time to elect a Chairman. It should be one election and not this committee to pick out the candidates for Chairman, but work some way to divide the Navajo country into four districts and have each district set up a candidate, and put up an election to elect those candidates for Chairman at the same time.

MR. FRYER: In other words, make four districts and each district will put up one candidate.

PETE TOTSONI: I was thinking just the way Mr. Dashne suggested, because if we go to work and nominate the candidates and put them up to the people we are going to be criticized for that. They will say that the retiring council nominated just certain ones of their friends.

CHAIRMAN: Let me ask this question. Who is going to nominate the candidates in these four districts?

DASHNE: We will suggest to the General Superintendent to set up four districts and each of those districts will set up a candidate as soon as possible so the people will know who the candidates are.

CHAIRMAN: The meeting stands adjourned until 1:00 o'clock.

AFTERNOON SESSION

Chairman: Henry Taliman   Monday May 2, 1938, 1:30 p.m.
Interpreter — Chick Sandoval

The meeting was called to order at 1:40 p.m. by Henry Taliman, Chairman. An explanation was given by him of the qualifications that the people should expect from the next Chairman of the Tribal Council. He explained to the delegates how their requesting these qualifications in the next Chairman would help them choose an outstanding leader. The qualifications that the next Chairman should have and which the people should demand he have, are:

1. He must have a good knowledge of what has been done by the Council in the past.
2. He must live on the reservation.
3. He should own stock or agricultural land.
4. His appointment should be approved by the Secretary of the Interior.

These suggestions were then discussed by the delegates among themselves.

Mr. Fryer explained to the delegates how Henry Taliman, Chairman, had come to suggest these qualifications be required of the next Chairman so that no criticism would be forthcoming from the delegates because the Chairman had brought these suggestions up.

Mr. Fryer suggested that the reservation be divided into four voting districts. From these four districts four candidates could be chosen, one from each district, for the Chairmanship of the next Tribal Council. This could be done by the present delegates. They could talk to their people and find out whom they wish to nominate for the Chairmanship. The delegates could then meet and elect the nominee from that voting district. His name could be sent in to Central Agency for having it placed on the voting ballot.

YAZZIE HOLMES, District #17 representative, stated that he believed Mr. Fryer's suggestions were the best — that conventions be held in each of the four voting districts and a Chairman be nominated from each of the districts.

Several of the delegates said they didn't quite understand what the suggestion was and wished to have it explained. The explanation was given by Mr. Tom Dodge.

YAZZIE HOLMES, representative of District #17, stated he understood the plan thoroughly, but that some of the other delegates still didn't understand it. He stated that he still believed the Chairman should be elected by popular vote.

FRANK MITCHELL, representative of District #10, explained that his understanding of the plan was that the names of the four nominees for the Chairmanship would be placed on the ballot at the same time that the names of the delegates for the next Tribal Council were placed on the ballot. They would then vote for the Chairman at the same time they were voting for the delegates. The entire Navajo Reservation would be divided into four voting districts by taking five Land Management Districts and calling them one voting district.

DASHNE, representative of District #12, stated that his understanding was the same as Frank Mitchell's and that he believed they ought to hold election of the new Tribal Council and also of the Chairman at the same time.

FRANK MITCHELL, representative of District #10, stated that he believed that this method proposed for holding the election would eliminate some of the criticism that has gone on in the past as to the manner of holding elections on the reservation.

The next question brought up was how the election of the Chief Delegate would be determined.

ADOLPH MALONEY, representative of District #3, stated he still maintained that the plan he had suggested during the morning session, that the delegates elected get together and determine who the Chief Delegate would be from each district was the best plan.

A general discussion was then held in Navajo among the delegates and was not translated.

FRANK MITCHELL, representative of District #10: I still maintain that the Chairman should be elected by the people by dividing the reservation into four parts. There will be one nominee from each voting district for the people to vote on for Chairman at the same time that they are voting for their delegates so that when the returns come in it will be known who has been elected Chairman at the same time that the delegates are elected. Districts 1, 2, 3, 4 and 5 would nominate one man for Chairman. Districts 6, 7, 8, 9 and 10 would nominate one man for Chairman. Districts 11, 12, 13, 14 and 15 would nominate one man for Chairman, and so would Districts 16, 17, 18, 19 and 20.

MR. FRYER enumerated to the delegates what they had agreed on so far as follows:

1. That the reservation be divided into four voting districts.
2. That each of these voting districts consist of five Land Management Districts.
3. That the present delegates of the present Tribal Council in each of these four voting districts call a meeting or a convention. That they, after determining the wish of the people they represent, nominate a candidate from this voting district for the Chairmanship of the Council.
4. The man receiving the highest vote in each of the four voting districts would be the candidate for their respective district. The names of the four candidates would appear on the ballot so that all the people would have a vote in choosing the Chairman.
5. The people in each Land Management District would vote for a delegate for his community and one Chairman.
6. The Council does not nominate the delegates but only the Chairman. The people nominate and elect their own delegates.

DASHNE: What Mr. Fryer explained is my motion. I make a motion that the Navajo Reservation be divided into four parts; each District consisting of five Land Management Districts. Each of these districts will nominate one man for Chairman. The name will be filed at the Agency here (Window Rock). The names of these candidates will be posted on the election ballot. When the election of the new Tribal Council takes place, the people will vote on the Tribal Council, the new Chairman, the Vice-Chairman and the delegates. The election would be done in one day instead of having it on different days.

YAZZIE HOLMES: I second the motion.

After the motion was made and seconded, it was put up for vote.

Vote results: Unanimously affirmative.

CHAIRMAN: The next question on the subject will be whether the new Executive Committee will be appointed by the Chairman or elected by the delegates from the new membership of the Council. Last year the Council gave me the authority to appoint an Executive Committee [man] from each district.

CHAIRMAN: Whether you want to have the new Council operate the same way as I did before or whether you want the new Council to elect the new Executive Committee from the next Council is the next question.

ADOLPH MALONEY: The delegates from each district should elect one from their delegates to be the Executive Committeeman.

ROBERT CURLEY: Last summer our suggestions were that wherever it could be done the delegates of the district select their own committeeman for their committee, but where they could not decide among themselves, the Chairman should pick the man out. I make this a motion.

FRANK MITCHELL: I second the motion.

After the motion was made and seconded a standing vote was taken.

Vote results: Unanimously affirmative.

CHAIRMAN: The next question open for discussion is whether or not the women should vote for the election of the Tribal Council, Chairman and delegates.

ROBERT CURLEY: I don't see why the women should be barred from voting. They have just as much right as men have. I make a motion that they be allowed to vote providing that they are twenty-one years of age or over.

FRANK MITCHELL: I second the motion.

After it was moved and seconded that the women, providing they were twenty-one years of age or over, be allowed to vote, a standing vote was taken.

Vote results: Unanimously affirmative.

CHAIRMAN: The next thing to be decided is the date of the election.

ROBERT CURLEY: Right at present there is much work such as lambing, shearing and lots of other work. I would suggest that the election be held sometime after the fourth of July. I make this a motion.

YAZZIE HOLMES: I make a motion that the election be held between the 4th and 15th of July.

DENET TSOSIE: I second the motion.

After the motion was made and seconded a standing vote was taken.

Vote results: Unanimously affirmative.

CHAIRMAN: The question has been brought up as to who is going to call the conventions in each of the four districts.

A general discussion was held by the delegates among themselves and it was agreed that a date would be agreed on after the regulations had been approved by the Washington Office and the people would be notified. It was also decided that the Chairman for the convention would not be chosen until the people had gathered at the convention.

Roy Kinsel, Vice-Chairman, replaced Henry Taliman at 3:55 p.m.

Before leaving the meeting Mr. Taliman explained to the delegates that an investigation had been made by himself, Mr. McClellan and others on the request to be presented from the San Juan County School Board for a permit to build a new schoolhouse on a certain parcel of land. He also stated that he believed it would be an advantage to the Navajo people if they would grant this request.

MR. MC CLELLAN: I have here an application presented by the San Juan County School Board for your action. They are requesting a school site on which to build a school. This is on Government land that was set aside a long time ago for Agency use. They want the approval of the Tribal Council for this site, and they would like to have word so that they can start construction work as soon as possible. They are going to use County money at present to build the building with. Some time ago I think this application was presented to the Council and they turned it down on account of the fact that it involved the sale of land. We are now presenting it with a different angle. They only ask for a permit for the use of this land. It will be on land just the same as the schools you have at Fort Defiance, Crownpoint and others. Shiprock does not have a public school. The employees have been sending their children about twenty miles by bus from Shiprock to school every morning. During this past year the San Juan County School Board has leased the Navajo Chapter House for use as a schoolhouse. There have been 14 to 16 Navajo children going to school there who belong to the different Navajo employees there. The School Board has not presented any bills to the Government for the schooling of these children.

The School Board want the Navajo people of Shiprock to send their children to public school − all those that wish to take advantage of this school.

This application was presented to me by the School Board for the action of you delegates. If there are any other questions that you want to ask, I will be glad to answer them.

CHEE DODGE: Where is that land?

MR. MC CLELLAN: It is land set aside for Government use a long time ago on a vacant lot next to the schoolhouse, a vacant lot between the school house and the school farm.

DASHNE: I am pretty well-acquainted with this so I will tell you. Most of you fellows know where the school is. The first time this was presented to us, of course at that time it was a sale that they asked, I was against it the same as all of you. Now I believe the granting of this request will be of benefit to us as the Navajo children have the advantage of picking up their English more quickly if they go to school with the White children. For that reason I make a motion that we approve this permit.

DINE TSOSIE: Did any of the people who have children in school there have anything to do with this request coming in?

MR. MC CLELLAN: No, but they are very pleased with the school and they want the school to continue. The reason this permit was requested is that they may not always be able to lease the Chapter House, and they would then have to discontinue the school.

HOSTEEN JESUS: I second the motion made by Dashne.

ADOLPH MALONEY: What would be the length of time for this permit?

MR. MC CLELLAN: This would have to go through the Washington Office. It would probably be a revocable permit and effective until such time as the school was discontinued, the same as these permits granted to these missions, traders, etc.

DASHNE: I want to make this statement before we take a vote on this thing. The Supervisors are stationed throughout the Navajo country and they are supposed to look for the advancement of the Navajo nation. The Navajo Indians should be taken into preference first before any other children should be considered for the reason that the White children we know need education and they have already advanced in their way of education. The Navajo children are just starting out in their life and don't know what the English language is. The Supervisors should take that into consideration and take the Navajo children in preference.

CHAIRMAN: It has been moved and seconded that the Tribal Council grant a permit for a school site on land as described by Mr. McClellan to the San Juan County School Board. All those in favor make themselves known by standing.

Vote: 14 Affirmative. 1 Negative.

Mr. McClellan told the delegates that his wife had been a teacher of Indian children for several years and was very much interested in getting the Navajo children educated. He assured them that Navajo children would be urged to attend this school at Shiprock.

The next subject brought up was to secure approval of a list of employable Navajos whom the delegates considered eligible for appointment as Judges whenever vacancies occurred. The resolution presented was unanimously approved without any changes.

NO MORNING SESSION
May 3, 1938

AFTERNOON SESSION

Tuesday, May 3, 1938, 2:00 p.m.

Roy Kinsel, Presiding
Tom Dodge, Interpreting

MR. FRYER: Let me ask this question — this is a very important question. I wonder if the group would be willing to have another council meeting before election at which the entire council will be assembled but at which meeting the members will serve without pay. There is no money with which to pay them, but if we could have a general meeting which everyone could attend, the members would have to come in of their own free will. They could not get per diem but we will provide food. It seems to me the Council would demand a meeting.

FRANK MITCHELL: I believe there should be a meeting of the Council before election for the reason the things we are discussing now are very important. There are too many white people on the outside of the reservation who are anxious to obtain some sort of foothold on the reservation and furthermore, the present administration has only two more years to go. The chances are with the next administration, there will be a different set of men and if the white people on the outside influence them with their ideas, there is great danger that they might be the type men who would throw the reservation open to white men as well as abolish the Indian Office. I would like for this Committee to adopt some resolution and at the general meeting we can take a stronger stand.

ROY KINSEL: As long as we have the majority of the Executive Committee here, I do not see what would hinder us from passing a resolution just as Frank Mitchell stated just now for the reason that the work we have to do at home will be coming up. The lambing season is on and right after that clipping and on top of that the planting season. Right at this time we have enough members and it will be just as well as to have the seventy-four and you executives have a right to pass a resolution right now so we will not have to come back for this other Tribal Council meeting. We do not mind paying out of our own pockets to discuss the Tribal affairs, but we have work to do at home. That is why I would like to have these executives act on it today.

HOSTEEN YAZZIE: I believe that we should adopt a resolution at this meeting of the Executive Committee because we all feel that the tribe should remain under the guardianship of Washington as it has been in the past. It is of vital importance that we take action at this time because the members of the next council may take a stand as well as action that would jeopardize the friendly relationship of the tribe and Washington. Furthermore, it may not be possible to have another meeting of the Tribal Council before election in view of the fact that this is the time of the year when the Navajos become very actively engaged in tilling the soil, attending to lambing, clipping of wool, and other activities.

DENET TSOSIE: Mr. Fryer, our Superintendent, has suggested that there should be a meeting of the Tribal Council before election. Apparently, he feels that our action here today would not be quite strong enough. He believes a similar action of the Tribal Council would be stronger and I believe that we should accept our Superintendent's suggestion.

FRANK MITCHELL: I know that an action of the Tribal Council has not the same force as a Government Regulation or Law and yet an action of the Tribal Council amounts to a suggestion to the Secretary of the Interior and if we adopt a resolution and send to the Secretary, he can act on our suggestion and let us know what action he wants to take. Nevertheless, we feel that our tribe needs to be protected against any movement started by the opposition, such as allotment of the reservation and turning it over to the tribe.

MR. FRYER: Let's let the matter stand as is. I will write the Commissioner and if the Commissioner thinks this might be strengthened by a general Council meeting, we will have one. If he thinks it would not, let's let it go without a meeting.

FRANK MITCHELL: I believe that is the feeling of this Committee and for that reason I am in favor of adopting a resolution at this meeting and then this resolution can be forwarded to the Commissioner of Indian Affairs along with other resolutions we adopted yesterday. Then, it will be up to the Commissioner to decide what action he wants to take on it.

MR. FRYER: I would suggest a petition.

(The following petition is outlined by Superintendent Fryer)

> The Executive Committee of the Navajo Tribal Council in an executive session at Window Rock on May 3, 1938, petitions the Commissioner of Indian Affairs to take whatever measures are necessary to prevent the encroachment of White Lawyers, and other Whites in this category, on the Navajo Reservation.
>
> These selfish and unethical Whites, by playing on the ignorance of our people regarding Bureau policies and other things which concern only the Navajos and the Government, are bringing untold damage to our people.
>
> They apparently have for their purpose, the abolishment of the Indian Bureau and are using the Navajos to gain this end. If some measures are not taken to stop this practice, no one can tell the effect their unwanted visitations might have.
>
> To accomplish their objectives, they hold meetings and take up collections of money which they use for their own support. They believe that the Navajos are discontented and will continue their generosities as long as they can keep them discontented.
>
> We are requesting the Commissioner to take whatever steps are necessary to prevent the encroachment of these Whites and other Whites in this class and allow their admittance on the Reservation only by a permit signed by the General Council and General Superintendent.

MR. FRYER: Anything else you want in the petition?
HOWARD GORMAN: That is the sentiment.

The petition addressed to the Commissioner of Indian Affairs was then unanimously approved by the Executive Committee of the Tribal Council.

Following this action, the meeting was adjourned.

APPENDIX D-2.

Chapters 1 — 5 of Department of the Interior Document
#85l43, "Law and Order Regulations," February 15, 1937

Misc.   UNITED STATES
DEPARTMENT OF THE INTERIOR
Office of Indian Affairs
Washington

The Honorable   February 15, 1937
The Secretary of the Interior

My dear Mr. Secretary:

Referring to the Law and Order Regulations which were approved by you under date of November 27, 1935, copy herewith, attention is invited to the second sentence of the third paragraph on page one, under the heading, "Application of Regulations," and which reads as follows: "Neither will these regulations apply to any tribe organized under the Act of June 18, 1934, except in so far as specific provisions thereof may be adopted and embodied in the constitution, bylaws, or ordinances of such an organized tribe."

As worded, the regulations now apply to Indian reservations (where Courts of Indian Offenses have been established) up to the time the tribe organizes, after which time they are not applicable to such organized tribe until law and order ordinances have been adopted by the tribe and have become effective. Therefore, at present, there is a hiatus between the time the tribal constitution is approved and the time when the tribal code becomes effective. Some of the tribes which have organized have not yet effectively adopted a Law and Order Code, but the Indian police and judges are attempting to enforce the Department code which is not, according to the code itself, applicable, and this might result in serious complications.

It is therefore recommended that said sentence two of paragraph three of the "Application of Regulations" be amended to read as follows:

These regulations shall continue to apply to tribes organized under the Act of June 18, 1934, (48 Stats. L. 984) until a Law and Order code has been adopted by the tribe in accordance with its constitution and bylaws and has become effective.

Respectfully submitted,

(Sgd) William Zimmerman, Jr.
Assistant Commissioner.

Approved and so ordered.
February 20, 1937

(Sgd) Charles West,

Acting Secretary of the Interior.

LAW AND ORDER REGULATIONS, Chapters 1-5

Application of Regulations

The following regulations relative to Courts of Indian Offenses shall apply to all Indian reservations on which such courts are maintained.

It is the purpose of these regulations to provide adequate machinery of law enforcement for those Indian tribes in which traditional agencies for the enforcement of tribal law and custom have broken down and for which no adequate substitute has been provided under Federal or State law.

No Court of Indian Offenses will be established on reservations where justice is effectively administered under State laws and by State law enforcement agencies. Neither will these regulations apply to any tribe organized under the Act of June 18, 1934, except in so far as specific provisions thereof may be adopted and embodied in the constitution, bylaws, or ordinances of such an organized tribe.

Chapter 1

Courts of Indian Offenses

Sec. 1 Jurisdiction

A Court of Indian Offenses shall have jurisdiction over all offenses enumerated in Chapter 5, when committed by any Indian, within the reservation or reservations for which the Court is established.

With respect to any of the offenses enumerated in Chapter 5 over which Federal or State courts may have lawful jurisdiction, the jurisdiction of the Court of Indian Offenses shall be concurrent and not exclusive. It shall be the duty of the said Court of Indian Offenses to order delivery to the proper authorities of the State or Federal Government or of any other tribe or reservation, for prosecution, any offender, there to be dealt with according to law or regulations authorized by law, where such authorities consent to exercise jurisdiction lawfully vested in them over the said offender.

For the purpose of the enforcement of these regulations, an Indian shall be deemed to be any person of Indian descent who is a member of any recognized Indian tribe now under Federal jurisdiction, and a "reservation" shall be taken to include all territory within reservation boundaries, including fee patented lands, roads, waters, bridges, and lands used for agency purposes.

All Indians employed in the Indian Service shall be subject to the jurisdiction of the Court of Indian Offenses but any such employee appointed by the Secretary of the Interior shall not be subject to any sentence of such Court, unless such sentence shall have been approved by the Secretary of the Interior.

Sec. 2 Appointment of Judges

A Court of Indian Offenses established for any reservation or group of reservations, shall consist of one or more chief judges, whose duties shall be regular and permanent, and two or more associate judges, who may be called to service when occasion requires, and who shall be compensated on a per diem basis.

Each judge shall be appointed by the Commissioner of Indian Affairs, subject to confirmation by a two-thirds vote of the Tribal Council.

Each judge shall hold office for a period of four years, unless sooner removed for cause or by reason of the abolition of the said office, but shall be eligible for reappointment.

A person shall be eligible to serve as judge of a Court of Indian Offenses only if he (1) is a member of a tribe under the jurisdiction of the said court; and (2) has never been convicted of a felony, or, within one year then last past, of a misdemeanor.

No judge shall be qualified to act as such in any case wherein he has any direct interest or wherein any relative by marriage or blood, in the first or second degrees, is a party.

Sec. 3 Removal of Judges

Any Judge of the Court of Indian Offenses may be suspended, dismissed or removed, by the Commissioner of Indian Affairs, for cause, upon the recommendation of the Tribal Council.

Sec. 4 Court Procedure

Sessions of the Court of Indian Offenses for the trial of cases shall be held by the Chief Judge, or, in case of his disability, by one of the associate judges selected for the occasion by all of the judges.

The time and place of court sessions, and all other details of judicial procedure not prescribed by these regulations, shall be laid down in Rules of Court approved by the Tribal Council and by the superintendent of the reservation.

It shall be the duty of the judges of each Court of Indian Offenses to make recommendations to the Tribal Council for the enactment or amendment of such Rules of Court in the interests of improved judicial procedure.

Sec. 5 Appellate Proceedings

All the judges of the reservation shall sit together, at such times and at such places as they may find proper and necessary for the dispatch of business, to hear appeals from judgments made by any judge at the trial sessions. There shall be established by Rule of Court the limitations, if any, to be placed upon the right of appeal both as to the types of cases which may be appealed and as to the manner in which appeals may be granted, according to the needs of their jurisdiction. In the absence of such Rule of Court any party aggrieved by a judgment may appeal to the full court upon giving notice of such appeal at the time of judgment and upon giving proper assurance to the trial judge, through the posting of a bond or in any other manner, that he will satisfy the judgment if it is affirmed. In any case where a party has perfected his right to appeal as established herein or by Rule of Court, the judgment of the trial judge shall not be executed until after final disposition of the case by the full court. The full court may render judgment upon the case by majority vote.

Sec. 6 Juries

In any case where, upon preliminary hearing by the court, a substantial question of fact is raised, the defendant may demand a jury trial.

A list of eligible jurors shall be prepared by the Tribal Council each year.

In any case, a jury shall consist of six residents of the vicinity in which the trial is held, selected from the list of eligible jurors by the judge. Any party to the case may challenge not more than three members of the jury panel so chosen.

The judge shall instruct the jury in the law governing the case and the jury shall bring a verdict for the complainant or the defendant. The judge shall render judgment in accordance with the verdict and existing law. If the jury is unable to reach a unanimous verdict, verdict may be rendered by a majority vote.

Each juror who serves upon a jury shall be entitled to a fee of fifty cents a day for each day his services are required in court.

Sec. 7 Witnesses

The several judges of the Courts of Indian Offenses shall have the power to issue subpoenas for the attendance of witnesses either on their own motion or on the request of the Police Commissioner or Superintendent or any of the parties to the case, which subpoena shall bear the signature of the judge issuing it. Each witness answering such subpoena shall be entitled to a fee of fifty cents a day for each day his services are required in court. Failure to obey such subpoena shall be deemed an offense as provided in Chapter 5, Sec. 36, of these regulations. Service of such subpoenas shall be by a regularly acting member of the Indian Police or by an Indian appointed by the Court for that purpose.

Witnesses who testify voluntarily shall be paid by the party calling them, if the court so directs, their actual traveling and living expenses incurred in the performance of their function.

Sec. 8 Professional Attorneys

Professional attorneys shall not appear in any proceeding before the Court of Indian Offenses unless Rules of Court have been adopted as set forth in section 4 of this Chapter prescribing conditions governing their admission and practice before the Court.

Sec. 9 Clerks

The Superintendent shall detail a clerk of court for each Court of Indian Offenses. The clerk of the Court of Indian Offenses shall render assistance to the Court, to the police force of the reservation and to individual members of the tribe in the drafting of complaints, subpoenas, warrants and commitments and any other documents incidental to the lawful functions of the Court. It shall be the further duty of said clerk to attend and to keep a written record of all proceedings of the court, to administer oaths to witnesses, to collect all fines paid and to pay out all fees authorized by these regulations, and to make an accounting thereof to the disbursing agent of the reservation and to the Tribal Council.

Sec. 10 Records

Each Court of Indian Offenses shall be required to keep, for inspection by duly qualified officials, a record of all proceedings of the Court, which record shall reflect the title of the case, the names of the parties, the substance of the complaint, the names and addresses of all witnesses, the date of the hearing or trial, by whom conducted, the findings of the Court or jury, and the judgment, together with any other facts or circumstances deemed of importance to the case. A record of all proceedings shall be kept at the agency office, as required by United States Code, Title 25, sec. 200.

Sec. 11 Copies of Laws

Each Court of Indian Offenses shall be provided with copies of all Federal and State laws and Indian Office regulations applicable to the conduct of Indians within the reservation.

Whenever the Court is in doubt as to the meaning of any law, treaty or regulation it may request the Superintendent to furnish an opinion on the point in question.

Sec. 12 Complaints

No complaint filed in any Court of Indian Offenses shall be valid unless it shall bear the signature of the complainant or complaining witness, witnessed by a duly qualified Judge of the Court of Indian Offenses or by the Superintendent or by any other qualified employee of such reservation.

Sec. 13 Warrants to Apprehend

Every Judge of a Court of Indian Offenses shall have the authority to issue Warrants to Apprehend, said warrants to issue in the discretion of the Court only after a written complaint shall have been filed, bearing the signature of the complaining witness. Service of such Warrants shall be made by a duly qualified member of the Indian Police or other police officer of the United States Indian Service. No Warrant to Apprehend shall be valid unless it shall bear the signature of a duly qualified Judge of the Court of Indian Offenses.

Sec. 14 Arrests

No member of the Indian Police shall arrest any person for any offense defined by these regulations or by Federal law, except when such offense shall occur in the presence of the arresting officer or he shall have reasonable evidence that the person arrested has committed an offense or the officer shall have a warrant commanding him to apprehend such person.

Sec. 15 Search Warrants

Every Judge of the Court of Indian Offenses of any Indian reservation shall have authority to issue warrants for search and seizure of the premises and property of any person under the jurisdiction of said Court. However, no warrant of Search and Seizure shall issue except upon a duly signed and written complaint based upon reliable information or belief and charging the commission of some offense against the tribe. No warrant for search and seizure shall be valid unless it contains the name or description of the person or property to be searched and describes the articles or property to be seized and bears the signature of a duly qualified Judge of the Court of Indian Offenses. Service of Warrants of Search and Seizure shall be made only by members of the Indian Police or police officers of the United States Indian Service.

No policeman shall search or seize any property without a warrant unless he shall know, or have reasonable cause to believe, that the person in possession of such property is engaged in the commission of an offense under these regulations. Unlawful search or seizure will be deemed trespass and punished in accordance with Chapter 5, Section 15 of these regulations.

Sec. 16 Commitments

No Indian shall be detained, jailed or imprisoned under these regulations for a longer period than Thirty-Six (36) hours unless there be issued a commitment bearing the signature of a duly qualified Judge of the Court of Indian Offenses. There shall be issued, for each Indian held for trial, a Temporary Commitment and for each Indian held after sentence a Final Commitment on the forms prescribed in these regulations.

Sec. 17 Bail or Bond

Every Indian charged with an offense before any Court of Indian Offenses may be admitted to bail. Bail shall be by two reliable members of any Indian tribe who shall appear before a Judge of the Court of Indian Offenses where complaint has been filed and there execute an agreement in compliance with the form provided therefor and made a part of these regulations. In no case shall the penalty specified in the agreement exceed twice the maximum penalty set by these regulations for violation of the offense with which the accused is charged.

Sec. 18 Definition of Signature

The term "signature" as used in these regulations shall be defined as the written signature, official seal, or the witnessed thumb print or mark of any individual.

Sec. 19 Definition of Tribal Council

The term "Tribal Council", as used in these regulations, shall be construed to refer to the council, business committee or other organization recognized by the Department of the Interior as representing the tribe, or where no such body is recognized, to the adult members of the tribe in council assembled.

Sec. 20 Relations with the Court

No field employee of the Indian Service shall obstruct, interfere with or control the functions of any Court of Indian Offenses, or influence such functions in any manner except as permitted by these regulations or in response to a request for advice or information from the Court.

Employees of the Indian Service, particularly those who are engaged in social service, health and educational work, shall assist the Court, upon its request, in the preparation and presentation of the facts in the case and in the proper treatment of individual offenders.

Chapter 2

Civil Actions

Sec. 1 Jurisdiction

The Courts of Indian Offenses shall have jurisdiction of all suits wherein the defendant is a member of the tribe or tribes within their jurisdiction, and of all other suits between members and nonmembers which are brought before the Courts by stipulation of both parties. No judgment shall be given on any suit unless the defendant has actually received notice of such suit and ample opportunity to appear in court in his defense. Evidence of the receipt of the notice shall be kept as part of the record in the case. In all civil suits the complainant may be required to deposit with the clerk of the Court a fee or other security in a reasonable amount to cover costs and disbursements in the case.

Sec. 2 Law Applicable in Civil Actions

In all civil cases the Court of Indian Offenses shall apply any laws of the United States that may be applicable, any authorized regulations of the Interior Department, and any ordinances or customs of the tribe, not prohibited by such Federal laws.

Where any doubt arises as to the customs and usages of the tribe the Court may request the advice of counsellors familiar with these customs and usages.

Any matters that are not covered by the traditional customs and usages of the tribe, or by applicable Federal laws and regulations, shall be decided by the Court of Indian Offenses according to the laws of the State in which the matter in dispute may lie.

Sec. 3 Judgments in Civil Actions

In all civil cases, judgment shall consist of an order of the Court awarding money damages to be paid to the injured party, or directing the surrender of certain property to the injured party, or the performance of some other act for the benefit of the injured party.

Where the injury inflicted was the result of carelessness of the defendant, the judgment shall fairly compensate the injured party for the loss he has suffered.

Where the injury was deliberately inflicted, the judgment shall impose an additional penalty upon the defendant, which additional penalty may run either in favor of the injured party or in favor of the tribe.

Where the injury was inflicted as the result of accident, or where both the complainant and the defendant were at fault, the judgment shall compensate the injured party for a reasonable part of the loss he has suffered.

Sec. 4 Costs in Civil Actions

The Court may assess the accruing costs of the case against the party or parties against whom judgment is given. Such costs shall consist of the expenses of voluntary witnesses for which either party may be responsible under Section 7 of Chapter 1, and the fees of jurors in those cases where a jury trial is had, and any further incidental expenses connected with the procedure before the Court as the Court may direct.

Sec. 5 Payment of Judgments from Individual Indian Moneys

Whenever the Court of Indian Offenses shall have ordered payment of money damages to an injured party and the losing party refuses to make such payment within the time set for payment by the Court, and when the losing party has sufficient funds to his credit at the agency office to pay all or part of such judgment, the Superintendent shall certify to the Secretary of the Interior the record of the case and the amount of the available funds. If the Secretary shall so direct, the disbursing agent shall pay over to the injured party the amount of the judgment, or such lesser amount as may be specified by the Secretary, from the account of the delinquent party.

A judgment shall be considered a lawful debt in all proceedings held by the Department of the Interior or by the Court of Indian Offenses to distribute decedents' estates.

Chapter 3

Domestic Relations

Sec. 1 Recording of Marriages and Divorces

All Indian marriages and divorces, whether consummated in accordance with the State law or in accordance with tribal custom, shall be recorded within three months at the agency of the jurisdiction in which either or both of the parties reside.

Sec. 2 Tribal Custom Marriage and Divorce

The Tribal Council shall have authority to determine whether Indian Custom Marriage and Indian Custom Divorce for members of the tribe shall be recognized in the future as lawful marriage and divorce upon the reservation, and if it shall be so recognized, to determine what shall constitute such marriage and divorce and whether action by the Court of Indian Offenses shall be required. When so determined in writing, one copy shall be filed with the Court of Indian Offenses, one copy with the Superintendent in charge of the reservation, and one copy with the Commissioner of Indian Affairs. Thereafter, Indians who desire to become married or divorced by the custom of the tribe shall conform to the custom of the tribe as determined. Indians who assume or claim a divorce by Indian custom shall not be entitled to remarry until they have complied with the determined custom of their tribe nor until they have recorded such divorce at the agency office.

Pending any determination by the Tribal Council on these matters, the validity of Indian custom marriage and divorce shall continue to be recognized as heretofore.

Sec. 3 Tribal Custom Adoption

The Tribal Council shall likewise have authority to determine whether Indian Custom Adoption shall be permitted upon the reservation among members of the tribe, and if permitted, to determine what shall constitute such adoption and whether action by the Court of Indian Offenses shall be required. The determination of the Tribal Council shall be filed with the

Court of Indian Offenses, with the Superintendent of the reservation and with the Commissioner of Indian Affairs. Thereafter all members of the tribe desiring to adopt any person shall conform to the procedure fixed by the Tribal Council.

Sec. 4 Determination of Paternity and Support

The Courts of Indian Offenses shall have jurisdiction of all suits brought to determine the paternity of a child and to obtain a judgment for the support of the child. A judgment of the Court establishing the identity of the father of the child shall be conclusive of that fact in all subsequent determinations of inheritance by the Department of the Interior or by the Courts of Indian Offenses.

Sec. 5 Determination of Heirs

When any member of the tribe dies leaving property other than an allotment or other trust property subject to the jurisdiction of the United States, any member claiming to be an heir of the decedent may bring a suit in the Court of Indian Offenses to have the Court determine the heirs of the decedent and to divide among the heirs such property of the decedent. No determination of heirs shall be made unless all the possible heirs known to the Court, to the Superintendent, and to the claimant have been notified of the suit and given full opportunity to come before the Court and defend their interests. Possible heirs who are not residents of the reservation under the jurisdiction of the Court must be notified by mail and a copy of the notice must be preserved in the record of the case.

In the determination of heirs the Court shall apply the custom of the tribe as to inheritance if such custom is proved. Otherwise the Court shall apply State law in deciding what relatives of the decedent are entitled to be his heirs.

Where the estate of the decedent includes any interest in restricted allotted lands or other property held in trust by the United States, over which the Examiner of Inheritance would have jurisdiction, the Court of Indian Offenses may distribute only such property as does not come under the jurisdiction of the Examiner of Inheritance, and the determination of heirs by the court may be reviewed, on appeal, and the judgment of the court modified or set aside by the said Examiner of Inheritance, with the approval of the Secretary of the Interior, if law and justice so require.

Sec. 6 Approval of Wills

When any member of the tribe dies, leaving a will disposing only of property other than an allotment or other trust property subject to the jurisdiction of the United States, the Court of Indian Offenses shall, at the request of any member of the tribe named in the will or any other interested party, determine the validity of the will after giving notice and full opportunity to appear in court to all persons who might be heirs of the decedent, as under Section 5 of this Chapter. A will shall be deemed to be valid if the decedent had a sane mind and understood what he was doing when he made the will and was not subject to any undue influence of any kind from another person, and if the will was made in accordance with a proved tribal custom or made in writing and signed by the decedent in the presence of two witnesses who also sign the will. If the Court determines the will to be validly executed, it shall order the property described in the will to be given to the persons named in the will or to their heirs; but no distribution of property shall be made in violation of a proved tribal custom which restricts the privilege of tribal members to distribute property by will.

Chapter 4

Sentences

Sec. 1 Nature of Sentences

Any Indian who has been convicted by the Court of Indian Offenses of violation of a provision of the Code of Indian Tribal Offenses shall be sentenced by the Court to work for the benefit of the tribe for any period found by the Court to be appropriate; but the period fixed shall not exceed the maximum period set for the offense in the Code, and shall begin to run from the day of the sentence. During the period of sentence the convicted Indian may be confined in the agency jail if so directed by the Court. The work shall be done under the supervision of the Superintendent or of an authorized agent or committee of the tribal council as the Court may provide.

Whenever any convicted Indian shall be unable or unwilling to work, the Court shall, in its discretion, sentence him to imprisonment for the period of the sentence or to pay a fine equal to $2 a day for the same period. Such fine shall be paid in cash, or in commodities or other personal property of the required value as may be directed by the Court. Upon the request of the convicted Indian, the disbursing agent may approve a disbursement voucher chargeable to the Indian's account to cover payment of the fine imposed by the Court.

In addition to any other sentence, the Court may require an offender who has inflicted injury upon the person or property of any individual to make restitution or to compensate the party injured, through the surrender of property, the payment of money damages, or the performance of any other act for the benefit of the injured party.

In determining the character and duration of the sentence which shall be imposed, the Court shall take into consideration the previous conduct of the defendant, the circumstances under which the offense was committed, and whether the offense was malicious or willful and whether the offender has attempted to make amends, and shall give due consideration to the extent of the defendant's resources and the needs of his dependents. The penalties listed in Chapter 5 of these regulations are maximum penalties to be inflicted only in extreme cases.

Sec. 2 Probation

Where sentence has been imposed upon any Indian who has not previously been convicted of any offense, the Court of Indian Offenses may in its discretion suspend the sentence imposed and allow the offender his freedom on probation, upon his signing a pledge of good conduct during the period of the sentence upon the form provided therefor and made a part of these regulations.

Any Indian who shall violate his probation pledge shall be required to serve the original sentence plus an additional half of such sentence as penalty for the violation of his pledge.

Sec. 3 Parole

Any Indian committed by a Court of Indian Offenses who shall have without misconduct served one half the sentence imposed by such Court shall be eligible to parole. Parole shall be granted only by a Judge of the Court of Indian Offenses where the prisoner was convicted and upon the signing of the form provided therefor and made a part of these regulations.

Any Indian who shall violate any of the provisions of such parole shall be punished by being required to serve the whole of the original sentence.

Sec. 4 Juvenile Delinquency

Whenever any Indian who is under the age of 18 years is accused of committing one of the offenses enumerated in the Code of Indian Offenses, the judge may in his discretion hear and determine the case in private and in an informal manner, and, if the accused is found to be guilty, may in lieu of sentence place such delinquent for a designated period under the supervision of a responsible person selected by him or may take such other action as he may deem advisable in the circumstances.

Sec. 5 Deposit and Disposition of Fines

All money fines imposed for the commission of an offense shall be in the nature of an assessment for the payment of designated court expenses. Such expenses shall include the payment of the fees provided for in these regulations to jurors and to witnesses answering a subpoena. The fines assessed shall be paid over by the Clerk of the Court to the disbursing agent of the reservation for deposit as a "special deposit, court funds" to the disbursing agent's official credit in the Treasury of the United States. The disbursing agent shall withdraw such funds, in accordance with existing regulations, upon the order of the Clerk of the Court signed by a judge of the Court, for the payment of specified fees to specified jurors or witnesses. The disbursing agent and the Clerk of the Court shall keep an accounting of all such deposits and withdrawals for the inspection of any person interested. Whenever such fund shall exceed the amount necessary with a reasonable reserve for the payment of the court expenses before mentioned, the Tribal Council shall designate, with the approval of the Superintendent, further expenses of the work of the Court which shall be paid by these funds, such as the writing of records, the costs of notices or the increase of fees, whether or not any such costs were previously paid from other sources.

Wherever a fine is paid in commodities, the commodities shall be turned over under the supervision of the Clerk of the Court to the custody of the Superintendent to be sold or, if the Tribal Council so directs, to be disposed of in other ways for the benefit of the tribe. The proceeds of any sale of such commodities shall be deposited by the disbursing agent in the special deposit for court funds and recorded upon the accounts.

Chapter 5

Code of Indian Tribal Offenses

Sec. 1 Assault

Any Indian who shall attempt or threaten bodily harm to another person through unlawful force or violence shall be deemed guilty of assault, and upon conviction thereof shall be sentenced to labor for a period not to exceed five days or shall be required to furnish a satisfactory bond to keep the peace.

Sec. 2 Assault and Battery

Any Indian who shall willfully strike another person or otherwise inflict bodily injury, or who shall by offering violence cause another to harm himself shall be deemed guilty of assault and battery and upon conviction thereof shall be sentenced to labor for a period not to exceed six months.

Sec. 3 Carrying Concealed Weapons

Any Indian who shall go about in public places armed with a dangerous weapon concealed upon his person, unless he shall have a permit signed by a judge of a Court of Indian Offenses and countersigned by the Superintendent of the reservation, shall be deemed guilty of an offense and upon conviction thereof shall be sentenced to labor for a period not to exceed 30 days; and the weapons so carried may be confiscated.

Sec. 4 Abduction

Any Indian who shall willfully take away or detain another person against his will or without the consent of the parent or other person having lawful care or charge of him, shall be deemed guilty of abduction and upon conviction thereof shall be sentenced to labor for a period not to exceed six months.

Sec. 5 Theft

Any Indian who shall take the property of another person, with intent to steal, shall be deemed guilty of theft and upon conviction thereof shall be sentenced to labor for a period not to exceed six months.

Sec. 6 Embezzlement

Any Indian who shall, having lawful custody of property not his own, appropriate the same to his own use with intent to deprive the owner thereof, shall be deemed guilty of embezzlement and upon conviction thereof shall be sentenced to labor for a period not to exceed six months.

Sec. 7 Fraud

Any Indian who shall by willful misrepresentation or deceit, or by false interpreting, or by the use of false weights or measures obtain any money or other property, shall be deemed guilty of fraud and upon conviction thereof shall be sentenced to labor for a period not to exceed six months.

Sec. 8 Forgery

Any Indian who shall, with intent to defraud, falsely sign, execute or alter any written instrument, shall be deemed guilty of forgery and upon conviction thereof shall be sentenced to labor for a period not to exceed six months.

Sec. 9 Misbranding

Any Indian who shall knowingly and willfully misbrand or alter any brand or mark on any livestock of another person, shall be deemed guilty of an offense and upon conviction thereof shall be sentenced to labor for a period not to exceed six months.

Sec. 10 Receiving Stolen Property

Any Indian who shall receive or conceal or aid in concealing or receiving any property, knowing the same to be stolen, embezzled, or obtained by fraud or false pretense, robbery or burglary, shall be deemed guilty of an offense and upon conviction thereof shall be sentenced to labor for a period not to exceed three months.

Sec. 11 Extortion

Any Indian who shall willfully, by making false charges against another person or by any other means whatsoever, extort or attempt to extort any moneys, goods, property, or anything else of any value, shall be deemed guilty of extortion and upon conviction thereof shall be sentenced to labor for a period not to exceed thirty days.

Sec. 12 Disorderly Conduct

Any Indian who shall engage in fighting in a public place, disturb or annoy any public or religious assembly, or appear in a public or private place in an intoxicated and disorderly condition, or who shall engage in any other act of public indecency or immorality, shall be deemed guilty of disorderly conduct and upon conviction thereof shall be sentenced to labor for a period not to exceed thirty days.

Sec. 13 Reckless Driving

Any Indian who shall drive or operate any automobile, wagon, or any other vehicle in a manner dangerous to the public safety, shall be deemed guilty of reckless driving and upon conviction thereof shall be sentenced to labor for a period not to exceed 15 days and may be deprived of the right to operate any automobile for a period not to exceed six months. For the commission of such offense while under the influence of liquor, the offender may be sentenced to labor for a period not to exceed three months.

Sec. 14 Malicious Mischief

Any Indian who shall maliciously disturb, injure or destroy any livestock or other domestic animal or other property, shall be deemed guilty of malicious mischief and upon conviction thereof shall be sentenced to labor for a period not to exceed six months.

Sec. 15 Trespass

Any Indian who shall go upon or pass over any cultivated or enclosed lands of another person and shall refuse to go immediately therefrom on the request of the owner or occupant thereof or who shall willfully and knowingly allow livestock to occupy or graze on the cultivated or enclosed lands, shall be deemed guilty of an offense and upon conviction shall be punished by a fine not to exceed $5, in addition to any award of damages for the benefit of the injured party.

Sec. 16 Injury to Public Property

Any Indian who shall, without proper authority, use or injure any public property of the tribe, shall be deemed guilty of an offense and upon conviction thereof shall be sentenced to labor for a period not to exceed thirty days.

Sec. 17 Maintaining a Public Nuisance

Any Indian who shall act in such a manner, or permit his property to fall into such condition as to injure or endanger the safety, health, comfort, or property of his neighbors, shall be deemed guilty of an offense and upon conviction thereof shall be sentenced to labor for a period not to exceed five days, and may be required to remove such nuisance when so ordered by the Court.

Sec. 18 Liquor Violations

Any Indian who shall possess, sell, trade, transport or manufacture any beer, ale, wine, whisky or any article whatsoever which produces alcoholic intoxication, shall be deemed guilty of an offense and upon conviction thereof shall be sentenced to labor for a period not to exceed 60 days.

Sec. 19 Cruelty to Animals

Any Indian who shall torture or cruelly mistreat any animal, shall be deemed guilty of an offense and shall be sentenced to labor for a period not to exceed thirty days.

Sec. 20 Game Violations

Any Indian who shall violate any law, rule or regulation adopted by the Tribal Council for the protection or conservation of the fish or game of the reservation, shall be deemed guilty of an offense and upon conviction thereof shall be sentenced to labor for a period not to exceed thirty days; and he shall forfeit to the Court for the use of any Indian institution such game as may be found in his possession.

Sec. 21 Gambling

Any Indian who shall violate any law, rule or regulation adopted by the Tribal Council for the control or regulation of gambling on any reservation, shall be deemed guilty of an offense and upon conviction thereof shall be sentenced to labor for a period not to exceed thirty days.

Sec. 22 Adultery

Any Indian who shall have sexual intercourse with another person, either of such persons being married to a third person, shall be deemed guilty of adultery and upon conviction thereof shall be sentenced to labor for a period not to exceed thirty days.

Sec. 23 Illicit Cohabitation

Any Indian who shall live or cohabit with another as man and wife not then and there being married shall be deemed guilty of illicit cohabitation and upon conviction thereof shall be sentenced to labor for a period not to exceed thirty days.

Sec. 24 Prostitution

Any Indian who shall practice prostitution or who shall knowingly keep, maintain, rent or lease, any house, room, tent, or other place for the purpose of prostitution shall be deemed guilty of an offense and upon conviction thereof shall be sentenced to labor for a period not to exceed six months.

Sec. 25 Giving Venereal Disease to Another

Any Indian who shall infect another person with a venereal disease shall be deemed guilty of an offense, and upon conviction thereof shall be sentenced to labor for a period not to exceed three months. The Court of Indian Offenses shall have authority to order and compel the medical examination and treatment of any person charged with violation of this section.

Sec. 26 Failure to Support Dependent Persons

Any Indian who shall, because of habitual intemperance or gambling or for any other reason, refuse or neglect to furnish food, shelter, or care to those dependent upon him, including any dependent children born out of wedlock, shall be deemed guilty of an offense and upon conviction thereof shall be sentenced to labor for a period not to exceed three months, for the benefit of such dependents.

Sec. 27 Failure to Send Children to School

Any Indian who shall, without good cause, neglect or refuse to send his children or any children under his care, to school shall be deemed guilty of an offense and upon conviction thereof shall be sentenced to labor for a period not to exceed ten days.

Sec. 28 Contributing to the Delinquency of a Minor

Any Indian who shall willfully contribute to the delinquency of any minor shall be deemed guilty of an offense and upon conviction thereof shall be sentenced to labor for a period not to exceed six months.

Sec. 29 Bribery

Any Indian who shall give or offer to give any money, property or services, or anything else of value to another person with corrupt intent to influence another in the discharge of his public duties or conduct, and any Indian who shall accept, solicit or attempt to solicit any bribe, as above defined, shall be deemed guilty of an offense and upon conviction thereof shall be sentenced to labor for a period not to exceed six months; and any tribal office held by such person shall be forfeited.

Sec. 30 Perjury

Any Indian who shall willfully and deliberately, in any judicial proceeding in any Court of Indian Offenses, falsely swear or interpret, or shall make a sworn statement or affidavit knowing the same to be untrue, or shall induce or procure another person so to do, shall be deemed guilty of perjury and upon conviction thereof shall be sentenced to labor for a period not to exceed six months.

Sec. 31 False Arrest

Any Indian who shall willfully and knowingly make, or cause to be made, the unlawful arrest, detention or imprisonment of another person, shall be deemed guilty of an offense, and upon conviction thereof shall be sentenced to labor for a period not to exceed six months.

Sec. 32 Resisting Lawful Arrest

Any Indian who shall willfully and knowingly, by force or violence, resist or assist another person to resist a lawful arrest shall be deemed guilty of an offense and upon conviction thereof shall be sentenced to labor for a period not to exceed thirty days.

Sec. 33 Refusing to Aid Officer

Any Indian who shall neglect or refuse, when called upon by any Indian Police or other police officer of the United States Indian Service, to assist in the arrest of any person charged with or convicted of any offense or in securing such offender when apprehended, or in conveying such offender to the nearest place of confinement shall be deemed guilty of an offense, and upon conviction, shall be sentenced to labor for a period not to exceed ten days.

Sec. 34 Escape

Any Indian, who, being in lawful custody, for any offense, shall escape or attempt to escape or who shall permit or assist or attempt to permit or assist another person to escape from lawful custody shall be deemed guilty of an offense, and upon conviction thereof shall be sentenced to labor for a period not to exceed six months.

Sec. 35 Disobedience to Lawful Orders of Court

Any Indian who shall willfully disobey any order, subpoena, warrant or command duly issued, made or given by the Court of Indian Offenses or any officer thereof, shall be deemed guilty of an offense and upon conviction thereof shall be fined in an amount not exceeding $180 or sentenced to labor for a period not to exceed three months.

Sec. 36 Violation of an Approved Tribal Ordinance

Any Indian who violates an ordinance designed to preserve the peace and welfare of the tribe, which was promulgated by the Tribal Council and approved by the Secretary of the Interior, shall be deemed guilty of an offense and upon conviction thereof shall be sentenced as provided in the ordinance.

NOTE: Chapter 6, "The Indian Police," and Chapter 7, "Legal Forms," were not of sufficient relevance to quote in this Appendix.

References

Aberle, David F.
    1966   The Peyote Religion Among the Navaho. Chicago: Aldine Publishing Company.

Adair, John
    1971   Personal Communication.

Akwesasne Notes
    1972   Summer Issue.

Antram, Father Cormac
    1963-1971 Personal Communication.

Bailey, L. R.
    1964   The Long Walk. Los Angeles: Westernlore Press.

Barnett, Clifford
    1962   Field Notes from Interview with Frank Mitchell on May 17.
    1971-1973 Personal Communication.
    n.d.   The Life History of Albert G. (Chic) Sandoval.

Bernally, Garnett
    1971   Personal Communication.

Bernheimer, Charles L.
    1923   Encircling Navajo Mountain with a Pack-Train. National Geographic Magazine 43, 2:197-224.
    n.d.   Field Notes for Canyon de Chelly National Monument. Extracts provided by Don Morris, Personal Communication.

Bosch, James
    1958   Personal Communication.
    1972   Personal Communication.

Bridgeman, Ruth N.
    1972   Personal Communication, May 5.

Brugge, David M.
    1963-1975 Personal Communication.
    1968   Navajos in the Catholic Church Records of New Mexico 1694-1875. Navajo Tribe Research Reports 1. Window Rock, Arizona: Navajo Tribe, Parks and Recreation Department, Research Section.

Brugge, David and Raymond Wilson
1976   Administrative History, Canyon de Chelly National Monu-
        ment, Arizona. United States Department of the Interior,
        National Park Service. NPS 577.

Bunnell, Gene A.
1966   Physicians, Medicine Men and Health of the Navajo Reserva-
        tion. B.A. Honors Thesis for Department of Anthropology,
        Wesleyan University.

Chiao, Chien
1965-1975 Personal Communication.
1971   Continuation of Tradition in Navajo Society. Nankang,
        Taipei, Republic of China: Institute of Ethnology, Academia
        Sinica.

Chinle Chapter
1944   Records on File at Our Lady of Fatima Mission [Franciscan],
        Chinle, Arizona.

Chinle Navajos
1930a   Petition to John G. Hunter, September 8. Copy provided by
        David Brugge.
1930b   Petition to John G. Hunter, October 8. Copy provided by
        David Brugge.

Coley, Kathryn T.
1963   Navajo Tribal Government: A Case History in the Persistence
        and Adaptation of Cultural Values. M.A. Thesis for Depart-
        ment of Anthropology, Wesleyan University.

Collier, John
1933   Letter to John Hunter, May 22. Copy on file at Saint
        Michaels Mission, Tribal Council Organizations Committee
        File.

Correll, Lee J.
1971-1975 Personal Communication.

Culin, Stewart
1898   Chess and Playing Cards. United States National Museum
        Annual Report for Year ending June 30, 1896:665-942.
1907   Games of the North American Indians. Bureau of American
        Ethnology, Annual Report 24.

Davis, Mary Mitchell
1963-1975 Personal Communication.

Day, Sam III
1971   Personal Communication.

Downs, James F.
1964   Animal Husbandry in Navajo Society and Culture. University
        of California Publications in Anthropology 1.

Dutton, Bertha
1971   Personal Communication.

Dyk, Walter
1938   Son of Old Man Hat: A Navaho Autobiography. New York: Harcourt, Brace and Company.
1947   A Navaho Autobiography. Viking Fund Publications in Anthropology 8. New York: Wenner-Gren Foundation.

Fort Defiance Agency
1888-1889 Letter Book 11, 7/13/88-1/15/89
1892-1893 Letter Book 17, 3/28/92-1/19/93
1893-1894 Letter Book 20, 10/11/93-2/9/94
1894a   Letter Book 21, 2/2/94-5/4/94
1894b   Letter Book 22, 5/5/94-7/21/94
1895-1898 Letter Book 25, 4/1/95-10/10/98
1898-1899 Letter Book 26, 10/20/98-9/4/99
1899-1900 Letter Book 27, 9/6/99-8/23/00
1902-1903 Letter Book 28, 7/1/02-4/11/03
1903-1904 Letter Book 29, 5/8/03-1/5/04
1903-1908 Letter Book 30, 1/2/03-6/1/08

Fort Defiance School
1907   Enrollment Record Book, Volume 1.

Franciscan Fathers
1910   An Ethnologic Dictionary of the Navaho Language. Saint Michaels, Arizona: Saint Michaels Press.

Frink, Maurice
1968   Fort Defiance & The Navajos. Boulder: Pruett Press.

Frisbie, Charlotte J.
1963-1975 Navajo Field Notes.
1967   Kinaaldá: A Study of the Navaho Girl's Puberty Ceremony. Middletown, Connecticut: Wesleyan University Press.
1968   The Navajo House Blessing Ceremonial. El Palacio 75, 3:26-35.
1970   The Navajo House Blessing Ceremonial: A Study of Cultural Change. Ph.D. dissertation for Department of Anthropology, University of New Mexico. Ann Arbor: University Microfilms.
1975a   Fieldwork as a "Single Parent": To Be or Not To Be Accompanied by a Child. In Collected Papers in Honor of Florence Hawley Ellis. Theodore R. Frisbie, Ed. Papers of the Archaeological Society of New Mexico 2:98-119. Norman: Hooper Publishing Company.
1975b   Observations on a Preschooler's First Experience with Cross-Cultural Living. Journal of Man 7, 1:91-112.

Frisbie, Theodore R.
1975   *Hishi* as Money in the Puebloan Southwest. *In* Collected
            Papers in Honor of Florence Hawley Ellis. Theodore R.
            Frisbie, Ed. Papers of the Archaeological Society of New
            Mexico 2:120-142. Norman: Hooper Publishing Company.

Gorman, Howard
1971   Personal Communication.

Grant, Campbell
n.d.   Four Views of Canyon de Chelly: Its Beauty, Its People, Its
            Explorers, Its Rock Art. Tucson: University of Arizona Press.
            In Press.

Hagerman, H. J.
1930   Letter to John G. Hunter, October 2. Copy provided by
            David Brugge.

Haile, Father Berard
1917   Some Mortuary Customs of the Navajo. Franciscan Missions
            of the Southwest 5:29-33.
1937a   With the Reorganization Committee of the Navajo Tribal
            Council 1936-37. 112 pp. MS, dated 4/19/37, on file at Saint
            Michaels Mission.
1937b   Some Cultural Aspects of the Navajo Hogan. Mimeographed.
1938   Origin Legend of the Navaho Enemy Way. Yale University
            Publications in Anthropology 17.
1942   Why the Navaho Hogan? Primitive Man 15:39-56.
1947   Head and Face Masks in Navaho Ceremonialism. Saint
            Michaels, Arizona: Saint Michaels Press.
1950   A Stem Vocabulary of the Navaho Language. Navaho-English.
            Saint Michaels, Arizona: Saint Michaels Press.
1951   A Stem Vocabulary of the Navaho Language. English-
            Navaho. Saint Michaels, Arizona: Saint Michaels Press.
1958   Personal Communication.

Harris, Sally P.
1964   Interview with Frank Mitchell, October 21, on Oral History
            of Canyon de Chelly. MS on file at National Park Service
            Office, Canyon de Chelly National Monument, Doris Duke
            American Indian History Project File.

Hegemann, Elizabeth C.
1963   Navaho Trading Days. Albuquerque: University of New
            Mexico Press.

Hester, James J.
1962   Early Navajo Migration and Acculturation in the Southwest.
            Museum of New Mexico Publications in Anthropology 6.
            Santa Fe: Museum of New Mexico Press.

Hill, W. W.
   1940   Some Aspects of Navajo Political Structure. Plateau 13:23-28.
   1956   Navajo Political Structure. *In* Societies Around the World. Irwin T. Sanders, Ed. One volume edition, Howard Becker, Ed. New York: Dryden Press.
   1964-1967 Personal Communication.

Hoffman, Virginia and Broderick H. Johnson
   1970   Navajo Biographies. Rough Rock, Arizona: Rough Rock Demonstration School.

Hoijer, Harry
   1971   Personal Communication.

Hunter, John G.
   1930   Letter to H. J. Hagerman, October 10. Copy provided by David Brugge.
   1931   Letter to Reuben Perry, February 24. Copy provided by Federal Records Center, Bell, California.

Jett, Stephen C.
   1971-1975 Personal Communication.
   1974   The Destruction of Navajo Orchards in 1864. Arizona and the West 16, 4:365-378.
   n.d.   Canyon de Chelly. Photographs by David Bohn and Clyde Childress.

Jett, Stephen C. and Virginia S. Harris
   n.d.   Navajo Architecture: Style, History, Geography.

Jewell, Donald P.
   1952   A Case of a "Psychotic" Navaho Male. Human Organization 40, 1:32-36.

Johnson, Broderick H. et. al. (Eds.)
   1969   Denetsosie. Rough Rock, Arizona: Rough Rock Demonstration School.

Kee, Geneva Mae
   1963-1965 Personal Communication.

Kennedy, Mary Jeanette
   1965   Tales of a Trader's Wife. Albuquerque: Valliant Company.

Kluckhohn, Clyde
   1940   Life Story of a Navaho Indian. 40-page MS.
   1944   Navaho Witchcraft. Papers of the Peabody Museum of American Archaeology and Ethnology, Harvard University 22, 2.
   1945   The Personal Document in Anthropological Science. *In* The Use of Personal Documents in History, Anthropology, and Sociology. Louis Gottschalk, Clyde Kluckhohn, Robert Angell, Eds. Social Science Research Council Bulletin 53:79-113.

1948	Conceptions of Death Among the Southwestern Indians. Harvard Divinity School Bulletin 66:5-19.
1956	A Navaho Personal Document with a Brief Paretian Analysis. *In* Personal Character and Culture Milieu. Douglas G. Haring, Ed. New York: Syracuse University Press. pp. 513-533.
1960	A Navaho Politician. *In* In the Company of Man. J. B. Casagrande, Ed. New York: Harper and Row Publishers. pp. 439-466.
1964	Navaho Women's Knowledge of Their Song Ceremonials. *In* Culture and Behavior. Richard Kluckhohn, Ed. New York: The Free Press of Glencoe. pp. 92-96.

Kluckhohn, Clyde, W. W. Hill and Lucy W. Kluckhohn
1971   Navaho Material Culture. Cambridge: Harvard University Press.

Kluckhohn, Clyde and Dorothea Leighton
1946   The Navaho. Cambridge: Harvard University Press.

Kluckhohn, Clyde and Janine Rosenzweig
1947   Two Navajo Children over a Five-Year Period. American Journal of Orthopsychiatry 19:266-278.

Kluckhohn, Clyde and Leland C. Wyman
1940   An Introduction to Navaho Chant Practice. Memoirs of the American Anthropological Association 53.

Langness, Lewis L.
1967   The Life History in Anthropological Science. Studies in Anthropological Method. New York: Holt, Rinehart and Winston.

Left-Handed Mexican Clansman et al.
1952   The Trouble at Round Rock. United States Indian Service, Navajo Historical Series 2. Phoenix: Phoenix Indian School.

Leighton, Alexander H. and Dorothea C. Leighton
1949   Gregorio, the Hand-Trembler. Papers of the Peabody Museum of American Archaeology and Ethnology, Harvard University 40, 1.

Link, Martin A. (Ed.)
1968   Navajo: A Century of Progress 1868-1968. Flagstaff: KC Publications.
1971   Personal Communication.

Lipps, Oscar H.
1909   The Navajos. Cedar Rapids: Torch Press.

Lister, Florence C. and Robert H. Lister
1968   Earl Morris & Southwestern Archaeology. Albuquerque: University of New Mexico Press.

Lister, Robert
1971-1972 Personal Communication.

Mandelbaum, David
1973   The Study of Life History: Gandhi. Current Anthropology
            14, 3:177-206 (includes Current Anthropology comment).

Matthews, Washington
1894   The Basket Drum. American Anthropologist 7:202-208.
1901   Navaho Night Chant. Journal of American Folklore
            14:12-19.
1902   The Night Chant. Memoirs of the American Museum of
            Natural History 6:1-332.

Mayes, Gay Ann
1971-1972 Personal Communication.

McAllester, David
1952   Texts of the Navajo Creation Chants. Pamphlet to accom-
            pany Album of Five Records. Cambridge: Peabody Museum
            of Harvard University.
1954   Enemyway Music. Papers of the Peabody Museum of
            American Archaeology and Ethnology, Harvard Univer-
            sity 41, 3.
1957-1975 Navajo Field Notes.

McClellan, George
1971   Personal Communication.

McNitt, Frank
1963   The Indian Traders. Norman, Oklahoma: University of
            Oklahoma Press. Second printing.
1964   Navaho Expedition. Norman, Oklahoma: University of Okla-
            homa Press.

Mindeleff, Cosmos
1898   Navaho Houses. Bureau of American Ethnology, Annual
            Report 17, 2:475-517.

Mitchell, Douglas
1963-1972 Personal Communication.

Mitchell, Frank
1931   Letter to Superintendent Reuben Perry, February 9. Copy
            on file at Our Lady of Fatima Mission, Chinle, Arizona, Old
            Chronicles – Daily File.
1957-1967 Personal Communication.

Mitchell, Howard
1963-1975 Personal Communication.

Mitchell, Isabelle
1963-1975 Personal Communication.

Mitchell, Mae
1963-1971 Personal Communication.

Mitchell, Rose
1963-1975 Personal Communication.

Mitchell, Seya
1963-1975 Personal Communication.

Morgan, William
1931   Navaho Treatment of Sickness: Diagnosticians. American
            Anthropologist 33:390-402.
1936   Human-Wolves Among the Navaho. Yale University Publica-
            tions in Anthropology 11:1-43.

Morgan, William, Sr.
1971   Personal Communication.

Morris, Ann Axtell
1933   Digging in the Southwest. Chicago: E.M. Hale and Company.
            Special Edition.

Morris, Don
1971-1972 Personal Communication.

Morris, Earl
1925   Exploring in the Canyon of Death. National Geographic
            Magazine 48:263-300.
1938   Mummy Cave. Natural History 42:127-138.
1948   Tomb of the Weaver. Natural History 57, 2:66-71.

Morrow, Don
1971   Personal Communication.

Narbona, Lieutenant Antonio
1805   Letter to Governor Chacón, January 24. New Mexico State
            Archives, Santa Fe.

Navajo Times
1967   May 18 Issue.
1973   June 7 Issue.
            July 19 Issue.
            November 29 Issue.

Navajo Tribal Constitutional Assembly
1937   Proposed Constitution of the Navajo Tribe, October 25. In
            Navajo Yearbook 8 (1961). Robert W. Young, Ed.
            pp. 400-407.

Navajo Tribal Council
1925   Minutes of July 7 meeting.
1930   Minutes of July 7-8 meeting.
1937   Minutes of April 9 meeting.
1938a   Proceedings of the Council and the Executive Committee,
            January 17-20.
1938b   Minutes of January 17-20 meeting.
1938c   Minutes of May 2-3 Executive Committee meeting.
1939   Minutes of November 20-21 meeting.
1945   Minutes of July 10-13 meeting.
1952   A Report on the Delegation to Washington, February 10-21.

Navajo Tribal Council *(cont.)*
1953   Minutes of July 22, 23, 31 meetings.
1954a   Minutes of February 23-26 meetings.
1954b   Minutes of March 2 meeting.

Navajo Tribe
1923   Regulations Relating to the Navajo Tribe of Indians, April 24. *In* Navajo Yearbook 8 (1961). Robert W. Young, Ed. pp. 395-397.
1927   Amendments to the Regulations Relating to the Navajo Tribe of Indians approved April 24, 1923. *In* Navajo Yearbook 8 (1961). Robert W. Young, Ed. pp. 397-398.
1928   Regulations Relating to the Navajo Indian Tribal Council, October 15. *In* Navajo Yearbook 8 (1961). Robert W. Young, Ed. pp. 398-400.
1928-1929   Window Rock Census.
1951a   Ballot for Tribal Council Election.
1951b   Report on Navajo Tribal Election, March 3-5.
1955   Ballot for Tribal Council Election.
1971   Census Records.

NeBoyia, Chauncey
1972   Personal Communication.

Olin, Caroline
1975   Personal Communication.

Ostermann, Father Leopold
n.d.   Mission at Chinle. 6 pp., typed MS. On file at Our Lady of Fatima Mission, Chinle, Arizona, Historical Folder.

Our Lady of Fatima Mission [Franciscan], Chinle, Arizona
n.d.   Baptismal Records.
n.d.   Birth and Death Records.
n.d.   Old Chronicles – Daily.

Padres' Trail
1961   November Issue.
1964   June-July Issue.
1973   February Issue.
            June-July Issue.
            October-November Issue.

Palmer, F. M.
1906   South West Society of the Archaeological Institute of America Dig at Antelope House. Album of Photography by Virgil Huff White. National Park Service Museum Catalog #3282, #17.

Paquette, Peter
1915   Census of the Navajo Reservation Under the Jurisdiction of Peter Paquette for the year 1915.

Parman, Donald L.
1971   Personal Communication.
1976   The Navajos and the New Deal. New Haven: Yale University Press.

Peri, David
1963   Personal Communication.
1971-1972 Personal Communication.

Plummer, E. H.
1894   Letter to Honorable Commissioner of Indian Affairs, February 1.

Puckett, Jo
1971   Personal Communication.
1975   Personal Communication.

Rademaker, Father Martan (Ed.)
1976a   Father Marcellus Troester. Padres' Trail (December 1975-January 1976): 2-13.
1976b   Father Emanuel Trockur, O.F.M. Padres' Trail (June-July): 2-17.

Reichard, Gladys A.
1928   Social Life of the Navajo Indians. Columbia University Contributions to Anthropology 7. New York: Columbia University Press.
1963   Navaho Religion. New York: Bollingen Foundation. Second Edition, in one volume.

Roberts, John M.
1951   Three Navaho Households: A Comparative Study of Small Group Culture. Papers of the Peabody Museum of American Archaeology and Ethnology, Harvard University 40, 3.

Saint Michaels Mission Census
n.d.   Records started by Father Marcellus Troester at Tohatchi in 1915.

Salsbury, Clarence G. with Paul Hughes
1969   The Salsbury Story. Tucson: University of Arizona Press.

Sanchez, Agnes Mitchell
1963-1975 Personal Communication.

Sandoval, Albert G. (Chic)
1963-1968 Personal Communication.

Sandoval, Augusta Mitchell
1963-1975 Personal Communication.

Sandoval, Cecilia
1963-1975 Personal Communication.

Shepardson, Mary
 1963   Navajo Ways in Government. Memoirs of the American
             Anthropological Association 65, 3 (2).
 1965a   Problems of the Navajo Tribal Courts in Transition. Human
             Organization 24, 3:250-253.
 1965b   Field Tapes of Interviews conducted during the fall with
             Frank Mitchell.
 1970-1975 Personal Communication.

Shirley, Ivonne
 1963-1971 Personal Communication.

Spencer, Virginia and Stephen C. Jett
 1971   Navajo Dwellings of Rural Black Creek Valley, Arizona-New
             Mexico. Plateau 43, 4:159-175.

Stewart, Irene
 1965   Interview with Frank Mitchell, July 17, on Oral History of
             Canyon de Chelly. MS (#965) on file at National Park Service
             Office, Canyon de Chelly National Monument, Doris Duke
             American Indian History Project File.
 1971   Personal Communication, July 8.

Thompson, Gerald
 1976   The Army and the Navajo: The Bosque Redondo Experiment
             1863-1868. Tucson: University of Arizona Press.

Trafzer, Clifford E.
 1973   Anglos Among the Navajos: The Day Family. *In* The
             Changing Ways of Southwestern Indians: A Historic Perspec-
             tive. Albert H. Schroeder, Ed. Glorieta, New Mexico: Rio
             Grande Press, Inc. pp. 259-274.

Trockur, Father Emanuel
 n.d.   History of the Ranch, about Seven Miles South of Ft.
             Defiance (Cienaga), Arizona, now Saint Michaels, Arizona.
             27 pp. MS, on file at Saint Michaels Mission, Saint Michaels
             Chronicle 1889-1905 file.
 1963-1975 Personal Communication.
 1964   Pioneer Doctor Dies. The Padres' Trail, June-July: 14-16.

Underhill, Ruth
 1953   Here Come the Navaho! United States Indian Service, Indian
             Life and Customs 8. Lawrence, Kansas: Haskell Institute
             Press.
 1972   Personal Communication.

United States - Navajo Treaty
 1868   Treaty Between the United States of America and the Navajo
             Tribe of Indians. Concluded June 1, 1868; Ratified July 25,
             1868; Proclaimed August 12, 1868. Introduction by
             Martin A. Link. Flagstaff: KC Publications (1968).

United States Department of the Interior
1937 Law and Order Regulations, February 15, Document #85143.
1938 Rules for the Navajo Tribal Council, July 26. *In* Navajo Yearbook 8 (1961). Robert W. Young, Ed. pp. 407-411. .

Van Valkenburgh, Richard
1938 A Short History of the Navajo People. Window Rock, Arizona: Navajo Agency. Mimeographed.
1941 Diné Bikéyah. United States Department of the Interior Navajo Service, Window Rock, Arizona. Mimeographed.

Vogt, Evon Z., Jr.
n.d. Life Histories of Fourteen Navajo Young Men. *In* Microcard Publications of Primary Records, Primary Records in Culture and Personality 1. Bert Kaplan, Ed. Madison, Wisconsin: Microcard Foundation.

Walker, John G. and O. L. Shepherd
1964 The Navajo Reconnaissance. L. R. Bailey, Ed. Los Angeles: Westernlore Press.

Wall, Leon and William Morgan
1958 Navajo-English Dictionary. Phoenix, Arizona: Phoenix Indian School Press.

Wallace, John
1971 Personal Communication.

Ward, Albert E. and David M. Brugge
1975 Changing Contemporary Navajo Burial Practice and Values. Plateau 48, 1-2:31-42.

Wassaja
1973 January Issue.

Watson, Editha
1971 Personal Communication.

Wilken, Robert L.
1955 Anselm Weber, O.F.M.: Missionary to the Navaho. Milwaukee: Bruce Publishing Company.

Williams, Aubrey W., Jr.
1970 Navajo Political Processes. Smithsonian Contributions to Anthropology 9. Washington, D.C.: Smithsonian Institution.

Wise, Melvin
1971 Personal Communication.

Witherspoon, Gary
1971 Review of Blessingway by Leland C. Wyman (1970). American Anthropologist 73, 6:1360-1361.
1974 The Central Concepts of Navajo World View: I. Linguistics 119:41-59.

Witherspoon *(cont.)*
1975a   The Central Concepts of Navajo World View: II. Linguistics
           161:69-87.
1975b   Navajo Kinship and Marriage. Chicago: University of Chicago
           Press.

Wyman, Leland C.
1962   The Windways of the Navaho. Colorado Springs: Taylor
           Museum.
1963-1975 Personal Communication.
1970   Blessingway (With three versions of the myth recorded and
           translated from the Navajo by Father Berard Haile). Tucson:
           University of Arizona Press.

Wyman, Leland C. and Clyde Kluckhohn
1938   Navajo Classification of Their Song Ceremonials. Memoirs of
           the American Anthropological Association 50.

Yazzie, Ruth Mitchell Shirley
1963-1975 Personal Communication.

Young, Robert W. (Ed.)
1961   The Navajo Yearbook 8 (1951-1961). Window Rock: Navajo
           Agency.
1972-1973 Personal Communication.

Acknowledgments

For the assistance received during the eighteen years of work that went into collecting and editing Frank Mitchell's life history material, the editors are indebted to numerous individuals, institutions and foundations.

Our greatest debt is to the Mitchell family of Chinle, Arizona. All through the many years of our study they provided such warm hospitality, friendship and good times that they became, for each of us, a second family of our own. We are keenly aware of our good fortune in finding in the late Frank Mitchell an outstanding singer who wished to preserve the record of his religious and personal life. He could not have been more generous with his time and with himself. He was at once our collaborator, our sponsor and our protector. Through him, we attended many other ceremonies in addition to his own and met a variety of other singers who broadened our understanding of Navajo religion. For all the years that we knew him, his wit and high spirits added a very special quality to our experience of Navajo life.

Frank's wife, Rose, and his youngest daughter, Isabelle, made us the beneficiaries of superb Navajo cooking and comfortable quarters. Isabelle's sense of fun was an additional reason that we looked forward with such pleasure to our visits with the Mitchell family.

Frank's six other children all contributed in numerous ways to our research and well-being. We are grateful to Mary Davis for many friendly visits and for genealogical information. Seya Mitchell, in long conversations, gave us encouragement and information on the extended Mitchell family. Agnes Sanchez, of Stockton, California, encompassed us in warm friendship during her visits to Chinle, and provided valuable counsel and family information. Ruth Yazzie opened her house to us for delicious meals, information, conversations and good times. Howard Mitchell was our generous mainstay in times of car trouble and other emergencies, and he was a helpful companion at a number of the ceremonies we visited. We thank him for unstinting friendship and for information on Navajo music and many aspects of Mitchell family life. Augusta Sandoval was one of our principal interpreters, and her home was another of our headquarters. She welcomed us to meals and provided a place to stay, and she has extended this welcome to a whole generation of students from Wesleyan University. She was our main correspondent when we were away from the reservation and assisted us at many times with suggestions concerning the project and with the actual data collection. It is to Augusta that we owe the inception of the whole project, since it was she, in the first place, who suggested that Frank's Blessingway ceremony should be recorded on film and tape.

Many of Frank's grandchildren were also extremely helpful, not only for the relaxing times and friendship they afforded, but also for valuable information on Navajo life and Mitchell family life in particular. We also appreciated their much-needed interpreting services at crucial moments. We want especially to thank Geneva Kee, Mae Mitchell, Ivonne Shirley, Cecilia Sandoval and the late Douglas F. Mitchell.

To our interpreters, the late Albert G. (Chic) Sandoval, Sr., Albert G. Sandoval, Jr., and Augusta Sandoval, goes our deep gratitude for the many, many hours of assistance in collecting, translating and checking this material. No words can express our thanks for the hospitality of Chic and his wife, Ethnobah Sandoval, and the interest, patience, good humor and serious commitment which all of our interpreters gave to the project. In a true sense these three individuals are co-authors, with Frank, of this book.

To Ted Frisbie and Susan McAllester, our respective spouses, our thanks for encouragement, inspiration and interest, and for forebearance with rearranged schedules and occasional preoccupations as the manuscript was prepared for publication. Frisbie would also like to express gratitude to her two children: Elizabeth, who shared the 1971 fieldwork with her mother, and Jennifer. Without their patience and cooperation, final preparation of the manuscript would have been exceedingly difficult.

Frisbie is deeply indebted to all of the many people who assisted her in collecting the material for the Notes and Appendixes. Foremost among these was David Brugge (formerly of the National Park Service, Ganado, Arizona), his wife, and family, all of whom provided hospitality, the opportunity for discussion, as well as valuable suggestions regarding available resources. For their warmth and friendliness toward Elizabeth, who accompanied her mother during the 1971 summer fieldwork at the age of three and one-half (Frisbie 1975a and b), Frisbie is particularly grateful.

To the many people associated with the Navajo Tribal Government in Window Rock, both Navajo Tribal and Bureau of Indian Affairs officials, Frisbie also offers thanks. Among those whose assistance was invaluable were: Lee Correll and the late Editha Watson of the Research Office; Melvin Wise and his staff of the Bureau of Information and Statistics; Frances Collins of the Judicial Department; Abraham Tucker, Department assistant area director of the Navajo Division of Education; Marian McLemore of the Census Office; Pauline Martinez of Tribal Operations; Chester Wilson of Budget Branch of the Administration Division of the Navajo Area Office in Gallup; Paul Hand, superintendent of the Chinle Agency; the late John Wallace, and Irene

Stewart, both of Chinle; Howard Gorman of Ganado; and William Morgan, Sr., of Navajo Community College, Tsaile, Arizona.

The Franciscan Fathers, both at Saint Michaels and Chinle, Arizona, provided invaluable assistance. Frisbie is particularly indebted to the late Father Emanuel (Trockur) of Saint Michaels and Father Cormac (Antram) of Houck, and formerly of Chinle, for years of untiring assistance and interest. Father John of Saint Michaels and Father Davin and Father Bart of Chinle also provided much help in locating mission records dealing with Frank Mitchell during the summer of 1971. McAllester was helped greatly by the late Father Berard Haile who provided access to his Blessingway manuscript (published by Wyman in 1970) and who gave much information and encouragement from his hospital bed in the spring of 1958. The Franciscans continue to maintain their deep interest in the Navajos as people, and their work among them and the records accumulated during this time have been invaluable for anthropologists and others interested in Navajo culture for more than sixty years.

Thanks are also due Martin Link of the Navajo Tribal Museum, Window Rock, Arizona; Kevin McKibbin, superintendent of the National Park Service at Ganado, Arizona, and his staff; and Leslie Cammack, superintendent of the National Park Service at Canyon de Chelly, Chinle, Arizona, and his staff, especially Jo Puckett, for help and suggestions.

Assistance was also made readily available by numerous anthropologists interested in the Navajos. Among them were John Adair, San Francisco State College, who gave Frisbie numerous helpful suggestions as well as inspiration, Mary Shepardson of San Francisco State College who made her own work with Frank Mitchell available to Frisbie, thus providing much clarifying information, and to Chien Chiao of Indiana University, who did likewise. Others who were also of assistance to Frisbie included the late W. W. Hill (University of New Mexico), Robert W. Young (University of New Mexico), Leland Wyman (Boston University), Bertha Dutton (formerly of the Museum of Navajo Ceremonial Art), Clifford Barnett (Stanford University, Stanford, California), Katherine Bartlett (Museum of Northern Arizona Research Center), Harry Hoijer (University of California at Los Angeles), Robert Lister (University of New Mexico), Caroline Olin (formerly of the Museum of Navajo Ceremonial Art) and Ruth Underhill (Denver, Colorado).

Thanks are also due Donald Parman of the History Department, Purdue University, for stimulating discussions and valuable suggestions during the 1971 fieldwork and to the following people for assistance in ethnohistorical research: Harold Pinkett of National Archives and Records Service, Washington, D.C.; Robert Sveningsen, Denver Federal Record Center, Denver, Colorado; Robert Jordan and Joseph Huld of the Los Angeles Federal Record Center, Bell, California; Don Morris of the Arizona Archaeological Center, University of Arizona, Tucson, Arizona and Stephen C. Jett, University of California at Davis.

Assistance in locating and preparing the illustrations was received from the following individuals, all of whom have our thanks too: Father Emanuel and Father John of Saint Michaels; Melvin Wise of the Bureau of Indian Affairs Information and Statistics Office in Window Rock; Garnett Bernally of Shiprock, New Mexico; Augusta Sandoval, Isabelle Mitchell and the late Douglas Mitchell of Chinle, Arizona; George McClellan of Fullerton, California; David Peri of Samona State College, Rohnert Park, California; John Adair of San Francisco State College, San Francisco, California; Bud Guadagnoli of Gallup, New Mexico; the late John Wallace of Chinle, Arizona; Sam Day III of Window Rock, Arizona; James and Mabel Bosch of Western Washington State University, Bellingham, Washington; Leland Wyman of Boston University; Gay Ann Mayes of the National Park Service at Ganado, Arizona; and Don Morrow of Bureau of Indian Affairs Instructional Service Center, Brigham City, Utah. The editors are also grateful to the late Mr. Charles F. Johnson, Jr., Frisbie's father, for assistance in preparing the illustrations for publication and to J. Michael Hodge for cartography.

Of substantial and continuing assistance were several foundations and institutions, whose financial help made the project possible and feasible. McAllester wishes to thank the John Simon Guggenheim Foundation for the year 1957-1958, the Museum of Navajo Ceremonial Art for their support during 1958, and the National Science Foundation for their research grant (GS-144), which provided financial assistance during 1963-65. He also thanks Wesleyan University for their generous support funds throughout the years.

Frisbie wishes to thank the National Science Foundation for the GS-144 grant which supported her work during 1963 and 1964, the University of New Mexico for their fellowship 1964-65, and the National Science Foundation for their Cooperative Fellowship from 1965 to 1967. Further research assistance from the American Association for University Women Shirley Farr Fellowship for 1967-68, and the American Philosophical Society Research Grant from the Penrose Fund, 1971-72 are also gratefully acknowledged. Frisbie also wishes to thank the Research and Projects Office of Southern Illinois University, Edwardsville, Illinois for support funds during 1971-76, the University's Graduate School for travel funds in 1975 and the School of Social Sciences at the same university for research typing assistance.

Both editors also wish to thank John Huie, former director of the Verde Valley School, for hospitality and the use of school facilities for two weeks in the summer of 1971, during which initial discussions about the book's final format took place, and indexing and editing procedures were begun. Frisbie also extends thanks for hospitality, friendship and inspiration to Joyce and Bill Griffen of Northern Arizona University, Flagstaff, Arizona; McAllester expresses appreciation for friendship and hospitality to Margaret and Willis Leenhouts, Sedona, Arizona.

The editors also want to express thanks to those who read the manuscript and offered criticisms: these included Augusta Sandoval of Chinle, Arizona; Agnes Sanchez of Stockton, California; Susan McAllester of Portland, Connecticut, and Theodore Frisbie, Joyce Aschenbrenner and Ernest Schusky of Southern Illinois University, Edwardsville. We are grateful to Ona Langer and Bonner McAllester for preparing the initial tape transcriptions, and to Valborg Proudman, Jane Haegele, Roben Kelley, Rita Petty, Donna Rees, Lynne Schmidt, Jeff Corbin and Ann Van Horn for draft copy typing. Special thanks for the preparation of final copy and numerous helpful suggestions go to Ann Van Horn of Southern Illinois University, Edwardsville.

Marshall Townsend, director, and other staff members of the University of Arizona Press contributed greatly in the metamorphosis from manuscript to book. We are indebted to Karen Thure in particular, for her imaginative and meticulous editing.

Last, and by no means least, the editors would like to express their appreciation of each other for ideas that became realities and hard work that bore fruit.

CHARLOTTE J. FRISBIE
DAVID P. MCALLESTER

Index